Textbook English

Studies in Corpus Linguistics (SCL)

ISSN 1388-0373

SCL focuses on the use of corpora throughout language study, the development of a quantitative approach to linguistics, the design and use of new tools for processing language texts, and the theoretical implications of a data-rich discipline.

For an overview of all books published in this series, please see *benjamins.com/catalog/scl*

Volume 116

Textbook English. A multi-dimensional approach
by Elen Le Foll

Textbook English

A multi-dimensional approach

Elen Le Foll
University of Cologne

John Benjamins Publishing Company
Amsterdam / Philadelphia

The paper used in this publication meets the minimum requirements of the American National Standard for Information Sciences – Permanence of Paper for Printed Library Materials, ANSI Z39.48-1984.

Cover design: Françoise Berserik
Cover illustration from original painting *Random Order*
by Lorenzo Pezzatini, Florence, 1996.

DOI 10.1075/scl.116

Cataloging-in-Publication Data available from Library of Congress:
LCCN 2024023006 (PRINT) / 2024023007 (E-BOOK)

ISBN 978 90 272 1493 5 (HB)
ISBN 978 90 272 4680 6 (E-BOOK)

John Benjamins Publishing Company · https://benjamins.com

To my teachers
and to all teachers who believe in their students

Table of contents

Acknowledgements

The truth is I have benefited, more or less directly, from the advice and scholarship of far too many people to mention them all here. Yet, at the risk of forgetting someone, I would like to extend special thanks to (in alphabetical order): Andrea Nini, Anna Fankhauser, Carolyn Blume, Dirk Siepmann, Douglas Biber, Gaëtanelle Gilquin, Janna Gerdes, Larissa Goulart, Luke Tudge, Martin Becker, Martin Schweinberger, Muhammad Shakir, Natalia Levshina, Peter Thwaites, Peter Uhrig, Stefan Gries, Stephanie Evert, Susanne Flach, Tatjana Winter, Thomas Prinzie, Ute Römer, and the developers and maintainers of all the open-source software that I have used as part of this project.

I am genuinely grateful to the editor of this series, Ute Römer, and to an anonymous reviewer for their insightful comments and suggestions on earlier versions of this manuscript. This book is a considerably reworked version of Chapters 1–3 and 7–8 of my doctoral thesis. As such, the long and rather more emotional acknowledgments of my thesis (Le Foll 2022c: ix–x) very much also apply here.

List of figures

List of tables

List of abbreviations

BNC	British National Corpus
COCA	Corpus of Contemporary American English
EAP	English for academic purposes
EFA	Exploratory factor analysis (see 5.3.5)
EFL	English as a foreign language
EGP	English for general purposes
ELF	English as a lingua franca
ENL	English as a native language
ESL	English as a second language
ESP	English for specific purposes
FA	Factor analysis (see 5.3.5)
FPV	Finite verb phrase (see 5.3.4)
Info Teens	Informative Texts for Teens Corpus (see 4.3.2.5)
L1	First language
L2	Second or more (foreign) language
MAD	Median absolute deviation
MFTE	Multi-feature tagger of English (see 5.3.2)
PCA	Principal component analysis (see 5.3.5)
pmw	per million words
POS	Part of speech
SD	Standard deviation
TEC	Textbook English Corpus (see 4.3.1)
Youth Fiction	Youth Fiction Corpus (see 4.3.2.4)

The full list of the linguistic features tagged by the MFTE and their abbreviations can be found in the Appendix C (see Online Supplements on elenlefoll.github.io /TextbookMDA and http://doi.org/10.17605/OSF.IO/JPXAE).

CHAPTER 1

Introduction

Asked "Where is Brian?", French nationals of a certain generation will immediately reply: "Brian is in the kitchen". Those with a particularly good memory may follow up with: "Where is Jenny, the sister of Brian?" – and, to those in the know, the correct answer is: "Jenny is in the bathroom".[1] There is hardly any need for an in-depth linguistic analysis to conclude that this interaction is highly unlikely to have ever taken place in a real English-speaking family home. To most teachers and learners, it will be evident that it is the result of a none too inspired attempt to model WH-question forms in a textbook dialogue aimed at beginner learners of English as a Foreign Language (EFL). Together with dull gap-fill exercises and photos of out-of-date technology, for many adults, the very mention of the word *textbook* evokes vivid memories of such artificially sounding, contrived and sometimes even nonsensical dialogues.

This raises the question of the status and nature of textbook language as a specific 'variety' of language, which is at the heart of the present study. It focuses on contemporary EFL textbooks in use in European secondary schools. Situated at the interface between linguistics and foreign language teaching, this study examines the linguistic content of these textbooks and seeks empirical answers to the questions: What kind of English do school EFL textbooks portray? And how far removed is this variety of English from the kind of English that learners can be expected to encounter outside the EFL classroom?

1.1 Research objectives and methodological approach

The above questions are critical because, as many adults' lingering memories of school foreign language lessons testify (see also, e.g., Freudenstein 2002: 55), textbooks play an absolutely central role in classroom-based foreign language learning. In the following, we will see that the dominance of textbooks in EFL school contexts persists to this day. According to Thornbury (in a response to Chong 2012: n.p.), they "(more often [than] not) instantiate the curriculum, provide the texts, and – to a large extent – guide the methodology". In lower secondary EFL

1. This dialogue can be found in *Speak English 6e série verte* (Benhamou & Dominique 1977: 167). It was made popular by stand-up comedian Gad Elmaleh.

instructional contexts, in particular, textbooks constitute a major vector of foreign language input. Yet, numerous studies have shown that "considerable mismatches between naturally occurring English and the English that is put forward as a model in pedagogical descriptions" (Römer 2006: 125–126) exist. These mismatches have been observed and sometimes extensively described in textbooks' representations of numerous language features ranging from the use of individual words and phraseological patterns (e.g., Conrad 2004 on the preposition *though*; Gouverneur 2008 on the high-frequency verbs *make* and *take*), to tenses and aspects (e.g., Barbieri & Eckhardt 2007 on reported speech; Römer 2005 on the progressive). More rarely, textbook language studies have also ventured into the study of spoken grammar (e.g., Gilmore 2004) and pragmatics (e.g., Hyland 1994 on hedging in ESP/EAP textbooks).

However, as we will see in Chapter 2, previous EFL textbook studies have tended to focus on one or at most a handful of individual linguistic features. Taken together, they provide valuable insights into "the kind of synthetic English" (Römer 2004b: 185) that pupils are exposed to via their textbooks; yet, what is missing is a more comprehensive, broader understanding of what constitutes 'Textbook English' from a linguistic point of view. Although corpus-based[2] textbook analysis can be traced back to the pioneering work of Dieter Mindt in the 1980s, the language of secondary school EFL textbooks (as opposed to that of general adult EFL or English for Specific Purposes [ESP] coursebooks) remains an understudied area.

The present study therefore sets out to describe the linguistic content of secondary school EFL textbooks and to survey the similarities and most striking differences between 'Textbook English' and 'naturally occurring English' as used outside the EFL classroom, with respect to a wide range of lexico-grammatical features.

To this end, a corpus of nine series of secondary school EFL textbooks (43 textbook volumes) used at lower secondary level in France, Germany, and Spain was compiled (see 4.3.1). In addition, three reference corpora are used as baselines for comparisons between the language input EFL learners are confronted with via their school textbooks and the kind of naturally occurring English that they can be expected to encounter, engage with, and produce themselves on leaving school. Two of these have been built specifically for this project with the aim of representing comparable 'authentic' (for a discussion of this controversial term in ELT, see 2.2) and age-appropriate learner target language.

2. Here the adjectives 'corpus-based' and 'corpus-driven' are used synonymously (see, e.g., Meunier & Reppen 2015: 499 for further information as to how these terms are sometimes distinguished).

A bottom-up, corpus-based approach is adopted (e.g., Mindt 1992, 1995a; Biber & Quirk 2012; Biber & Gray 2015; Carter & McCarthy 2006a). A broad range of linguistic features are considered: ranging from tenses and aspects to negation and discourse markers. We will pay particular attention to the lexico-grammatical aspects of Textbook English that substantially diverge from the target learner language reference corpora and examine these with direct comparisons of textbook excerpts with comparable texts from the reference data.

1.2 Outline of the book

The following chapter outlines the background to and motivation behind the present study. Chapter 3 then provides a literature review of state-of-the-art research on the language of school EFL textbooks. It is divided in two parts. Part 1 is a methodological review in which the various methods employed so far to analyse, describe, and evaluate Textbook English are explained and illustrated with selected studies. Part 2 summarises the results of existing studies on various aspects of Textbook English, including lexical, grammatical and pragmatic aspects. Based on the methodological limitations and the gaps identified in the existing literature, Chapter 4 elaborates the specific research questions addressed in the present study. These research questions informed the decision-making processes involved in the compilation of the Textbook English Corpus (TEC) and the selection/compilation of three reference corpora designed to represent learners' target language. These processes and their motivations are explained in the remaining sections of Chapter 4.

Chapter 5 describes the multivariable statistical methods applied to describe the linguistic nature of Textbook English on multiple dimensions of linguistic variation. It begins by explaining the well-established multi-feature/dimensional analysis (MDA) method pioneered by Biber (1988, 1995; see also Berber Sardinha & Veirano Pinto 2014, 2019), before outlining the reasoning for the modified MDA framework applied in the present study. Chapter 6 presents the results of an MDA model of Textbook English which highlights the sources of linguistic variation within EFL textbooks across several dimensions of intra-textbook linguistic variation. Chapter 7 presents the results of a second MDA model that shows how Textbook English is both, in some respects, similar to and, in others, different from the kind of English that EFL learners are likely to encounter outside the classroom.

Chapter 8 explains how the two models contribute to a new understanding of the linguistic characteristics of Textbook English. This, in turn, has implications for teachers, textbook authors, editors, publishers, and policy-makers. These implications are discussed in Chapter 9. It first considers the potential impact of the substantial gaps between Textbook English and the target reference corpora before making suggestions as to how teachers, textbook authors, and editors may want to improve or supplement unnatural sounding pedagogical texts using corpora and corpus tools. Chapter 10 focuses on the study's methodological strengths and limitations. It explains how the modified MDA framework presented and applied in this study may be of interest to corpus linguists working on a broad range of research questions. Chapter 11 concludes with a synthesis of the most important take-aways from the study. It also points to promising future research avenues.

CHAPTER 2

Context and rationale

Why study textbook English?

This chapter outlines the underlying pedagogically-driven and theoretical motivations for this study beginning, in 2.1, with the status of English as a foreign language (EFL)[3] at secondary school level, with a focus on continental Europe. This is followed by a summary of some of the controversies around the contentious concept of 'authenticity' in 2.2. An overview of the linguistic and language development theories that motivated the present study is represented in 2.3, followed by a section highlighting the centrality of input in foreign language learning and teaching in 2.4. Section 2.5 turns to language input in lower secondary school EFL contexts, whilst 2.6 focuses on secondary school EFL learners' main source of English input: their textbooks. Finally, Section 2.7 situates the present study and its methodological framework within the growing body of "pedagogically-driven corpus-based research" (Gabrielatos 2006:1).

3. Note that, throughout this book, the term 'English as a foreign language' (EFL) is used to refer to learning English in countries and regions where English is not an official or otherwise widely used language (e.g., France, Germany, and Spain). For non-native English speakers learning English in countries/regions where English is an official or widely used language, the term 'English as a second language' (ESL) is preferred. Where both learning contexts are meant, English 'L2' is used, regardless of whether English is in fact an individual's second, third, or more non-native language. I recognise that all of these terms – 'native' vs. 'non-native' or 'foreign' and 'L1' vs. 'L2' – are inherently problematic with regards to their epistemology, operationalisations and underlying assumptions (see, e.g., Birkland et al. 2022; Holliday 2005; Ramjattan 2019). For lack of a better generalisable categorisation system, however, the terms 'English native speaker'/'English L1 user' and 'EFL learner'/'English L2 user' are used throughout as an imperfect means of differentiating between two typically very different language acquisition contexts in full recognition that such a dichotomisation represents a vast oversimplification of what are frequently much more complex language biographies and learning experiences.

2.1 English as a foreign language at secondary school level

As the most widely taught foreign language and the *lingua franca* of choice in business and academia, the utmost relevance of English as a Foreign Language (EFL) in the 21st century need not be explained. In mainland Europe, too, English is by far the most widely taught foreign language. At lower secondary school level, defined here as level 2 from the International Standard Classification of Education (hereafter ISCED; OECD, European Union, UNESCO Institute for Statistics 2015), almost all students (97.3% according to the latest available figures from 2014) attend English classes (European Commission, EACEA & Eurydice 2017: 13).

In Germany, English is a mandatory subject during compulsory secondary education in nine out of the sixteen *Bundesländer* (European Commission, EACEA & Eurydice 2017: 44). As of 2013, 97.8% of students were learning English in the *Sekundarstufe I* (lower-level secondary school, i.e. ISCED 2). Similarly high rates were recorded in France (98.6%) and Spain (100%) in 2016 (European Commission, EACEA & Eurydice 2017: 164).

In France and Germany, the expected minimum level of attainment based on the Common European Framework of Reference for Languages (hereafter CEFR; Council of Europe 2020) is B1 by the end of lower secondary, and B2 by the end of general upper secondary level, whilst in Spain it is A2 and B1 respectively (European Commission, EACEA & Eurydice 2017: 122–123). This difference in target proficiency level is reflected in the minimum annual instruction time for EFL as a compulsory subject: in the eighth year of compulsory schooling, it ranges from 111 hours per school year in Spain to 154 in Germany and 216 in France (European Commission, EACEA & Eurydice 2017: 107–108).[4]

Up until recently, the competence-based descriptors of the CEFR made frequent mentions of an idealised native speaker as the reference point. For instance, at B2 level, learners were expected to be able to "interact with a degree of fluency and spontaneity that makes regular interaction with native speakers quite possible without strain for either party" (Council of Europe 2001: 24) and to "sustain relationships with native speakers without unintentionally amusing or irritating them or requiring them to behave other than they would with a native speaker" (Council of Europe 2001: 76). However, the updated guidelines (Council of Europe 2020), like most current European school curricula, no longer explicitly mention native speakers as the target norm.

4. For Spain and Germany, these figures correspond to the weighted average annual instruction time as calculated on the basis of the number of students enrolled in each educational authority and type of school (European Commission, EACEA & Eurydice 2017: 107–108).

In Germany, the national 'core curriculum' stresses the need for learners of English to learn to deal with "authentic texts", in particular in listening and reading comprehension, as well as in mediation tasks (Kultusministerkonferenz 2012: 12, 15, 18). In Spain, too, the focus lies on the transferability of competences acquired in the classroom to genuine communicative situations:

> El enfoque orientado a la acción adoptado en el currículo se concentra en el estudiante, que es quien aprende, construye sus competencias y las utiliza, tanto para llevar a cabo las tareas de aprendizaje en el aula como las que demanda la comunicación real [The action-oriented approach adopted in the curriculum focuses on the learner, who is the one who learns, builds his or her competences and uses them, both to accomplish the learning tasks in the classroom and those afforded by real communication].[5]
>
> (Consejería de Educación, Juventud y Deporte de Madrid 2015: 133)

The French curriculum also makes clear that the priority of school English instruction should be enabling students to interact with authentic materials in all language skills (Conseil supérieur des programmes 2015).

Up until recently, there was no doubt that EFL teaching was expected to follow native-speaker norms. European foreign language curricula now generally refrain from referring to any specific native-speaker varieties. For instance, the German Education Standard for the general higher education entrance level (*Abitur*) states that:

> Sprachlicher Orientierungspunkt sind *Standardsprache(n)* sowie Register, Varietäten und Akzente, deren Färbung ein Verstehen nicht generell behindert [The linguistic point of reference is *standard language(s)*, as well as registers, varieties and accents, whose distinctiveness do not generally impede comprehension].
>
> (Kultusministerkonferenz 2012: 14 emphasis added)

In practice, however, this typically amounts to either a 'standard' British or a US-American English norm. Using similar terminology, the curriculum of the Autonomous Community of Madrid refers to "*una variante estándar de la lengua*" [a standard variety of the language] (Consejería de Educación, Juventud y Deporte de Madrid 2015: 432). At this stage, the repeated use of the word 'standard' begs the question: What is meant by 'standard varieties of English' in such educational contexts? This question has sparked controversies since at least the 1980s, when debates concerning the variety of English to be taught as part of the National Curriculum of England and Wales raged (Tony 1999: 1). Quirk (1995: 5)

5. Unless otherwise noted, all translations mine.

provided an early, succinct summary of the main concerns associated with the term 'Standard English':

> There are few enough (not least among professional linguists) that would claim the existence of a single standard within any one of the ENL [English L1] countries: plenty that would even deny both the possibility and the desirability of such a thing. Recent emphasis has been on multiple and variable standards (insofar as the use of the word 'standard' should be ventured): different standards for different occasions for different people – and each as 'correct' as each other.

The plurality of different 'standard' registers, varieties and accents to which Quirk refers is echoed in the German Education Standard cited above – as opposed to the excerpt from the Madrilenian curriculum which uses the singular article *una* implying that a single standard variety should be taught. Regardless of whether a single or multiple 'standards' are to be taught, in practice, what does or does not constitute a 'standard' form of any widely used language is notoriously difficult to define (for book-length discussions on Standard English, see, e.g., Crowley 2003; Milroy & Milroy 2012; Tony 1999). What most linguists, education scholars and, indeed, teaching practitioners would likely agree on, however, is that 'standard varieties' can be equated to prestige varieties (Tony 1999: 7) and prestige is usually associated with 'correctness'. This notion is confirmed in the German Education Standards, which states:

> Die Entwicklung der funktionalen kommunikativen Kompetenzen ist bezogen auf die *geläufige* und *korrekte* Verfügung über die sprachlichen Mittel in den Bereichen: Aussprache und Intonation, Orthographie, Wortschatz, Grammatik. [The development of functional communicative competence [in a foreign language] refers to the *typical/frequent* and *correct* use of linguistic features in the areas of: pronunciation and intonation, spelling, vocabulary and grammar].
> (Kultusministerkonferenz 2003: 9; emphases added)

Thus, despite not (officially) adhering to any (specific) native-speaker norm(s), the objectives set out by school educational authorities stipulate that pupils are expected to be taught *correct, typical*, and *frequent* English forms. Whilst measures of correctness necessarily involve some subjective judgements, objective measures of typicality and frequency of occurrence in English as it occurs naturally "in the wild" can be made on the basis of corpus data. At the same time, it is clear that such measures of frequency and typicality will differ depending on the situational context of language use. In sum, modern European secondary school curricula appear to advocate for the teaching of real-world, naturally occurring, idiomatic or, what has often been termed "authentic" English.

2.2 Authenticity in EFL teaching

'Authenticity' is a particularly challenging concept in ELT, especially in EFL contexts. Definitions abound – as do their interpretations (see Gilmore 2019 for an overview). One understanding, which is not infrequently encountered among English teachers, is that authentic input is input created by native speakers for native speakers (see, e.g., Little, Devitt & Singleton 2002). At the other end of the spectrum, some adopt very broad definitions such that essentially any text with a "true" communicative objective is deemed to be authentic (e.g., Swaffar 1985: 17). Since teaching and learning a language can easily be argued to constitute genuine communicative objectives, such definitions imply that all pedagogical texts are 'authentic'. In practice, this is clearly not the case: learners, teachers and researchers frequently unite to deplore the contrived, artificial-sounding texts typically found in EFL textbooks, which often feature pragmatically highly unlikely sentences of the type: *Where is Jenny, the sister of Brian?*, *Are you swimming in the sea?*[6] and *There's grass in the garden.*[7]

The crux of the problem is that authenticity can be understood either as a characteristic of a text, the participants of the text, its communicative intent, social or cultural context, or any combination of these. Hence, authenticity need not refer solely to the linguistic elements of the texts presented to learners. Indeed, some authors have (re)defined authenticity to include the relationship of the texts offered to the learners' culture (e.g., Prodromou 1992), learners' interaction with texts and the tasks associated to them (e.g., Widdowson 1978), and the learners' personal engagement with the texts (e.g., van Lier 2013). Given this wealth of definitions, Mauranen (2004a: 201–202) suggests that it may be advantageous to distinguish between "subjective" and "objective" authenticity. Such a distinction appears reasonable at first glance. However, according to Mauranen, subjective authenticity would reflect learners' perceptions of the materials, whilst teachers' and/or researchers' evaluation would be objective. This assumption that teachers' and researchers' evaluations are inherently objective is, however, highly questionable, given that even foreign language education scholars cannot agree on an operationalisable definition.

Indeed, though space precludes a detailed discussion of the many controversies around the term and its various meanings, this very brief introduction to the issue will argue that authenticity is simply too difficult to define for anyone to be expected to make objective classifications (for more detailed discussions of authenticity in foreign language teaching and materials design, see, e.g., Widdowson 1989;

6. From *Achievers Pre-intermediate* (see Table 5).

7. From *Green Line 1* (see Table 5).

Mishan 2005; Trabelsi, Tomlinson & Masuhara 2010; Tomlinson 2013a; Gilmore 2019; Nelson 2022). Part of the problem is that many of the debates on authenticity in ELT implicitly assume that a text either *is* or *is not* "authentic". Yet, authenticity need not be a dichotomous variable or, indeed, a uni-dimensional one (see also Bendix 1997: 23; Day & Bamford 1998: 58–59). That said, in the present study, the terms 'authentic', 'real-world', and 'naturally occurring' are used synonymously to refer to texts that have not been specifically produced nor modified or adapted with L2 learners in mind.

As for the pedagogical impact of authentic materials on L2 learners, some scholars have argued that the simplification and contrivance of teaching materials facilitates learning (e.g., Widdowson 1984: 218) whilst others have countered that they deprive learners of opportunities for naturalistic learning and can therefore hamper progress (e.g., Siepmann 2011: 29; Sinclair 1983; Wolff 1984). Others, still, have advocated for simplified or otherwise pedagogically modified texts that nonetheless retain the "natural qualities of authenticity" (Day & Bamford 1998: 59). The notion of 'enriched input' (also sometimes termed 'flooded input') has also been proposed: it refers to pedagogical texts employed in a meaning-focused activity, in which a target structure has artificially been multiplied to raise learners' awareness of the structure in context (see, e.g., Reinders & Ellis 2009).

The most common socio-functional argument put forward by detractors of contrived pedagogical materials is that authentic materials boost learners' motivation (e.g., Ahmad & Millar 2020; Gilmore 2011; Ghanbari, Esmaili & Shamsaddini 2015; Liedke 2013; Little, Devitt & Singleton 1989; Peacock 1997; Rüschoff & Wolff 1999; Sun 2010; Varmış Kiliç & Genç İlter 2015). However, others reject this argument claiming that the opposite is true: authentic texts demotivate learners because they make too many assumptions about known lexical, grammatical, and cultural knowledge (e.g., Freeman & Holden 1986; Prodromou 1996; Richards 2001: 252–54; Vielau 2005; Widdowson 2003: 107). Given how difficult it is to define (let alone: operationalise!) authenticity, conducting valid and reliable studies to measure the impact of authentic vs. non-authentic materials on learners' motivation (or, indeed, learning outcomes) constitutes a near impossible feat. Yet, motivation remains a popular argument both *for* and *against* the use of authentic materials. The textbook publishing industry has seemingly learnt to make the best of both worlds by, on the one hand, frequently plastering claims of "authentic English" and "authentic texts" on its book covers and marketing materials and, on the other, featuring plenty of pedagogically contrived texts within its coursebooks (Gilmore 2007: 106). Perhaps the most convincing claim is that acquiring the skills to engage with authentic materials may, in itself, be motivating for learners (e.g., Little, Devitt & Singleton 1989; Skehan 2014). In other words, intrinsic motivation may arise from the process of engaging with the materials, rather than the materials themselves being the cause of the motivation (see also Gilmore 2007: 108).

At any rate, knowing that authenticity is so notoriously difficult to define certainly relativises the contentious claims made by both proponents and critics of the use of authentic materials in the EFL classroom. Hence, rather than quibble over what *does* or *does not* constitute a genuinely 'authentic' or 'real-world' text in the EFL classroom, or to what degree, let us focus on a more relevant and, at least theoretically, operationalisable question: What kind of language do learners need to be exposed to and engage with in order to acquire typical, idiomatic English that will equip them with the linguistic, pragmatic, discourse, and sociocultural means to thrive outside the classroom? To do so, this study turns to usage-based approaches to language and language learning (see, e.g., Barlow & Kemmer 2000; Bybee & Hopper 2001; Bybee 2007; Ellis, Römer & O'Donnell 2016; Robinson & Ellis 2008; Tomasello 2005; Tyler et al. 2018).

2.3 Usage-based theories to L2 learning and teaching

A usage-based understanding of L2 learning and teaching naturally draws on a range of approaches, including various branches of usage-based linguistics, foremost, cognitive linguistics (Croft & Cruse 2004; Geeraerts 2006; Goldberg 1995, 2006; Lakoff & Johnson 2003; Langacker 1987, 2008), as well as emergentism (Bybee & Hopper 2001; Ellis 1998; Ellis & Larsen-Freeman 2006; Elman et al. 1996; MacWhinney 2006), constructionism (Harel & Papert 1991; Papert 2020; Piaget 2013), and complex dynamic systems theory (de Bot, Lowie & Verspoor 2007; Fogal & Verspoor 2020; Larsen-Freeman 1997; Verspoor 2017; Verspoor, Lowie & van Dijk 2008). These approaches are, in turn, based on decades of research in several related disciplines, including linguistic theory, psycholinguistics, cognitive and educational psychology and, more broadly, cognitive science (for a recent overview, see Ellis 2019). At the heart of all these approaches is the central notion that: "Language and its use are mutually inextricable; they determine each other" (Ellis & Larsen-Freeman 2009: 91). Language use therefore constitutes "the foundation for language learning" (Tyler & Ortega 2018: 5).

Usage-based linguistic theories place a strong emphasis on the centrality of meaning. Meaning is, of course, also a core tenet of contemporary communicative language teaching approaches. However, in usage-based language acquisition models, the centrality of meaning implies that all aspects of language, from lexis to syntax to discourse, are acquired as form-meaning pairings. These form-meaning pairings are conceptualised as constructions of various levels of complexity and abstraction: the most concrete and specific constructions are individual words and their concrete meaning in the real world, whilst more abstract ones consist of, for example, grammatical phenomena such as the present perfect or syntactic patterns such as verb argument structures, e.g., the ditransitive construction (Ellis & Ferreira-Junior 2009a: 188; see also, e.g., De Knop & Gilquin 2016; Herbst, Schmid & Faulhaber 2014; Goldberg 2006, 1995; Hoey 2005; Lewis 2009; Siepmann 2007; Sinclair 1991 on the concept of lexicogrammar).

Language is acquired as a result of exposure to these form-meaning mappings, or constructions, in "iterative usage events" (Tyler & Ortega 2018: 7; see also Barlow & Kemmer 2000) – in other words, when language users are exposed to, engage with, and produce surface-level linguistic patterns that convey specific meaning in genuine communicative situations. It is through these usage experiences that linguistic knowledge becomes entrenched in the learner's mind (see, e.g., Blumenthal-Dramé 2012). As such, and contrary to generative, rule-based theories of language acquisition (as postulated by, e.g., Chomsky 1995, 2002), humans are not endowed with any universal or innate abstract grammar rules. Consequently, language acquisition processes are not concerned with the setting of any parameters for pre-supposed innate grammar rules, but rather language users naturally construct rules as they gradually make generalisations on the basis of the linguistic patterns they encounter over time. This, in turn, means that language structure – in the form of various kinds of constructions, e.g., words, collocations, grammar, and discourse – cannot be successfully acquired if dissociated from meaning. Hence, following a usage-based approach to language acquisition, pedagogically contrived textbook texts and contextless sentences exemplifying grammar rules are not thought to be the most successful means to learn a language.

Language learning is a process and, in this paradigm, the ability to generalise over individual language usage events and to induce meaningful categories are understood as examples of domain-general cognitive processes, i.e., abilities that are not specific or restricted to language learning (e.g., Cohen & Lefebvre 2017; Murphy 2003), but which are rather at the heart of all aspects of human learning. For language acquisition, these general cognitive mechanisms (such as memorisation, pattern finding, abstraction, induction, categorisation and schematisation) have been shown to be driven by various aspects of the input language users are exposed to; in particular, they are known to be exquisitely sensitive to frequency effects (e.g., Ellis 2002). Indeed, the degree of entrenchment of any one construction in the learner's mind is thought to be proportional to the frequency of usage (e.g., Bybee & Hopper 2001; Bybee 2007; Ellis 2002; Tomasello 2005). This means that, in a usage-inspired L2 instruction paradigm, both the quantity and the quality of language input are crucial.

2.4 Input and frequency

Input is, in fact, central to all theories of L2 learning and teaching and: "no model of second language acquisition does not avail itself of input in trying to explain how learners create second language grammars" (Gass 1997:1; for more on the "input hypothesis" in SLA, see Krashen 1982, 1985). In usage-based accounts, input is understood as a wealth of information that captures both the frequencies at which various linguistic patterns occur in natural usage and the contexts in which they are most likely to (co)occur (Bybee & Hopper 2001; Bybee 2007). Numerous psycholinguistic, corpus- and computational-linguistic studies have now demonstrated that "the acquisition of constructions is input-driven and dependent on learners' experience with form-meaning mappings in context" (Ellis & Larsen-Freeman 2009:92). For instance, experiments (e.g., Elio & Anderson 1981, 1984; Posner & Keele 1968, 1970) have shown that the learning of categories from prototypical exemplars is optimised when learners are exposed to language input in which the distribution of specific exemplifications of a construction are skewed towards one prototypical exemplar (e.g., the verb *give* in ditransitive constructions). As they are exposed to more input, learners continually redefine the bounds of each construction category (Ellis & Larsen-Freeman 2009:95). Corpus studies (e.g., Ellis, Römer & O'Donnell 2016; Goldberg, Casenhiser & Sethuraman 2004) have demonstrated that the natural distributions of constructions follow Zipf's law (Zipf 1935, 1949), whereby one exemplar is by far the most frequent and the frequency of the second most frequent exemplar can be expected to be approximately half the frequency of the first exemplar and so on (for a succinct explanation with clear illustrations, see Brezina 2018:44–46). These highly frequent, semantically prototypical exemplars are thought to serve a 'pathbreaking' function facilitating the generalisation of a construction to more abstract instantiations (Goldberg 2006; Ninio 1999).

These effects have been demonstrated in both L1 and L2 acquisition contexts (e.g., Goldberg, Casenhiser & Sethuraman 2004; Lavi-Rotbain & Arnon 2022; Römer & Berger 2019). For instance, Ellis and Ferreira-Junior (2009a, 2009b) analysed ESL adult learners' use of three types of verb-argument constructions over a period of 32 months and found that participants' first use of each verb-argument construction was indeed with a 'pathbreaker' verb, which corresponds to the most frequent verb type of each construction in the learners' language input. Moreover, these pathbreaker verbs appear to "seed" the construction so that, over time, learners begin to use more (semantically similar) verbs as part of the process of mental abstraction of the construction. The results of these studies (see also Wulff et al. 2009) suggest that the naturally skewed distributions of construction type/token frequencies in natural language input optimises not only L1 but also L2 learning by providing one very high-frequency exemplar that is also prototypical in meaning and widely applicable in a broad range of contexts (cf. Hu & Maechtle 2021).

Thus, usage-based linguistic theories and the results of empirical studies converge to show that language learning is largely driven by frequency. That said, it is not by any means the only factor that contributes to successful language learning. Just like in all other non-linguistic learning processes, socio-emotional factors are also considered in usage-based approaches to language learning. These include surprise value, learner attention, transfer, overshadowing and blocking (see, e.g., Ellis 2002, 2006, 2008). Other important factors include the salience of a construction to comprehend or produce a particular utterance, as well as the prototypicality, generality or redundancy of a construction. Suffice to say, however, that, in naturalistic input, these aspects very often, though by no means always, correlate strongly with frequency of use. For instance, the most frequent forms are unlikely to be redundant and, as explained above, it is typically the most frequent exemplar of a construction that gives that construction its prototypical meaning (e.g., *give* in ditransitive constructions).

2.5 Input in lower secondary school EFL contexts

As we have seen, input is central to almost all SLA models and, in particular, to usage-based approaches, yet empirical research on the impact of input on L2 learning development remains relatively sparse (Gurzynski-Weiss et al. 2018: 292). Part of the issue is that, whilst the role of input in early L1 acquisition can be relatively easily examined by analysing the language of a young learner's main caretaker language (e.g., Behrens 2006; Clark & Casillas 2016; Kuhl & Meltzoff 1996), capturing the language L2 learners are exposed to is rather more complex:

> Rather than a single or limited set of caretakers, second language (L2) learners are exposed to numerous native and nonnative speakers, making it nearly impossible to accurately characterize all sources of input.
>
> (Gurzynski-Weiss et al. 2018: 291)

The few studies that have attempted to do so have, however, concluded that input is equally important in L2 as in L1 acquisition (see, e.g., Moyer 2008 on phonological attainment). Whilst capturing the total language input of (adult) learners in ESL contexts is particularly tricky, in lower secondary school EFL contexts, L2 input is rather more restricted and thus easier to capture. At lower secondary school level in France, Germany, and Spain extracurricular exposure to and interaction with English remains, on average, fairly limited (Berns, de Bot & Hasebrink

2007). Note, however, this is not the case everywhere (see, e.g., Henry 2014 for the case of Sweden) and that the situation is rapidly evolving. Indeed, recent surveys have shown that the proportion of teenagers in Germany who consume English-medium media is on the rise: 43% of 12- to 19-year-olds in Germany report watching YouTube videos in a language other than German – overwhelmingly English – at least once a week (Feierabend et al. 2020: 48). The percentages reported at lower secondary school level are only marginally lower: 32% for 12–13-year-olds and 39% for 14–15-year-olds (Feierabend et al. 2020: 48). We can expect similar trends in France and Spain: as teenage EFL learners' English proficiency grows, so does their consumption of media in English and engagement in English-medium (online) communication – making it increasingly difficult to discern how much of their L2 input is classroom-based.

At the time of writing, however, formal classroom-based English input remains the dominant source of English input for most pupils at lower secondary school level in the three countries of interest (more on this in 2.6). This input consists foremost of the content of the textbook (that is: the student's coursebook, associated audio and video materials and potentially also a workbook and/or vocabulary book), teacher talk, peers' production, and, if used, any additional teaching materials. The present study was thus motivated by the combination of the centrality of input in L2 acquisition processes and the fact that a substantial proportion of that input in lower secondary school EFL contexts comes from textbooks. Indeed, although other sources of classroom-based L2 input have just been listed, large proportions of these sources are in fact directly or indirectly influenced and/or mediated by textbook content. For instance, much of teacher talk at secondary school level revolves around the textbook, its explanations, instructions, and tasks, and much of learner writing, learner-teacher and learner-learner spoken interactions are produced on the basis of these same textbook tasks, prompts, and models (see, e.g., Huang 2019: 87).

2.6 Textbooks in the EFL classroom

Although statistics are hard to come by (Schaer 2007: 255), textbooks are widely recognised as the primary source of formal L2 input in European lower secondary school EFL contexts. In fact, textbooks are almost universally "considered to be the backbone of second and foreign language teaching" (Tateyama 2019: 404; see also, e.g., Diepenbroek & Derwing 2014; Oelkers 2008). Richards (2015: 594) goes as far claiming that they largely determine teachers' teaching practice. Across all EFL instructional contexts, it has been deplored time and again, by language education scholars and teacher trainers alike, that teachers are heavily dependent on textbooks and that there is *de facto* no distinction between textbook and syllabus (e.g., Schaer 2007: 256; Sinclair & Renouf 1988: 145). According to Vellenga (2004: n.p.; see also, e.g., Hyland 1994; Kim & Hall 2002), textbooks constitute both "the centre of the curriculum and syllabus in most [EFL] classrooms". Thornbury (in a response to Chong 2012: n.p.; see also Bragger & Rice 2000: 107) goes further and claims that:

> the reason that coursebooks are so often in the line of fire is that they do to a large extent dominate and determine so many aspects of a teacher's day-to-day professional life. They (more often [than] not) instantiate the curriculum, provide the texts, and – to a large extent – guide the methodology.

This view is echoed in the following observations:

> Together with teaching methodologies, [textbook] materials represent the interface between teaching and learning, the point at which needs, objectives and syllabuses are made tangible for both teachers and students. They provide most of the input and language exposure that learners receive in the classroom [...].
> (Hyland 2013: 391)

As Usó-Juan and Martínez-Flor (2010: 424) stress, textbooks have always tended to be "[t]he main source of input presented in classroom settings" (see also Tono 2004: 45); hence, this is not a new phenomenon but, in spite of much criticism of textbooks, it is also not one that appears to be changing in any significant way.

Virtually all European lower secondary EFL classrooms are equipped with textbooks. Thus, the overwhelming dominance of the textbook as a source of L2 input that has been observed in general, global EFL contexts is likely to be also true of lower secondary school EFL education in mainland Europe. Regarding the secondary school German context specifically, Kurtz (2019: 116) speaks of the "großenteils lehrwerkorientierte Alltagspraxis des Englischunterrichts [largely textbook-oriented everyday practice of teaching English]", especially in the "*Sekundarstufe I*" (Kurtz 2019: 122; see also Hermes 2009: 9), i.e., in the first five years of secondary school. Similarly, Volkmann (2010: 235) reports that:

> das traditionelle Leitmedium des Unterrichts, das Lehrwerk, insbesondere das Lehrbuch (Schülerbuch), bleibt in der Phase des Spracherwerbs (also vor allem in der Sekundarstufe I) das oftmals absolut dominante Medium der Instruktion) [as the medium which has traditionally guided and organised teaching, the textbook, especially the coursebook (i.e., the pupil's book), often remains the absolutely dominant medium of instruction in the language acquisition phrase (i.e., especially at lower secondary school level)].

In some *Bundesländer*, this reliance on textbooks is, in fact, more or less directly prescribed in the curriculum. The English curriculum for *Gymnasium* in Hessen, for instance, proclaims that, at lower secondary level (*Sekundarstufe I*) the textbook is *the* "Leitmedium" (Hessisches Kultusministerium 2010: 4).

Referring to the German context more generally, Siepmann (2007: 59) points to a noticeable overlap between textbooks, syllabus and vocabulary teaching methodology when he notes that:

> [i]n der Sekundarstufe I verlassen sich die Lehrer auf das Wörterverzeichnis und die Grammatik des Lehrbuchs; die ausgeprägte Einzelwortorientierung dieser Lernhilfen wird im Unterricht übernommen [at lower secondary school level, teachers rely on the textbook's vocabulary and grammar sections; the strong emphasis on individual words that these materials promote is mirrored in vocabulary teaching and explanation].

Over in Spain, Alejo González et al. (2010: 61) observes that:

> Spanish secondary school students meet English first and foremost in the language classroom and the coursebook that they use is likely to be their primary source of English language input.

The situation in France is particularly interesting as teachers' perceived over-reliance on textbooks has led to calls to abandon textbooks altogether or, at the very least, to adapt and/or supplement textbook materials with 'authentic' texts (see 2.2). In particular, teachers in their post-studies qualification stage are often told by teacher trainers and assessors to avoid relying on a textbook in their observed (and assessed) classes. This backlash has led many French EFL teachers to resorting to a mix-and-match approach – combining texts and activities from several textbooks and additional resources, rather than relying on a single textbook series (personal communication with practising teachers, see also forum discussions on neoprofs.org 2016; Séré & Bassy 2010: 10–11). Nonetheless, even when surveyed by the Ministry of National Education, French EFL teachers report that, at *collège* level [lower secondary school, see Table 3], textbooks are "*indispensable*" (Leroy 2012: 62).

The palpable tension concerning the use of textbooks in French EFL classrooms is, in fact, symptomatic of a far more universal love-hate relationship with textbooks in ELT. Indeed, in spite of the undeniable popularity of EFL textbooks, as demonstrated by their widespread use in foreign language classrooms across the world and the great range of publications on offer, detractors have regularly criticised the "superficial and reductionist" content of textbooks that impose "uniformity of syllabus and approach" and remove "initiative and power from teachers"

(Tomlinson 2001: 67). Following this line of thought, Prabhu (1989) argues that textbooks rob teachers of the freedom to freely order, use and localise materials.

Another important factor to consider is that most EFL textbook publishing houses are commercial, for-profit businesses. Some have therefore claimed that textbook publishers do not always have learners' best interests at heart since, at the end of the day, learners are rarely involved in textbook selection processes (in fact, it is not rare for teachers to be entirely excluded from textbook selection processes, too, see, e.g., Friederici 2019; Stein et al. 2001: 5–6; Stranks 2013: 338). It has been argued that privately outsourcing such a crucial aspect of EFL education has the potential to stall the implementation of recent research findings in applied linguistics, second language acquisition, and other relevant disciplines. Some claim that "the economic imperative" incites publishers to "clone previously best-selling coursebooks rather than risk investment in more principled innovations" (Tomlinson 2013b: 541; see also the conclusions of Burton 2023 whose analysis of the "canon of pedagogical grammar" in ELT textbooks combines textbook content analysis and interviews with textbook authors, editors and publishers). Tomlinson (2013b: 3) summarises the situation as follows:

> Publishers obviously aim to produce excellent books which will satisfy the wants and needs of their users but their need to maximize profits makes them cautious and conservative and any compromise with authors tends still to be biased towards perceived market needs rather than towards the actual needs and wants of learners.

This is not to say that attempts at innovation have not been made – on the contrary. For example, the 'lexical approach' (Lewis 1993, 1997, 2009), that challenges the all-empowering centrality of grammar in the L2 syllabus, inspired the design of several commercially published textbooks (e.g., Dellar & Hocking *Innovations*, 2000; Dellar & Walkley, *Outcomes*, 2011). These emphasised the importance of conceptualising language as 'grammaticalised lexis' as opposed to the customary 'lexicalised grammar' approach (Lewis 1993: 34) using corpus-informed texts and activities. Presumably these were not great commercial successes, however, because a brief tour of the tables of contents of today's most popular EFL textbooks shows that these continue to treat grammar and vocabulary as two distinct areas of language teaching and learning (see also Tan 2003). Again, it is easy to see how school textbook publishers would be placing themselves at a competitive disadvantage if they were the first to remove what has come to be an expected feature of foreign language textbooks and has, so far, proved to be an attractive selling point. The constraints associated with the commercial production of ELT materials have been extensively discussed in, among others, Bell & Gower (2011);

Richards (2015) and Gray (2010). Although these publications tend to focus on the global ESL/EFL textbook market, most often targeted at adult learners, continental European publishers producing school textbooks for their respective domestic markets face many of the same constraints.

An additional constraint, and one that may be more specific to the European textbook market, is that European foreign language curricula and syllabi are now expected to be aligned with the CEFR. Indeed, the CEFR has established itself as an unavoidable pedagogical framework for language learning and teaching in European schools and, as such, has had a major influence on textbook and task design (Hallet & Legutke 2013: 8) (though the framework is not without its critics; for the German context, see, e.g., Bausch 2005; Vogt 2011).

Given the widespread criticism of textbooks for a multitude of reasons, we may ask: why *are* textbooks nonetheless so ubiquitous in ELT and even considered "indispensable" (Leroy 2012: 62) by many secondary school EFL teachers? As any practising teacher can attest, textbooks are, first and foremost, a much-needed timesaver when teachers' timetables are packed and classes full (see, e.g., Nordlund 2016: 48). Recognising a genuine need to reduce teachers' preparation load, textbook publishers have responded by adapting their business models and are now marketing all-encompassing "multidimensional packages" (Dat 2013: 409) which go well beyond what was traditionally understood as a textbook. For each textbook within a textbook series, these packages now frequently include, in addition to the pupil's coursebook, an activity workbook and a teachers' manual with often very detailed lesson plans, step-by-step instructions, extra photocopiable worksheets, answer sheets, as well as optional related games, quizzes, and assessments, vocabulary apps, audio recordings, videos, graded readers, etc. (Dat 2013: 410–411). Given the wealth – and, it is worth highlighting, the often high quality – of these materials, it is easy to see how, in particular inexperienced, teachers can quickly come to rely on them so much.

In general, the textbook (package) is perceived as a trustworthy authority (e.g., Abello-Contesse & López-Jiménez 2010; Brown 2014; Chien & Young 2007; Ghosn 2013). There is often a sense that, if it is followed to the letter, teachers can be reassured that their lessons will cover all aspects of the curriculum and syllabus (Nordlund 2016: 48). Textbooks therefore contribute to standardising learning outcomes (Anton 2017: 13). In many cases, textbooks also act as a mark of credibility vis-à-vis ever-more demanding parents. Furthermore, textbooks are frequently seen – by learners, teachers, and parents alike – as an ideal way to present contents in a well-structured and systematically organised order, following tried-and-tested progressions (Burton 2019, 2020; Möller 2016). This leads to:

> a circle (whether vicious or virtuous), whereby publishers provide their customers with the kind of teaching materials that they are asking for, and their customers continue to ask for the same kinds of teaching materials as they feel that what they have seen before represents the norms they should be following.
> (Burton 2019: 220–221)

The fact that these norms and progressions may be the product of decades of innovation stagnation rather than the conclusion of any empirical studies on learners' development of linguistic competence in instructional EFL settings is usually overlooked. On the contrary, textbooks are often perceived as "Innovationsträger [drivers of innovation]" that bring pedagogical research findings and new teaching methods to the foreign language classroom (Anton 2017: 14).

Given the rapid growth in technology-based ELT and, more generally, computer-assisted language learning (CALL; see, e.g., Chapelle 2010), it may seem rather inconceivable that, in the late 2010s and early 2020s, secondary school learners' main source of formal English input still comes in the form of book publications (Bezemer & Kress 2016: 477). Vague claims and slogans such as "*Die Perspektive des Schulbuchs ist digital* [The future of the textbook is digital]" (Landesregierung Nordrhein-Westfalen 2016: 8, 25) found in North-Rhine Westphalia's *Leitbild 2020 für Bildung in Zeiten der Digitalisierung* [Mission statement for 2020 for education in the day and age of digitalisation] are frequently heard. Yet, to date, the vast majority of so-called "digital textbooks" and their accompanying e-materials are essentially replicas of the same textbooks, graded readers, grammar books and flashcards that publishers still successfully sell in paper form. Hence, although all major school textbook publishers now promote various digital textbook packages (Kurtz 2019: 119), for now, these digital textbooks offer little more than digitised versions of their paper counterparts. They typically represent little to no change in terms of content or teaching methodologies (see, e.g., Gehring 2013; Richards 2015: 594; Stranks 2013: 348–349; Schildhauer, Schulte & Zehne 2020: 30–31). The obvious lack of suitable digital materials (as well as, crucially, teacher training in using existing digital resources and, in many cases, the necessary equipment and infrastructure) made headlines during the (partial) school closures triggered by the COVID-19 pandemic (see, e.g., Blume 2020; Fominykh et al. 2021; Kerres 2020; Starkey et al. 2021; van de Werfhorst, Kessenich & Geven 2020). Whilst the urgency of the pandemic is likely to have accelerated both the development and the acceptance of new digital teaching materials compatible with online, on-site, and hybrid instructional settings, genuine advances in commercial materials development can nevertheless be expected to remain slow. Indeed, academic research has been churning out innovative, evidence-based ideas for new digital L2 teaching materials for the better part of a decade (see, e.g., Biebighäuser, Zibelius & Schmidt 2012; Meurers et al. 2010,

2019); however, few of these ideas have been translated into any of the best-selling secondary school EFL textbook series examined as part of the present study. In the textbook industry, innovation remains a commercial risk.

As this section has shown, Vellenga's (2004: n.p.) claim that "textbooks remain the most important tools and resources in the EFL classroom" still rings true today – in spite of their many shortcomings (see also Möller 2016). In addition, it has concluded that textbooks continue to play a particularly important role at lower secondary school level – accounting for a substantial, if not the largest, proportion of L2 input that EFL learners are exposed to. Gaining a comprehensive understanding of the language that modern secondary school EFL textbooks present to learners is therefore of high pedagogical value. This is precisely what the present study sets out to achieve.

The approach adopted to do so is corpus-based. In other words, the totality of texts from a representative sample of EFL textbooks used at lower secondary school level in France, Germany, and Spain (see Table 5) is analysed as a "learners' L2 [input] corpus" (Gabrielatos 1994: 13; see also Meunier & Gouverneur 2007: 122). Thus, rather than following a page-by-page textbook analysis approach, the language of this corpus of Textbook English (see 4.3.1 for details of its composition) is examined as a variety of English, much like Academic English, Australian English, or Aviation English.

2.7 Corpus linguistics and foreign language education

The present corpus-based textbook analysis study follows in the footsteps of a now decades-long tradition of "pedagogy-driven corpus-based research" (Gabrielatos 2006: 1). Corpus-based methodologies rely on the exploration of language corpora, principled computerised collections of real-world, authentic texts, to investigate patterns of language use. Corpus linguistics is characterised by its empirical basis, analysing (usually large) collections of texts using automatic and interactive data retrieval techniques, and by its application of mixed quantitative and qualitative analytical methods. Drawing on corpus data without (too many) assumptions allows linguists to observe language features, e.g., lexico-grammatical patterns and other phenomena, which have not necessarily been previously explored or described (Hunston 2002: 1). For example, analyses of corpora of spoken British English revealed highly frequent lexico-grammatical features in spoken English which had previously not been considered in traditional grammars (see, e.g., Carter & McCarthy 1995; McCarthy & Carter 1995; Carter, Hughes & McCarthy 1998; Hughes 2010; McCarthy 1998).

As a discipline, corpus linguistics has, from the outset, positioned itself as a decisively applied subdiscipline of linguistics. Pedagogical applications have been at the heart of many strands of corpus-linguistic research and corpus methods[8] are now widely used in numerous areas of applied linguistics relevant to second language acquisition and foreign language education. In particular, corpus-linguistic methods have now become the norm in (learner) lexicography (see, e.g., Granger 2018; Rundell 2008; Runte 2015) and, since the 1990s, have had a major impact on the development of reference and learner grammars of English (e.g., Biber et al. 1999; Conrad, Biber & Leech 2011 for English; see also Siepmann 2018a, 2019; Siepmann & Bürgel 2022 for a corpus-based learner grammar of French). For instance, the second edition of the *Longman Grammar of Spoken and Written English* (Biber et al. 1999) relied exclusively on empirical data drawn from corpus analyses (Conrad 2000: 548–549). Moreover, corpora of learner language, both written and spoken, have been used in contrastive studies comparing learner language to native and/or non-native expert language use to investigate the influence of learners' L1s on their L2 productions (e.g., Bruyn & Paquot 2021; Granger, Hung & Petch-Tyson 2002; Tracy-Ventura & Paquot 2020), as well as in a host of natural language processing (NLP) applications, e.g., to automatically score and mark learner texts, perform proficiency level classification, error detection and/or correction (e.g., Ballier, Díaz Negrillo & Thompson 2013; Leacock et al. 2010; Meurers 2015; Reder, Harris & Setzler 2003).

According to Granger (2004: 136), the main fields of pedagogical application of corpus data are classroom methodology and materials and syllabus design. However, Granger (2004: 136) adds that "with the exception of ELT dictionaries, the number of concrete corpus-informed achievements is not proportional to the number of publications advocating the use of corpora to inform pedagogical practice". Recent studies appear to confirm that this statement is, unfortunately, very much still valid today (see, e.g., Callies 2019; Chambers 2019; Jablonkai & Csomay 2022; Karlsen & Monsen 2020; Kavanagh 2021).

Concerning the impact of corpus data on pedagogical methods, most research has so far focused on data-driven learning, i.e. learners' interaction with corpus data. However, in spite of the wealth of publications on data-driven learning going back to the work of Tim Johns from the 1980s onwards (e.g., Johns 1986, 1993, 2002, 2014) and a myriad of studies pointing to its effectiveness in a wide range of teaching contexts (summarised in Boulton & Cobb 2017; Lee, Warschauer & Lee 2019), the direct use of corpora in the foreign language classroom has yet to become more than an exception to the norm (Barbieri &

8. For more on the debate of corpus linguistics as a discipline vs. a methodological framework, see, e.g., Stefanowitsch (2020: 21–60) and Taylor (2008).

Eckhardt 2007:320; see also Callies 2019; Leńko-Szymańska & Boulton 2015; Leńko-Szymańska 2017; Mukherjee 2004).

As for the application of corpus data in materials and syllabus design, corpus linguists have long sung the merits of incorporating corpus-based findings in L2 materials in a way that will inevitably require some modifications to traditional foreign language syllabi (e.g., Biber & Reppen 2002; Conrad 2000; Frazier 2003; Harwood 2005; Holmes 1988; Granger 2004; McCarthy & Carter 1995; Nelson 2022; Timmis 2013); yet, in spite of the growing availability of freely accessible corpora and corpus research findings, very few EFL textbooks are advertised as corpus-informed, let alone corpus-based. In the rare cases where corpora do inform EFL textbook design, it tends to be in the context of English for Special Purposes (ESP) and English for Academic Purposes (EAP) textbooks (Meunier & Gouverneur 2009:180–81). General EFL textbooks, by contrast, appear to remain largely unaffected by such moves (for a notable exception see the *Touchstone* series by McCarthy et al. 2005).

When Prowse asked ELT materials designers how they approached textbook writing back in 1988, textbook authors stressed the creative nature of the writing process. Prowse (1998:137) concluded that most textbook authors:

> appear to rely heavily on their own intuitions viewing textbook writing in the same way as writing fiction, while at the same time emphasizing the constraints of the syllabus. The unstated assumption is that the syllabus precedes the creation.

A few decades later, Burton (2012) conducted a case study survey of fifteen EFL coursebook authors, which revealed that authors still largely relied on their intuition. Accessibility issues, lack of relevant skills and knowledge, and time constraints were all cited as reasons for their lack of corpus use in designing ELT materials. Given the wealth of English-language corpora and accessible, user-friendly tools that became available over the past few decades, this lack of innovation is regrettable. Indeed, as corpus-based English grammars such as the *Longman Grammar of Spoken and Written English* (Biber et al. 1999, see also 2021 for a more up-to-date corpus-based English learner grammar) have since shown:

> Unfortunately, decisions about the sequencing of material, typical contexts, and natural discourse are not served as well by intuition and anecdotal evidence as judgments of accuracy are. (Biber & Conrad 2010:1)

Analysing in-depth interviews with four ELT editors employed by Cambridge University Press (CUP), Curry et al. (2022) yielded more recent insights into what textbook editors currently perceive as the advantages and limitations of corpus linguistics for ELT materials development. It transpired that the perceived limitations are largely traceable to limited knowledge about existing corpora (including what kind of corpus metadata are available and how they can be exploited) and corpus tools.

The conclusions of this most recent survey are particularly sobering considering that CUP likely represents a notable exception in the ELT publishing world; indeed, it has a long tradition of collecting and processing data for the (co-)development of language corpora. Most notably, it has been instrumental in the development of the Cambridge Learner Corpus, which is used by CUP authors to target common learner errors in ELT publications, including textbooks. In this respect, it also constitutes an exception to the rule that Granger (2015: 494) describes as learner corpora's "more nominal than real" impact on textbooks.

If corpora and the insights of corpus-linguistics studies have yet to be taken on board by EFL textbook authors, editors and publishers, it is nonetheless possible to examine and evaluate the language of textbooks using corpus-linguistic methods. This is what the present study sets out to do. As will be shown in the following literature review chapter, it is not, by any means, the first study to attempt to do so (see also Nelson 2022).

CHAPTER 3

Research on the language of school EFL textbooks

The state of the art

Having established that both the frequency and quality of input is fundamental to L2 acquisition and that, at least in the context of European secondary schools, textbooks account for a large proportion of learners' language input, the following question arises: Are secondary school textbooks providing the kind of language input that will promote 'authentic' language acquisition, or, to quote the Standing Conference of the German Ministers of Education (Kultusministerkonferenz 2003: 9) "the correct use of typical and frequent linguistic elements"? To shed light on this question, the present chapter will present previous research on the language of EFL textbooks. Only where methodological innovations or specific fields have been left out in English for General Purposes (EGP) textbook studies, will the occasional reference to textbooks of other foreign languages, or textbooks for other levels and learning contexts be made.

Textbooks have long been a cherished object of study in a wide range of disciplines applying an equally diverse array of methods. As "social-cultural-political artefact[s]" (Singapore Wala 2013: 120), foreign language textbooks may also be considered as "sources not only of grammar, lexis, and activities for language practice, but, like Levi's jeans and Coca Cola, commodities which are imbued with cultural promise" (Gray 2000: 274). As such, it is quite natural that the broad spectrum of EFL textbook studies should include fields of research as disparate as the pragmatics of politeness in German EFL textbooks (Limberg 2016), semiotic approaches to the representation of culture in Hungarian EFL textbooks (Weninger & Kiss 2013), and the evaluation of interactional metadiscourse in Iranian EFL textbooks (Alemi & Isavi 2012), using an equally broad range of different methods. Though research on EFL textbooks extends well beyond "the linguistic nature of their content" (Littlejohn 2011: 182), the present study focuses exclusively on the language of textbooks – as opposed to the pedagogical reasoning behind the textbooks' tasks and activities and their effectiveness (see, e.g., Harwood 2005; Jacobs & Ball 1996; Ranalli 2003), their layout or the nature of content topics chosen by the textbook authors (see, e.g., recent special issue of *Language, Culture and Curriculum*; Canale 2021; also Siegel 2014), or its adherence and fulfilment of specific educational standards (e.g., Cools & Sercu 2006 on the extent to which the tasks and topics of two German as a Foreign Language textbooks are aligned with the CEFR) – hence the studies reviewed in the present chapter all focus on the linguistic content of EFL textbooks, hereafter referred to as 'Textbook English'.

The present literature review does not claim to cover the full breadth of past and current research on the language of EFL textbooks. To the author's best knowledge, no systematic review of Textbook English studies has been attempted so far. This is likely due to the incredibly diverse range of methods and linguistic foci that characterise this field of study, as well as the many different types of English textbooks that cater for different instructional settings, proficiency levels, and regional markets and are therefore not readily comparable. The most comprehensive overview of Textbook English research to date can be found in Meunier and Gouverneur (2009: 183–184). A total of 27 studies, spanning from 1990 to 2009, are summarised in a tabular format. The overview not only covers the linguistic content of textbooks, e.g., its "authenticity", grammar, and vocabulary, but includes a few studies on non-linguistic aspects of textbook research, e.g., task design.

Following a similar approach, all the relevant studies surveyed as part of this literature review are summarised in an interactive table in Appendix A ⟨elenlefoll.github.io/TextbookMDA/AppendixA⟩. It presents the results of a non-exhaustive survey of Textbook English studies published over the past four decades, summarising some of the key information on each study, including its main language focus, methodological approach, information on the textbooks investigated, and, if applicable, on any reference corpora used. Empty cells represent fields that are either not applicable to this particular study or for which no information could be found. Intended as a dynamic resource, this searchable and filterable table lists over 80 studies on the language content of English L2 textbooks, thereby demonstrating the breadth of Textbook English studies published to date.

In light of the sheer number of publications on the subject, the present chapter can only aim to provide key insights from a selection of studies. To this end, this chapter is divided into two main parts. Part one (3.1) focuses on the methodologies applied from the 1980s to the present day with the aim of investigating the authenticity and/or pedagogical relevance of various features of Textbook English. Summaries of individual studies serve to exemplify the methodological approaches described. In this first part, the results of studies are only presented to illustrate the advantages and limitations of each method. Part two (3.2) then reports on key results from a range of relevant Textbook English studies, including the ones outlined in the methodological part of the chapter (3.1). Since some aspects of Textbook English have been at the heart of more than one study, this second half is organised in sections that roughly correspond to the different types of linguistic features examined in these studies (tense, aspect, lexis, etc.), rather than by chronological order. The chapter concludes with a list of implications for the present study that concern both the choice of data and methods and the language focus of the ensuing analyses (3.3).

3.1 Methodological review

3.1.1 Intra-textbook approaches

The studies outlined in the following sections focus exclusively on describing Textbook English without relying on any form of comparison with other sources of English. Such 'intra-textbook' approaches are illustrated in the following sections with, first, check-list approaches (3.1.1.1), second, largely qualitative page-by-page surveying methods (3.1.1.2), and third, corpus-based intra-textbook methods that rely more on quantitative analyses (3.1.1.3).

3.1.1.1 *Checklist approach to textbook evaluation*

Perhaps the most common approach to evaluating textbooks, and one that will be familiar to many practising teachers, consists in choosing, adapting, or developing and then applying checklist-based evaluation frameworks. Typical EFL textbook checklists can feature anything from a dozen (e.g., Garinger 2002) to over a hundred criteria (e.g., Tomlinson et al. 2001). They usually resort to *ad hoc* considerations of the pedagogical and linguistic content of the textbooks, rather than apply any form of empirical measures. Thus, practitioners are expected to be able to answer questions such as: "*Do the exercises and activities in the textbook promote learners' language development?*" (Garinger 2002: 2) or "*Are the grammar rules presented in a logical manner and in increasing order of difficulty?*" (Miekley 2005: n.p.) without resorting to any concrete norms, standards, methodologies, or tools.

It goes without saying that attempting to construct a checklist designed to objectively evaluate foreign language textbooks across all dimensions constitutes a truly monumental task. By way of illustration, Tomlinson et al. (2001) devised a set of 133 criteria and used them to each, independently, evaluate eight adult EFL textbooks. The results of their analysis are derived from the mean scores of the four researchers' criteria scores, yet they concede that "the same review, conducted by a different team of reviewers, would almost certainly have produced a different set of results" (Tomlinson et al. 2001: 82). Thus, if checklists are completed without any comparison benchmarks, the results of such checklist-based evaluations risk being largely based on subjective judgement. An advantage of this method, however, is that checklists can easily be adapted to specific teaching contexts. However, this very advantage also entails a risk: rarely are these custom-made checklists thoroughly evaluated in terms of their reliability and validity (Mukundan 2010: 271). For a comprehensive review of checklist-based evaluation frameworks for EFL textbooks, see Mukundan and Ahour (2010).

3.1.1.2 *Page-by-page intra-textbook analysis*

Before the advent of computer-readable corpora, manual page-by-page surveying of publications was the only way to conduct textbook language studies. In fact, for some types of investigations, this approach is still popular (e.g., Cullen & Kuo 2007; Timmis 2003; Vellenga 2004). By way of illustration, the following section considers the manual intra-textbook methodology applied in Vellenga's (2004) study on pragmatic information featured in EFL grammar textbooks and integrated skills textbooks.

The study is largely qualitative in nature, though Vellenga (2004) includes some quantitative metrics gleaned from manually counting the number of pages containing pragmatic information (defined as "any information related to culture, context, illocutionary force, politeness, appropriacy and/or register", Vellenga 2004: n. p.) as compared to the total number of pages in each textbook. This page-by-page counting approach is not without its problems and, indeed, Vellenga warns that the resulting "percentages of pages featuring pragmatic information" are somewhat misleading, since, in most cases, pragmatic information only comes in the form of one or two sentences on any one page, so that the page-counting method is prone to producing inflated percentages. In each of the textbooks investigated, Vellenga also counts the number of explicit mentions and metapragmatic descriptions of 21 different speech acts, such as requests, apologies and complaints. Furthermore, instances of metalanguage in the textbooks[9] are identified and coded according to four types of functions: description, instruction, introduction, and task-related. Using this data, Vellenga proceeds with descriptive analyses of the types of sentences used in the metalanguage – imperative, declarative and interrogative – and makes *ad hoc* observations about the use of pronouns in metalanguage.

In addition, Vellenga conducted telephone interviews with four experienced EFL/ESL teachers to inquire whether they thought that the textbooks presented issues of politeness and contextual language use in an appropriate manner, and to ask whether the interviewees supplemented textbook materials with additional pragmatic information. Such methodological triangulation can be a very mean-

9. Note that, here, Vellenga only considered texts "used to preface activities and explain grammatical points" for the analysis of metalanguage, since, as she points out, "[t]he entire contents of a textbook, by its very nature, can be considered metalinguistic" (2004: n. p.).

ingful addition to such an intra-textbook page-by-page analysis but nevertheless bears the same risks observed with the checklist method in terms of reliability and validity.

3.1.1.3 *Corpus-based intra-textbook analysis*

One of the conclusions of Vellenga's (2004) study is that some of the worrying observations in the representations of pragmatic information in EFL textbooks would merit further exploration in a larger study. This could be achieved by replicating the analysis on a large corpus of EFL textbooks using (partially) automated corpus queries and other corpus-linguistic methods. However, it is questionable as to whether a larger, more quantitative, intra-textbook study would yield results of any greater linguistic or pedagogical significance.

This is illustrated with an example from a corpus-based intra-textbook study assessing the distribution patterns of articles and of their colligation patterns (e.g., *a* + singular count nouns, *the* + ordinal) in a corpus of Malaysian ESL textbooks (Mukundan, Leong Chiew Har & Nimehchisalem 2012). Information on the frequency and distribution of articles and their colligation patterns was extracted automatically from the corpus data. The authors concluded that, in the five textbooks analysed, the article '*an*' is considerably less frequent than the articles '*the*' and '*a*' (see first columns of Table 1). The article subsequently claims that teachers should therefore "create appropriate teaching materials to expose the learners more to the article 'an'" (Mukundan, Leong Chiew Har & Nimehchisalem 2012: 67). However, a quick query of the British National Corpus 1994 (hereafter BNC1994; Burnard 2007) suffices to show that the proportional article frequencies observed in these Malaysian textbooks are, in fact, very comparable to the proportions of article frequencies found in a balanced corpus of naturally occurring English (see Table 1).

There may well be pedagogical arguments as to why including more explicit teaching material on the article '*an*' may be beneficial but, given that this is far from the case in real-world English usage, textbook authors can hardly be expected to feature all three articles in equal proportions.

Another interesting form of intra-textbook analysis worth mentioning is found in Moreno (2003), in which accounts of causal metatext (lexico-grammatical features that explicitly signal causal relations) featured in eleven English for Academic Purposes (EAP) textbooks are compared to the actual expression of causal coherence relations in authentic essays, or extracts of essays, featured in the same textbooks. The author claims to have only included "authentic essays" in these comparisons, but the report does not explain how such an "authentic status" was determined. This is problematic given that it is common for texts featured in textbooks to be presented as "authentic", even if they have been purposefully written

Table 1. Distribution of the articles *a, an* and *the* in the five Malaysian textbooks examined by Mukundan et al. 2012 (as reported in Table 1, p. 69) and in the BNC1994 (as calculated using Sketch Engine)

	a	*a* (%)	*an*	*an* (%)	*the*	*the* (%)
Textbook 1	1,097	25.88%	141	3.33%	3,001	70.79%
Textbook 2	1,271	32.61%	130	3.34%	2,496	64.05%
Textbook 3	1,630	31.95%	162	3.18%	3,309	64.87%
Textbook 4	1,894	27.90%	209	3.08%	4,685	69.02%
Textbook 5	1,762	25.92%	256	3.77%	4,779	70.31%
Textbook series (Textbooks 1–5)	7,654	28.54%	898	3.35%	18,270	68.12%
BNC1994	2,136,923	25.31%	333,044	3.94%	5,973,437	70.75%

as pedagogical material. At the very least, these texts can be expected to have been purposefully chosen to illustrate the linguistic features explained in these textbooks so that their authentic representativeness of general, here Academic, English can be called into question.

3.1.2 Comparative approaches

The previous section explored non-comparative methods to describe Textbook English and, citing Mukundan et al.'s (2012) investigation of articles in Malaysian EFL textbooks and Moreno's (2003) analysis of causal coherence relations in EAP textbooks as examples, pointed to the risks of making pedagogically motivated evaluations from analyses of textbook language alone. The methods described hereafter involve comparing aspects of the language presented in EFL textbooks with real-world, naturally occurring language data, usually in the form of a reference corpus (3.1.2.3), but also of corpus-based frequency lists (3.1.2.1), or of semi-staged re-enactments of the situations portrayed in the textbook dialogues (3.1.2.5). In particular, the methodologies of two pioneers in the field, Magnus Ljung and Dieter Mindt, will be detailed.

In the mid-1980s and early 1990s, Ljung (e.g., 1990, 1991) conducted an early corpus-driven analysis of the English vocabulary taught in upper secondary EFL classes in Sweden. As part of a large project, his team collected 56 Swedish TEFL publications (designed for the final three years of secondary education) and converted their entire content to machine-readable text. The COBUILD corpus (the main and reserve corpora totalling some 18 million words of mostly written texts; Sinclair et al. 1990) was chosen as a reference corpus, as – at the time – a large collection of contemporary mostly British non-specialist texts. Both corpora were lemmatised and Ljung (1991) subsequently extracted the most frequent 1,000 words in both the pedagogic material corpus and the COBUILD corpus in order to investigate the nature of words unique to either top-frequency word lists, as well as the differences in frequencies between shared words.

Within the confines of this top 1,000-word frequency band, the two corpora shared 796 words. Ljung (1991) analysed the nature of words unique to the TEFL high-frequency list and concluded that the majority of nouns and verbs denote physical objects, processes and human actions, whilst the adjectives express "either emotional judgement (*terrible, wonderful*), physical characteristics (*soft, bright*), or feelings (*angry, glad*)". In contrast, a large proportion of the nouns exclusively found on the COBUILD high-frequency list denote abstract concepts (*argument, decision, difficulty*), or can be classified as terms from the semantic fields of society or politics (*community, council, campaign, tax*). The high-frequency verbs are predominately used to evaluate human behaviour (*achieve, argue*). Moreover, the majority of the adjectives found in the COBUILD list do not denote physical characteristics (*international, basic, central*).

As for the observed differences in the frequencies of the shared words, in effect, these do little else but reveal that the reference corpus used in these early comparative corpus-based Textbook English studies features mostly elaborate, professionally written and published written texts often on topics quite far removed from those of school textbooks, whereas the pedagogical material appears to have a strong focus on spoken or spoken-like texts. For instance, Ljung (1991) notes that contractions are far more frequent in the TEFL corpus than in the COBUILD. Similarly, first-, second- and third-person pronouns are reported to be more frequent in the TEFL materials. Though certainly no mean feat in the 1990s, these results essentially point to the fundamental necessity of drawing on an appropriate reference corpus for the results of such comparative corpus-based textbook analyses to be in any way meaningful.

3.1.2.1 *Word-frequency list approaches*

In the decades following Ljung's pioneering work, analyses of the vocabulary of EFL textbooks have continued to rely on comparisons of the words found in textbooks to corpus-derived frequency word lists. The following section describes more recent and, given modern computing power, less work-intensive, corpus-based methods involving the computation of frequency lists and rates of word repetition in EFL textbooks. The studies chosen to illustrate this approach deal with phrasal verbs (Zarifi & Mukundan 2012) and prepositions (Mukundan & Roslim 2009); however, the method is applicable to any other kind of lexico-grammatical unit.

Zarifi and Mukundan's (2012) study on phrasal verbs examines a corpus of the spoken sections of five Malaysian secondary school ESL textbooks. First, all occurrences of 19 particles were located using the wordlist function of the software WordSmith Tools (Scott 2011). The researchers then manually identified and tagged the occurrences of phrasal verbs (as opposed to, for example, prepositional uses of these particles). This procedure led to the identification of 108 instances of a total of 66 different *verb + particle* constructions in the spoken textbook corpus. These were then compared to data from the BNC1994 (Burnard 2007).

There are several issues with the presentation and interpretation of the results. First, the quantitative results should be viewed with caution as the textbook corpus explored was relatively small and no statistical testing was carried out so that is it unclear whether many of the observed differences between the textbook and reference corpora may simply be due to random variation. Second, the interpretation of the results seems somewhat removed from the original pedagogically orientated aim of the study. For instance, Zarifi and Mukundan (2012: 13) report that 67% of all phrasal verb occurrences in their textbook corpus involve the particles *up, down* and *out.* The authors go on to suggest that these results "can be viewed as a deviation of the textbooks from natural use of the language since combination [sic] of 8 particles with 20 lexical verbs has been reported to account for about half of all the combinations in natural language" (Zarifi & Mukundan 2012: 13). However, the study they refer to, Gardner and Davies (2007), reports that the most productive verb particles in British English are, indeed, in the following order: *out, up, back* and *down.* Adding the relevant frequencies presented in Gardner and Davis (2007: 346) reveals that *up, down* and *out* account for 58% of all phrasal verb occurrences in the BNC1994, which is not far off the 67% figure observed in the textbook corpus.

It is also worth bearing in mind that both the token frequencies of phrasal verbs and the number of different types of phrasal verbs varies greatly across different text registers (see, e.g., Liu 2011). It is striking that Zarifi and Mukundan's (2012) textbook corpus only includes textbooks' representations of spoken English, whereas the BNC1994 consists of 90% written registers. Thus, a more meaningful comparison benchmark for this particular Textbook English study may have involved Liu's (2011) study, which reports on the frequency counts of the 150 most frequent phrasal verbs across different registers of the BNC1994 and the Corpus of Contemporary American English (hereafter COCA; Davies 2009, 2010). In fact, from the detailed results provided in Liu's (2011) appendix, it is possible to calculate that about two-thirds of the most frequently occurring phrasal verbs in spoken registers feature the particles *up, down* and *out.*

Other studies comparing frequency lists across a textbook corpus and a reference corpus have sometimes relied on differences in frequency ranks to evaluate the linguistic content of EFL textbooks. Mukundan and Roslim (2009), for instance, discuss supposed differences in the representations of prepositions between Textbook English and naturally occurring English by comparing the frequency ranks of a corpus of ESL textbooks and frequency rank data from the BNC1994. As illustrated in Table 2, the reported rank comparisons do not include the actual frequencies; hence, it is impossible to grasp how large any observed difference in rank actually is. In addition, it is quite reasonable to assume that register differences between the textbooks and the BNC1994 data alone could account for such discrepancies in frequency order. For instance, the high percentage of complex, professionally written texts in the BNC is likely to contribute to a higher frequency of noun phrases and consequently to more frequent occurrences of the preposition *of*, as reported in Table 2.

Table 2. Comparison of the order of the most frequent prepositions in the BNC1994 and three Malaysian ESL textbooks (reproduced from Mukundan & Roslim 2009: 24)

Rank	BNC	Textbooks
1	*of*	*to*
2	*in*	*of*
3	*to*	*in*
4	*on*	*on*
5	*by*	*from*
6	*at*	*at*
7	*from*	*by*
8	*after*	*after*
9	*between*	*before*
10	*under*	*between*
11	*before*	*near*
12	*behind*	*under*
13	*near*	*behind*
14	*in front of*	*in front*

In sum, whilst such corpus-based frequency list comparisons between textbook and reference corpora can produce interesting and pedagogically valuable results, great care must be taken to choose a suitable baseline unit and the appropriate reference corpus, featuring comparable registers – lest the comparison resemble that of apples and pears. Furthermore, providing detailed quantitative results and/or applying robust statistical testing is essential to the generation of authoritative results.

3.1.2.2 *NLP methods*

This section attempts to shed light on how corpus-derived word frequency lists may also be used in combination with more complex statistical and natural language processing (NLP) methods to investigate the language of English textbooks. This is illustrated with a method designed to evaluate the development of linguistic complexity across three series of high school Taiwanese ESL textbook series (Chen 2016, 2017).

The method first involves calculating several well-established readability measures for each of the main reading texts of the textbooks. Some of these measures involve phonological analyses of the texts (which require a tool to identify syllable boundaries) whilst others attempt to account for the complexity of the grammatical structures (which usually requires part-of-speech tagging or dependency parsing). These measures are combined with an analysis of the vocabulary coverage of the textbook texts. This is computed by extracting the content words from each text and comparing them to a list of the most frequent content words in the BNC1994. Counted from the top of this corpus-based frequency list, the coverage rates of each 1,000-word band is calculated as a percentage. This calculation is repeated for the top thirteen 1,000-word frequency bands, with each percentage representing the proportion of the words in each text that is found in these 1,000-word bands from the BNC1994 list. A variability neighbour-based clustering algorithm is then applied to evaluate the text's complexity on the basis of all of these different measures calculated for each text.

The aim of the method is to tease out relative differences in text difficulty between the textbook texts across the various textbook volumes within each textbook series. Contrary to Chen's (2016) hypothesis that the progression of lexical difficulty ought to be unidirectional – in other words, that both the range of vocabulary and textual structure complexity of the reading texts should increase volume by volume – the results point to some striking non-linear developmental stages of text difficulty across the volumes of the three-textbook series.

An advantage of such a method is that it combines a large number of linguistic complexity metrics into one measure that can be used to easily compare the linguistic complexity of texts across different textbooks and textbook series. However, like all of the frequency-list approaches discussed so far, the method requires a suitable reference corpus to produce meaningful results. Furthermore, such methods always involve some arbitrary assumptions as to the appropriate size of the frequency bands employed (i.e., should the analysis focus on the 100, 500, 1,000, or 5,000 most frequent words in any one category?). Hence, no matter how complex, the validity and reliability of such methods remain difficult to ascertain.

Chen (2017) developed an alternative metric, which instead of relying on readability measures, attempts to model the lexical sophistication of textbook texts by examining trigrams, i.e., strings of three consecutive word forms, e.g., *a lot of*. In accordance with previous research, Chen (2017) concludes that textbook volumes for advanced learners do not necessarily feature higher degrees of lexical sophistication than less advanced textbooks in the same series. An advantage of using trigrams to model linguistic complexity is that they also capture valuable information on probabilistic estimates for multiword expressions, thus potentially also revealing relevant developmental trends in the representations of collocation and colligation patterns across textbook texts, volumes, and series.

One methodological issue that remains, however, is that the results of such models are dependent on the number of texts per textbook volume, as well as text length and sentence length. Whilst it may be countered that the latter two are, in fact, desirable features since text length and sentence length may be considered valid factors of lexical and grammatical complexity in their own right, the models nevertheless conflate several variables, thus severely complicating the interpretation of the results that emerge from them. More generally, a major disadvantage of basing Textbook English descriptions and/or evaluation on such complex statistical methods is that the results are highly opaque. If a break in the progression of linguistic complexity across a textbook series is observed, as Chen (2016, 2017) does, it is very difficult to determine which of the many variables entered in the model made consequential contributions to this break to understand how improvements could potentially be made. This limits the pedagogical value of such methods. Access to such methods is furthermore complicated by the slow uptake of Open Science practices in computational linguistics (see, e.g., Belz et al. 2021; Wieling, Rawee & van Noord 2018). Regrettably, it remains relatively common to present new innovative NLP-based methods at conferences and in publications, without ever publishing the corresponding code that would enable (corpus) linguists to apply and assess the methods on new data and research questions (see also 4.2.2).

3.1.2.3 *Corpus-based comparisons of 'real-world' language to textbook language*

The corpus-based methodologies outlined thus far have relied on corpus-based frequency lists and have thus tended to revolve around the word level. By contrast, the following sections outline comparative corpus-based methodologies applied to the study of Textbook English with the aim of arriving at quantitative and qualitative descriptions of more complex lexico-grammatical features, their functions, and pragmatic uses. We begin with Dieter Mindt's pioneering corpus-driven method for the analysis of Textbook English, first described in a monograph on the usage and teaching of future constructions in English (Mindt 1987).

Mindt's interest in textbook language stems from his belief that foreign language textbooks are traditionally based on a pre-conceived grammatical syllabus, rather than on an empirical grammar of actual usage by native speakers (Mindt 1987: 11). Mindt claims that both the grammar syllabus and its content – i.e., the functions of the different grammatical structures – are constructed from two non-empirical, indeed almost anecdotal, sources. He identifies the first as "a long-standing tradition of English language teaching" and the second as "the accepted grammatical knowledge as we find it in current handbooks of English grammar" (Mindt 1997: 40), thus pointing to the cyclical nature of traditional pedagogical grammars. Although these textbook corpus analyses focus on German EFL textbooks, Mindt believes this notion of a grammatical syllabus to also be true of EFL textbooks published in other countries (Mindt 1997: 40–41, see also Burton 2023).

At the most basic level, the idea behind Mindt's (1987: 9) approach to the analysis of Textbook English is:

> Ein aus Analysen von Sprachkorpora gewonnenes Bild der sprachlichen Realität des heutigen Englisch wird verglichen mit dem Abbild der englischen Sprache, wie es in zwei verbreiteten Lehrwerken dargeboten wird [to compare the results of analyses of authentic English usage that provide a picture of the linguistic reality of present-day English with that of the English language as it is presented in two series of popular [German EFL] textbooks].

As described in 3.1.1.2, page-by-page analysis of textbook language is a difficult, error-prone, and time-consuming process. The development of digital data storage and retrieval enabled Mindt to pioneer a new approach to language textbook analysis work using computer-readable textbook corpora. The first step consists in compiling a corpus of naturally occurring, and in Mindt's case, native speaker English. From this data, Mindt extrapolates an empirical grammar of future time expressions that is exclusively based on the observed phenomena, thus breaking with the tradition of introspection-based, deductive grammars. In a third phase, the frequencies, functions, and co-occurrences of future expressions found in a corpus of two series of popular German EFL textbooks are compared with those of an 'authentic' corpus, the latter representing target learner language. Mindt's (1987, 1992) study of future time expressions in English exemplifies this methodology.

In this first, corpus-driven Textbook English study, Mindt explores the future constructions featured in textbooks designed for lower secondary school. The reference corpus used for comparisons combines a corpus of English conversation (34 spontaneous recordings of conversations of native British English speaking adults, ca. 170,000 words) and a corpus of contemporary British plays, which he considered to be written representations of natural, spoken language (totalling some 184,000 words). Mindt (1987: 50) justifies his choice of a spoken English reference corpus by arguing that the German education authorities stipulate that foreign language teaching at this level should aim to enable students to be able to communicate in everyday situations. The analysis focuses exclusively on the language presented in the coursebooks, excluding accompanying material such as workbooks, test materials, vocabulary books, and, notably, the transcripts of the listening exercises (Mindt 1987: 53).

Mindt's approach begins with a comparison of the two reference subcorpora before comparing these results with those from the analysis of the textbook corpus. Hierarchal and centroid-based cluster analyses are applied to group both reference subcorpora. To test the homogeneity of the clusters, i.e., whether differences between the various independent groups are significant, chi-square tests are applied. Mindt (1987: 62–73) argues that the combination of these two procedures produces a "core description" of the frequencies and co-occurrences of future expressions in spoken British English, which he goes on to compare to the claims made in major English grammar works and, finally, to the language presented in two popular series of German EFL textbooks. Thus, Mindt's approach involves inferring an empirical grammar inductively, moving from language data to grammatical generalisation, as opposed to the more traditional, deductive approaches that rely on previously ascertained prescriptive rules. Empirical grammars may then be drawn upon to generate pedagogical grammars.[10]

Since Mindt (1987) first exemplified the method by investigating the representations of the future in German EFL textbooks, numerous Textbook English studies have emerged which have, at least partially, been inspired by the Mindtian approach: comparing computer-readable, real-world L1 corpora with textbook corpora. So far, these have also focused on specific, individual lexico-grammatical features, such as support verb constructions (Sinclair & Renouf 1988), the indefinite pronouns *any* and *some* (Tesch 1990), modal auxiliaries (Römer 2004a), the progressive aspect (Römer 2005) and *if*-conditionals (Gabrielatos 2013, 2019; Römer 2004b, 2007). Key insights from these studies will be presented in part two (Section 3.2).

10. In the following, the term 'pedagogical grammar' will be used according to Dirven (1990: 1) for whom the term 'pedagogical grammar' covers both learning and teaching grammars.

3.1.2.4 *Corpus-based comparisons of textbook language to 'real-world' language*

Another approach to exploring the lexico-grammatical content of language textbooks is to manually extract groups of lexico-grammatical features from EFL textbooks and compare these and their frequencies to a reference corpus. This methodology may be perceived as a reversal of Mindt's methodology described in 3.1.2.3. Instead of deriving an empirical grammar of specific features of English from an English L1 corpus to then compare it to the way these features are presented in EFL textbooks, this approach begins with the textbook grammar and attempts to apply it to data extracted from a corpus of naturally occurring English. In the following, Koprowski's (2005) analysis of lexical phrases featured in EFL textbooks and Gabrielatos' (2003, 2006, 2013) explorations of textbooks' typologies of conditionals will serve to exemplify this approach.

In an investigation on the usefulness of the lexical phrases presented in contemporary textbooks, Koprowski (2005) manually extracted all the lexical phrases explicitly presented in three intermediate EGP coursebooks. The resulting 822 lexical items were then compared to data retrieved from five subcorpora of the COBUILD corpus. To this end, a "usefulness score" was calculated for each lexical item extracted from the textbooks. This score relies on two criteria: frequency, arguing that "the commonest units in the language are the ones most likely to be met by learners outside the classroom and should therefore be at the centre of the learning program" (Koprowski 2005: 324) and range, which refers to the number of text types in which a phrase is commonly found, on the grounds that "a unit which exists in a wide variety of registers is generally considered much more useful than an item found in just one, even if that item is highly frequent" (Koprowski 2005: 324). Koprowski's (2005) results are rather disconcerting: 14% of the lexical phrases explicitly featured in the coursebooks were found to be entirely absent from the COBUILD corpus (Sinclair et al. 1990) (see 3.2.1.2 for more details of the results).

Similar, 'reversed Mindtian' approaches have also been applied to analyses of Textbook English focusing on grammar and here, too, have pointed to the inadequacy of pedagogical grammars in EFL textbooks. For instance, Gabrielatos (2003, 2006, 2013) examined the typologies of conditional sentences presented in a range of intermediate to advanced EFL textbooks. Gabrielatos identified five types of ELT typologies and concluded that the majority of the coursebooks examined largely follow a simple conditional typology consisting of three types: first conditional with *will*, second and third conditionals with *would*. The most elaborate ELT typologies also include the so-called *zero* conditional, the use of epistemic modals, imperatives, and a range of tenses in all the conditional types. Next, Gabrielatos extracted a random sample of *if*-sentences from the written sections of the BNC1994 and annotated them according to their conditionality, tense and aspect marking, time reference, modality, etc. Using these annotations, the author calculated the number of naturally occurring *if*-sentences that can accurately be described according to the ELT conditional typologies presented in EFL textbooks. Using the most basic typology, only 15% of the *if*-sentences from the BNC could be successfully classified. Most strikingly, even with the most complex and inclusive of the ELT typologies identified in the textbooks, 22% of all sentences are still unaccounted for. These results lead Gabrielatos (2006: 2) to conclude that the typology explicitly taught in textbooks "provides learners with an incomplete, and in some cases distorted, picture of *if*-conditionals".

Contrary to Mindt's studies, Gabrielatos' approach only explores ELT grammar as presented in the textbooks' grammar sections, rather than, more holistically, to the totality of the language to which learners are exposed via their textbooks. Methodologically, such 'reversed Mindtian' approaches have the disadvantage of pointing to the inadequacy of Textbook English without providing textbook authors and EFL teachers with those "useful" (to keep with Koprowski's terminology) linguistic features that are missing from or grossly underrepresented in textbooks but which corpus-based studies have shown are in fact highly frequent and salient.

Though a much more time-consuming undertaking, the compilation of a textbook corpus, in addition to the qualitative analysis of their grammar sections, allows for the analysis of how specific linguistic features are represented in the textbooks' reading passages, exercises, instructions and listening exercises. Following such an approach, Winter and Le Foll (2022) revealed that a remarkably large proportion (between 43% and 53% depending on the typology applied) of *if*-conditionals featured in 14 secondary school EFL textbooks did not fit the conditional typologies presented in these same textbooks; thus highlighting a significant gap between what is taught in textbooks and what is practiced by textbook authors within these same textbooks (on conditionals in EFL/ESL textbooks, see also Gabrielatos 2006, 2013; Römer 2004b, 2007; Tesch 1990).

3.1.2.5 *Elicitation approaches*

The previous section explained how lexical units or grammar rules extracted from EFL textbooks can be compared to reference corpus data to form judgements as to how "useful" (e.g., Koprowski 2005) or "accurate" (e.g., Gabrielatos 2003, 2006, 2019) textbook input is likely to be for foreign language learners. In the following, a different approach to evaluating the authenticity of textbook language will be described. It relies on the re-creation of communicative situations simulated in the textbooks. In this respect, it can be said to share some characteristics with the 'reversed Mindtian' approach described in the previous section.

In a study of spoken discourse features in Textbook English, Gilmore (2004) investigated the authenticity of the language presented in service encounter dialogues (e.g. hiring a car from a rental shop, or asking for directions in the street) in ten EFL textbooks published between 1981 and 2001. To this end, the author selected one such dialogue from each textbook and extracted, in note form, all the questions asked by the information receiver in each dialogue. The questions were then reformulated and used as a basis for real conversations in the genuine settings imagined by the textbook authors. The real dialogues were recorded and transcribed and subsequently used to compare the use of discourse features in the textbook dialogues and their 'authentic' re-creations.

Gilmore's (2004) method is highly original, but it is difficult to generalise results based on just seven textbook dialogues and seven enactments. Critically, the authentic nature of semi-staged service encounter dialogues (and, though this is not specified in the publication, perhaps even with the researcher acting as the information receiver in each of the re-created dialogues) may be questioned. Furthermore, it would be interesting to investigate to what extent discourse features of the conversations would differ if the information receiver were a non-English native speaker, given that the majority of these service encounter dialogues are intended to present typical communicative situations that tourists may face in an English-speaking country.

In a similar vein, Schauer and Adolphs (2006) explore the possibility of using native speakers' responses to discourse completion tasks, rather than large-scale native speaker corpora to inform the teaching of formulaic sequences in the EFL classroom. Expressions of gratitude featured in four EFL textbooks were compared to those elicited in discourse completion tasks, as well as to thanking formulae retrieved from the spoken CANCODE corpus. Unsurprisingly, the researchers observe notable differences between the controlled, elicited responses and the natural conversations of the corpus. They argue that the first type of data can facilitate the acquisition of more recent language pattern changes, whilst the latter can generally provide "[a] much broader picture" such as "insights into the procedural aspects of expressing gratitude", which may materialise in the form of collaborative negotiation or re-lexicalisation of another speaker's utterance (Schauer & Adolphs 2006: 130).

In sum, it is tempting to conclude that constructed dialogues, whether in the form of semi-staged re-enactments of textbook dialogues or discourse completion tasks, are unlikely to yield sufficiently robust data to reliably evaluate the authenticity of textbook language. Nonetheless, such methodological approaches can point towards aspects of textbooks that may need to be updated or re-organised. They can thus provide valuable starting points for further investigations.

3.1.2.6 *Adding learner corpora to the equation*

A number of studies explore Textbook English with a view to better understanding learners' interlanguage. Since textbooks constitute a major source of secondary school learners' L2 input (see 2.5), it may be speculated that learners' over-, underuse, or misuse[11] of specific lexico-grammatical features may be (at least partly) attributed to their textbooks' treatment of these features. In order to investigate such potentially causal relationships, some studies have attempted to triangulate results derived from textbook vs. reference corpora comparisons with insights from learner corpora (e.g., Fujimoto 2017; Gabrielatos 2013; Le Foll 2023b; Möller 2020; Rankin 2010; Vine 2013; Winter & Le Foll 2022). The potential and limitations of such methodologies are exemplified in the following.

An example of a study drawing on textbook data to glean insights into English learners' difficulties is Rankin's (2010) study of adverb placement in L2 essay writing. In this study, 37 English essays written by Austrian university students were surveyed for adverb placement errors. The errors were checked against the Louvain Corpus of Native English Essays (LOCNESS; Granger 1998) and tagged. In parallel, all the pedagogic material used during the students' English language course (the duration of which is not mentioned) was gathered; materials and exercises specifically dedicated to adverbs were tallied. In other words, Rankin's study exclusively looks at explicit practice of adverbial usage, rather than at all the lexico-grammatical constructions involving adverbs to which learners were exposed in class. In the qualitative part of the analysis, Rankin (2010) compares the students' adverb placement errors with the classroom input material. The results suggest that whilst the adverb grammar exercises provided often require learners to choose appropriate adverbs for particular gaps in gap-filling exercises, they do little to address the issue of adverb placement within sentences. The author stresses that "residual problems with adverb placement are not due to any major deficiencies in basic grammar but rather to the fact that appropriate variation in adverb placement for special discourse and pragmatic contexts has not been mastered" (Rankin 2010: 214).

In another example of an English Textbook study involving learner corpus data, Fujimoto (2017) examines the use of the present perfect simple with and without temporal adverbials across three corpora: a longitudinal learner corpus of Japanese university students' academic writing assignments, a textbook corpus consisting of "reading passages" drawn from six high school English textbooks and a reference corpus consisting of the fiction and general prose subcorpora of

11. Note that, unlike 'misuse', the terms 'overuse' and 'underuse' are descriptive, rather than prescriptive terms: they merely refer to the fact that a linguistic form is found significantly more or less in the learner corpus than in the reference corpus.

the Freiburg-LOB Corpus of British English (FLOB; Hundt, Sand & Siemund 1998) and Freiburg-Brown Corpus of American English (Frown; Hundt, Sand & Skandera 1999). The frequencies of the co-occurrences of the present perfect simple with temporal adverbials in the reference corpora are compared to the corresponding frequencies extracted from both the learner corpus and the textbook corpus. As Fujimoto demonstrates, such L1 vs. textbook vs. learner corpora comparisons can provide relevant insights into the source of learners' difficulties with regards to specific lexico-grammatical features. However, in this case, it may be argued that the FLOB and Frown fiction and general prose subcorpora are questionable baselines for comparisons of reading texts from secondary school textbooks and student academic writing. Academic writing is known to follow register-specific lexico-grammatical patterns and the study fails to account for such register discrepancies.

Following a similar procedure, Vine (2013) computed the frequency of four high-frequency category ambiguous words (*down, like, round* and *up*) across English native language (hereafter ENL) corpora (spoken and written British English and New Zealand English), learner English corpora (spoken and written) and an EFL textbook corpus. Comparisons of the frequencies of occurrences of each of these four words sorted in terms of the grammatical category of each use revealed considerable variations across all the corpora. It is interesting to note that whilst Vine subdivides all of her results into the spoken and written subcorpora for the ENL and the learner English corpora, this register differentiation is not made for the textbook corpus, even though language textbooks typically include registers as diverse as conversation, newspaper writing, and fiction (see 4.3.1.3). Here, too, it is difficult to draw any meaningful conclusions from the results of this analysis since the frequencies reported for each part-of-speech use also vary greatly across the different reference subcorpora. Nevertheless, it would appear that the frequencies of the learner corpora are considerably closer to those of the textbook corpus than to those observed in the reference ENL corpora. Such observations lend tentative support to the hypothesis that, given they represent a major source of L2 input, textbooks play a crucial role in EFL learners' language acquisition processes (see 2.5–2.6). At the same time, they also remind us that mode and register differences need to be accounted for when describing and evaluating the language of EFL textbooks.

3.1.2.7 *Textbook language as learner target language*

As in the previous section, this section presents a methodological approach to the study of Textbook English that also compares data from a learner corpus to that of a textbook corpus. However, this particular approach not only adds a layer of cross-linguistic comparison using an L1 (Japanese) corpus, it also turns the equation around by assuming textbook language to be the learners' target language.

In stark contrast to the corpus-based comparative approaches reviewed so far, Tono (2004: 51) claims that "textbook English is a useful target corpus to use in the study of learner language". He convincingly argues that comparing learner language to texts produced by native speaker professionals makes little sense. Indeed, all of the well-known general English corpora used in most of the Textbook English studies reviewed so far (e.g., BNC1994, Brown, FLOB, etc.) predominantly feature professionally written or spoken texts such as newspaper articles, extracts of novels, and political speeches. Whilst Tono recognises that the use of such reference corpora may make sense when it comes to supporting advanced L2 learners or professional translators, he argues that the majority of English learners in Japan have no such aspirations:

> In the present case, it is certainly not the language of the BNC that the Japanese learners of English are aiming at, but, rather, a modified English which represents what they are more exposed to in EFL settings in Japan. (Tono 2004: 51)

Although Tono acknowledges that Textbook English often does not reflect actual language use, he nevertheless contends that, since Textbook English is constructed so as to facilitate learning, it makes sense to apply Textbook English as a benchmark when investigating EFL attainment.

In the Japanese context, Tono (2004) emphasises the fact that textbooks represent the primary source of English language input, noting that even when teachers use English as medium of instruction, they tend to restrict themselves to the structures represented in the textbooks. As such, "it is fair to say that the English used in ELT textbooks is the target for most learners of English in Japan" (2004: 52). Whilst I am not convinced that Textbook English necessarily is (see also Timmis 2003) or should be the learners' target (see 3.1.2.7), Tono undoubtedly raises an important point: the need to reflect on the suitability of using general English corpora such as the BNC as benchmark reference corpus when analysing both textbook and learner language (see Winter & Le Foll 2022 for an example of a study that justifies the use of only specific subcorpora of the BNC in such a comparative analysis).

In a study on the acquisition of English argument structures by Japanese learners, Tono (2004) compares three different types of corpora: (a) an interlanguage corpus of free compositions written by Japanese learners of English, (b) a native language corpus consisting of English newspaper articles, and (c) an EFL textbook corpus. First, sentence frame patterns with the three most frequent verbs (except *have* and *be*) are extracted from all three corpora. For each high-frequency verb use, several variables are collected, e.g., frequency in the textbook corpus, number of learner errors, learners' year group, Japanese equivalents of the verb constructions. Log-linear analysis is then used to tease out the most important factors influencing Japanese learners use of these sentence frame patterns. To this end, all frequencies are converted to categorical data (i.e., to high, mid, or low occurrence); which inevitably reduces the degree of accurateness and adds a layer of arbitrariness in the statistical analysis. The results of the best fitting models show that the learners' school year exerts the most influence on learners' idiomatic production of sentence frame patterns. Interestingly, the second most influential factor is the frequency of a pattern in the textbook corpus. Strong two-way interaction effects between the factors 'school year' and 'textbook frequency' are also observed. By contrast, 'learner error' only significantly interacts with 'school year' in one case (for the verb *get*). This suggests that textbook frequencies mostly impact students' overuse or underuse of a particular verb pattern, rather than their rate of success in producing the pattern idiomatically. In addition, the results also show that whether or not a verb argument structure has a comparable equivalent structure in Japanese has less impact on Japanese L1 learners' production of the target structures than how often the structure is featured in the textbooks they learn from.

Although working from radically different premises, both this section and the one preceding it have revealed the value of integrating learner corpora in Textbook English description and evaluation. At least since the late 1990s, a number of academics have advocated integrating observations gleaned from learner corpora into the design of new EFL publications (e.g., Granger 2015). Indeed, some major textbook publishers have now latched onto the idea; as mentioned in 2.7, Cambridge University Press now draws on the error-tagged Cambridge Learner Corpus, which was compiled on the basis of student responses taken from Cambridge English Language Assessment examinations.

3.1.3 Evaluating the impact of textbook language

Most of the studies of Textbook English outlined thus far have aimed to describe the linguistic input of EFL textbooks. By contrast, this section examines studies that also aim to evaluate the potential pedagogical impact of this textbook-based input. Of course, language teachers regularly reflect on the quality of the textbook materials they introduce in class and will thus periodically conduct at least impressionistic retrospective analyses of textbook content. However, attempts to formalise and quantify such retrospective evaluations on the effectiveness of foreign language textbooks have tended to examine the nature of the tasks and activities featured in the textbooks (see, e.g., Ellis 1997), rather than focus on the quality and usefulness of their linguistic input. This section presents two studies that investigate the linguistic content of EFL publications with regards to their impact on learners in terms of learning outcomes and efficacy. As an extension of comparative corpus-based approaches described in 3.1.2.3, the methodology of the first study (Alejo González et al., 2010) will be familiar to the reader. The methodology of the second study (Gouverneur 2008), however, relies on the analysis of a corpus of textbook activities annotated with a complex pedagogical annotation scheme.

Alejo González et al. (2010) delve into both the implicit and explicit mentions of phrasal verbs in textbooks, focusing on the learning efficacy gains for the textbook users. To this end, they select eight popular EFL textbooks targeted at the Spanish secondary school market. Their research on the likelihood of incidental learning of phrasal verbs in the ELT material is based on frequency counts within the textbooks and on frequency comparisons with the BNC1994. They report that the vast majority of the phrasal verbs featured in the examined textbooks only appear once or twice in any one textbook, and thus do not occur nearly frequently enough to warrant incidental learning. Moreover, comparisons of the frequencies of the 25 most frequently occurring phrasal verbs from the BNC1994 with the data from the textbooks show that while two of those phrasal verbs (*go out* and *look after*) are vastly over-represented in the ELT material, many others are largely under-represented (e.g., *go back, point out* and *take over*), if not entirely absent (*carry on*).

The explicit part of the investigation examines the metalanguage used to describe phrasal verbs and related phenomena in the textbooks, as well as the types of exercises designed to encourage the acquisition of these lexical items. Referring to pedagogical approaches inspired by cognitive linguistics (see 2.3), Alejo González et al. (2010) deplore that none of the textbooks examined organise explicit mentions of phrasal verbs in a way that is likely to facilitate acquisition by encouraging learners to understand the 'motivated' nature of the particles in combination with their corresponding lexical verbs (for more on the cognitive linguistics' view that phrasal verb particles display a certain degree of compositionally, see, e.g., Condon 2008; Spring 2018; Torres-Martínez 2019; Tsaroucha 2018). Alejo González et al. (2010: 72) argue that "[i]f materials create too few opportunities for incidental uptake, then this should be compensated by explicit targeting" and conclude that their sample of eight Spanish secondary school EFL textbooks fail to adequately do so.

Based on a large-scale learner corpus study on collocation, Nesselhauf (2005: 238) also postulates that collocations are not taught in a way that spurs on their idiomatic acquisition since there appears to be no correlation between the number of years of classroom teaching and the idiomaticity of the collocations learners produce. Although Gouverneur (2008) does not directly compare Textbook English to learner language, she takes Nesselhauf's (2005) corpus-based learner error analysis as her starting point and designs a study that aims to tease out whether "learners' deficiencies in the production of phraseological patterns of simple verbs might be teaching-induced or, more precisely, material-induced" (Gouverneur 2008: 224). To do so, Gouverneur (2008) draws on a textbook corpus (TeMa; Meunier & Gouverneur 2009) which includes the full pedagogical materials from each textbook series including the reading texts, transcripts, vocabulary exercises and instructions from both student's coursebooks and workbooks. Uniquely, the TeMa corpus also includes detailed pedagogical annotation of the subcorpora containing the vocabulary exercises with some 80 codes referring to various aspects of task design and content (Meunier & Gouverneur 2009). As part of this study, all the instances of the lemmas MAKE and TAKE were automatically retrieved from the vocabulary exercise subcorpora and the results were manually sorted for meaning and collocational patterns. High-frequency verbs are found to feature prominently in the context of restricted collocations in all the textbooks, thus suggesting that material designers had taken due care "to include a significant number of phraseological uses [of MAKE and TAKE] in the exercises" (Gouverneur 2008: 234).

Next, all instances of restricted collocations identified were categorised according to the degree of focus on the collocation in the corresponding exercises. It transpires that direct, explicit focus on these lexical units was largely found in the intermediate level textbooks. Gouverneur (2008: 235) notes that, in more advanced textbooks, these collocations are no longer dealt with explicitly. This trend was found to be true for all three textbook series examined. Gouverneur (2008: 235) concludes that this "lack of direct focus on restricted collocations at the advanced level might well be one of the reasons why more proficient learners have so many problems dealing with high-frequency verbs".

The vocabulary exercises were also annotated according to eight types of pedagogical activities, which were themselves grouped into four larger categories corresponding to the cognitive processes they are (presumably) designed to activate. According to this annotation scheme, whilst 12% of the intermediate learning activities on collocations of MAKE and TAKE are designed to activate understanding, such activities are entirely absent from the advanced textbooks (Gouverneur 2008: 236–237). Another striking finding is that fewer than 20% of all the advanced exercises require learners to produce an answer that requires full retrieval from the mental lexicon. Most exercises merely require students to select the correct solution from a given list of words or expressions (Gouverneur 2008: 236–237).

3.2 Key findings of Textbook English studies

Part one of this literature review chapter provided an overview of the wide range of methodologies that have so far been applied to survey the linguistic content of EFL textbooks, reporting on the results of individual studies to illustrate the advantages and potential weaknesses of the various methods. Part two, by contrast, homes in on some of the key results of previous studies examining the language of English textbooks. Whenever possible, emphasis is placed on the results of secondary school EFL textbooks but, in language areas where studies are sparse, the results of relevant adult EFL, ESL and EAP textbook studies are also mentioned.

The following section falls into three subsections. The first summarises the results of studies principally exploring the lexis of Textbook English. The second presents studies investigating more complex lexico-grammatical features denoting verb tense, aspect, and argument structures, whilst the third reviews the results of the few Textbook English studies focusing on pragmatics and discourse. Note that the categorisation of the examined linguistic phenomena into these sections only serves organisational purposes. Indeed, and as will be made evident in the discussion of the studies' results, many of the examined linguistic features straddle any artificial boundaries between lexis, grammar, discourse, semantics, and pragmatics.

3.2.1 Lexis

Perhaps the most immediately obvious aspect of Textbook English is its vocabulary – in other words, the range of words and multi-word units presented in English textbooks. In the following, the results of a small selection of studies focusing on the lexis of English textbooks are laid out. Subsection 3.2.1.1 focuses on individual words whilst 3.2.1.2 looks at the treatment of multi-words units such as collocations, phrasal verbs, and lexical bundles in Textbook English.

3.2.1.1 *Individual words*

The tradition of examining the vocabulary of EFL textbooks goes back a long way. The results of Ljung's (1990, 1991) analysis of the vocabulary featured in upper secondary school Swedish EFL publications have already been discussed in 3.1.2.1. As a reminder, the studies pointed to an overrepresentation of concrete words to the detriment of abstract ones and deplored the poor representation of lexical units commonly used in communicative interaction and in the establishment of social relationships.

As part of another early corpus-based Textbook English study, Renouf (1984; cited in Sinclair & Renouf 1988) investigated learners' vocabulary input in nine major EFL coursebooks. The analysis showed that, in the first coursebook of each series, the number of different word forms introduced ranged from just over 1,000 to nearly 4,000 – thus representing an incredibly wide variation. The average rate of re-occurrence of each word form across the different textbook series was also calculated. Here, too, the patterns of reinforcement also ranged widely: from six to 17 times.

Based on an analysis of the same textbook series, Sinclair and Renouf (1988) explored learners' exposure to delexical constructions (also frequently referred to as support verb constructions). The authors concluded that such constructions are mostly neglected in Textbook English, despite their preponderance in ENL corpora. This study, however, disregards occurrences of delexical constructions occurring within "the rubric of the text" as of secondary importance, rather than as an integral part of the teaching programme (Sinclair & Renouf 1988: 153). Thus, whilst Sinclair and Renouf (1988) deplore that ditransitive uses of the verb *give* are not explicitly highlighted in the coursebooks, they acknowledge that such patterns are featured within the coursebooks' "text rubrics".

A few decades later, Reda (2003) conducted a large-scale analysis of (adult) EGP textbooks designed for the global EFL market. The study concludes that the vast majority of textbooks across all proficiency levels are largely based on a "limited number of 'general interest' topics", such as *cooking, food and drink* or *holidays and travel* (Reda 2003: 264). Hence, in spite of the rise of English as an international language in the context of globalisation, the lexical syllabus taught in the EFL/EIL textbooks examined confines itself to "the basic area of the English vocabulary – the 'visitors' wing'" (Reda 2003: 268). Even the more advanced coursebooks in each series do not depart from these "basic topics" of "general interest".

Whilst Reda's (2003) analysis of English textbooks targeted at adults appears to point to a common understanding by textbook publishers as to the "topics of general interest" to be covered in EFL textbooks, Catalán and Francisco (2008) conclude that the textbook authors of EFL textbooks used at two levels in Spain (6th grade of primary education and 4th grade of secondary education) disagree on the concrete vocabulary items that learners ought to acquire at these stages. The authors measure the number of tokens and types for each textbook and compare type-token ratios. Moreover, they compute lists of the 50 most frequent content words from each textbook. Comparisons of these frequency lists show that Spanish learners of English are exposed to very different words and with varying frequencies depending on which textbook they have been assigned. Catalán and Francisco (2008: 161–62) conclude that textbook authors appear to lack a systematic approach to vocabulary selection and presentation.

Whilst the studies reviewed so far have focused on the breadth of vocabulary covered by English textbooks, the following studies examine three specific functional categories of words: linking adverbials (Conrad 2004), definite articles (Yoo 2009), and adjectives (Biber & Reppen 2002). Conrad (2004) focuses on the frequencies and usage of linking adverbials of contrast and concession in two registers (conversation and academic prose), comparing data from the *Longman Grammar of Spoken and Written Language* (Biber et al. 1999) to the coverage of the adverbial *though* in four American ESL textbooks. The study concludes that textbook coverage does not match native corpus evidence. For instance, Conrad (2004) notes that three out of the four textbooks fail to include the use of *though* as a linking adverbial, and that the only textbook that mentions it presents it as a means of showing contrast but neglects its usage as a means of expressing concession. Although it occurs frequently in L1 conversation, all four textbooks fail to mention *though* as a means of softening disagreement between speakers. Conrad (2004) observes that only one textbook suggests a number of contrast linking adverbials to use in conversation, but that this textbook misleads learners into thinking that *however* and *on the other hand* are commonly used in conversation, whereas they, in fact, occur far more frequently in academic prose than in any other register. Indeed, numerous Textbook English studies have pointed to the predominance of lexico-grammatical features typical of written registers in textbook dialogues designed to emulate spontaneous spoken interaction (see 3.2.4 on spoken grammar in Textbook English).

In a study following a very similar approach, Yoo (2009) compared the treatment of definite articles in six EFL/ESL grammars with corpus findings reported in the *Longman Grammar of Spoken and Written English* (Biber et al 1999). The results suggest that whilst most ESL/EFL grammars extensively describe the anaphoric and associative uses of the definite article (e.g., *Let's go to the Indian restaurant. The food is delicious.*), its situational (e.g., *Can I have the chutney, please?*) and cataphoric uses (e.g., *At the beginning of my PhD*) are neglected. The findings potentially have important pedagogical implications since corpus data shows that the situation and cataphoric uses of the definite article are more common than its anaphoric use in a number of text registers that English learners are most likely to be confronted with: namely, conversation, newspaper language and academic prose (Yoo 2009: 273–276).

In sum, the results of these case studies on the presentation of *though* and *the* in textbook grammars serve as a reminder as to the central importance of production modes, registers, and text types in the (contextual) use of specific lexico-grammatical features. It therefore follows that these factors must be taken into consideration, both in the elaboration and evaluation of Textbook English (see 4.1). The final case study on individual words reviewed as part of this section,

Biber and Reppen (2002), illustrates how the proficiency levels that textbooks are targeted at must also be considered when modelling Textbook English.

Among other lexico-grammatical phenomena, Biber and Reppen (2002) focus on the role of adjectives in Textbook English. To this end, they compare the frequencies of different types of nominal premodifiers in a large general English corpus with how they are presented in six popular ESL/EFL grammar textbooks. The results suggest that the pedagogical materials over-emphasise the prevalence of participial adjectives (e.g., *an exciting game, an interested couple*) whilst underestimating the pervasiveness of nominal premodifiers (e.g., *a grammar lesson*) (Biber & Reppen 2002: 201–202). As far as teaching beginner-level conversation is concerned, a focus on attributive adjectives (e.g., *the big house*) appears to be justified. At higher levels of proficiency, however, the authors argue that students would likely benefit from greater exposure to the use of nouns as nominal premodifiers since corpus-based findings have shown that these are conspicuously frequent in both newspaper and academic writing (Biber & Reppen 2002: 202). Thus, these results point to the necessity of not only accounting for mode and register differences, as highlighted in the discussion of Conrad's (2004) and Yoo's (2009) results, but also textbook proficiency levels when describing and evaluating the language of textbooks. It is worth noting that the vast majority of Textbook English studies reviewed as part of this chapter do not account for either of these potential sources of variation.

3.2.1.2 *Multi-word units*

Though 3.1.2.1 has shown that the study's methodology is not without its flaws, Zarifi and Munkundan (2012) certainly point to a disconcerting gap between the phrasal verbs featured in the 'spoken' sections of Malaysian ESL textbooks and the most frequent phrasal verbs in the BNC1994. For instance, they report that the most frequently occurring phrasal verbs in their textbook corpus, *clean up* and *melt down*, do not, in fact, belong to the most frequent 100 phrasal verbs in the BNC1994. The results also reveal that other highly frequent and more pedagogically valuable phrasal verbs – such as *work out, turn over* and *go over* – do not appear at all in this corpus of textbook dialogues (Zarifi & Mukundan 2012: 13).

The comparative corpus-based methodology employed in Koprowski's (2005) exploration of multi-word lexical units in Textbook English was laid out in 3.1.2.4. Among the most striking results was the fact that more than 14% of the lexical phrases explicitly featured in the three EGP coursebooks examined were entirely absent from the selected reference corpus, the COBUILD (Sinclair et al. 1990). Such phrases include *cheap steak, mild cigarette, imprisoned man, recommend fully* and *on its last feet* (Koprowski 2005: 328). Based on this small-scale investigation, Koprowski (2005: 329) draws the provocative conclusion that: "the more lexical phrases in a course[book], the less useful the items tend to be on average". It would thus appear that textbook authors frequently attempt to supply excessively comprehensive sets of lexical phrases of a single type or on a single topic which leads to the inclusion of some highly infrequent, sometimes outright implausible, collocations. In addition, and just like Catalán and Francisco's (2008) study of individual words in school EFL textbooks, Koprowski (2005) points to a striking lack of consensus as to what constitutes a meaningful lexical curriculum at intermediate level since less than 1% of the lexical phrases collected are shared by any of the textbooks under study (Koprowski 2005: 330). From a detailed analysis of multi-word units featuring the high-frequency verb MAKE in textbook dialogues, Le Foll (2022b) also concluded that EFL textbook authors do not appear to follow any systematic criteria when selecting the few multi-word units that are featured in textbook conversation. In Le Foll's corpus of 43 European EFL textbooks (the TEC, see 4.3.1), phrasal verbs with MAKE, as well as causative and delexical MAKE constructions associated with the semantic field of speech and communication were found to be underrepresented in textbook conversation as compared to the Spoken BNC2014 (Love et al. 2017).

Another strand of Textbook English studies is concerned with phrasemes (also referred to as lexical bundles, lexical clusters and n-grams), i.e., recurrent sequences of words such as *the fact that, I want you to* and *which is why*. Even though they often do not represent a complete structure nor are they necessarily idiomatic in meaning, these multi-word units nevertheless capture important discourse functions in both written and spoken registers (Biber 2006: 134–135; Biber & Barbieri 2007: 264) and are thus very relevant to the description and evaluation of Textbook English.

Siepmann (2014) compared the phrasemes featured in the vocabulary sections of two series of German secondary school EFL textbooks with a revised version of Martinez and Schmitt's (2012) list of the most frequent "non-transparent phrasemes" found in the BNC1994. Across these entire textbook series spanning five years of EFL instruction, only 12% (for *Green Line*) and 16% (for *G21*) of the phrasemes of the revised corpus-based list were mentioned at least once. Siepmann (2014) concludes that the selection of phrasemes in these textbooks is seemingly not based on frequency or, in fact, on any other systematic set of criteria. In addition, and contrary to expectations, it was also not the case that the number of phrasemes featured in these textbooks rose as students' proficiency level increased.

Aside from the aforementioned study, most Textbook English research to have taken a phraseme or lexical bundle perspective have examined English for Academic Purposes (EAP) and English for Specific Purposes (ESP) textbooks. These materials are designed to equip non-native speakers of English with the necessary skills to cope with the demands of academic reading and writing at English-speaking universities and/or (future) professional activities in English. A number of studies have attempted to describe and/or evaluate the language of such textbooks by examining the types and frequencies of lexical bundles they feature (e.g., Biber et al. 2002; Biber 2006; Chen 2010; Grabowski 2015; Wood 2010; Wood & Appel 2014).

Wood (2010), for instance, investigates the frequency of lexical clusters in six intermediate and advanced EAP textbooks. This corpus-based analysis of the textbook materials reveals that textbook instructions feature considerably more lexical clusters than the reading passages. Wood (2010) advances the theory that publishers aim for a certain amount of consistency in the formulation of the tasks, thus leading to a high frequency of lexical clusters in the instructional texts. The reading passages, on the other hand, contain fewer lexical clusters and their frequencies of occurrence within any one textbook are such that the author believes that it is unlikely that learners can acquire them solely through reading. Wood's (2010) page-by-page analysis of the pedagogical treatment of formulaic language in the examined textbooks strengthens this hypothesis, as no attempt appears to be made to focus learners' attention on these lexical units.

The presentation of lexical bundles in EAP and ESP textbooks is also the focus of Wood and Appel's study (2014) in which they first extracted the most frequent three and four-word bundles in a corpus of ten first-year business and engineering textbooks, and then queried a corpus of five intermediate and advanced EAP textbooks to examine which of those bundles appear in the EAP textbooks. Depending on the EAP textbook, between 35% to 47% of the most frequently occurring lexical bundles from the subject textbooks were found at least once in the EAP textbooks. However, the authors deplore that none of the formulaic sequences are dealt with pedagogically, i.e., presented as units worth learning or highlighted in any way that might raise learners' awareness of their potential.

Focusing on one discipline only, electrical engineering, Chen (2010) also compares the frequency and nature of multi-word units in entry-level university electrical engineering textbooks and ESP textbooks especially designed for students of this same discipline. In contrast to Wood and Appel (2014), however, Chen not only compiled a list of the most frequent lexical bundles found in the introductory subject-specific textbooks, but also one for the ESP textbooks. As a result, she was able to compare the types, frequencies, and pragmatic functions of lexical bundles featured in both types of textbooks. The results match those of Wood and Appel (2014) in that only a third of the lexical bundles identified in the electrical engineering introductory textbooks occur at least once in the corresponding ESP textbooks. Furthermore, a qualitative analysis of the pragmatic functions of the bundles demonstrates that entire subcategories of stance bundles (e.g., *can be used to, it is important to*) are missing from the ESP textbooks. When it comes to referential bundles (e.g., *is referred to as, a great deal of*), Chen concludes that "the ESP textbooks underrepresent quantity and spatial specifications but overemphasize referential information which is not central in target language use, such as the introduction to new concepts/definitions and provision of time information" (Chen 2010: 123).

3.2.2 Tense and aspect

Having presented some of the observations derived from a range of studies on the lexis of Textbook English, this section now turns to the representation of tenses and aspects in EFL publications. To this end, it seems natural to begin with one of the earliest comparative corpus-based studies already mentioned in 3.1.2.3: Mindt's (1987, 1992) study on the prevalence, functions, and lexico-grammatical patterning of future constructions in German EFL textbooks.

3.2.2.1 *Future constructions*

As explained in 3.1.2.3, Mindt (1987, 1992) undertook to study the future constructions presented in textbooks designed for the first few years of German secondary schools with those produced in speech by British native speakers. The results show that the examined German EFL textbooks under-represented *will*, over-represented *going to* and left out *shall* as a means of expressing future situations altogether (Mindt 1992: 189). Mindt (1992: 37) also observed that, compared to his reference corpus of (pseudo-)spoken English, the contracted forms of *going to* were considerably under-represented in the spoken passages of the textbooks. Furthermore, Mindt (1992: 35, 41) interprets the absence of *gonna* and *ain't* in the examined textbooks as a misrepresentation of English language usage at the time of the study.

3.2.2.2 *The present perfect*

Following a similar approach, Schlüter (2002) published a book-length corpus-driven analysis of the use of the present perfect in spoken and written ENL. From this data, Schlüter (2002) established a so-called 'empirical grammar' (see also Dirven 1990; Mindt 1995a) of the present perfect and contrasted it to existing traditional (EFL) grammars that are known to mostly rely on introspection, as well as to the grammar sections of two popular series of secondary school EFL textbooks used in Germany, together with their accompanying grammar and activity books. The textbooks are found to present the functions of the present perfect in substantially different ways (Schlüter 2002: 219–328). For example, textbooks fail to explain that the present perfect progressive is often used to refer to iterative actions or events rather than continuous ones.

In order to investigate Japanese EFL learners' difficulties with the use of the present perfect, Fujimoto (2017) triangulated results from three corpora: a reference corpus of general American and British English, an English learner corpus of Japanese L1 speakers, and a corpus of EFL textbooks designed for Japanese high schools. Fujimoto (2017) reports that English L2 learners overuse the present perfect with temporal adverbials as compared to the reference corpus. The six textbooks examined vary greatly in their use of the simple present perfect both with and without temporal adverbials. However, the two textbooks that radically over-represent the simple present perfect with temporal adverbials, as opposed to without, do so principally in the exercises, rather than in the extended reading passages. Fujimoto (2017) suggests that this may explain why, in their own writing, Japanese learners of English are more comfortable using the present perfect with temporal adverbials than without. Their over-representation in EFL textbook exercises may mean that Japanese learners of English have internalised their use as lexical markers that trigger the use of the present perfect.

3.2.2.3 *The progressive*

In an in-depth, corpus-driven analysis of the progressive aspect, Römer (2005) examined how the progressive is represented in the dialogues of two popular textbook series also designed for German secondary schools. Römer's study broadly follows Mindt's methodology described in 3.1.2.3. A noteworthy difference, however, is that Römer (2005) only examines occurrences of the progressives in the textbook passages intended to reflect spoken language use (printed dialogues, speech bubbles, transcripts of audio materials, etc.). By comparing these with how the progressive is used in everyday conversation among L1 speakers, Römer's study is one of the few investigations of Textbook English to date that genuinely accounts for the fact that mode and register are likely to impact how such a grammatical construction is used in context (see also Le Foll 2021c, 2022a, 2022b).

For each occurrence of the progressive in her corpora, Römer (2005) surveyed a wide range of contextual features including tense forms, contraction, polarity, clause type, adverbial specification, verb lemma, subject and object of progressive verb phrases, as well as functional features including time reference, continuousness, repeatedness, and framing. Among other findings, Römer (2005: 244–245) reports that contracted forms of the auxiliary BE are under-represented among the progressive forms encountered in the textbook dialogues. Furthermore, *he* and *she* are found to be over-represented in subject positions of progressives, whilst *I*, *it*, *we* and *they* are underused (Römer 2005: 246–248). With respect to the core functions of the progressive, Römer (2005: 260–266; see also Römer 2010: 22–24) notes that proportionally too few occurrences of textbook progressives convey the sense of "repeatedness". Römer (2005) also attempted to compare the results of some of her analyses across the most frequent verb lemmas; however, the textbook corpus surveyed being relatively small (108,000 words), such comparisons of the contextual use of specific verb lemmas in the progressive are inescapably explorative in nature. Le Foll (2022a) applied collostructional analysis to explore differences in the verb lemmas most attracted to or repelled by the progressive in textbook dialogues and real-world conversation as captured in the Spoken BNC2014 (Love et al. 2017). The results show that textbook dialogues under-represent typically stative verbs (e.g., LOVE, LET and WANT) in the progressive, as well as a number of relatively fixed discourse-structuring phrasemes that feature present or past progressive forms such as *I'm/was thinking, she was saying, what I'm trying to say is*, etc.

3.2.2.4 *Modals*

In an earlier study, Römer (2004) applied a comparative corpus-based methodology following Mindt (see 3.1.2.3) to compare the frequencies, co-occurrence patterns, and functions of modal verbs in authentic spoken British English and in the German secondary school EFL textbook series: *Learning English Green Line New*. As electronic versions of the coursebooks were unavailable, Römer (2004) decided against the compilation of a "pedagogic corpus" containing all the texts featured in the coursebooks, opting, instead, for the non-random selection of 32 texts from the textbook units in which one or more modals are specifically taught. Combined with all the grammar sections from the same textbook series and the content of a grammar book for the same level (*Learning English Grundgrammatik)*, the 32 texts were considered to represent "a sample of EFL textbook language – the kind of language pupils are exposed to in the EFL classroom" (Römer 2004: 190). Striking discrepancies were observed between the textbook data and the reference L1 corpus. For instance, whereas Römer's analysis of the spoken BNC1994 shows that the modal *would* (and its contracted form *'d*) is the second most frequent modal, it only comes in fifth position in the textbook data (Römer 2004: 193). In general, modals in Textbook English more frequently refer to ability than in naturally occurring conversation. Thus, for *could* and *may*, the meaning of possibility tends to be under-represented in the textbook data. Furthermore, *must* expresses an inference/deduction in over a third of the BNC concordance lines examined, yet this meaning is only very rarely featured in textbooks (Römer 2004: 194). Textbooks also tend to over-represent certain negated modals whilst others are never presented in a negated form in the textbook materials examined (Römer 2004: 194). Römer (2004) notes further mismatches between the two corpora in the context of questions and *if*-sentences featuring modals (Römer 2004: 195).

3.2.2.5 *Conditionals*

Frazier (2003) surveyed eight ESL textbooks for their coverage of hypothetical and counterfactual conditionals. The study concludes that the textbooks largely neglect hypothetical and counterfactual *would*-clauses that are removed from their presumed *if*-clauses and rarely present such clauses in larger units of discourse. To demonstrate the prevalence of such *would*-clauses, Frazier (2003) also conducted a mixed-methods analysis of 467 instances of *would*-conditionals in one written and two spoken corpora of American English. Frazier (2003: 451) concludes that "much more often than not, conditional and hypothetical clauses with the modal *would* are not accompanied by *if*-clauses anywhere near them, much less in the same sentence".

Based on Frazier's (2003) corpus-driven data, Yoo (2013) investigated how *would*-clauses are presented in five Korean high school EFL textbooks which account for approximately 70% of the EFL textbook market share in Korea. All 253 occurrences of *would*-clauses from the textbook corpus were extracted and annotated. Yoo then compared the lexico-grammatical patterns in which the *would*-clauses were embedded and compared their frequencies with Frazier's (2003) analysis of naturally occurring English corpus data. Great disparities between the textbook sentences and naturally occurring language were observed. For instance, Yoo notes that despite its wide usage, all the textbooks explored fail to include the combination of *would* with the copula verb *seem* (Yoo 2013: 54), thus neglecting to expose learners to this potentially highly useful double-hedging construction. Moreover, no single example of an infinitive-*would* pattern is found in the textbook corpus (Yoo 2013: 81) despite attested frequent occurrence in naturally occurring English as demonstrated by Duffley's (2006) corpus study.

Gabrielatos' (2003, 2006, 2013) approach to evaluating the authenticity of *if*-sentences as described in EFL textbooks has already been presented in 3.1.2.4. These studies clearly demonstrate that a large proportion of *if*-sentences found in natural L1 speech and writing cannot be accounted for by the consensual typologies of conditionals typically taught in EFL/ESL textbooks. Remarkably, this is true even when taking account of all the rules and examples featured in the most advanced textbooks examined. On the basis of these pedagogically-driven corpus-based studies, Gabrielatos (2013: 155) draws the worrying conclusion that "the pedagogical information in the coursebooks, taken collectively, presented learners not only with a partial picture of the variety of types of conditionals and their respective morphosemantic features, but also a distorted one".

Using the same textbook corpus as for Römer's (2005) analysis of the progressive, Römer (2004b) also conducted a study on conditionals in Textbook English. In this study, the focus lies on the sequences of clauses and tenses in conditional sentences and collocational patterns within *if*-clauses. Römer (2004b: 158) reports that a higher proportion of *if*-sentences begin with the *if*-clause in the authentic data than in the textbook corpus. The results also show that three tense form sequences are vastly over-represented in the textbooks as compared to the corpora of naturally occurring speech. These tense sequences correspond to what EFL textbooks and grammar books usually refer to as Type 1, Type 2, and Type 3 conditionals. Conversely, Römer (2004b: 159–60) demonstrates that the most frequent tense combinations in *if*-sentences in the spoken component of the BNC1994 (simple present + simple present), as well as a number of other frequent tense sequences appear to be significantly under-represented in Textbook English (for similar results, see also Gabrielatos 2003, 2006, 2013; Möller 2020; Winter & Le Foll 2022).

3.2.2.6 *Reported speech*

Applying a manual page-by-page approach (see 3.1.1.2), Barbieri and Eckhardt (2007) surveyed how reported speech is taught in seven popular ESL/EFL grammar textbooks. They report that the textbooks largely focus on indirect reported speech and find a general consensus on the 'backshifting rule' for pronouns, adverbials and tense. Whilst all the textbook authors seem to agree that, in general, the verb in the embedded clause should be "backshifted" to the past, there is no agreement as to which specific cases constitute exceptions to this rule. Barbieri and Eckhardt (2007) compared these results to two corpus-based studies on direct (Barbieri 2005) and indirect (Eckhardt 2001) reported speech in real-world language use, mobilising conversation and newspaper corpora as their data basis. They drew on the most striking discrepancies between the textbooks' "grammar rules" and the patterns of use that emerge from the authentic data to make ten suggestions to improve the authenticity of EFL textbook's portrayal of reported speech. Barbieri and Eckhardt (2007) convincingly argue that indirect reported speech should not be taught as a transformation of direct speech (i.e., following the well-known backshifting rule), since the two constructions follow distinctive lexico-grammatical patterning and discourse functions and are used in different communicative situations and registers. Consequently, the authors suggest that indirect reported speech should be taught in the context of newspaper writing, whilst direct reported speech ought to be taught in the context of conversation. Barbieri and Eckhardt (2007) also make recommendations concerning the range of reporting verbs that ought to be associated with certain types of reported speech constructions in EFL/ESL textbooks and encourage textbook authors to highlight the grammatical patterns and discourse functions associated with less frequent tense sequences. Furthermore, they advocate the inclusion of informal quotatives such as *be like, go* and *be all*, together with context regarding their discourse-pragmatic function and sociolinguistic associations.

3.2.3 Pragmatics

This section examines aspects of discourse and pragmatics in Textbook English. The selected studies are discussed in chronological order.

In English, doubt and certainty can be expressed in a variety of ways including using modal verbs, adjectives, tag questions, and specific intonation patterns, as well as paralinguistic and non-linguistic devices. The fact that many lexical markers of doubt and certainty are highly polysemous further adds to the complexity of the task. This motivated Holmes (1988) to conduct a survey on the coverage of lexical items commonly employed to express doubt in two EFL/ESL reference grammars and two coursebooks. To this end, Holmes (1988) compared the epistemic lexical items illustrated in the four textbooks with information on the range and frequency of the same lexical devices as retrieved from four different native corpora. In addition to these corpus-based comparisons, Holmes (1988) also referred to previous research findings and to native-speaker acceptability judgments to evaluate the choices of the pedagogical material designers. Holmes' (1988) study concludes that some textbooks paint an entirely misleading picture of epistemic modality compared to real-world English usage, whilst other textbooks neglect the topic altogether. Although corpus data clearly shows that, when expressing doubt, native speakers of English do not confine themselves to modal verbs, Holmes (1988: 40) observes that the majority of textbook authors "devote an unjustifiably large amount of attention to modal verbs, neglecting alternative linguistic strategies for expressing doubt and certainty".

In academic writing, doubt is frequently expressed in the form of hedging. Hyland (1994) explored the representations of hedging devices in 22 EAP/ESP textbooks designed to help L2 English users acquire Academic English writing skills. Following a page-by-page approach (see 3.1.1.2), Hyland (1994) first drew a list of markers of uncertainty and tentativeness that a number of previous studies have found to be salient in academic writing and proceeded to manually check the EAP/ESP textbooks for evidence of coverage of these hedging devices. The evaluation of the textbooks' coverage of these devices is based on both the number of exercises devoted to these devices and the quality of the information provided on them (Hyland 1994: 244). Hyland's (1994: 250) study concludes that, in general, "the presentation of hedges in published [EAP/ESP] materials is not encouraging, with information scattered, explanations inadequate, practice material limited". Echoing Holmes' (1988) conclusion, Hyland (1994: 244) criticises the fact textbooks hardly present any alternatives to modal verbs for hedging.

Vellenga (2004) selected four EFL integrated skills textbooks and four ESL grammar textbooks that are frequently used in university settings in non-English-speaking countries to examine how pragmatic information is presented in English textbooks. The study's methodology has already been detailed in 3.1.1.2. The results can only be considered exploratory but seem to point towards a general paucity of metapragmatic and metalinguistic information in EFL and ESL textbooks. Vellenga notes that metalinguistic information is mostly presented in the form of imperative directives for learners to complete an activity in the textbook. Pronominal reference is often absent. The author deplores the pragmatic inadequacy of the treatment of most speech acts in the textbooks explored. In particular, Vellenga points to the danger of providing unique speech act–grammatical form associations as they may prove misleading and restricting for learners. The study (Vellenga 2004: n.p.) concludes that the "distribution of speech act types across ESL and EFL textbooks did not appear to be patterned, nor based on frequency of speech act occurrence in natural language". Finally, interviews conducted with four experienced EFL/ESL teachers lead the author to the disconcerting conclusion "that textbooks do provide the majority of input, and that even professional teachers rarely have the time, inclination, or training to include supplementary pragmatic information in their lessons" (Vellenga 2004: n. p.).

Cheng (2007) examined a corpus of spoken English produced by competent English speakers from Hong Kong (the *Hong Kong Corpus of Spoken English*; Cheng, Greaves & Warren 2005) for instances of interruption in the form of initiation of simultaneous talk in conversations. Both the functions of the interruptions and their linguistic realisations were compared to phrases that eleven popular English textbooks used in Hong Kong secondary schools suggest are appropriate for interrupting. Cheng's (2007) results make clear that, by and large, the phrases suggested in the textbooks do not accurately reflect real-language use: the majority of the phrases taught in the textbooks (e.g., *Excuse me, but…, Sorry to interrupt…, If I could just come in here…, I want to say something, please)* do not occur even once in the 800,000-word corpus of naturally occurring Hong Kong English corpus queried.

Drawing on the same reference corpus, Cheng and Warren (2007) evaluated textbook authors' perception and presentation of strategies for monitoring and checking understanding in 15 upper-secondary ESL/EFL textbooks. Their manual analysis of the pedagogic texts shows that the textbook authors emphasise the role of the listener in checking understanding, often providing example phrases encouraging the listeners to "seek clarification", "ask for repetition", "say they don't understand", etc. Only four of the 15 textbooks examined also propose strategies for the speaker to "check others' understanding" and "clarify". The analysis of the authentic conversation data reveals that the primary responsibility in ensuring that understanding has taken place rests with the speaker, rather than with the listener. However, some of the phrases suggested by the textbooks to explicitly ask the listeners whether they have understood (e.g., *Are you with me?* and *Do you understand me?*) do not appear a single time in the *Hong Kong Corpus of Spoken English*. Although the simple backchannel *okay* is found to be the third most frequent form of checking understanding in the corpus of real-world Hong Kong English, it is widely under-represented in textbook examples. Thus, Cheng and Warren (2007: 202) conclude "that textbooks contain language forms that are rarely, if ever, used in the real world and are overly influenced by academic genres". From a pedagogical point of view, it is worth noting that the most frequent forms in Hong Kong English "are both simpler and less explicit than those included in the textbooks" (Cheng & Warren 2007: 202).

In a similar vein and, again, relying on the same corpora, Cheng and Warren (2005, 2006) reveal that Hong Kong textbook authors' intuitions on forms used to express disagreement (Cheng & Warren 2005) and to give opinions (Cheng & Warren 2006) do not match real language use as documented in the *Hong Kong Corpus of Spoken English*. In sum, the Textbook English studies surveyed in this section suggest that textbook authors' intuitions and portrayal of the functions and linguistic realisations of a wide range of learner-relevant speech acts largely fail to match evidence from corpora of naturally occurring English. Unlike the vast majority of corpus-based textbook language studies examined so far, the aforementioned studies carried out in Hong Kong rely on a reference corpus that consists of culture-specific spoken interactions between Hong Kong Chinese speakers and speakers of languages other than Cantonese in a range of communicative situations that English learners are likely to be confronted with. Thus, contrary to many of the previously described Textbook English studies that rely on general L1 corpora of sometimes doubtful relevance to anyone but highly advanced learners of English (see Tono 2004), the *Hong Kong Corpus of Spoken English* can reasonably be considered to constitute the target learner language of secondary school students in Hong Kong.

3.2.4 Spoken grammar

The final section of this literature review focuses on how spoken grammar is represented in EFL/ESL textbooks. Attitudinal research indicates that learners of English are generally very interested in acquiring at least receptive knowledge of spoken grammar, whereas teachers and textbook authors are more divided on the subject (Timmis 2003). According to Timmis (2003), EFL textbooks tend to ignore lexico-grammatical features typical of spoken English such as the *get*-passive, discourse dimensions of past-aspect choices, certain reported speech forms, and ellipsis structures. This observation would certainly merit empirical verification.

One original methodological approach to evaluating the linguistic features of spoken interactions in EFL textbooks was already presented in 3.1.2.5. As a reminder, Gilmore's (2004) evaluation of the authenticity of spoken textbook language involved the comparison of re-creations of communicative situations simulated in textbooks with the textbook dialogues themselves. Nine discourse features were selected for comparison: lexical density, false starts, repetition, pauses, terminal overlap, latching, hesitation devices, and backchannels. Gilmore (2004) reports that the 'authentic' enactments of the dialogues (see caveats in 3.1.2.5) are almost twice as long as their textbook counterparts. Additionally, the lexical density of textbook dialogues is higher than that of authentic conversations (though it may be argued that the difference, based on 200-word samples from only seven examples, does not appear to be great, nor is this claim backed by the results of any statistical testing). In particular older textbooks were found to hardly feature any of the discourse features typical of spontaneous spoken interactions.

In a page-by-page survey, Cullen and Kuo (2007) focused on explicit mentions of features of spoken grammar in 24 global EFL textbooks covering all levels from beginner to advanced. Focusing their investigations on three categories of features of spoken grammar, Cullen and Kuo (2007: 361) conclude that "where spoken grammar is dealt with at all, there tends to be an emphasis on lexico-grammatical features, and common syntactic structures peculiar to conversation are either ignored or confined to advanced levels as interesting extras". One could argue, however, that such structures are more likely to be taught implicitly than in an overt manner and that, as a consequence, a corpus-based textbook study that includes the written dialogues and transcripts of the listening materials accompanying the textbooks may paint a rather different picture.

The results of the studies outlined above confirm that, despite a strong focus in syllabi on speaking skills and communicative language learning, textbooks seemingly continue to present a misleading picture of spoken language. Barbieri and Eckhardt (2007: 321) conclude that textbooks "neglect important and frequent features of the language spoken by real language users, present a patchy, confusing, and often inadequate treatment of common features of the grammar of the spoken language, and, in sum, do not reflect actual use". However, this section has shown that studies on representations of spoken English in EFL/ESL textbooks have, so far, either only focused on individual linguistic features (e.g., Römer on *if*-conditionals [2004; see 3.2.2.5] and the progressive [2005; see 3.2.2.3]), on explicit mentions of spoken grammar features only (e.g., Cullen & Kuo 2007), or on a very small sample of textbook dialogues (e.g., Gilmore 2004).

3.3 Conclusions

This review strongly suggests that, as suspected by many (former) learners of English as a foreign language in instructional contexts, Textbook English may indeed constitute a distinct variety of English that, in many respects, differs substantially from real-life, naturally occurring English. Section 3.2.2.5 highlighted the fact that some grammar rules promulgated in textbooks are, in fact, not even respected in the extended written passages of the textbooks themselves; thus, pointing to striking intra-textbook inconsistencies and, more generally, to a genuine gap between prescriptive grammars of English and extracurricular, 'real-world' usage.

Section 3.2.3 showed that the results of most studies examining pragmatics in Textbook English stress that textbooks are not providing learners with adequate input to develop pragmatic competences. In spite of some improvements found in studies comparing older with more recent publications (e.g., Gilmore 2004; Jiang 2006; Usó-Juan 2008), critics argue that newer publications do little more than simply lengthen the list of linguistic structures to be used in the context of specific speech acts, yet provide next to no contextual information as to their usage in real language use (Usó-Juan & Martínez-Flor 2010: 426).

In terms of methods, we have seen that linguists have, thus far, mostly strived to compare Textbook English to naturally occurring English as produced by native speakers; however, even comparisons of local ESL textbooks with that of English produced by local proficient ESL speakers have shown that the language input learners obtain from their textbooks remains far removed from what they are expected to later engage in outside the classroom (see 3.2.3).

To better grasp this apparent mismatch between the language of pedagogical materials and target learner language, let us consider the factors that may contribute to this gap. The first argument that textbook authors would presumably advance is that their task is to simplify real-world language use to make it accessible to language learners. In fact, a distinct limitation of many of the studies surveyed as part of this literature review is that they examine Textbook English as a single, monolithic variety of English, ignoring potential variation related to the different proficiency levels of the textbooks. Whilst there is no doubt that proficiency level must be accounted for in future descriptions of Textbook English (see 4.1), advocates of usage-based L2 instruction models would counter that the most important factors in the construction of Textbook English ought to be the relative frequencies of occurrence and salience of linguistic features in naturally occurring English (see 2.4). In practice, however, it would appear that the majority of textbook authors still rely on long-established grammar conventions and/or their intuition, rather than on empirical insights from actual language usage (see 2.7). Many of the conclusions of the Textbook English studies summarised in this chapter thus remind us that: "Tradition, even if it is most venerable, cannot serve as a substitute for research" (Mindt 1997: 41). This was most apparent in the studies that compared the coverage of key lexical items in different textbooks targeted at the same proficiency level and found very little agreement across different textbook series (e.g., Koprowski 2005; see 3.2.1.2).

Furthermore, many of the studies surveyed as part of this literature review have concluded that textbooks tend to present lexico-grammatical patterns as if they were generalisable across all registers, thus failing to acknowledge crucial differences between different production modes, text types, and discourse-context-specific uses (see also Barbieri & Eckhardt 2007: 321). The studies summarised in 3.2.3 and 3.2.4, in particular, suggest that the language of EFL textbooks is predominantly based on norms pertaining to written text registers. Indeed, textbook dialogues appear to largely fail to account for the processing conditions of spontaneous spoken interaction (e.g., lack of planning, reciprocity, shared environment). The resulting disregard of syntactic and lexico-grammatical features that are typical of unplanned speech contributes to this prevailing lack of fit between many aspects of Textbook English and real-world language use. At the same time, however, this criticism can be turned on its head. As this chapter has shown, numerous Textbook English studies suffer from severe methodological limitations. Crucially, many of the conclusions drawn on the basis of comparisons between Textbook English and naturally occurring English are likely flawed due to the use of inappropriate or only partially suitable reference corpora (e.g., comparing textbook dialogues to the entire BNC1994).

Despite some limitations, the studies outlined in this chapter, collectively, provide substantial evidence for the frequently idiosyncratic use of specific lexico-grammatical features in Textbook English. They reveal pedagogically questionable gaps between the language input that textbooks provide and what learners are expected to eventually produce and engage with. That said, our understanding of Textbook English remains patchy – not least because no study has yet attempted to provide a comprehensive linguistic description of Textbook English across a broad range of linguistic features and registers, based on appropriate reference corpora and a sufficiently large corpus of EFL textbooks. The present study sets out to contribute to bridging this gap by investigating a broad range of lexico-grammatical features in a large corpus of contemporary EFL textbooks widely used in secondary schools in France, Germany, and Spain. The following chapter explains how this literature review informed both the methodological approach of the present study (4.1–4.2) and the design of the corpora used in its comparative corpus-based analyses (4.3).

CHAPTER 4

Research aims and corpus data

The present chapter begins by drawing conclusions from the outcomes of the literature review summarised in Chapter 3. Based on these insights, Section 4.2 outlines the methodological framework of the present study. The research questions that guide the analyses are formulated in 4.2.1. They are concerned with the linguistic nature of Textbook English and the factors that may mediate variation within this variety of English. The second half of the present chapter outlines the many decision-making processes involved in the compilation of the Textbook English Corpus (TEC; 4.3.1) and the three reference corpora (4.3.2) and provides descriptive statistics on their compositions.

4.1 Insights from the literature review

Taken together, the studies surveyed in Chapter 3 provide valuable insights into "the kind of synthetic English" (Römer 2004a: 185) that EFL learners are exposed to via their English textbooks. However, the literature review revealed some problematic aspects that have commonly been neglected in past endeavours to study the language of textbooks and which the present study aims to address.

First, throughout the literature review, concerns were raised as to the suitability of the reference corpora used in comparative corpus-based analyses. Whilst some have argued that English native speaker standards are not suitable for most EFL learners (for more on this, see 4.3.2.1), the more pressing issue resides in the fact that many of the reference corpora used in previous Textbook English studies do not match the communicative aims and/or target audiences of the textbook texts. Many of the surveyed studies relied on general English corpora such as the British National Corpus (BNC1994; Burnard 2007), which is made up of 90% written language, mostly penned by professional writers with an adult readership in mind and edited by professionals for publication. Thus, the present study aims to find and, if necessary, compile the most appropriate reference corpora possible for maximally meaningful comparisons.

Second, though it has long been established that situational characteristics of texts are a major driver of linguistic variation (see, e.g., Biber 2012; Gray & Egbert 2019; Goulart et al. 2020), Chapter 3 repeatedly showed that potential register differences between the various types of texts typically featured in school

EFL textbooks have largely been brushed aside. Given that, on any double page, a school EFL textbook may feature, for example, an extract of a short story, a dialogue, instructions, and exercises, the present study hypothesises that Textbook English cannot be meaningfully described without taking a register-based approach. Up until now, however, register variation within EFL textbooks has largely been ignored (exceptions include Le Foll 2021c; and Miller 2011 in the context of university-level ESL textbooks). In the few cases where register has been considered in the analysis of EFL textbooks, the focus has almost exclusively been on representations of spoken language, e.g., Mindt (1987, 1995a), Le Foll (2022a, 2022b) and Römer (2004b, 2005), who all compared the dialogues of secondary school EFL textbooks to corpora of spoken/ pseudo-spoken native speaker English. However, other sources of register variation in school EFL textbooks have yet to be adequately explored.

Another frequently neglected aspect concerns interactions between the frequencies of individual linguistic features. This is important because usage-based approaches to language acquisition (see 2.3–2.4) postulate that the co-occurrence information that learners perceive in language input "is stored as points in a multi-dimensional space at coordinates, and that speakers process this stored linguistic information in ways that allow them to identify (under certain conditions and defined by various types of frequency occurrences) abstract linguistic patterns" (Rautionaho & Deshors 2018: 229). Thus, whilst some influential studies have helped us to understand how EFL/ESL learners can be misled by their textbooks to make unidiomatic use of specific linguistic features (e.g., the progressive aspect; Römer 2005), only a multivariable approach can paint the full picture as to how Textbook English – as a whole – differs from the English that English learners will later encounter and be expected to produce outside the classroom. In fact, even within a case-study approach describing and/or evaluating the representation of a single linguistic feature in Textbook English, potential interactions between different variables ought to be taken into consideration. For instance, if a study reports that certain lexical verbs in the present progressive are under-represented in textbook dialogues as compared to naturally occurring conversation among L1 speakers, this could mean that these verbs are, overall, under-represented in EFL textbooks, across all tenses and aspects. It could, however, equally mean that the present progressive is under-represented as compared to other tenses and aspects. Alternatively, it could point to a genuine under-representation of a specific combination of tense, aspect, and verb type. The problem is that most Textbook English studies, to date, have not accounted for such possible interactions between the linguistic variables that they have investigated.

Such multivariable analyses of corpus data, however, call for appropriate statistical methods. The methodological review reported on in 3.1, however, concluded that statistical tests have only rarely been conducted in the context of quantitative, comparative corpus-based analyses of Textbook English. When they have, chi-squared tests have been favoured (see, e.g., Römer 2005: 60). These statistical tests, together with other tests popular in corpus linguistics such as log-likelihood and Fisher's exact tests (Brezina 2018: 112–15), can help researchers conclude with a certain degree of certainty that frequencies observed in textbook language differ from the probabilistically expected frequencies (drawn from, e.g., a reference corpus) because of genuine differences between the corpora, rather than due to random, chance variation (Levshina 2015: 201–13; Wallis 2020: Chapter 8). Many studies that report tests such as chi-squared tests, however, only report whether the test returned a *p*-value below a pre-defined threshold (usually 0.05, corresponding to 5% probability that the same test result or a more extreme one could have been obtained if there were no actual difference between the compared populations). Here, the problem is twofold. First, *p*-values do not inform the reader as to how large (let alone: relevant!) these supposed differences actually are and, second, they are dependent on sample size. Thus, given very large corpus datasets, statistically significant results (i.e., with very small *p*-values) will almost inevitably be returned (Baroni & Evert 2009: 787; Gries 2005; or simulate some data to observe this effect on https://shinyapps.org/apps/p-hacker/ [Schönbrodt 2016]). With small datasets, by contrast, only extremely large differences between two sets of frequencies will return significant results. In other words, studies with small sample sizes are often underpowered and therefore cannot be used to reliably detect anything but huge effects (Winter 2019: 171–175). Another issue is that when conducting individual tests on potential differences between the mean frequencies of many different linguistic variables, *p*-values ought to be corrected to account for multiple comparisons (Wallis 2020: 274–275; Winter 2019: 175–177). To date, this has rarely been done in corpus-based analyses of Textbook English.

On a related matter, previous quantitative corpus-based studies of textbook language have usually been undertaken at the corpus level (rather than at the textbook volume, chapter, unit, or individual text level), thus implicitly assuming that Textbook English is a homogenous variety of English in which the linguistic features under study are dispersed evenly within the textbook corpora. Just like learner Englishes have been shown to vary across different registers, tasks, proficiency levels, individual learners, etc., so can Textbook English be expected to vary across different textbook series, targeted textbook audience/instructional setting, proficiency levels, text registers, etc.

4.2 The present study

The present study is based on Mindt's comparative, corpus-based methodology (see 3.1.2.3). As explained in the previous chapter, such an approach requires the compilation of two corpora: a textbook corpus and a reference corpus of naturally occurring English representative of the target language students can be expected to aspire to. In addition, various methods that have been proposed to account for the multifactorial/-variate and multilevel structure of learner corpus data (Gries 2013, 2018; Gries & Deshors 2020; Paquot & Plonsky 2017; Möller 2017; Wulff & Gries 2021) have inspired the methodological approaches followed in the present study in an attempt to account for the nested nature of textbook language data. Thus, this study attempts to model the potential impact of the different text registers typically found in EFL textbooks, their varying target proficiency levels, and any potential idiosyncrasies of textbook authors, editors, or publishers, as well as how these variables may interact with each other.

4.2.1 Research aims and questions

In sum, the present study attempts to describe both the linguistic specificities of Textbook English as a variety of English, as well as to model its internal variation. More specifically, the project addresses the following research questions:

1. How homogenous is Textbook English as a variety of English? Which factors mediate intra-textbook linguistic variation?
2. To what extent are French, German, and Spanish secondary school pupils confronted with varying English input via their textbooks?
3. To what extent is the language of current EFL textbooks used in secondary schools in France, Germany, and Spain representative of 'real-world' English as used by native/proficient English speakers in similar communicative situations? To what extent are some registers more faithfully represented than others?
4. What are the defining linguistic features that characterise Textbook English registers as compared to these target language registers? To what extent are these stable across entire textbook series? To what extent are some of these defining features specific to certain proficiency levels?

This study aims to provide an empirical, multivariable description of the language of a large sample of secondary school EFL textbooks. It is hoped that it can contribute to raising awareness of what constitutes the main variety of English that secondary school students are formally exposed to: 'Textbook English'. Ultimately, both the results and some of the methods employed may be used to evaluate future EFL teaching materials. In addition, the results may help EFL teachers, textbook authors, and editors to improve existing teaching materials in order to better equip learners with the necessary linguistic knowledge and skills to succeed in the English-speaking world outside the classroom.

4.2.2 Open Science statement

Among the wealth of Textbook English publications summarised in Chapter 3 (see also Appendix A), very few have included the data and, where relevant, the code necessary to reproduce or replicate the findings that they report (thereby reflecting current sharing practices in linguistics more broadly, see Bochynska et al. 2023).[12]

Although the terms are sometimes used interchangeably (for a comprehensive glossary of Open Science terminology, see Parsons et al. 2022), 'reproducibility' is used here to refer to the ability to obtain the same results using the researchers' original data and code, whilst 'replicability'[13] entails repeating a study and obtaining compatible results with different data analysed with either the same or different methods (see also Berez-Kroeker et al. 2018: 4; Porte & McManus 2018: 6–7). Not only does not sharing data and materials mean that published results are not reproducible, hereby making it difficult to assess their reliability, it also makes it very difficult to attempt to replicate the results to gain insights into the extent to which they are generalisable, e.g., across a different set of EFL textbooks used in a different educational context (see also Le Foll 2024b; McManus in press).

A major barrier to the reproducibility of (corpus) linguistic research is that it is often not possible for copyright or, when participants are involved, data protection reasons to make linguistic data available to the wider public. However, both research practices and the impact of our research can already be greatly improved if we publish our code or, when using GUI software, methods sections detailed enough for an independent researcher to be able to perfectly repeat the full procedure. If this is done, it is possible to conduct detailed reviews of our methodologies and replicate the effects reported in the published literature using different data.

12. This is also true of my own earlier work on the language of EFL textbooks (Le Foll 2021c, 2022a, 2022b). More recent work conducted as part of this project, however, has been published alongside with the data and code (Le Foll 2022c, 2023c, 2024a).

13. Confusingly, other terms are also frequently used to refer to the same or related concepts, e.g., *repeatability, robustness* and *generalisability* (see, e.g., Belz et al. 2021: 2–3; Parsons et al. 2022).

Aside from data protection and copyright restrictions, there are, of course, many more reasons why researchers may be reluctant to share their data and code (see, e.g., Al-Hoorie & Marsden 2024; Gomes et al. 2022). It is not within the scope of this monograph to discuss these reasons; however, it is important to acknowledge that, in many ways, such transparency makes us vulnerable. At the end of the day: to err is human. Yet, the risks involved in committing to Open Science practices are particularly tangible for researchers working on individual projects, like me, who have had no formal training in project management, programming, or versioning and have therefore had to learn "on the job". Nonetheless, I am convinced that the advantages outweigh the risks. Striving for transparency helps both the researchers themselves and others reviewing the work to spot and address problems. As a result, the research community can build on both the mishaps and successes of previous research, thus improving the efficiency of research processes and ultimately contributing to advancing scientific progress.

It is with this in mind that I have decided, whenever possible, to publish the data and code necessary to reproduce the results reported in the present monograph following the FAIR principles (i.e., ensuring that research materials are Findable, Accessible, Interoperable and Reusable; Wilkinson et al. 2016). For copyright reasons, the corpora themselves cannot be made available. However, the full, unedited tabular outputs of the tool used for automatic corpus annotation (the MFTE Perl; see 5.3.2) are published in the Online Supplements ⟨https://elenlefoll.github.io/TextbookMDA/⟩. Together with the commented data analysis scripts also published in the Online Supplements, as well as in the associated GitHub repository ⟨https://github.com/elenlefoll/TextbookMDA/⟩ and archived version on the OSF ⟨https://doi.org/10.17605/OSF.IO/JPXAE⟩, these tables allow for the computational reproduction of all of the results and plots discussed in the following chapters.

In describing the study's methodology, maximum transparency is strived for by reporting on how each sample size was determined and on which grounds variables and data points were excluded, manipulated, and/or transformed. Most of these operations were conducted in the open-source programming language and environment R (R Core Team 2022). The annotated data processing and analysis scripts have been rendered to HTML pages (viewable in the Online Supplements) thus allowing researchers to review the procedures followed without necessarily installing all the required packages and running the code themselves. Furthermore, these scripts include additional analyses, tables, and plots that were made as part of this study but which, for reasons of space, were not reported on in detail here. Whenever data, packages or other open-source scripts from other researchers were used, links to these are also provided in the Online Supplements (in addition to the corresponding references in the bibliography).

4.3 Corpus data

The second half of this chapter describes the corpora drawn upon to explore the characteristics of Textbook English as a variety of English. The first part (4.3.1) explains the rationale behind the many decision processes involved in the creation of the Textbook English Corpus (TEC), while the second part (4.3.2) is devoted to the three reference corpora used to compare and contrast Textbook English with naturally occurring 'real-world' language deemed to be representative of the kind of English that secondary school L2 English learners can be expected to understand and produce on leaving secondary school.

4.3.1 The Textbook English Corpus (TEC)

The present study aims to examine the English language content EFL learners are exposed to in secondary school settings. To conduct a corpus-based analysis of this input, it would be necessary to compile a pedagogic corpus, which Hunston (2002: 16) defines as:

> A corpus consisting of all the language a learner has been exposed to. For most learners, their pedagogic corpus does not exist in physical form. If a teacher or researcher does decide to collect a pedagogic corpus, it can consist of all the course books, readers, etc., a learner has used, plus any tapes etc they have heard. [...] It can also be compared with a corpus of naturally occurring English to check that the learner is being presented with language that is natural-sounding and useful.

Collecting data for a pedagogic corpus as defined by Hunston is undoubtably a highly ambitious project. Although not explicitly mentioned, Hunston's definition implies that it should also include all teacher-student and student-student interactions in the L2 and would thus be specific to each and every class group and, even, learner. If, however, in "input-impoverished EFL context[s]" (Meunier & Gouverneur 2007: 122), textbooks do indeed account for such a large proportion of the learner language input, it follows that the textbooks themselves can be considered as a kind of "learner input corpus" (see also Gabrielatos 1994: 13). In 2.5, textbooks were shown to be a key source of language input in school EFL classroom settings. This formed the starting point for investigating the language of EFL textbooks used at lower secondary school level in France, Germany, and Spain. In designing and compiling any corpus, several aspects must be carefully considered: these include the corpus specification, the data collection sampling frame and considerations pertaining to corpus size, representativeness, and balance, all which are explained in the following sections.

4.3.1.1 *Selection of textbooks*

No matter how large, corpora tend to represent only a sample of a target population, with few exceptions such as corpora of individual authors' complete published works. In this study, the target population is defined as the English language content of all the textbooks from which all lower secondary school students in France, Germany, and Spain were learning English as a second or foreign language between 2016 and 2018. Since the school systems are organised differently across the three countries of interest, lower secondary school is defined here for comparison as the equivalent to ISCED 2 (OECD, European Union, UNESCO Institute for Statistics 2015), i.e., the stage where pupils are usually expected to be aged between 11–12 to 15–16 years. In most OECD countries, this period coincides with compulsory secondary education. The corresponding educational levels and year groups for France, Germany, and Spain are displayed in Table 3 (data from Fournier, Gaudry-Lachet & DEPP-MIREI 2017). To compare textbooks aimed at similar levels and year groups across these different educational systems, an additional universal "country-neutral" textbook level variable is used throughout this study (see first column of Table 3). Textbooks for more advanced secondary school English L2 learner were not included in the corpus because textbooks tend to be used more sparingly beyond the first four to five years of secondary school EFL instruction. Although still present in many European classrooms, they are often supplemented with other 'real-world' materials (see, e.g., Leroy 2012: 72 for the French context).

Table 3. The levels of the Textbook English Corpus (TEC)

TEC Level	France		Germany		Spain		Pupil age (approx.)
A	*Collège*	*6e*	*Sekundarstufe I*	*5. Klasse*	*Educación Primaria*	*6°*	11
B		*5e*		*6. Klasse*	*Educación Secundaria Obligatoria (ESO)*	*1° ESO*	12
C		*4e*		*7. Klasse*		*2° ESO*	13
D		*3e*		*8. Klasse*	*ESO Secundo Ciclo*	*3° ESO*	14
E	*Lycée*	*2e*		*9./10. Klasse*		*4° ESO*	15

Since the French, German, and Spanish educational authorities do not prescribe the use of any particular textbooks in state schools, a vast number of different textbook series from a range of publishers are currently in use. For a textbook corpus to capture the full variability of lower secondary school EFL textbooks used in France, Germany, and Spain, it would have to include all the textbooks in use, including possibly some older or little-known editions favoured by individual schools or teachers. However, the principle of representativeness (Egbert, Biber & Gray 2022) also implies that the corpus ought to be representative of the textbook language to which as many pupils as possible are exposed, so that conclusions drawn from the sample of textbooks contained in the corpus may be confirmed in a larger sample of textbooks. This, in turn, implies that the most popular textbooks used in the majority of classrooms ought to be included in the corpus. Since textbook sale figures are not publicly available, informal surveys were conducted with local teachers (in EFL teacher Facebook groups), bookshop assistants, and publisher representatives to establish a list of the most widely used school EFL textbooks in France, Germany, and Spain.

Table 4 summarises the results of these informal market surveys, which revealed differences between countries in school textbook market dynamics. In Germany, the textbook market is dominated by three publishers (Klett, Cornelsen, and Diesterweg), which each offer one major English textbook series per school form (e.g., *Hauptschule, Realschule, Gesamtschule*, and *Gymnasium*) and which, to a lesser extent, may be adapted to match the requirements of specific *Bundesländer*.[14] By contrast, France has a centralised national educational system. That said, schools and teachers are also free to choose whether to use textbooks at all, and if so, which. In general, there is a tendency to be more critical of textbooks than on the other side of the Rhine, with some trainee teachers instructed not to use any commercial textbooks, or at least to design their own lesson units selecting suitable materials from a range of textbooks and authentic materials, rather than religiously following one series (see 2.6). In practice, however, it appears that the majority of English teachers in French lower secondary schools largely rely on one textbook per year group (Leroy 2012: 62) and, indeed, the school textbook market in France continues to experience record growth (Syndicat national de l'édition 2021), despite the concerns of critics.

Whilst the textbooks used in French and German secondary schools are usually published in France and Germany, Spanish schools, teachers (and parents?) seem less convinced of the quality of their locally published textbooks and, as a result, the textbook market is largely dominated by Anglo-Saxon publishers. We may speculate that such "imported textbooks" are favoured for the same reasons as they are in Southeast Asia, where Dat (2008) reports that they are perceived as being more visually and thematically appealing, linguistically accurate, and systematic in their pedagogical approaches compared to "domestic textbooks". Since

14. In Germany, education is devolved to the *Bundesländer* (federal states), which means that each *Bundesland* is, within the limits defined in the German constitution, responsible for its own system of organising public education.

the only Spanish publisher of school English textbooks featured in the informal survey list did not wish to contribute textbooks to the present project and was technically unable to sell digital textbooks without a Spanish ID number, only Anglo-Saxon published textbook series could be included in the Spanish textbook subcorpus. These textbook series are generally the result of a core "global course-book" sold to a number of target countries with "differentiated supplementary materials [...] often written by local authors with specific local knowledge [...] to give the teachers 'a better fit'" (Gray 2002: 165).

In designing the sampling frame of the Textbook English Corpus (TEC), the aim was to select three recently published textbook series per country, ideally by three different major publishers, from the list compiled from the informal surveys (see Table 4). The selection was based on the following, ordered opportunistic criteria:

1. Availability of the textbooks in
    a. Text/PDF format
    b. Other digital formats and
    c. Print
2. Price

Price was particularly relevant for French and Spanish textbooks as some publishers were only willing to sell digital textbooks in bundles of 20 textbooks or more. Availability may seem an odd criterion in an interconnected globalised world, but in some cases buying even a single digital copy of a Spanish textbook requires a valid Spanish ID number. Digital textbook formats also raised technical issues. Whilst PDF textbooks are relatively easy to convert to text using standard optical character recognition (OCR) software, many digital textbooks are only available as complex flash files designed for use with smartboards and/or tablets. These had to be converted to PDF on a page-by-page basis (though this was automated with a script) before they could be converted to text. Finally, two textbook series were obtained in print and scanned to PDF for further OCR processing.

The textbooks included in the TEC are listed in Table 5 (the full bibliographic metadata is available on doi.org/10.5281/zenodo.4922819). To ease comparisons across different educational systems, whenever possible, five textbooks per series were included. As a result, two French textbook series designed for use in *collèges* (corresponding to the first four years of secondary school education, see Table 3 – note, also, that French school years are counted backwards) are complemented with a fifth textbook aimed at first year *Lycée* students in *Seconde* (2e; see Table 3) from the same publisher. This was not possible in the case of the most recent textbook series, *Piece of Cake*, since this relatively new publisher had, as of autumn 2018 when the corpus was finalised, not yet penetrated the *lycée* textbook market.

Table 4. Most widely used lower secondary school textbook series (publisher in brackets) according to the informal market surveys conducted in 2016 with teachers, bookshop assistants, and publishers in France, Germany, and Spain

France
Hi there! (Bordas)
Join the team (Nathan)
New Enjoy (Hatier)
E for English (Didier)
Piece of Cake (Le Livre Scolaire)
New Connect (Hachette)
Spain
High Achievers (Richmond)
Fast Track (Richmond)
Action! (Burlington)
Real English (Burlington)
English in Use (Burlington)
English in Mind for Spanish Speakers (Cambridge University Press)
English File (Oxford University Press)
Germany
Gymnasium
Green Line (Klett)
Access G (Cornelsen)
Camden Town (Diesterweg)
Gesamtschule
Orange Line (Klett)
Lighthouse (Cornelsen)
Hauptschule
Blue Line (Klett)
Realschule
Red Line (Klett)

In terms of its marketing concept, *Piece of Cake* is rather different from the other textbook series featured in the TEC since it was co-authored by, at the time of writing, over 100 school English teachers and is available online in its entirety for free on ⟨https://www.lelivrescolaire.fr⟩. Though it was still relatively new when the

TEC was compiled, the informal market study revealed it to already be a popular series in French secondary schools.

Every effort was made to also include all the (tran)scripts of the audio and video materials belonging to the textbooks of the corpus. When they were not provided by the publishers themselves, this involved trawling through teachers' books and textbook home pages to access the materials. Unfortunately, transcripts could not be sourced for the older version of *Green Line* (Klett, 2006–2009 edition) or *Achievers* (Richmond). None of the textbooks' accompanying workbooks were included. This decision was based on pragmatic time and resource constraints and is justified by the fact that many schools do not require parents to buy the workbooks and many teachers do not, or only rarely, use them. Of the textbooks featured in the TEC, the only series advertised as "corpus-informed" is *English in Mind* from Cambridge University Press. However, many of the other textbook series claim to include a large proportion of "authentic materials".

4.3.1.2 *Corpus processing and mark-up*

The nine selected textbook series, or 43 textbook volumes (see Table 5), were processed so as to include as much of the textual content as possible. All PDF files were processed with high-performing OCR software (ABBYY FineReader 14 Corporate). The results were saved as text (.txt) files for future processing with corpus analysis software. All non-text elements such as images, symbols, font specifications, etc. were discarded.

To ensure maximum compatibility across operating systems and software, the corpus files were saved using UTF-8 encoding. In keeping with standard corpus practice, eXtensible Markup Language (XML) was used for the markup and annotation. However, in line with Atkins et al.'s (1992) advice to aim for "a level of mark-up which maximizes the utility value of the text without incurring unacceptable penalties in the cost and time required to capture the data" (Atkins, Clear & Ostler 1992: 9; see also Hardie 2014), the standards usually advocated for XML corpus mark-up, such as the Corpus Encoding Standard (CES; Ide 1996) and the Text Encoding Initiative (TEI; Burnard, Lou & Bauman 2021), were deemed unnecessarily detailed and too labour intensive for this project. Since it was not relevant to the research question at hand, the textbooks' structural and formatting elements (e.g., paragraphs, font formats, section dividers) were not annotated to keep the design of the XML schema as simple as possible.

The metadata associated with each textbook was encoded in a simple XML header at the start of each textbook file in the following format:

<doc sign="POC4" series="Piece of cake" level="C" publisher="Livre scolaire" year="2017" country="France">

Table 5. Composition of the Textbook English Corpus (TEC) (the full bibliographic metadata is available on https://doi.org/10.5281/zenodo.4922819)

Country of use	Publisher	Textbook series	Volume	Level	Publication date
France	Bordas	*Hi There*	6ème	A	2012
			5ème	B	2013
			4ème	C	2014
			3ème	D	2015
		New Mission	2nde	E	2014
	Nathan	*Join the Team*	6ème	A	2010
			5ème	B	2011
			4ème	C	2012
			3ème	D	2013
		New Bridges	2nde	E	2010
	Le Livre Scolaire	*Piece of Cake*	6ème	A	2017
			5ème	B	
			4ème	C	
			3ème	D	
Germany	Klett	*Green Line*	1	A	2006
			2	B	
			3	C	2007
			4	D	2008
			5	E	2009
	Klett	*New Green Line*	1	A	2014
			2	B	2015
			3	C	2016
			4	D	2017
			5	E	2018
	Cornelsen	*Access G*	1	A	2013
			2	B	2014
			3	C	2015
			4	D	2016
			5	E	2017
Spain	Richmond	*Achievers*	A1+	A	2015
			A2	B	

Table 5. *(continued)*

Country of use	Publisher	Textbook series	Volume	Level	Publication date
			B1	C	
			B1+	D	
			B2	E	
	Cambridge University Press	*English in Mind*	Starter	A	2010
			1	B	
			2	C	
			3	D	2011
			4	E	
	Oxford University Press	*Solutions*	Elementary	A	2014
			Pre-Intermediate	B	2016
			Intermediate	C	2017
			Intermediate Plus	D	2017

Each file header includes:

i. A unique file name (doc sign)
ii. The name of the textbook series
iii. The textbook proficiency level (according to the country-neutral scale introduced in 4.3.1.1 and Table 3)
iv. The publisher
v. The date of publication
vi. The country in which the textbook is used (i.e., France, Germany, or Spain).

This simple metadata markup schema makes it possible to restrict corpus searches to subsections of the corpus, choosing for instance one or more level(s), publisher(s), series, country, a publication date range, or any combination of these parameters in off-the-shelf corpus software such as Sketch Engine (Kilgarriff et al. 2014), as well as via custom scripts in, e.g., R or Python.

4.3.1.3 *Register annotation*

A major pedagogical implication to emerge from corpus linguistics research is "the centrality of register for studies of language use" (Conrad & Biber [2001] 2013: 334). Thus, before outlining the register annotation process, a brief excursus on register is called for. This is because, at all linguistic levels, corpus studies have consistently shown that lexico-grammatical patterns are distributed systematically differently according to the communicative purposes and situations of use of the texts under study (e.g., Biber 1988; Biber et al. 1999). Pedagogical approaches to language description, however, have, if at all, tended to focus on linguistic variation across national (and more rarely regional and sociocultural) varieties of English only. This is highly problematic given that the few studies that have attempted to quantify both generic and geographic dimensions of variation have consistently found that text genre/register is a much more powerful predictor of variation than geography (e.g., Bohmann 2021). Similarly, textbook language evaluations have traditionally either considered textbook language as one register (e.g., Ljung 1990), thus disregarding major intra-textbook register variations, or focused solely on textbook dialogues (e.g., Le Foll 2022a, 2022b; Mindt 1995b; Römer 2005). Aiming for a comprehensive lexico-grammatical analysis of Textbook English, this study accounts for the different registers featured in school EFL textbooks, in recognition of the fact that "[s]trong patterns in one register often represent only weak patterns in other registers, and, consequently, few descriptions of language are adequate for a language as a whole" (Barbieri & Eckhardt 2007: 325). As a result, the present study aims to explore the lexico-grammatical specificities of a range of typical textbook registers. To this end, the main textbook registers featured in school EFL textbooks were first identified. Before this procedure is described, a few definitions are in order.

Numerous attempts have been made to tease apart the often partly overlapping terms *genre, register* and *text type*. For many researchers, the use of the term *genre* or *register* is a matter of tradition or personal choice; both have been used to refer to text varieties associated with specific situations of use and communicative purposes (Egbert, Biber & Davies 2015). Biber and Conrad's (2019) framework, however, distinguishes between the two terms. *Genres* are text categories whose definitions are based on their conventional structures. In general, *genre* studies have tended to focus on socio-cultural aspects (Biber 2006: 11). *Registers*, on the other hand, are text categories that are defined according to their situational characteristics, such as their communicative purpose, the type of interaction and participants they involve, and topic (though the latter is controversial, see Lee 2001) (e.g., Biber 2006; Egbert, Biber & Davies 2015; Biber & Conrad 2019).[15] *Register* studies home in on the typical lexico-grammatical features of particular registers, thus revealing the systematic use of specific features in particular

15. It is worth mentioning, however, that in pedagogically-motivated systemic functional linguistics (SFL), the term *genre* has frequently been used to refer to what most other SFL research refers to as *register* (this is particularly true of the Sydney School, e.g., Martin & Rose 2008; Martin 2009; Rose & Martin 2012).

contexts of use. Finally, the term *text type* refers to text varieties which are initially defined according to similarities in linguistic form, i.e., in the co-occurrences of lexico-grammatical features. In other words, the terms *genre, register*, and *text type* refer to different, external, or internal, yet complementary, perspectives on text varieties (for a more detailed discussion, see Lee 2001). For the purposes of this study, the term *register* is preferred because the different text varieties found in the textbooks are initially distinguished according to their situational features, before being functionally analysed on the basis of their specific linguistic features. Put differently, it is assumed that a register's defining lexico-grammatical features serve a functional purpose within a particular situational context of use.

As highlighted in 4.1, textbook corpus research has largely evaded the question of register in textbook language. This is possibly due to the emphasis placed on the text unit in text-linguistic research that has traditionally been based on the assumption that "texts are nested within registers, but the opposite is not true: registers are not nested within texts" (Egbert & Mahlberg 2020: 75). In an article entitled 'Fiction – one register or two?', Egbert and Mahlberg (2020) break away from this tradition by analysing the linguistic variation within novels whilst distinguishing between passages of narration and fictional speech in fictional writing. As a result, coherent texts were divided into text segments that, while situationally different, remain contextually interdependent. To a certain extent, subdividing textbooks into texts of different registers may also be interpreted as dividing whole, coherent texts into text segments. In actual fact, defining text units, as required in text-linguistic corpus approaches where each text represents one observation (Biber et al. 2016: 357), is particularly tricky when it comes to textbooks. Indeed, typical school textbooks offer a range of plausible units of observation: the textbook series, textbook volume, chapter/unit, subchapter/unit, right down to the individual text (Le Foll 2020b). This study applies the smallest of these units where any one exercise, reading passage, explanation, instruction, dialogue or transcript corresponds to one observation. At the same time, each text observation is nested within one of the 43 textbook volumes and nine textbook series of the corpus (see Table 5).

Text subdivision and annotation was performed manually. As part of this process, each text was manually annotated for register. First, however, it was necessary to identify meaningful register categories for all the texts featured in the 43 textbooks of the corpus. To the author's best knowledge, this had not been attempted in this form before. The most detailed textbook mark-up scheme that I am aware of is that of the TeMa project (Meunier & Gouverneur 2009). The TeMa corpus consists of 32 English for General Purposes (EGP) textbook volumes. Both the coursebooks and workbooks of each textbook are subdivided into four subcorpora: texts, transcription of the tape scripts, vocabulary exercises, and the guidelines to these exercises (Meunier & Gouverneur 2009:7). In previous studies, textbook instructional language had often been annotated for separate analysis or entirely removed from textbook corpora. For instance, in an exploration of lexical clusters in EAP textbooks, Wood (2010) organised his textbook corpus into two subcorpora: one containing the main textual elements of textbooks, and the other capturing the instructional material. Wood also pruned the raw text data of titles, headings, tables of content, prefaces, etc., thus obtaining a textbook corpus of approximately 580,000 tokens, of which 68% consisted of instructional material. In a different study comparing business and engineering textbooks with EAP textbooks, Wood and Appel (2014) acknowledged the difficulty arising from the wide range of registers found in textbooks. They therefore removed all instructional language from their business and engineering textbooks and annotated their EAP textbook corpus so as to create two subcorpora: one for the reading texts, and a second for all "instructional language" including vocabulary and comprehension exercises (which accounted for ca. 42% of the total word count).

The present study aims to account for, among other factors, register-based variation in modelling Textbook English so that a binary division of (reading/listening) text vs. instructional language is not satisfactory. Suitable textbook text register categories were inferred following a cyclical categorisation process (inspired by Mayring 2010:84–85). In order to reduce the manual annotation workload as well as the risk of inattention errors, short macros were created using the automation tool Keyboard Maestro (v. 7.3.1), enabling the two annotators (the author and a student research assistant) to automatically annotate manually identified portions of the text files with the appropriate XML syntax as shown in (1) (see also Le Foll 2020b for more details and a video demonstration). The final annotated version of the TEC corpus contains over 52,000 individual "div type" tags for register annotation.

(1) <div type="instructional"> Try to guess what each piece of information refers to. </div><div type="individual words or sentences">Olivia Timothy Liverpool London nd of March Fiona Loudon 4 Ella Steven Spielberg Casino Royale going to the theatre </div><div type="instructional"> Then listen to him speak about his life and check if you were right. </div>

Although this register annotation process was very time-consuming, it also served to thoroughly check the OCR process across all the textbooks. This was important because the use of unusual fonts and the frequently complex formatting of blocks of texts on individual pages of the textbooks meant that it was often necessary to correct OCR mistakes and in some cases re-type or re-organise sections of the processed text files. In other words, the register annotation process also contributed to the cleaning of the raw data.

The cyclical categorisation process ultimately led to the creation of the eight textbook register categories listed in Table 6: 'Conversation', 'Informative writing', 'Fiction', 'Personal correspondence' (letters, diary entries, social media posts, and e-mails), 'Instructional' (instructions and explanations), 'Poetry' (songs and poems), 'Other texts' (timetables, recipes, to-do lists, etc.), and 'Individual words or sentences'. Tags were also added to identify textbook passages in languages other than English (i.e., explanations or translations in the students' L1/school language).

Table 6. Distribution of textbook register categories in the TEC

Register	Words	Share of wordcount
Conversation	508,370	16.81%
Fiction	253,836	8.39%
Individual words or sentences	913,331	30.20%
Informative texts	302,739	10.01%
Instructional texts	591,743	19.57%
Personal correspondence	67,050	2.22%
Poetry	26,174	0.87%
Other texts in English	14,379	0.48%
Non-English texts	346,336	11.45%
Total	**3,023,958**	**100%**

The reliability of the annotation scheme and method was tested by having both coders blind-annotate three full textbook volumes and comparing the results. The only systematic issue consisted in distinguishing between 'individual sentences' as opposed to 'isolated words/phrases'; hence these two categories were merged into one in the final annotation scheme. This resulted in an inter-rater agreement rate of 96.65%. In the following, each register category and its rationale are briefly explained with an example text excerpt.

In this study, all dialogues, scripts and transcripts of the audio and video materials accompanying the textbooks purporting to be unscripted were annotated as one register labelled 'Conversation', e.g.:

(2) Nice of you to let us come to your barbie, Mike.
No worries. Great you're here. – Hey Cam! Come and meet a couple of new mates. They're staying at the hostel.
Hey, how're you doing? [...] <TEC: New Green Line 5>[16]

16. All corpus excerpts include a reference to its source in angle brackets. The corpus abbreviation is followed by a colon and then a file identifier. In the case of excerpts from the TEC, each corpus file corresponds to a textbook, hence the name of the textbook volume is printed.

The 'Informative' register tag was used to annotate factual articles, newspaper-like writing, reports (including scripted oral reports featured in video and audio materials) and texts from informative websites, e.g.:

(3) English is an official language in over seventy-five countries in the world. More than two billion people speak English. Fifty-four English-speaking countries are members of the Commonwealth of Nations, an association of independent countries. Queen Elizabeth II is head of the Commonwealth. 31% (percent) of the world's population live in the Commonwealth. [...]
<TEC: Hi There 5[e]>

'Fiction' narrative texts in lower secondary school EFL textbooks are mostly found in the form of short stories and extracts of novels, e.g., (4). To keep the integrity of the texts, direct speech passages in these narrative texts were not annotated separately (for a different approach, see Mindt 1995a: 7).

(4) With my backpack in my hands, I stepped off the train onto the crowded platform. It was 7:30 in the evening. People were hurrying home. A mother and her two young children were sitting on a bench. The mother was talking to the boy, but he wasn't looking at her. [...] <TEC: Solutions Pre-intermediate>

Singapore Wala (2013: 134) describes textbooks' "narratorial voice [...] as the formal and most powerful means of structuring the relationship between coursebook and learner". As such, the coursebook narrator is responsible for informing, instructing learners to carry out learning tasks and asking questions to seek information for learners to meet their learning objectives. Here, the textbooks' "narrative voice" was annotated as 'Instructional', regardless of the exact function of the narrative voice at any point in time, e.g., (5). As has been shown by Wood (2010) and Wood and Appel (2014), this register makes up a large proportion of school EFL textbooks and, as textbook metalanguage is a major source of linguistic input for EFL learners (Kim & Hall 2002), it seemed essential to include it in this comprehensive exploration of Textbook English.

(5) a. In the film, the girl shows us her hometown. Watch the film. What did she show us? Choose A or B.
b. Watch the film again. What other things and places can you see in the film? Make a list. <TEC: Access G 1>

The register category 'Personal correspondence' includes diary and blog entries, personal e-mails, and letters, e.g., (6). Since formal letters and e-mails may serve somewhat different communicative purpose, they were originally allocated to a separate category. However, as lower secondary school textbooks contain very few such texts, they were later relegated to the category 'Others' as part of the second annotation cycle.

(6) Ally McKoene > WestHigh Bros
December 1 near University Heights, IA via mobile
Your best feature is definitely your kindness and I'm sure everyone else agrees! You have tons of kindness in your heart and your compliments can light up anyone's face. You guys are some of the kindest people I've met and I'm so glad that you guys do what you do. Your compliments can make anyone's day :) keep it up! <TEC: New Mission 2^{e}>

Though not included in the original annotation scheme, the first cycle of the categorisation process revealed that songs, poems, and rhymes feature heavily in lower secondary school EFL textbooks used in France, Germany, and Spain, thus justifying the need for a separate 'Poetry' register category, e.g.:

(7) School friends
Welcome to my school!
Welcome to my school!
Come in, and be cool!
Good morning, you can all sit down! <TEC: Join the Team 6^{e}>

Finally, the register tag "Individual words or sentences" was used to label example words, phrases, or sentences that were designed to illustrate particular lexico-grammatical phenomena and are not embedded in a cohesive text (e.g., (8)), as well as contextless words, phrases and sentences featured in exercises. Note that the glossaries printed at the back of many coursebooks were not included in the TEC.

(8) a. You are in a home, not a hotel!
b. Questions are better than mistakes.
c. It's important to be polite. <TEC: Green Line 2>

In addition, the manual annotation process revealed that the textbook series differ considerably in their use of students' L1/school language to provide instructions and explain grammatical points. As a result, it was thought worthwhile to keep track of the use of a language other than English across the various textbooks series and different proficiency levels. All extended passages in languages other than English were thus annotated with the register tag 'Non-English', e.g., (9).

(9) Regarde la légende du document. a. Identifie la date. b. Cherche des informations à propos de l'artiste sur internet. B c. Lis le titre, regarde le tableau et devine le sens du mot *shiner*. <TEC: Hi There 3e>

It is worth noting that, although the TEC was constructed as a balanced corpus of textbooks with three series from each country, the number of texts and words are not distributed equally across each textbook series, or country of use. This is illustrated in Figure 1, which displays the distribution of words in the TEC per textbook volume.[17] It shows the number of words in the Conversation, Fiction, Informative, Instructional, and Personal correspondence texts of the TEC (i.e., those included in the intra-textbook analysis presented in Chapter 6). As we can reasonably expect the number and length of texts to increase as learners become more proficient in English, the bars of the plot are sorted by textbook proficiency level.

In the following sections and chapters, the register subcorpora of the TEC are frequently referred to as separate entities. To differentiate the general reference to typical texts of a particular register found in textbooks from, specifically, a register subcorpus of the TEC, the word 'Textbook' and the first word of the register category are capitalised in Table 6 are used to denote the latter, i.e., 'Textbook Conversation' and 'Textbook Personal' refer to the Conversation and the Personal correspondence subcorpora of the TEC, respectively.

4.3.2 The reference corpora

As has been noted in Chapter 3.3, when analysing the frequency, use, and function of individual lexico-grammatical features of Textbook English, a realistic reference benchmark is of the upmost importance. It has been argued that target learner language is, for instance, unlikely to resemble professional journalistic writing, and that such comparisons are thus unhelpful indicators when evaluating the lexico-grammatical content of Textbook English. This is also an argument advanced by Harwood (2005), who criticises studies that compare ESL textbooks to general reference corpora. Striking a similar tone, Miller (2011: 34) rightly argues that "we must carefully consider measures (e.g., comparison corpora) upon which we are gauging our evaluation so that conclusions drawn are indeed fair and useful". Thus, it is not necessarily meaningful to compare learner language to professional native-speaker writers and radio presenters, using such general corpora as the British National Corpus (BNC; Burnard 2007), since this is not what secondary school students are expected to aspire to. On the basis of

17. Note that wordcount totals are difficult to compare across entire textbook series. This is because, on the one hand, one of the textbook series used in Spain (*Solutions*) and one of the French ones (*Piece of Cake*) feature only four rather than five volumes and, on the other, because the TEC does not include all the transcripts of additional audio/video materials for one German and one Spanish series (the older version of *Green Line* and *Achievers*) (see Table 5 and doi.org/10.5281/zenodo.4922819 for details).

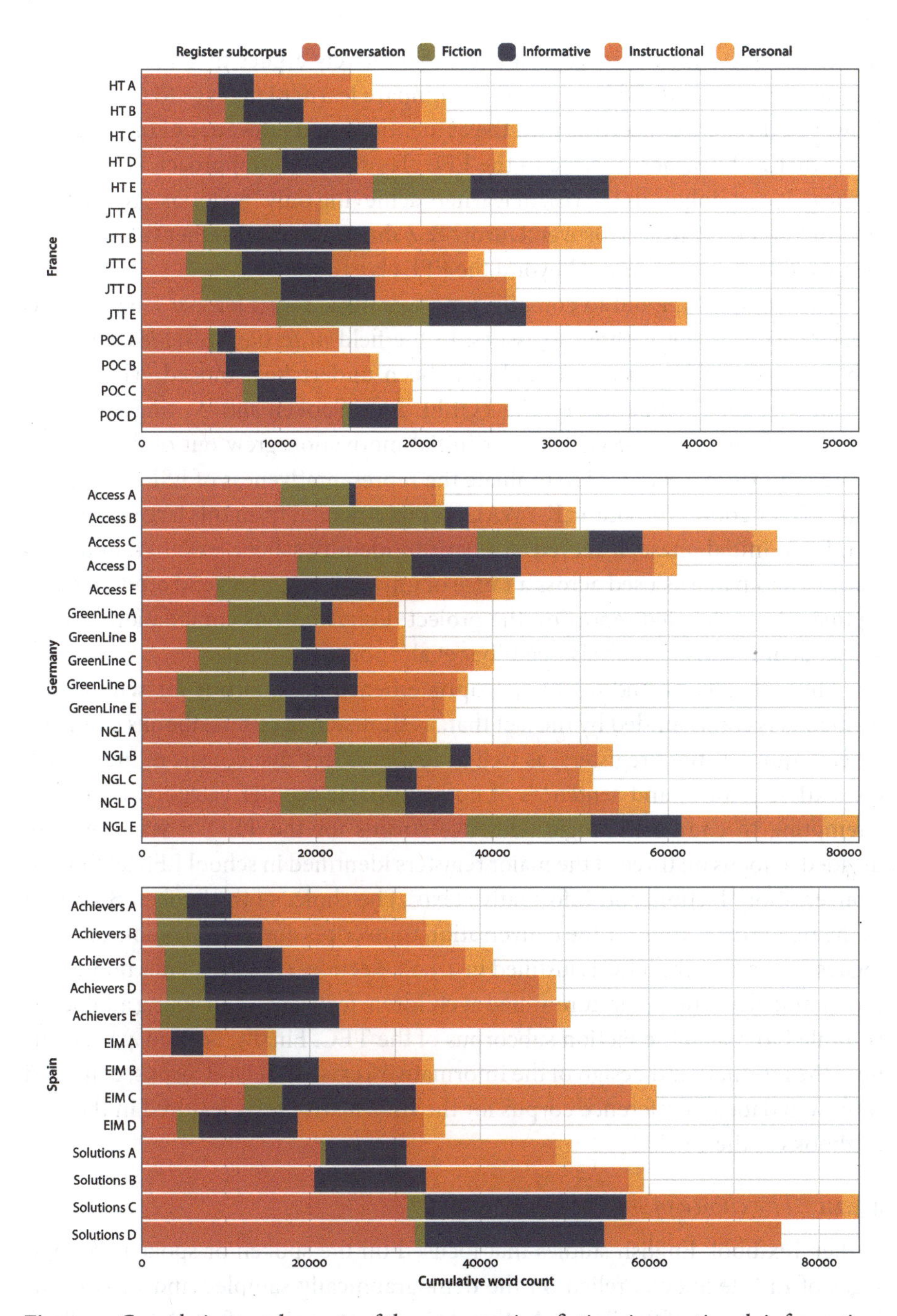

Figure 1. Cumulative word counts of the conversation, fiction, instructional, informative, and personal correspondence subcorpora of the TEC per textbook volume

this claim, Tono (2004) somewhat counterintuitively argues that Textbook English itself may be a useful benchmark to compare learner language to (see 3.1.2.7). However, if we are concerned with the authenticity and relevance of the language input that EFL learners receive in the EFL classroom, this approach is evidently cyclical. It certainly runs the risk of learners achieving only "textbook proficiency" (to borrow a term from Dörnyei, Durow & Zahran 2004: 87) rather than the language competences required beyond the EFL classroom.

That said, setting out to compile a more realistic target learner language reference corpus is not without its issues. In the field of tertiary-level learner English, however, such a project has already been undertaken. Indeed, when Biber et al. (2002, 2004) embarked on the TOEFL 2000 Spoken and Writing Academic Language Project (T2K-SWAL), their initial motivation grew out of the need to create "an external standard to evaluate the representativeness of ESL/EFL materials" (Biber 2006: 20). The T2K-SWAL corpus emerged from this large-scale project. In an initial phase, it served as a basis to identify salient lexico-grammatical features and patterns used across a range of university registers and academic disciplines (for a detailed report on the project design, corpus compilation, and its subsequent linguistic analysis, see Biber et al. 2004).

The difficulty of finding an appropriate benchmark corpus for school EFL textbooks is compounded by the fact that, as shown in 4.3.1.3, textbooks comprise several, quite distinct registers, as well as text passages that consist of individual, contextless phrases and sentences of no identifiable register category. Instead of attempting to compile a single reference corpus for the TEC, it was therefore decided to focus on three of the major registers identified in school EFL textbooks: Conversation, Fiction, and Informative texts. The choice of the Spoken BNC2014 as the reference corpus for the conversation transcripts and conversation-like dialogues featured in the TEC is justified in 4.3.2.1. Section 4.3.2.4 explains how a corpus of modern fiction literature aimed at children, teenagers, and young adults was compiled to match the Fiction subcorpus of the TEC. Finally, Section 4.3.2.5 outlines the rationale and design of the Informative Texts for Teens Corpus, compiled from web data as a reference corpus for the Informative texts featured in the EFL textbooks of the TEC.

4.3.2.1 *The choice of the Spoken BNC2014*

Earlier Textbook English studies that focused on the spoken or spoken-like passages of EFL textbooks relied on the demographically-sampled and/or context-governed sections of the British National Corpus 1994 (hereafter BNC1994; BNC Consortium 2007) as a reference corpus for comparisons between textbook vs. authentic language use (e.g., Römer 2005). In the present study, Textbook Conversation is compared to the equivalent demographically-sampled section of the latest version of the British National Corpus: the Spoken BNC2014 (Love et al. 2017, 2018). The new Spoken BNC2014 is an 11.4-million-word corpus of orthographically transcribed conversations among L1 speakers in the UK (covering a range of self-reported regional dialects). The recordings were made by the speakers themselves using their own smartphones between 2012 and 2016 (Love, Hawtin & Hardie 2018: 4–5). In total, the corpus features 668 speakers in a total of 1,251 recordings (Love, Hawtin & Hardie 2018: 1).

The Spoken BNC2014 was chosen because, to date, it is the largest publicly accessible corpus of contemporary spoken English and one of the very few to reflect unscripted, informal conversation on everyday topics, which was identified as a key register in Textbook English (see 4.3.1.3). In choosing the Spoken BNC2014 as a reference corpus for Textbook Conversation, two additional choices were made: the choice of a native English variety as a reference for Textbook Conversation on the one hand, and the choice of British English over US-American or any other L1 English variety, on the other. The thoughts and reflections that motivated these two choices are explained in the following brief excursus.

4.3.2.2 *Excursus on the use of L1 norms in English language teaching*

Traditionally, EFL instruction in Europe has largely relied on British English norms (see, e.g., Bieswanger 2008; Forsberg, Mohr & Jansen 2019; Gilquin 2018). However, over the past few decades, "the whole notion of *nativeness* has become murky, if not downright controversial" (Moyer 2013: 91, emphasis original). In ESL contexts, the hegemonic, colonial implications that lie at the heart of many native vs. non-native distinctions are no longer tenable. In EFL instructional contexts such as those found in most of continental Europe, too, the relevance of native speaker models has increasingly been questioned as a result of the ever-growing use of English as a *lingua franca* (ELF) and English as an International Language (EIL) in the business world and beyond (e.g., Jenkins 1998, 2000, 2003; Gnutzmann & Intemann 2008; Prodromou 1992). If 21st century English teachers aim to follow a communicative language teaching approach, they will evidently need to equip their students with the (socio-)linguistic and pragmatic knowledge to communicate with both native and non-native speakers of English from various regional and socio-cultural backgrounds (Bieswanger 2008: 27). This is why many have called for a definition of "authentic" foreign language exposure that recognises "the reality of language use which learners will encounter outside and after their course[s]" (Tomlinson 2013b: 476). In the case of EFL teaching in continental European schools, this post-instruction context will likely involve interacting with native and non-native speakers of English in both professional and personal ELF contexts. Thus, there are many convincing arguments for deciding against the exclusive reliance on native-speaker norms in EFL instruction.

Correspondingly, Mauranen (e.g., 2003, 2004a, 2004b; Mauranen et al. 2010) advocates for the use of ELF reference corpora for pedagogic purposes (such as the English as a Lingua Franca in Academic Settings Corpus [ELFA]) which Mauranen claims contains "good international English spoken in academic and professional contexts" (Mauranen 2004a: 207). However, compiling such a reference corpus is not without its issues. It goes without saying that selecting "good speakers" (see also Prodromou 2003 on the notion of "successful users of English") to include in such a corpus will inevitably involve some subjective and/or normative judgements which will, themselves, be based on the researchers' own (naturally biased) norms and standards (cf. Mauranen 2004a: 207). This problem is, of course, not limited to the compilation of non-native language corpora. It can easily be argued that many native speakers of English are, in fact, not particularly eloquent speakers or talented writers (cf. McCarthy & Carter 2001: 339). And when it comes to written registers, even fewer L1 users are expert writers of the kinds of professionally written texts featured in most general L1 corpora such as the two versions of the BNC or COCA. Suffice to say that the idea of capturing the language of proficient or expert language users regardless of their native-speaker status is – no matter how theoretically or pedagogically meaningfully – rather difficult in practice.

Whilst recognising the need to raise awareness of and embrace the diversity of plural native, non-native, standard, and non-standard English varieties in use around the globe, some English education scholars argue that EFL teachers and their students nevertheless need "a standard for pedagogical consistency" (Moyer 2013: 92). Thus, although native speaker norms are no longer explicitly mentioned in European secondary school EFL curricula (see 2.1), they nevertheless remain the most practical and reliable way of evaluating whether students are exposed to and themselves produce "authentic" and "correct" English – to quote two adjectives still frequently found in secondary school EFL curricula (see 2.1). On the other hand, staunch advocates of communicative foreign language teaching approaches argue that such a strict understanding of "authentic" and "correct" language use writes off too many unidiomatic learner usage cases as "inauthentic" and "incorrect" when they are, in fact, frequent in ELF contexts and do not hinder communication among native or non-native speakers of English. Mauranen (2004a: 208) illustrates this with an example from Altenberg and Granger's (2001) investigation of L2 speakers' use of collocations with the verb MAKE: she concludes that many, when compared to L1 use, so-called "collocation errors" are actually irrelevant for daily communicative needs and should therefore not be highlighted as deviant.

At the opposite end of the spectrum, Siepmann et al. (2011: 4) remind critics of native speaker norms in (advanced) foreign language teaching of "the age-old insight that the lower you set your sights, the less you will ultimately achieve". Returning to the example of collocates of MAKE mentioned above, they argue that:

> the word combination 'make a claim' could theoretically mean 'invent a claim', but there is a common-sense convention which assigns to it the meaning 'utter an assertion'. There is, of course, nothing that prevents foreign-born writers [L2 English users] from using 'make a claim' creatively to mean 'invent a claim'; the snag is that their (unidiomatic) use of the word combination is certain to be misinterpreted by both native and non-native speakers of English.
> (Siepmann et al. 2011: 4)

Going further, Siepmann et al. (2011: 4) warn that "[o]nce you start turning a blind eye to [standard L1 norm infringements], it is difficult to say where to draw the line" – an argument that echoes that of the difficulty of reliably distinguishing between (very) proficient and so-called "non-proficient" speakers of English (regardless of their native-speaker status). Gilmore (2007: 106) adds that taking the production of even highly proficient (however this may be defined) L2 speakers as the reference norm runs "the risk of providing learners with 'dumbed down' models of English which, although perhaps meeting their transactional needs, fail to illustrate the true expressive potential of the language".

A further argument in favour of L1 norms can be found in attitudinal research, which has repeatedly shown that both EFL teachers and, crucially, EFL learners still largely aim for native-speaker norms in spite of the generalisation of ELF/EIL (e.g., Edwards 2016; Forsberg, Mohr & Jansen 2019; Mohr, Jansen & Forsberg 2019; Scales et al. 2006; Timmis 2003). Even when their foreseen use of English is more likely to be with other non-native speakers in international ELF contexts, English L2 learners nevertheless most often aim for norms aligned with those of Inner Circle English varieties, i.e., from regions with largely monolingual English-speaking populations (Kachru & Smith 2008). Of course, there is no denying that students' opinions will be shaped by all kinds of societal pressures including their teachers' (actual or presumed) preferences. Nonetheless, the results of such attitudinal research should be taken into consideration if we are to attempt to break away from the customary paternalistic approach that tends to cast aside the opinions and wishes of learners as irrelevant.

In addition, some ELF agendas (as laid out, for instance, in Jenkins 2000; Seidlhofer 2001) risk dissociating learning to communicate in English from the (arguably also highly relevant) sociocultural contexts of the language – a critical aspect repeatedly highlighted as "intercultural (communicative) competence" in the EFL curricula of the educational authorities of France, Germany and, to a lesser extent, Spain (see, e.g., Conseil supérieur des programmes 2015; Consejería de Educación, Juventud y Deporte de Madrid 2015; Kultusministerkonferenz

2003, 2012), as well as the CEFR (Council of Europe 2001, 2020) on which European national and regional school curricula are increasingly based on.

Bearing these three factors in mind – the pedagogical need for (at least some) consistency, respecting learners' wishes (whilst acknowledging that these are undeniably influenced by those of their peers, teachers, parents and society as a whole) and the curricular requirements to also teach English for intercultural competence, in addition to the pragmatic considerations mentioned above (in particular: what constitutes a "good/proficient" ELF speaker?), no attempt was made to create an ELF reference corpus for this project. This is not to say that students' language production cannot or should never be assessed against an ELF norm (however hard that may be to define). Finally, it is important to remember that the present study of Textbook English focuses on the evaluation of students' language *input* rather than their own *output* or production.

Given that the three educational systems represented in the TEC are situated in Europe, the choice of British English over the other dominating L1 English varieties in EFL instructional contexts – American English – seemed natural. As mentioned at the beginning of this section, British English has been, and continues to be, the most commonly used target English variety in Europe, even though the relevant national/regional curricula no longer explicitly refer to a single British English norm (see 2.1). In the Netherlands, a large survey concluded that British English remains the English model of choice for over half of the Dutch population, whilst just 15% claimed to aim for an American English norm (Edwards 2016: 81). Similarly, the results of an attitudinal study conducted in Spain suggest that learners prefer Standard British English (RP) rather than American English and aim to emulate this variety themselves (Carrie 2017). In practice, all the textbook series featured in the TEC focus on England, both in terms of language use (most noticeably, of course, in the pronunciation in the audio and video materials – though this is not the focus of this study) and cultural contextualisation. That said, individual activities and textbook units do attempt to feature other L1 speaker varieties, most notably US-American,[18] Australian, Irish, and South African Englishes (see Scheiwe 2022 on how realistic the portrayals of such accents, usually produced by British actors, are in German textbooks). British English is clearly the *de facto* standard as deviations from British English are marked. For instance, in most glossaries within the textbooks of the TEC, terms such as *movie* and *cellphone* are annotated as "American English" or "AmE".

As its name suggests, the Spoken BNC2014, which was chosen as the reference corpus for Textbook Conversation, is most representative of British Eng-

18. In fact, in the G8 [*Gymnasium* in eight years] system in Germany, Year 8 is devoted to US-American English and culture.

lish – though it covers a range of regional dialects. The corpus features 566 English L1 speakers from all over the UK, 17 from outside the UK, and this optional speaker metadata is unavailable for 88 speakers (who, together, account for about 10% of the total word count) (Love, Hawtin & Hardie 2018: 24). The remaining two reference corpora, Youth Fiction and Info Teens, are also biased towards British English but considerably less so than the reference corpus for spoken English. Thus, 55% of the novels of the Youth Fiction corpus are by British authors, 31% by US-American authors, and the remaining 14% by authors from eleven different countries. The reference corpus for the informative texts of the TEC mostly contains texts of unknown authorship. However, the web domains from which they were sourced are principally from the UK and the USA, with a smaller percentage of texts from Australia and New Zealand. Hence, both these reference corpora can also be said to largely represent L1 English usage. Details of the composition of these corpora can be found in 4.3.2.4 and 4.3.2.5.

4.3.2.3 *Processing of the Spoken BNC2014*

The Spoken BNC2014 is richly annotated with detailed metadata on the speakers and the context of each conversation. In the untagged XML version of the corpus, which served as the basis for the preparation of the version used in the present study, the metadata is listed in the files' headers. The analyses carried out in the context of this study do not take this metadata into consideration; hence the headers were removed. The corpus also includes numerous other metatags, e.g., for paralinguistic sounds, pauses, and overlaps. These were also removed. Table 7 summarises the regular expressions featured in the R script which was used to pre-process the untagged XML files of the Spoken BNC2014, see also Appendix B.2.1; ⟨elenlefoll.github.io/TextbookMDA/AppendixB⟩. Many of these pre-processing steps were necessary because the data contributed to the Spoken BNC2014 has been fully anonymised and therefore contains many tags corresponding to anonymised words and phrases. These tags were replaced with placeholders designed to ensure that the POS-tagger and dependency parser used to further process the corpus would correctly label their word class and function. In addition, truncated words, which are rarely correctly identified by lemmatisers and POS-taggers, were removed.

In contrast with the BNC1994, the transcription scheme of the Spoken BNC2014 makes minimal use of punctuation and in fact only allows for question marks (Love, Hawtin & Hardie 2018: 37–38). Since automatic taggers and parsers are usually trained with punctuated texts, placeholder full stops were added at utterance boundaries that did not end in a question mark to reduce the potential for tagging errors resulting from a lack of punctuation. However, it is worth noting that these full stops markers were not used in any further linguistic analyses.

Hereafter, the text files generated after these replacements are referred to as the "John and Jill in Ivybridge" version of the Spoken BNC2014 corpus (see 'Replacement' column in Table 7 as to why this name was chosen).

Table 7. Summary of the regular expressions (regex) used to process the Spoken BNC2014 (see Appendix B.2.1 for full script)

Description of tag	Search regex	Replacement
Header with full metadata	<header>.*</header>	[nothing]
Anonymised male name	<anon type=\"name\" nameType=\"m\"/>	John
Anonymised female name	<anon type=\"name\" nameType=\"f\"/>	Jill
Anonymised neutral name	<anon type=\"name\" nameType=\"n\"/>	Sam
Anonymised place	<anon type=\"place\"/>	IVYBRIDGE
Anonymised telephone number	<anon type=\"telephoneNumber\"/>	0123456789
Anonymised address	<anon type=\"address\"/>	ADDRESS
Anonymised e-mail address	<anon type=\"email\"/>	anonemail@email.com
End of utterance not immediately preceded by a question mark	(?<!\\?)</u>	.
Truncated word	<trunc>.{0,12}</trunc>	[nothing]
Anonymised financial details	<anon type=\"financialDetails\"/>	FINANCIAL DETAILS
Anonymised social media name	<anon type=\"socialMediaName\"/>	@SAM
Anonymised data of birth	anon type=\"dateOfBirth\"/>	DOB
Other anonymised personal information	<anon type=\"miscPersonalInfo\"/>	PERSONAL INFORMATION
All other remaining tags	<.*?>	[nothing]

4.3.2.4 *The Youth Fiction corpus*

Off-the-shelf corpora of English fiction exist, e.g., the English subcorpus of the PhraseoRom Corpus (Novakova & Siepmann 2020), and most general English corpora include a literature subcorpus of extracts of novels, e.g., the BNC1994. However, for a meaningful comparison of Textbook Fiction with authentic fiction texts to be possible, it was decided that both the communication purposes and the intended target audiences of the texts ought to be matched. Thompson and Sealey (2007) report a number of significant differences between adult and children fiction in the frequencies and contextual uses of the most frequent types, parts-of-speech, lexical verbs, 4 grams, and POS-grams. They also highlight strikingly different representations of world and self in children and adult fiction. Their results confirm the need for creating a dedicated Youth Fiction Corpus to be used as a comparison corpus for the Fiction subcorpus of the TEC: Textbook Fiction.

Since the TEC consists of textbooks intended for ca. 11- to 16-year-olds, the aim was to compile a balanced and representative corpus of English-language fiction books suitable for children, teenagers, and young adults. Unlike films, books are not usually explicitly labelled as being suitable or targeted at particular age groups; it was therefore necessary to find alternative selection criteria. In an attempt to achieve sample representativeness and balance, the books to be included in the reference Youth Fiction corpus were selected from seven online lists:

- The List: 100 Best Children's Books of All Time (published on 8 January 2015) ⟨http://time.com/100-best-childrens-books/⟩
- LIST: The 100 Best Young Adult Books of All Time (published on 8 January 2015) ⟨http://time.com/100-best-young-adult-books/⟩
- The 100 best children's books of all time (published on 19 July 2018) ⟨https://www.telegraph.co.uk/books/childrens-books/100-best-childrens-books-time⟩
- The Guardian Children's Fiction Prize Winners (from 2000–2016) ⟨https://en.wikipedia.org/wiki/Guardian_Children%27s_Fiction_Prize⟩
- The School Reading List – Suggested reading books for primary and secondary aged children in the UK (Years 7 and 8) (by Jan Tolkien, last updated on 20 January 2019 when accessed on 31 January 2019) ⟨https://schoolreadinglist.co.uk/category/reading-lists-for-ks3-pupils/⟩
- What Book Got You Hooked? (user-contributed list, accessed on 30 January 2018 with 9,003 contributors at the time) ⟨https://www.goodreads.com/list/show/651.What_Book_Got_You_Hooked_⟩
- Your Favorites: 100 Best-Ever Teen Novels (user-contributed list with 75,220 contributors, published on 7 August 2012) ⟨https://www.npr.org/2012/08/07/157795366/your-favorites-100-best-ever-teen-novels?t=1539242729260⟩

The lists were chosen to represent the choices made by respected British and US-American media, as well as those made by the wider internet community, as represented in the two dynamic user-contributed lists from goodreads.com and NPR.org. Although such best-of lists undoubtedly represent subjective choices, in the absence of book sale numbers, they provided a useful starting point. Picture books clearly aimed at children younger than 10 years were excluded, as were translations of books originally in languages other than English. The final selection from the lists was opportunist and entirely based on the immediate availability of the books[19] in digital format (Epub or PDF). In part, however, it can

19. Many thanks to the PhraseoRom team (in particular Johan Didier and Susanne Dyka) who kindly provided text versions of the titles already included in the PhraseoRom corpus.

be assumed that the availability of the books in digital format generally testifies to their popularity. The digital books were subsequently converted to UTF-8 text using the same OCR software as for the TEC and automatically cleaned of unwanted characters and systematic OCR errors using custom Python scripts (Van Rossum & Drake 2009).

In total, 300 books were collected, amounting to over 20 million words. The majority of the novels in the corpus are by British authors (166 books), a large proportion by US-American authors (92 books) and the rest from eleven other countries including Australia, India, and Ireland. The full list of works included in the corpus may be found in the Appendix B.2.3 ⟨lenlefoll.github.io/TextbookMDA/AppendixB⟩.

The Youth Fiction corpus consists of four random samples of approximately 5,000 words (splitting was performed at sentence boundaries, hence the slightly varying word counts) extracted from each of the 300 books collected and processed for the corpus, except for three very short books, which were only sampled once in full. With a total of 1,191 Youth Fiction texts, this procedure resulted in a number of texts comparable to that of the Spoken BNC2014.

4.3.2.5 *The Informative Texts for Teens Corpus (Info Teens)*

Whilst corpora of children's or young adults' fiction do exist, it was clear from the outset that the reference corpus for the Informative subcorpus of the TEC would have to be compiled specifically for this project. The aim was to find informative texts that are targeted at English-speaking teenagers of the kinds of topics typically featured in school EFL textbooks. To this end, a list of 20 quality informative websites for teenagers from various English-speaking countries was compiled.

The web scraping process was facilitated by Sketch Engine's (Kilgarriff et al. 2014) corpus-building tool, which relies on WebBootCaT (Baroni et al. 2006), to create a text corpus from the list of selected websites. Sketch Engine automatically downloads the text materials from webpages, removes non-text elements, boilerplates, and duplicates to produce (relatively) clean text files. Of the 20 originally chosen websites, four were later discarded as they did not permit text scraping. Post-duplication removal, Sketch Engine retrieved and cleaned 17,014 files from the remaining 16 web domains. These texts were not distributed evenly among the websites. To remedy this, the corpus as originally compiled with Sketch Engine was downloaded as a single XML file without part-of-speech tagging and lemmas for further off-line processing. Off-line processing was performed in Python. Regular expressions were employed to remove erroneous XML tags, non-UTF-8 characters, indices and tables of contents, any remaining boilerplates and adverts, texts containing language puzzles (e.g., crosswords), marking schemes and past exam papers (only in the texts from revisionworld.com), and user comments (especially in the texts extracted from dogonews.com, teenvogue.com and teen .wng.org). The resulting XML file (totalling nearly one million lines) was split into the individual texts of the corpus and saved as separate plain text files with file-names incorporating relevant metadata on the web domain and title of each web-page, as available in the corresponding XML tags. This was achieved with the *beautifulsoup* library (Richardson 2015), which was found to cope relatively well with such a large, malformed XML file.

This procedure led to the creation of 10,104 individual text files, of which 4,895 were under 400 words and were therefore discarded as too short. To achieve a more balanced corpus, a stratified sampling approach was followed: 100 texts from each web domain were randomly selected for inclusion in the corpus. For two domains, fewer than 100 texts longer than 400 words had been retrieved; for these, the full domain datasets were retained. The final selection thus consists of 1,414 text files (see Table 8) – a number comparable to both the total number of conversation files in the Spoken BNC2014 (see 4.3.2.1) and text samples in the Youth Fiction Corpus (see 4.3.2.4).

Table 8. Composition of the Informative Texts for Teens Corpus

Domain name	Nb. texts	Nb. words
bbc.co.uk/history	100	74,722
dogonews.com	100	60,762
heatres.com	100	67,894
encyclopedia.kids.net.au	100	74,566
factmonster.com	100	60,395
historyforkids.net	100	71,955
quatr.us	100	62,254
revisionworld.com (GCSE only)	100	74,301
sciencekids.co.nz	100	57,097
sciencenewsforstudents.org	100	82,258
teen.wng.org	85	45,515
teenkidsnews.com	100	81,765
teenvogue.com	100	82,117
tweentribune.com	29	26,166
whyfiles.org	100	85,492
Total	**1,414**	**1,007,259**

CHAPTER 5

Methodology

Adapting the multi-dimensional analysis (MDA) framework

The literature review (Chapter 3) concluded that previous research on Textbook English has tended to focus on individual lexico-grammatical features. Collectively, these studies have provided us with a vast patchwork of evidence demonstrating how individual linguistic features are (frequently mis-)represented in ESL/EFL textbooks as compared to various interpretations of what is often termed 'real', 'natural', or 'authentic' English. However, the review concluded that such individual-feature studies cannot account for relevant interactions between features. In addition, we saw that potential differences between textbooks catering to different proficiency levels and, across texts, between the various registers typically featured in English textbooks have yet to be adequately explored.

The present study aims to overcome these limitations by using a multivariable statistical analysis method aimed at reducing a large set of potentially relevant grammatical, lexical, and semantic features to a parsimonious set of meaningful factors of linguistic variation. Thus, the objective is to provide a more comprehensive view of the defining characteristics of Textbook English and of the linguistic variation found within school EFL textbooks. To this end, Biber's multi-feature/multi-dimensional analytical (MDA) framework of register variation is applied to the study of Textbook English. Section 5.1 begins by laying out the principles behind the MDA framework (for more detailed accounts, see Biber 1984, 1988: Chapter 5–6; Biber et al. 2004: Section 4.4–4.5; Biber & Conrad 2019: Chapter 2; Friginal & Hardy 2014). Section 5.2 describes how MDA has already been successfully applied to the exploration of textbook language in EFL (5.2.1) and English L1 (5.2.2) contexts. The rest of this chapter (5.3) presents the details of the method as it was adopted in the present study, together with the reasoning behind the changes made to the 'standard' MDA framework.

5.1 The MDA framework

The MDA framework was pioneered by Douglas Biber (1984, 1988, 1995) to capture the underlying dimensions of variation across different registers of natural languages. It is based on the theoretical assumption that "differences in registers include patterns of co-occurring lexico-grammatical features" (Halliday 1988: 162), which result from texts having register-specific contexts of use and communicative goals (Biber & Conrad 2001; see also Hymes 1984). MDA is used to reduce these large matrices of linguistic co-occurrence patterns to a few core functional dimensions of systemic, situational variation. Thus, it allows for the conceptualisation of register variation as a continuous phenomenon, which varies along multiple fundamental dimensions. It has been successfully applied to tease out register differences at different levels of granularity, e.g., between a broad range of registers as different as face-to-face conversation and official documents (e.g., Biber 1988), but also between academic writing across different disciplines (e.g., Gray 2015), and student essay writing across different levels of proficiency (e.g., Friginal & Weigle 2014).

MDA is an exploratory method and therefore makes no a priori assumptions about how the registers explored may differ from one another. As in any corpus-based analysis, in conducting an MDA, the first step consists in selecting, collecting, and sampling the texts to be analysed in conjunction with the relevant metadata. The corpus ought to be representative of the variety and full range of the registers to be explored. In parallel, potentially relevant linguistic features need to be determined. At this stage, the aim is to be as inclusive as possible, so as not to omit any inconspicuously relevant features that may not have been identified in previous studies (Egbert & Staples 2019: 132). Biber's (1988) pioneering study of spoken and written registers of English included 67 lexical, grammatical and semantic features, ranging from first-person referents to verbal contractions and downtoners (see Conrad & Biber [2001] 2013: 18–19 for full list). Due to the large number of features and texts involved, the features chosen are best operationalised such that they can be automatically identified (i.e., tagged) and counted. Given that not all potentially relevant linguistic phenomena can reliably be automatically detected, this approach inevitably limits the types of linguistic features that can be entered in an MDA. That said, modern taggers of English are remarkably powerful, so that the benefits of being able to count a wide range of features across very many texts largely outweigh the drawbacks (but see 5.3.2–5.3.3 for details and limitations).

Once the texts have been automatically tagged (or partially automatically tagged, cf. Gray 2019) for the chosen linguistic features, the total number of occurrences of all the features selected are counted in each text of the corpus. These raw counts are then normalised to a common denominator (e.g., 100 words) to enable comparisons across texts of different lengths, as illustrated in Table 9. Excerpts of the texts (10)–(12), in which an example selection of eight features were counted, can be found below.

Table 9. Selected normalised feature counts (per 100 words) in three texts (see Excerpts (10)–(12) below)

	Excerpt (10)	Excerpt (11)	Excerpt (12)
Attributive adjectives	4.20	7.92	7.41
Causative subordination	0.66	0.21	0.13
Contractions	5.97	0.00	3.84
First person referents	5.34	0.00	7.41
Negation	2.12	0.43	1.85
Nominalisations	0.54	2.78	0.00
Prepositions	5.04	13.49	6.35
Second person referents	4.15	0.00	3.57

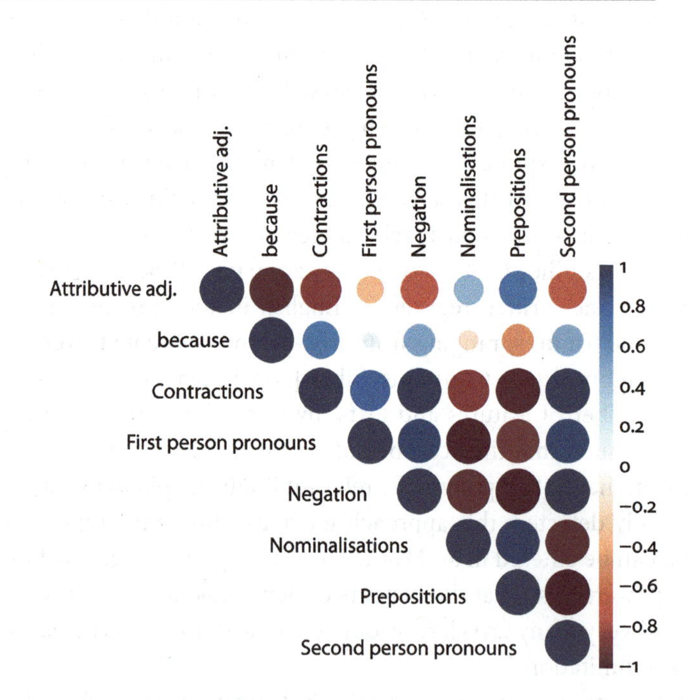

Figure 2. Correlation matrix of the normalised counts in Table 9

A correlation matrix of all the normalised feature counts is then computed (see Figure 2, in which the strength of the correlation between any two features is represented by the size and colour density of the circle, whilst its colour indicates the sign of the correlation). Since language features are not randomly distributed, but rather according to contextual usage and communicative aims, we expect to observe many significant correlations. Indeed, Figure 2 shows that a text with many occurrences of first and second-person referents is also likely to feature more negated verbs and contracted verb forms. Such positive correlations, marked in blue in Figure 2, are frequently found in involved, spontaneous spoken conversations, as illustrated in (10), in which these features have been highlighted in bold.

(10) **I just** did these well **I just** did these staid really laboured monologues which **you'd get** from textbooks and
yeah yeah yeah
and it was cringe cringeworthy John what **I** taught and **I'm** thinking why **didn't I** think? But that's that's but that's because **you're not**
because that's the problem **you're not** encouraged to think the the teaching language teaching industry **doesn't** encourage **you** to think it encourages **you** to use textbooks textbooks
it **no** but yeah because I was a newly qualified TEFL teacher **I** was obsessed with sticking to the plan
yeah
and the techniques that **I'd** been taught but they **didn't** teach **me** to use **my** knowledge and to say what do people really say in English **you** know?
<BNC2014: SHJJ>

By contrast, high normalised frequencies of nominal forms ending in *-tion, -ment, -ness*, and *-ity* tend to correlate negatively with the features highlighted in (10), but correlate positively with prepositions and attributive adjectives (see Figure 2), as well as higher lexical densities. Such clusters of features are typical of edited, information-dense texts, as illustrated in (11).

(11) Ionesco, Eugène özhĕn´ yŏnĕs´kō, 1912–94, **French** playwright, b. Romania. Settling **in** France **in** 1938, he contributed **to** Cahiers du Sud and began writing **avant-garde** plays. His works stress the **absurdity** both **of bourgeois** values and **of** the way **of** life that they dictate. They express the **futility of human** endeavor **in** a universe ruled **by** chance. His play La Cantatrice chauve (1950; tr. The Bald Soprano, 1965) was suggested **by** the **idiotic** phrases **in** an English language textbook; it has become an enormously **popular** classic **of** the heatre **of** the absurd. ⟨Info Teens: factmonster.com⟩

Naturally, the normalised counts of the linguistic features mentioned above can also be calculated for an excerpt from a textbook dialogue (12), to compare these frequencies to those counted in 'real-world' English in (10) and (11). Thus, in this toy example, we can see that, although Text (12) purports to represent spoken interaction, it features almost as many attributive adjectives as an informative text from the Info Teens corpus (see reported frequencies for Text (11) and Text (12) in Table 9). The textbook dialogue (Text (12)) also features fewer causative subordinators, verbal contractions, negated verbs, and second-person referents than the conversation transcript from the Spoken BNC2014 (Text (10)). MDA facilitates these kinds of comparisons across large numbers of texts and variables.

(12) **Jennifer:** Hi Grandpa!

Grandpa: **Good** morning, honey!

Jennifer: What are **you** doing?

Grandpa: **I'm** looking at my **old** fairy tale book ...

Jennifer: It's beautiful!

Grandpa: What's **your favourite** tale?

Jennifer: **I** think the **funniest** tale is The three **little** pigs.

Grandpa: **I** agree with **you**! The **Big Bad** Wolf is so ridiculous!

Jennifer: Yes, it is. **I** like **Sleeping** Beauty too. It's the most **romantic** story and Prince Charming is so handsome! <TEC: Piece of Cake 6[e]>

More precisely, MDA is applied to tease out the quantitative relationships – in statistical parlance referred to as the 'shared variance' – between linguistic features (variables) across a large corpus of texts. This is achieved on the basis of a correlation matrix of normalised variable counts, similar to that presented in Figure 2, albeit much larger. The statistical method used to this effect is called exploratory factor analysis (EFA). EFA is used to extract factors that correspond to clusters of frequently co-occurring linguistic features. In theory, a factor analysis can continue to extract factors until all the shared variance has been accounted for; indeed, once the first factor has been determined, the second factor accounts for the maximum amount of shared variance remaining, as does the third, etc. However, beyond the first few factors, additional factors are unlikely to account for more than nontrivial amounts of shared variance and may therefore be disregarded. It is up to the researcher to determine how many factors account for a sufficient amount of shared variance and can meaningfully be interpreted. In his seminal MDA of general English, Biber (1988) extracted seven factors, which, together, account for 51.9% of the total shared variance.

Several linguistic features contribute to, or load on, each of the extracted factors. The strengths of their relationship to a factor are captured by the factor loadings. Factor loadings thus reflect the amount of variance a feature has in common with the total pool of shared variance accounted for by any one factor. Features with a factor loading above a certain cut-off point are considered relevant contributors to the factor. Biber (1988: 87) included all features with an absolute factor loading of > 0.35 in the final model. This resulted in a final factor solution involving 60 (out of the original 67) linguistic features loading onto seven factors. This solution is summarised in Table 10, which lists the salient co-occurring features that constitute the seven factors along with their factor loadings. Note that the positive and negative signs of the loadings on any one factor serve to identify features that occur in a complementary pattern. Thus, as observed in Excerpts (10) and (11), when a factor's features with positive loadings frequently co-occur within a text, those with negative loadings are, on average, also markedly less frequent (or even entirely absent), and vice versa. Features listed in brackets on Table 10 were not included in Biber's (1988) final model because they have a higher loading on a different factor and, in order "to assure the experimental independence of the factor scores" (Biber 1988: 93), each feature was only included in the computation of a single factor score.

The next step in an MDA involves the functional interpretation of each factor, with its co-occurrence patterns of features and their loadings, as an underlying dimension of variation. To this end, a functional micro-analysis of the individual features is conducted, seeking the shared function(s) of the clusters of features loading on each factor. Functionally interpreted factors are then referred to as 'dimensions'.

Table 13 summarises the functional interpretation of Biber's (1988) six dimensions of general English and their associated linguistic features.[20] It was derived from a qualitative analysis of the linguistic features that load on each factor listed in Table 10. For instance, features with positive factor loadings on the first factor include those identified as particularly frequent in Text (10): first and second-person pronouns, negated verbs, and contractions. In terms of a functional interpretation, it can be said that these features are "associated with an involved, non-informational focus, related to a primarily interactive or affective purpose and on-line production circumstances", (Conrad & Biber [2001] 2013: 24). Thus, texts with a high proportion of nouns, prepositions, and attributive adjectives, as well as long words and a high type/token ratio will be assigned a negative score on Biber's (1988) Dimension 1. Such texts are typical of highly informational texts with precise lexical choices, as illustrated in (11). Consequently, Biber (1988)

20. Although Biber (1988: 114) originally extracted a seven-factor solution, the seventh factor was not included in the final model because it comprises only one feature that loads above the pre-determined threshold.

Table 10. Features with a minimum factor loading of ±0.35 that make up Biber's (1988) seven-factor solution

Factor 1	**Loading**
Private verbs	.96
that-deletion	.91
Contractions	.90
Present tense verbs	.86
Second-person pronouns	.86
DO as pro-verb	.82
Analytic negation	.78
Demonstrative pronouns	.76
General emphatics	.74
First-person pronouns	.74
pronoun *it*	.71
BE as main verb	.71
Causative subordination	.66
Discourse particles	.66
Indefinite pronouns	.62
General hedges	.58
Amplifiers	.56
Sentence relatives	.55
WH-questions	.52
Possibility modals	.50
Non-phrasal coordination	.48
WH-clauses	.47
Final prepositions	.43
(Adverbs)	(.42)
Nouns	−.80
Word length	−.58
Prepositions	−.54
Type/token ratio	−.54
Attributive adjectives	−.47
(Place adverbials)	(−.42)
(Agentless passives)	(−.39)
(Past participle WHIZ deletions)	(−.38)

Table 10. *(continued)*

Factor 2	Loading
Past tense verbs	.90
Third-person pronouns	.73
Perfect aspect verbs	.48
Public verbs	.43
Synthetic negation	.40
Present participial clauses	.39
(Present tense verbs)	(–.47)
(Attributive adjectives)	(–.41)
Factor 3	**Loading**
WH-rel. clauses on object positions	.63
Pied piping constructions	.61
WH-rel. clauses on subject positions	.45
Phrasal coordination	.36
Nominalizations	.36
Time adverbials	–.60
Place adverbials	–.49
General adverbs	–.46
Factor 4	**Loading**
Infinitives	.76
Prediction modals	.54
Suasive verbs	.49
Conditional subordination	.47
Necessity modals	.46
Split auxiliaries	.44
(Possibility modals)	(.37)
Factor 5	**Loading**
Conjuncts	.48
Agentless passives	.43
Past participial clauses	.42
by-passives	.41
Past participial WHIZ deletions	.40
Other adverbial subordinators	.39

Table 10. *(continued)*

Factor 6	**Loading**
that-clauses as verb complements	.56
Demonstratives	.55
that-relative clause on object positions	.46
that-clauses as adjective complements	.36
Factor 7	**Loading**
SEEM/APPEAR	0.35

interpreted the first factor as the 'Involved vs. Informational Discourse Dimension', whereby positive Dimension 1 scores correspond to involved texts and negative Dimension 1 scores to informational discourse.

Finally, for each text in the corpus, dimension scores for each of the dimensions identified are usually computed. Before doing so, however, the normalised counts are standardised to a mean of zero and a standard deviation of one (resulting in *z*-scores) to prevent particularly frequent features from having a disproportionate impact on the computed dimension scores. The importance of using standardised frequencies is illustrated with a simplified example, in which a dimension has six features, with present tense, discourse particles, negation, and causative adverbial subordinators loading positively, and nouns and type/token ratios (TTR) loading negatively. As shown in Table 11, if we simply added the normalised frequencies of the positively loading features and subtracted the negative ones to calculate the dimension scores of these three texts, we would conclude that Texts (10) and (12) are very similar to each other on this dimension. Yet a closer look at the normalised frequencies presented in Table 11 reveals that, across all six features, Texts (10) and (11) are, in fact, much more similar to each other than Texts (10) and (12) are. However, because nouns are overall much more frequent than the other five features, any small relative differences in the noun counts will unduly influence the dimension scores whenever normalised, rather than standardised, frequencies are used.

In Table 12, by contrast, the dimension scores are based on standardised frequencies (*z*-scores). These have been calculated on the basis of the mean and standard deviation of the normalised frequencies of each feature (see Table 11). The dimension scores thus computed in Table 12 make evident that Text 1 is, indeed, more like Text 2 than Text 3. Hence, with standardised frequencies, the features with the highest relative frequencies, here nouns, no longer exert undue influence on the dimension scores. In other words, standardised frequencies "give each feature a weight in terms of the range of its variation, rather than in terms of its absolute frequency" (Biber 1988: 95).

Table 11. The computation of dimension scores on the basis of normalised frequencies

	Present tense	Discourse particles	Negation	*because*	Nouns	TTR	Dimension score
Text (10)	4.93	0.68	1.53	0.17	37.91	0.53	−31.13
Text (11)	4.80	0.64	1.60	0.16	41.00	0.53	−34.33
Text (12)	5.67	0.81	3.24	0.81	41.31	0.34	−31.12
Mean	*5.13*	*0.71*	*2.12*	*0.38*	*40.07*	*0.47*	
SD	*0.47*	*0.09*	*0.97*	*0.37*	*1.88*	*0.11*	

Table 12. The computation of dimension scores on the basis of standardised frequencies (*z*-scores)

	Present tense	Discourse particles	Negation	*because*	Nouns	TTR	Dimension score
Text (10)	−0.43	−0.34	−0.61	−0.56	−1.15	0.58	−1.37
Text (11)	−0.71	−0.79	−0.54	−0.59	0.49	0.58	−3.70
Text (12)	1.14	1.13	1.15	1.15	0.66	−1.15	5.07
Mean	*0.00*	*0.00*	*0.00*	*0.00*	*0.00*	*0.00*	
SD	*1.00*	*1.00*	*1.00*	*1.00*	*1.00*	*1.00*	

Once dimension scores have been computed for each text, these can be compared to explore register-based linguistic variation across a corpus. Figure 3 plots the mean Dimension 1 scores of the registers included in Biber's (1988) analysis. We see that on Biber's first 'Involved vs. Informational Discourse' dimension, highly involved, spontaneously produced texts, such as telephone and face-to-face conversations, score very high and information-dense official documents and academic writing obtain low negative scores, whilst fiction scores around zero.

Biber's first and the many subsequent MDAs have shown that text registers cluster in different configurations along different dimensions, thereby revealing the truly multi-dimensional nature of registers, which are characterised by several groups of linguistic features (Thompson et al. 2017: 155).

Table 13. Summary of Biber's six dimensions of English (1988)

Dimension	Description	Features
1. *Involved vs. Informational Discourse*	Low scores indicate informationally dense discourse, e.g., official documents and academic writing, whereas high scores indicate that the text is affective and interactional, e.g., face-to-face and telephone conversations.	Involved production features: private verbs, *that*-deletions, contractions, present tenses, second-person pronouns, DO as pro-verb, analytic negations, demonstrative pronouns, emphatics, first-person pronouns, *it*, BE as main verb, causative subordinations, discourse particles, indefinite pronouns, hedges, amplifiers, sentence relatives, WH-questions, possibility modals, non-phrasal coordination, WH-clauses, stranded prepositions. Informational production features: nouns, longer words, prepositions, higher type/token ratio, attributive adjectives.
2. *Narrative vs. Non-Narrative Concerns*	Works of fiction score high on this dimension, whereas official documents, academic prose and broadcasts score lowest.	Narrative concerns features: past tense, third-person pronouns, perfect aspect, public verbs, synthetic negations, present participial clauses.
3. *Explicit vs. Situation-Dependent Reference*	Low scores indicate dependence on the context, as is the case in sport broadcasts and conversations, whereas high scores indicate independence from context, e.g., academic prose and official documents.	Explicit Reference features: WH-relative clauses on object position, pied-piping relatives, WH-relative clauses on subject position, phrasal coordination, nominalisations.
4. *Overt Expression of Persuasion*	Texts with high scores explicitly mark the author's point of view and attempt to persuade, e.g., professional letters and editorials, as opposed to factual broadcasts and press reviews, which score low.	Overt expression of persuasion features: infinitives, prediction modals, suasive verbs, conditional subordinations, necessity modals, split auxiliaries.
5. *Abstract vs. Non-Abstract Information*	The higher the score on this Dimension the higher the degree of technical and abstract information, as for example in scientific discourse.	Abstract information features: conjuncts, agentless passives, past participial clauses, *by*-passives, past participial WHIZ deletion relatives, other adverbial subordinators.
6. *On-Line Informational Elaboration*	High scores on this Dimension indicate that the information expressed is produced under certain time constraints, as for example in speeches.	On-line informational elaboration features: *that* clauses as verb complements, demonstratives, *that* relative clauses on object position, *that* clauses as adjective complements.

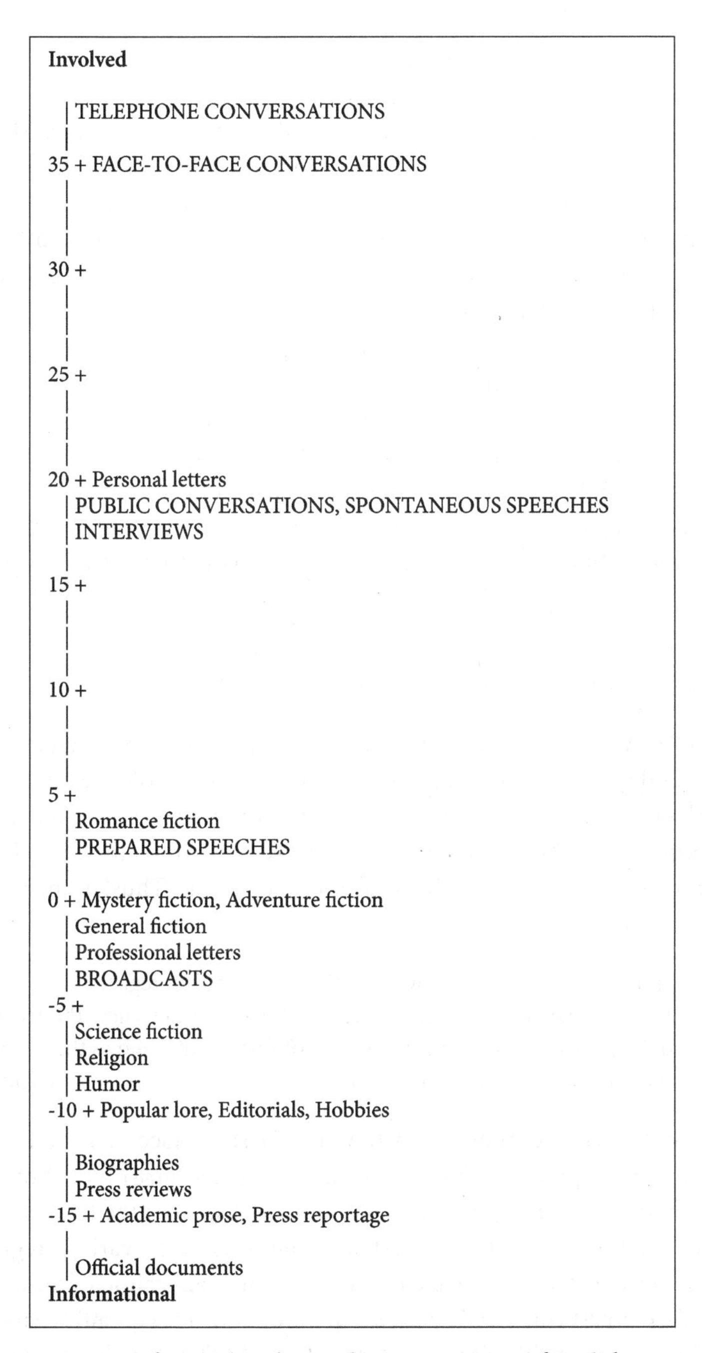

Figure 3. Mean scores of general spoken and written registers of English on Biber's (1988) Dimension 1 (as summarised in Biber & Conrad 2019: 292)

5.2 MDA and textbook language

Post-1988, two approaches to register variation studies applying MDA have emerged. One approach involves comparing one (or more) new, specialised register(s) relative to the dimensions of an earlier analysis of registers (most commonly Biber's 1988 model): this is referred to as 'additive MDA' (Berber Sardinha et al. 2019). The second approach consists in conducting a new, 'full MDA', following the steps outlined in Chapter 5.1 for an entire (new) set of registers (cf. Friginal & Hardy 2014; Egbert & Staples 2019). Given enough data, researchers can choose between these two approaches to analyse textbook language using MDA. In the following, Le Foll's (2021c, 2022c: Chapter 6) analysis of linguistic variation across different text registers featured in school EFL textbooks will briefly illustrate the use of additive MDA to explore Textbook English, whilst Reppen's (1994, [2001] 2013) study of Elementary School English will serve to point to the potential of conducting a full MDA in the context of pedagogically-driven corpus-based research.

5.2.1 Exploring textbook English using additive MDA

Biber's (1988) MDA study led to the elaboration of a model of language variation in spoken and written English that can now be used for predictive purposes. With a detailed, empirical validation of its generalisation to new texts using the Brown corpus, Nini (2014, 2019) demonstrated its robustness (though see Le Foll 2023c for issues in replicating the six dimensions on new data). Thus, in theory at least, this means that:

> it is possible to determine how a 'text' corpus, or even register behaves linguistically in comparison to other registers of English. In essence, the [Biber's 1988] model represents a base-rate knowledge of English that allows the description or evaluation of other texts or registers. (Nini 2019: 70)

Drawing on the same corpora as in the present study (see 4.3), Le Foll (2021c, 2022c: Chapter 6) applied additive MDA using Biber's (1988) model of variation in spoken and written English as the 'base-rate' to tease out the linguistic characteristics of Textbook English. In a first step, the texts of the various register subcorpora of the TEC (see 4.3.1) were processed with a replication of the algorithms used in Biber (1988) (the MAT; Nini 2014, 2019) and subsequently mapped onto the six dimensions of Biber's model (see Table 13). These analyses revealed that by far the most important driver of linguistic variation within secondary school EFL textbooks is register – thus confirming the need to account for this variable when describing and/or evaluating the linguistic content of textbooks. As was to be expected, the target proficiency level of the textbooks also proved to have a significant impact on linguistic variation within textbooks on several dimensions. However, this factor proved difficult to examine with additive MDA as many of the short texts of the TEC returned zero counts for the rarer features that load on Biber's fourth, fifth and sixth dimensions, leading to flooring effects in the corresponding dimension scores (Le Foll 2022c: Chapter 6). In a second, 'comparative additive MDA', the first three dimensions of Biber's (1988) model were used to compare the defining features of three major textbook registers with the three reference corpora described in 4.3.2. As illustrated in Figure 4, the results suggest that considerably less linguistic variation within EFL textbooks can be attributed to register than across situationally similar 'real-world' target language texts.

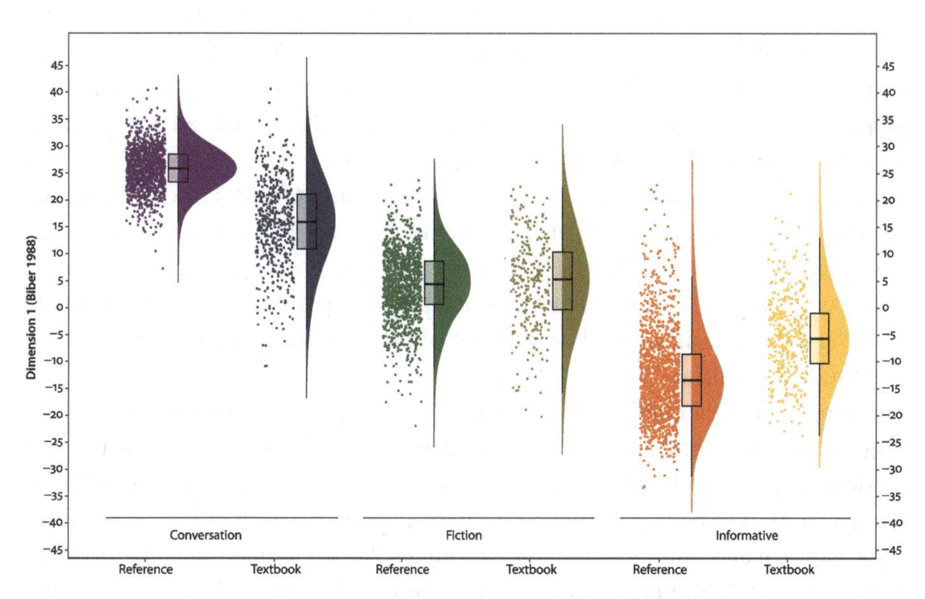

Figure 4. Comparison of the conversation, fiction and informative texts from the TEC with the three corresponding target language reference corpora on Biber's (1988) Dimension 1 (as calculated by the MAT) (Le Foll 2021. Zenodo. http://doi.org/10.5281/zenodo.4732334)

On average, the informative texts of the TEC were found to be more interactional and spoken-like than the texts on the informative websites targeted at English-speaking teenagers (as captured in the Info Teens corpus). On most dimensions, the fictional, narrative texts of the intermediate and advanced textbooks of the TEC scored closest to their corresponding reference corpus of Youth Fiction novels. The greatest discrepancies between the registers of the textbooks and those of the reference target language variety were observed in the conversation register. However, the extent of these differences could not be fully examined due to the type and operationalisation of several linguistic features included in Biber's (1988) model (Le Foll 2021c, 2022c: Chapter 6). Thus, whilst these additive MDAs hinted at the potential of applying MDA to the analysis of Textbook English, they also shed light on several limitations inherent to relying on a model that is not well suited to the specific constraints of Textbook English.

5.2.2 Exploring textbook English by conducting a full MDA

Within the MDA framework, the alternative to situating textbook language relative to other written or spoken registers of English is to conduct a new, 'full' MDA with a corpus of textbooks or a corpus that, among other types of texts, includes textbook materials. This second approach was adopted by Reppen (1994, [2001]2013) in her extensive study of (English L1) elementary student speech and writing. Reppen compiled a corpus of spoken and written texts either produced or consumed by fifth-graders in the USA that included, among other texts, 10,000 words from elementary school science and social studies textbooks and 5,000 words from basal readers commonly used at that level in Arizona. Following the procedure described in Chapter 5.1, five factors were extracted. The linguistic features associated with each factor and their factor loadings were functionally interpreted to arrive at a lexico-grammatical description of the variation of registers in Elementary Student English.

Reppen was then able to both compare the registers of Elementary Student English to one another and, in a second step, the dimensions of 'Elementary Student English' to those of 'Adult English' (as captured in Biber 1988). The comparisons revealed that textbooks share linguistic features typical of edited informational and non-personal uninvolved discourse (Reppen 1994, [2001]2013). In both the adult and elementary student models, the first and strongest dimension depicts an oral-written continuum, reflecting production circumstances and the density of informational content. The two models also feature a second dimension pertaining to narrative vs. non-narrative discourse. There are, however, some notable differences. Reppen (2013: 196) observes that many of these differences reflect developmental processes because, although fifth-graders' communicative goals largely match adults', ten- to eleven-year-olds rely on a more limited set of linguistic resources to pursue the same objectives. Students presumably acquire the necessary linguistic resources to construct subtle arguments and persuade at a later stage because features associated with these communicative aims are largely absent from Reppen's dimensions of elementary school English. Moreover, Reppen (2013: 197–198) notes that some of the tasks elementary students are asked to complete at school, e.g., describing hypothetical scenarios, involve clusters of lexico-grammatical features that are not found to co-occur in adult registers, suggesting that – at least from a linguistic point of view – the pedagogical relevance of such school tasks may be called into question.

In sum, both Le Foll's (2021c, 2022c: Chapter 6) additive MDAs and Reppen's (1994, [2001] 2013) full MDA of elementary school language point to the considerable potential of MDA in the context of textbook language studies.

5.3 A modified MDA framework: MDA as applied in the present study

The MDA framework (Biber 1984, 1988, 1995) may date back to the 1980s but it remains a highly influential and popular method of multivariable linguistic variation analysis (see, e.g., Berber Sardinha & Veirano Pinto 2014, 2019; Goulart & Wood 2021). The following section outlines the various linguistic, computational, and statistical decisions made as part of the design of the multi-feature/multi-dimensional method applied in the present chapter. In sum, this methodology is strongly inspired by Biber's MDA framework (see 5.1) but departs from the way it is traditionally applied in significant ways. Modifications to the framework have been implemented as a result of general, methodological issues associated with multivariable corpus-linguistic methods, specific ones related to the MDA framework, as well as in response to specific problems arising from the nature of Textbook English and the research questions outlined in 4.2.1. In subsequent chapters, the method described in this section will be referred to as 'the modified MDA framework'.

The main modifications are explained in the following sections, which detail the method used in the present study. Section 5.3.1 begins by outlining the selection of text samples for the present MDAs. This is followed in 5.3.2 by the process of feature selection, which led to the development of a new Multi-Feature Tagger of English (the MFTE), and a discussion on tagger accuracy in 5.3.3, which includes an evaluation of the MFTE on a sample of data used in the present study. The procedure applied to normalise the frequency counts entered in the analyses is explained and justified in 5.3.4. Section 5.3.5 focuses on the choice of PCA over EFA as the central statistical method for the present MDA study. Details of the methods applied to deal with skewed feature distributions can be found in 5.3.6. The methods used to compute and compare the dimension scores are explained in 5.3.7 and 5.3.8, whilst considerations regarding the presentation of the results are outlined in 5.3.9. The chapter ends with a brief discussion of the measures undertaken to improve the reproducibility and replicability of the analyses in 5.3.10.

5.3.1 Selection of text samples

The design of the Textbook English Corpus (TEC) and of the three target language reference corpora (Spoken BNC2014, Youth Fiction, and Info Teens) was already described in 4.3.2. In text-linguistic research designs, as typically adopted in MDA studies, the units of analysis are the individual texts within a corpus, with each text representing one observation (Egbert, Larsson & Biber 2020: 18). Thus, to begin, the individual texts identified as part of the manual annotation of the TEC (see 4.3.1.2) were extracted as single text files. This process, however, resulted in texts with a wide range of text lengths including a multitude of extremely short ones (in the case of instructional texts, often single sentences), for which no meaningful or reliable normalised feature counts can be computed. The risk is that, with so few opportunities to occur, most linguistic features will end up having discrete rather than continuous distributions.

Linguists attempting to apply MDA to social media texts often face the same problem. To solve this issue in MDAs of Twitter data, Clarke and Grieve (2017) developed a 'short-text version of MDA' (for details, see Clarke 2019, 2020, 2022). It relies on multiple correspondence analysis (MCA) which processes binary feature frequencies (i.e., whether a feature is present or absent within a tweet) rather than relative frequencies as in EFA. If, as Clarke and Grieve did, one considers a single tweet (as opposed to a thread of tweets) as a single text, this approach is very sensible because single tweets are, by corpus-linguistic standards, very short (at the time of writing, the maximum length was 280 characters) and as a result, relative frequencies would largely depend on tweet length. The case of textbook texts, however, is much more complex: whilst many textbook texts are as short as a tweet (e.g., task instructions, short rhymes), countless others run well over 1,000 words (e.g., short stories, news articles, transcript of dialogues). Indeed, defining text units in school EFL textbooks is a particularly challenging task. Numerous possibilities arise. Up until now, entire textbook volumes (or even textbook series!) have usually been treated as single texts. However, as explained in 4.1, such an approach entirely ignores the variety of text registers encountered within each textbook volume/series. A second approach might consider all the texts of one register found within a chapter or unit of a textbook volume to constitute one text. In some cases, this may be justified because texts within a textbook unit will often be thematically related and may therefore form a coherent whole; however, this will depend on the textbook series and is not always consistent across an entire textbook series, either (see Le Foll 2020b).

In addition to the problem of defining text units and counting them, the great variety of text lengths encountered in school EFL textbooks must also be considered. Short texts may not present enough opportunities for many linguistic features to occur. In other words, even if a feature is not particularly rare, a text may simply be too short for it to occur. In many corpus-linguistic studies, it is often tacitly assumed that normalising counts of occurrences generally solves this problem. In the case of zero counts, however, it evidently does not. This is easily illustrated by imagining a short informative textbook text totalling 100 words that might feature 20 nouns and six present tense verbs but not a single adverb or relative clause. If we normalise these counts to 1,000 words, we are implying that a longer version of this informative text would feature 200 nouns, 60 present tense verbs and still zero adverbs and zero relative clauses! As this example makes clear, the minimum text length must therefore be determined based on the frequency of the least frequent linguistic feature to be counted in an MDA. For the present study, several minimal text lengths were compared in an exploratory pilot phase before settling on 400 words. This decision also facilitates the comparability of the present results with the previous additive MDAs carried out on the same textbook and reference corpora (Le Foll 2021c, 2022c: Chapter 6).

In light of both the great variety of text lengths encountered in school EFL textbooks and the fact that many texts are under 400 words, shorter texts within each textbook volume and register were collated into longer text files. This means that, for example, a number of short, consecutive instructional texts from any one textbook volume were combined until a total word count of at least 400 words was reached. Concatenation was performed sequentially within each textbook volume so that short texts from within a chapter/unit or across directly adjacent chapters/units were grouped together. Hence, the collated text files also correspond to the progression that the learners are expected to make. Although it may be considered a limitation, it is not unusual for text samples of longer texts (e.g., as in Biber 1988: 66) or collations of shorter texts within one text category of interest (e.g., as in Coats 2016: 188) to be entered in MDAs. Whilst there is a clear theoretical advantage to working with entire, self-contained texts, where samples are long enough to be representative of the full texts from which they were sampled, and the collated texts relatively homogeneous within the text category they represent, they can provide adequate data to describe both the central tendency of a category and variation within it.

Having defined text units, another question arises: What is the minimum number of texts that needs to be entered in an MDA to obtain robust results? As a general rule of thumb, factor analysis is said to require a dataset of at least five times as many observations (i.e., here, texts)[21] as independent variables (i.e., linguistic

21. As explained above, in the present study, some of these 'texts' are in fact concatenation of several short texts made according to systematic criteria that reflect how the textbooks are constructed and used in the EFL classroom.

features) to be included in the analysis (Hair et al. 2019: 133). This would imply that, when using Biber's original 67 lexico-grammatical features, a minimum of 335 texts is needed to conduct a full MDA. That said, a high ratio of number of texts to independent variables is desirable (Hair et al. 2019: 133; in the context of MDA specifically, see Friginal & Hardy 2014: 304) and increases the robustness and replicability of the results (Costello & Osborne 2005; Osborne & Fitzpatrick 2005). As will become evident in the following, the ratios of text to linguistic feature in the following analyses are considerably higher than five.

Text concatenation as part of the pre-processing of the TEC for MDA resulted in the exclusion of texts categorised as Poetry from thirteen textbook volumes, Fiction texts from seven volumes, and Informative texts from two volumes because the texts of these registers within these volumes did not add up to at least 400 words. As a result, there were ultimately too few Poetry text files for this register category to be meaningfully included in the present MDAs. Hence, following these data preparation steps, 1,977 textbook text files from five major registers could be entered in the analyses presented in this study (see Table 14 for details).

Table 14. Textbook English Corpus (TEC) text files included in this study

Textbook registers	Number of text files	Number of words*
Conversation	593	505,147
Fiction	285	241,512
Informative texts	364	304,695
Instructional texts	647	585,049
Personal correspondence	88	69,570
Total	**1,977**	**1,705,973**

* As counted by the MFTE (Le Foll 2021d).

5.3.2 Selection of linguistic features

Having compiled a corpus suitable for MDA, the next step consists in selecting the linguistic features to be counted in the texts of extracted from the corpora. Given that MDA typically relies on (relatively) large corpora and dozens of linguistic features, feature identification and counting must be performed automatically. Biber (2019: 14) emphasises that "[a]lthough its importance is not widely recognized, the computer program used for grammatical tagging provides the foundation for MD studies". This is because the tagging software determines both the kinds of features entered in an MDA and the reliability of their counts.

In Biber's original MDA design, the 67 linguistic features were chosen based on the results of previous literature on linguistic variation across general spoken and written registers of English (Biber 1988: 71–72). Although Biber and others have always made clear that the range of features entered in MDAs ought to be as broad as possible so as to have the potential to unearth hitherto unseen patterns of variation (Conrad & Biber [2001] 2013: 15; Egbert & Staples 2019: 127), such an approach nevertheless risks introducing biases (Diwersy, Evert & Neumann 2014: 174). Altenberg (1989: 173) best illustrates this risk with what he calls the "stylistic 'predisposition'" of a few of Biber's (1988) categories (see also McEnery & Hardie 2011: 112–115). For instance, Biber (1988) included both a 'conjuncts' category (which includes *alternatively, consequently, further, hence, however,* etc.) and a 'discourse markers' category (which includes *anyway(s), anyhow, now, well,* etc.). Altenberg (1989: 173) argues that the two categories are functionally equivalent and that the distinction between the two is situational – the first being specific to literate genres, whilst the second is typical of spoken interactions (see also Siepmann 2004). Although this issue only concerns a handful of features from the 1988 version of the Biber tagger, it highlights the difficulty of conceptualising linguistically interpretable features that are not in any way situationally determined.

To counter the risk of circularity that arises from the top-down selection of features, some (foremost computational linguistic) studies have opted for bottom-up approaches to feature selection (an approach in line with "corpus-driven research", see, e.g., Meunier & Reppen 2015: 499; Xiao 2009: 993–996). Such approaches reject "*prima facie* those theories, axioms and precepts that were formulated before corpus data became available" (Tognini-Bonelli 2001: 179), hereby aiming to avoid as many types of linguistic preconceptions as possible, including those concerning lexico-grammatical categories, e.g., parts-of-speech. Arguably the most data- or corpus-driven approaches to the selection of features involve character n-grams.[22] However, studies based on character n-grams frequently reveal relatively trivial topic-related patterns rather than more generalisable linguistic ones (Baroni & Bernardini 2005: 264; Popescu 2011: 638; Volansky, Ordan & Wintner 2015: 111). Additionally, character n-grams can be argued to lack "direct linguistic motivation or interpretation" (Argamon 2019: 111) and, like token/word n-gram-based methods, largely fail to account for polysemy. All other 'data-driven', 'bottom-up' approaches inevitably involve some form of theory-dependent pre-processing steps such as tokenisation, lemmatisation, part-of-speech tagging, (shallow) syntactic parsing, or combinations thereof. It can be argued that such

22. The first three character tri-grams of this footnote are: *the he_* and *e_f*. Note that in many computational linguistic studies relying on character n-grams, however, whitespaces and/or cross-token n-grams are ignored. When adopting the latter option, the method is arguably no longer truly data-driven as it requires an initial layer of tokenisation.

tools add layers of biases in that they rely on specific, pre-established theoretical models of language analysis (see, e.g., Sinclair 1992: 385–390).

In sum, seeking to entirely eliminate bias in the feature selection and operationalisation process whilst nevertheless arriving at a linguistically meaningful and generalisable set of linguistic features is likely an unattainable objective. McEnery and Hardie (2011: 114) suggest that bias can be reduced by ensuring that the selection is "both *principled* and *exhaustive*". The present study relies on the feature portfolio of a new lexico-grammatical tagger specifically designed for the analysis of situational variation in general spoken and written registers of English: the Perl version of the Multi-Feature Tagger of English (hereafter: MFTE; Le Foll 2021d). Whilst the MFTE makes no claim to have an entirely "*principled* and *exhaustive*" feature portfolio, various steps were undertaken to reduce bias in both the selection and operationalisation of the features. For the selection of features, simplified Hallidayian system networks were examined to ensure that no major aspect of English lexicogrammar would be overlooked (for details, see Le Foll 2021d, cf. Matthiessen 2019; and Whitelaw & Argamon 2004). Ultimately, however, the final choice of features was necessarily restricted by both practical and computational constraints. In particular, the large number of texts usually entered in MDAs means that only features that can relatively reliably be retrieved using automated queries were ultimately included in the feature portfolio of the MFTE. To cite but one example, these constraints resulted in a tagger that makes no distinction between *that*-relative clauses and other *that*-subordinate clauses (unlike the Biber tagger, whose output, however, is often manually "fix-tagged" for such problematic features; see, e.g., Gray 2019).

Crucially for the interpretability of the dimensions that emerged from the present multi-feature analyses, the MFTE was developed with the aim of arriving at a set of features that can be both identified to a high degree of accuracy in a variety of written and spoken registers of English, as well as meaningfully interpreted in terms of their function. In other words, the aim was that all the features' "scale and values represent a real-world language phenomenon that can be understood and explained" (Egbert, Larsson & Biber 2020: 24). Whilst no automatic tool can ever pretend to be able to achieve this perfectly, several tagger development-evaluation cycles were completed to arrive at a set of rule-based algorithms that best fulfils this criterion. The manifold decisions involved in the selection and operationalisations of these features are detailed in the user documentation of the MFTE Perl (Le Foll 2021d).

Appendix C ⟨elenlefoll.github.io/TextbookMDA/AppendixC⟩ provides a comprehensive list of the final set of over 80 features of the MFTE feature portfolio for which the texts of the TEC and the three reference corpora were tagged for the present analyses (see Table 15 for an extract). Note that, although the table in

Appendix C is subdivided into broad linguistic categories (see also the first column of Table 15 for illustration purposes), these merely serve organisational purposes and do not seek to represent any specific theoretical or functional categorisation. Indeed, many features could equally well be subsumed under a different category. The second column (see also Table 15) provides a very brief description of each linguistic feature. The third corresponds to the tag codes assigned by the MFTE. These codes are also used in the tables and figures presented in the following chapters. Examples of different language patterns illustrating these features are found in the fourth column. Finally, the operationalisation column contains simplified, written-out explanations of the combinations of regular expressions used to identify each feature. For more details, the interested reader is invited to examine the tagger source code available on GitHub ⟨https://github.com/elenlefoll/MultiFeatureTaggerEnglish⟩.

Table 15. Excerpt of Appendix C: Operationalisation of 'DO as an auxiliary' (DOAUX)

Category	Feature	Code	Examples	Operationalisation
Verb semantics	*DO auxiliary*	*DOAUX*	*Should take longer than it* ***does****. Ah you* ***did****. She needed that house,* ***didn't*** *she? You* ***don't*** *really pay much attention,* ***do*** *you? Who* ***did*** *not already love him.*	Assigned to *do, does* and *did* as verbs in the following patterns: (a) when the next but one token is a base form verb (VB) (e.g., *did it work?, didn't hurt?)*; (b) when the next but two token (+3) is a base form verb (VB) (e.g., *didn't it work*); (c) when it is immediately followed by an end-of-sentence punctuation mark (e.g., *you did*?); (d) when it is followed by a personal pronoun (PRP) or *not* or *n't* (XX0) and an end-of-sentence punctuation mark (e.g., *do you? He didn't!)*; (e) when it is followed by *not* or *n't* (XX0) and a personal pronoun (PRP) (e.g., *didn't you?*); (f) when it is followed by a personal pronoun followed by any token and then a question mark (e.g., *did you really? did you not?*); (g) when it is preceded by a WH question word. Additionally, all instances of *DO* immediately preceded by *to* as an infinitive marker (TO) are excluded from this tag.

The MFTE performs feature extraction over several iterations over the texts of a corpus. First, each text is tagged for part-of-speech with the Stanford Tagger (bidirectional version 3.9.2; Toutanova & Manning 2000; Toutanova et al. 2003). Next, rule-based algorithms are run to identify linguistic features necessary for the identification of other features, e.g., DO auxiliaries are first identified on the basis of various combinations of POS tags and forms of the verb DO, before imperatives can be tagged. This ensures that imperative forms of the verb DO can be disambiguated from auxiliary forms, in particular those included in *yes/no* questions where the *do/does/did* frequently occur after an end-of-sentence punctuation mark (see Appendix C for details). Since the Stanford Tagger provides the first layer of linguistic annotation (tokenisation and POS tagging), the accuracy of the feature extraction is heavily dependent on the accuracy of the Stanford Tagger. Whilst it is a well-tested and robust model, it is by no means perfect (Toutanova et al. 2003; Spoustová et al. 2009; Manning 2011). As a result, some of the feature operationalisations include more tags and/or loops than would be necessary if the POS-tagging process were failproof. For instance, since the Stanford Tagger was found to frequently fail to differentiate between past tense (VBD) and past participle forms (VBN), the algorithms designed to capture passives (PASS and PGET) and the perfect aspect (PEAS) include syntactic patterns with either the VBN or the VBD tag to improve recall rates whenever past participles have been erroneously tagged as VBD. Whilst using a POS-tagger as the basis for the feature extraction process reduces the reproducibility of the method as different tagging software (and versions) will inevitably produce different results (Bohmann 2017: 165), the gain in recall and precision is huge and many of the linguistic features of the MFTE's feature portfolio simply cannot be extracted without this initial annotation layer.

Although the MFTE was designed as an all-purpose tagger of general English, its first intended use was for the present project. As a result, some of the features and feature operationalisations could be adapted to the specificities of the corpora under study. An example of such tailoring concerns the imperative verb feature. To begin with, the MFTE assigns the imperative tag (VIMP) to tokens identified by the Stanford Tagger as base form verbs (VB), which have not previously been tagged as DO auxiliaries (DOAUX) by the MFTE and are immediately preceded by a punctuation mark other than a comma, or the combination of such a punctuation mark and an adverb. Textbook instructions often begin with a verb in the imperative; however, these are not always proceeded by an end-of-sentence punctuation mark. Instead, tasks are frequently delimited by a symbol or icon of some kind. These frequently cause OCR issues and produce tokens which are inconsistently identified by the Stanford Tagger as symbols (SYM), list markers (LS), or foreign words (FW). Consequently, the MFTE was designed to also assign to the imperative variable base form verbs which occur after such tokens. It was also noticed that the Stanford Tagger often considers sentence-initial *please* to be a base verb form (VB), hence exceptions were added for the tokens *please* and *thank*. Having identified these sentence-initial imperatives, a second loop then searches for a potential second imperative verb which may occur after *and* or *or* with up to two optional intervening tokens, e.g., (13) to (15). Finally, it was noticed that *work* in the phrase *work in pairs*, which occurs more than 700 times in the TEC, is almost invariably identified by the Stanford Tagger as a noun (NN). As a result, this phrase, together with several other frequently occurring phrases which also proved problematic for the POS-tagger were implemented as additional exceptions in the version of the MFTE used for the present analyses (version 3.1 ran on Perl v.5.22.1 built for x86_64-linux-gnu-thread-multi).

(13) **Describe** or **draw**

(14) **Listen** carefully and **repeat**

(15) **Read** the text and **answer** the questions

5.3.3 Evaluation of the reliability of the feature counts

Although the robustness of any statistical method that relies on counts of features evidently hinges on the high accuracy of these counts, very few MDA studies mention tagger reliability (major exceptions deserving of mention include Biber & Gray 2013; Gray 2015). The present MDA relies on the MFTE Perl (Le Foll 2021d), whose documentation includes a full evaluation of the tagger's accuracy against texts of diverse registers randomly sampled from the BNC2014 (Brezina, Hawtin & McEnery 2021; Love et al. 2017). To account for the specificities of the registers examined in the present study, the accuracy of the MFTE was also evaluated on samples of the TEC and the reference corpora. The full report of this evaluation can be found in Le Foll (2022c: 277–281) and is summarised below.

The overall accuracy rate for the TEC and the three reference corpora, excluding unclear tokens, punctuation, and symbols, is estimated to be around 96.38% [95% CI: 96.13–96.62%]. However, when reporting the accuracy of a tagger to be used for MDA, it is imperative to consider not just the overall accuracy of a tagger, since this will be heavily skewed towards very frequent tags (many of which are particularly easy to tag, e.g., punctuation marks and determiners), but also the tagger's per-feature accuracy. Figure 5, which presents the MFTE's per-feature accuracy rates for the data analysed in this study, was used to check that the models reported in Chapters 6 and 7 were not overly influenced by features with low accuracy rates.

For each feature, Figure 5 displays three different accuracy metrics. The three metrics are formally defined in Table 16. Tagger evaluations typically only report 'precision', i.e., the percentage of correctly assigned tags within a category. This is for practical reasons as precision is much easier to spot-check than 'recall', i.e., the percentage of a particular feature that is correctly identified as such by the tagger. In practice, however, both precision and recall are crucial for the results of MDAs to be reliable and robust, which is why the combined accuracy 'F1' metric (see Table 16) is also reported in Figure 5 and Le Foll (2022c: 277–281). The full breakdown of the evaluation results and the corresponding code can be found in the Appendix D ⟨elenlefoll.github.io/TextbookMDA/AppendixD⟩.

Table 16. Summary of the terminology used in the evaluation of the MFTE

Term	Definition
True positive	Feature correctly tagged by the MFTE as X
False positive	Feature incorrectly tagged by the MFTE as X
False Negative	Feature incorrectly not tagged by the MFTE as X
Precision	True positive count / (true positive count + false positive count)
Recall	True positive count / (true positive count + false negative count)
F1 score	2 * (precision * recall) / (precision + recall)

5.3.4 Normalisation of feature counts

Even with a minimum word count of 400 (see 5.3.1), the texts of the TEC and the three reference corpora of the present study (see 4.3) vary greatly in length. This is potentially problematic given that counts of linguistic features in texts of different lengths cannot be directly compared. To illustrate this, let us imagine a short business e-mail of 200 words that features four occurrences of the word *if* and compare it to an imaginary novel of, say, 20,000 words in which the word *if* is observed eight times across the entire book. Comparing these raw counts, we may naively be tempted to conclude that *if* is twice as frequent in fictional writing as in professional e-mails. Evidently, however, this comparison does not account for the vastly different number of potential opportunities of use of the word *if* in the two texts. To remedy this, the *de facto* standard in corpus linguistics has so far consisted in normalising raw counts to a common word-based denominator. For example, the count of four *ifs* in our hypothetical e-mail can be divided by the total number of words in the e-mail (200) and the count of eight in the book by the length of the novel (20,000) before multiplying both results by a common denominator, e.g., by 1,000 words. In our example, this approach results in nor-

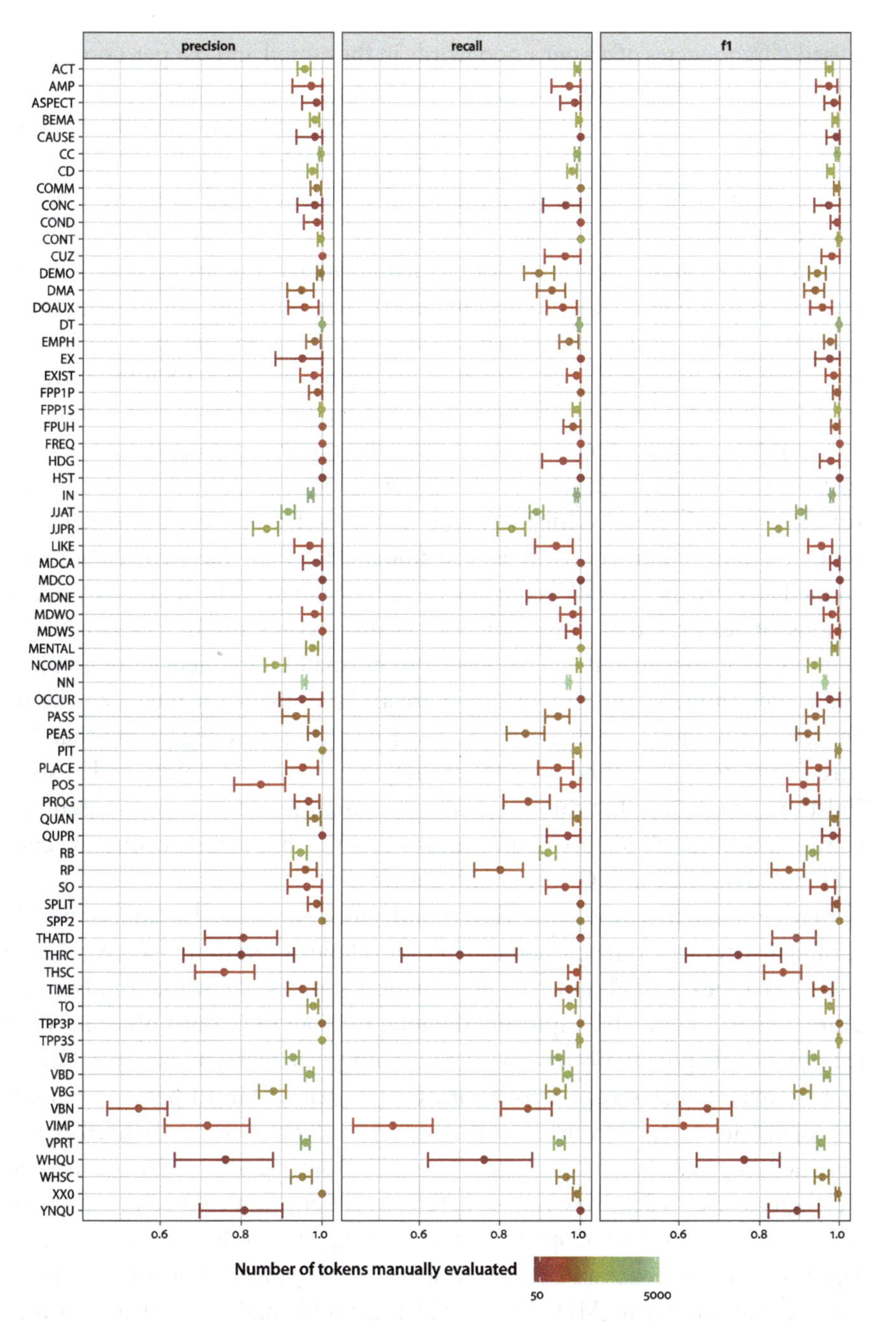

Figure 5. Per-feature accuracy measures (and bootstrapped 95% confidence intervals) of the MFTE on samples of the TEC, the Spoken BNC2014 and data comparable to the Youth Fiction and Info Teens (for details, see Le Foll 2022c: 277–81)

malised *if* frequencies of 20 per 1,000 words in the e-mail and 0.4 per 1,000 words in the novel. In other words, once normalised on a per-word basis, we might conclude that *if* is in fact 50 times more frequent in professional e-mails than in novels! Typical word-based denominators in corpus linguistics are 100, 1,000, 10,000 and a million words and the resulting numbers are referred to as 'normalised', 'normed', or 'relative' frequencies.

In MDA research, the use of word-based normalisation for all linguistic features results in a potentially problematic overlap between the covariation of features due to functional and/or situational variation on the one hand, and covariation due to grammatical structure on the other (Grieve-Smith 2007; Lee 2000). Consider the linguistic features that load on Biber's (1988) first dimension: at the positive, 'involved' end, these include the number of verbal contractions, negated verbs, and present tense verbs per 1,000 words, which all correlate strongly with each other. Whilst it is true that these features are particularly frequent in spoken interactions, it is also undeniable that these correlations are also mediated by the overall frequency of verbs. Similarly, the high positive correlations of features that contribute to negative scores on Biber's (1988) first dimension (e.g., between the per-1,000-word normalised frequencies of nominalisations, determiners, and prepositions) are all "grammatically mediated" by the frequency of nouns. Grieve-Smith (2007: 6) goes as far as suggesting that "the entire Dimension 1 [in Biber's (1988) model] measures nominal vs. verbal style". Whilst not suggesting that this is actually the case, the use of a word-based normalisation unit for all feature counts means that this hypothesis cannot be completely ruled out (see also Grieve-Smith 2007: 7).

In response to this problem, Grieve-Smith (2007) proposes the adoption of the sociolinguistic, variationist principle of the "envelope of variation" (see, e.g., Labov 2004: 7) as a means of eliminating grammatical sources of covariation. For each feature, this would involve capturing the total number of opportunities in which the feature could potentially have occurred in any given text. For example, Grieve-Smith (2007: 13) suggests operationalising the frequency of third-person pronouns as a proportion of all occurrences of all pronouns, except those used in fixed expressions such as *you know, you see* and *if you will*. However, this approach assumes that language users effectively choose to refer to either a first-, a second- or a third-person topic. It excludes the option that, depending on extralinguistic factors, language users may, for example, also choose to refer to more or fewer topics. In the context of a multi-register MDA, this is evidently problematic given that: "Speakers do not typically 'say the same thing' in conversation as in lectures, reports, academic papers, and congratulatory telegrams" (Biber & Finegan 1994: 6).

Reflecting on the quantification of linguistic measures in general terms, Schegloff (1993: 103) speaks of the need to account for "environments of possible *rel-*

evant occurrence" (emphasis original) and argues that "quantitative analysis requires an analytically defensible notion of the denominator". In the context of MDA specifically, I have argued that measuring feature frequencies as a proportion of all 'grammatically possible' options is both theoretically and practically inappropriate (Le Foll 2021d: 21–23; see also Biber 2012; Bohmann 2019: 43).

Instead, I proposed a solution which falls somewhere between the text-linguistic and the variationist approaches: the implementation of what Wallis (2020: 62) refers to as a "plausible baseline" on his methodological continuum of normalisation baselines. In Wallis' example of measuring the frequency of *shall* as a modal, the 'plausible baseline' suggested is the total number of tensed verb phrases. It is argued here that, for the purposes of MDA, a linguistically motivated 'plausible baseline' suffices to (approximately) eliminate grammatical covariation whilst allowing for the theoretical possibility that language users frequently make language choices that are not restricted to a finite set of alternatives.

Ultimately, however, the choice of normalisation baseline always depends on both theory and the feasibility of reliably counting what is considered to be the most meaningful unit (Wallis 2020: 69–70). For instance, as a denominator for the counts of *if*, the total number of sentences or clauses in a given text might seem like the most linguistically meaningful or "analytically defensible" unit. However, whilst identifying sentences is relatively trivial in written registers, not only can this unit be argued to not make much linguistic sense in spoken registers, but it is also impossible to reliably implement with spoken corpora whose transcription scheme do not include any sentence boundaries (e.g., the Spoken BNC2014). As for automatically identifying clauses, this would require dependency parsing, which, to date, remains woefully unreliable for transcriptions of spontaneous spoken language, and which would, in any case, certainly result in units that would be equally difficult to compare across different modes and registers.

The present analyses rely on the normalisation baselines as implemented in the "mixed normalisation" output of the MFTE (see Le Foll 2021d for details). For this output, the MFTE normalises counts of most features including conditional conjunctions (*if* and *unless*), modal verbs, contractions, negation, aspect, tenses, and different types of questions to 100 finite verb phrases (hereafter: FVP). The number of finite verb phrases is approximated to a satisfactorily high degree of accuracy by the MFTE by adding the counts for present tense, past tense, imperatives and all the modal verbs together. Five features, attribute adjectives, *s*-genitives, noun compounds, quantifiers, and determiners, are normalised to 100 nouns, whilst only the remaining 19 features, e.g., emoji and emoticons, discourse markers and nouns, are normalised to 100 words. This approach is by no means considered to be perfect, but it is hoped that it will reduce the amount of variance explained by MDA-based models that can be attributed to grammatical covariation alone.

5.3.5 Factor analysis method

MDA relies on factor analysis to reduce a large set of associations of normalised counts of many different linguistic features across a large number of texts to a more parsimonious set of underlying, or latent, variables. These summarising variables are first referred to as 'factors' and then, once they have been functionally interpreted, as 'dimensions'. Thus, MDA makes use of factor analysis to reduce complexity and "consolidate variables in a principled manner" (Loewen & Gonulal 2015:183) in order to more concisely describe, and ultimately hopefully understand, the relationships among the linguistic features. The underlying belief is that such parsimonious solutions will have greater external validity and will therefore be more likely to replicate (Henson & Roberts 2006:394).

At this stage, it should be noted that the terminology is often used ambiguously and that statisticians disagree as to what exactly does or does not constitute 'factor analysis' (see, e.g., Henson & Roberts 2006:398; Jolliffe 2002:150). In the present study, 'factor analysis' will be used as an overarching term that encompasses both 'common factor analysis' and 'principal component analysis'. This choice was made to facilitate the discussion on issues that apply to both methods. Though other methods have been used, the factor-extracting method of choice in MDA studies has traditionally been exploratory factor analysis (EFA) (Goulart & Wood 2021:124), which is a common factor analysis method.

Within the standard MDA framework, determining the number of factors to extract has been described as an "important part of the iterative process between statistical procedure and subjective researcher interpretation" (Egbert & Staples 2019:130). Comparing the interpretability of the various combinations of factors that emerge from different factor solutions is part of the method. Indeed, Egbert and Staples (2019:130) recommend that "[i]f particular factor solutions ([with a] greater number or smaller number [of factors]) are more interpretable than others, then it should be considered as a more favorable solution". Whilst this qualitative approach to selecting the number of factors is entirely justifiable, it nonetheless entails potentially problematic "researcher degrees of freedom" (Simmons, Nelson & Simonsohn 2011). The issue is particularly relevant for the replicability of MDA results based on EFA because the factor solutions produced by EFAs are not computationally stable (see, e.g., Costello & Osborne 2005; Velicer & Jackson 1990). In other words, using the same data, researchers will obtain different results for the first three factors of an EFA solution depending on whether they decide to extract three, four, five, or more factors (see also

Clarke 2020: 317–318). This issue is well-documented in the applied statistics literature. As a result, all best-practice guidelines on how to conduct EFAs (e.g., Tabachnick & Fidell 2014: 696–699; Loewen & Gonulal 2015: 194–197) devote a section to various (more or less objective) factor retention criteria. The problem is that, whilst methods to determine the number of factors to retain abound (e.g., Kaiser-1 rule, Joliffe's criteria, visual inspection of the scree plot, parallel analysis, machine learning methods), they frequently produce different results. This is problematic as "[d]etermining the number of factors in exploratory factor analysis is arguably the most crucial decision a researcher faces when conducting the analysis" (Goretzko 2022: 444).

This is one of the reasons why Diwersy et al. (2014) and Neumann and Evert (2021) advocate for the use of principal component analysis (PCA) rather than EFA in multi-dimensional linguistic research. Whilst researchers conducting a PCA still need to choose one of the many methods to decide on how many summarising, latent variables (referred to as 'principal components' in PCA) to retain and interpret, the results themselves will remain the same regardless of how many components are deemed to be worthy of further analysis and (linguistic) interpretation (Jolliffe 2002: 159–160).[23]

PCA is also a dimensionality-reduction statistical method. However, mathematically, EFA and PCA differ in that PCA accounts for all the variance in the data, thus pooling together shared (or 'common') variance between variables, the variance due to error and the variance that is unique to each variable. By contrast, EFA attempts to estimate the specific variance and the error variance to eliminate these sources of variance and thus focus exclusively on the shared (or 'common', hence the term 'common factor analysis') variance. Whilst the latter may produce factor solutions that are more readily interpretable, the computing of the factors themselves is rather opaque. By contrast, the components produced by PCA are linear functions directly derived from the observed variables, i.e., in the present context, from the normalised frequencies of each linguistic feature in each text of the corpora.

Theoretically, too, EFA and PCA differ in that EFA produces latent variables that are assumed to represent real-life constructs. Conceptually, these constructs are thought to "cause" the distributions of the variables to be as they are observed in the dataset, whereas in PCA it is the resulting components that are "caused by" or that "produce" the observed variables. Thus, the components of PCA can be said to be empirically real factors that directly represent aggregates of the observed correlated variables but that do not necessarily reflect any underlying constructs

23. Note, however, that this is no longer true if the PCA solution is rotated (see, e.g., Husson, Lê & Pagès 2017: 29).

or processes (Tabachnick & Fidell 2014: 662). This is why EFA is often assumed to offer a higher degree of generalisability to other, unsampled variables (Velicer & Jackson 1990: 17). In practice, however, the more reliable the measured variables and the greater the number of variables included in the analysis, the less pronounced the differences in outputs between PCAs and EFAs tend to be (Henson & Roberts 2006: 398). MDAs typically include far more linguistic features than the number of variables typically involved in factor analysis studies in psychology. This is likely why preliminary comparative EFAs and PCAs conducted on the TEC and its three reference corpora yielded very comparable results.

PCA has already been successfully used for the multi-feature and multi-dimensional analysis of linguistic variation (notably, Biber & Egbert 2016, 2018; Diwersy, Evert & Neumann 2014; Neumann & Evert 2021; Sigley 1997). For the present study, PCA was chosen for its computational stability (reducing researcher degrees of freedom) and its (relative) ease of interpretation. The latter is also true of the feature weights (loadings) which, in PCA, simply represent correlation coefficients between the observed variables and the components, whereas the factor loadings that emerge from EFAs are factor score estimations. These are mathematically more complex and, although they fulfil a very similar function, are more difficult to interpret accurately.

To make the most of different visualisation options, two different R packages are used to conduct the PCAs: *stats* for its *prcomp* function that allows for 3-D visualisation of the results via *pca3d* and *PCAtools* for its highly customisable *pairsplot* and *biplot* functions for 2-D graphs. Visual inspection of eigenvalues scree plots is used as an initial step to determine how many components are to be analysed. The components are not subject to any rotation (details of all the packages, functions, and parameters used can be found in the Online Supplements on https://elenlefoll.github.io/TextbookMDA/).

5.3.6 Dealing with skewed distributions of features

As a family of statistical methods, dimensionality-reduction methods are known to be very sensitive to outliers and skewed distributions. Tabachnick and Fidell (2014: 665) claim that "problems created by missing data, and degradation of correlations between poorly distributed variables all plague FA [factor analysis] and PCA". In the context of MDA, it is perfectly possible for linguistic features to be entirely absent from some of the texts in the corpora under study, thus creating the impression of "missing data" in the frequency matrices to be entered in such analyses. Of course, the data is not "missing" in the traditional sense but rather the rate of occurrence of these features is simply zero. There are, in theory, three reasons why this might be the case. The first is quite simply that a text genuinely does not feature this particular lexico-grammatical unit. For instance, it is easily conceivable that a novel may not include a single emoji. Thus, especially linguistic features that have "strong stylistic discriminating properties" (Lee 2000: 173), such as emojis, question tags, or interjections, will necessarily follow very skewed distributions across multi-register corpora. Moreover, texts as long as an entire novel are rarely entered in an MDA (see 5.3.1). Second, therefore, we may envisage a situation in which a particular feature is absent from a text sample, thus returning a count of zero, but can actually be observed in other parts of the full text. For instance, a short sample of a novel may not happen to include a single verb in the passive voice, yet it is highly unlikely that the entire novel does not feature a single verb in the passive. Similarly, if a complete text is very short it is also likely to have zero occurrences of many of the least frequent linguistic features, even though this may not be representative of the text register/variety more generally. Ultimately, both these issues tie back to the discussion of an appropriate minimum text length for MDA studies (see 5.3.1). Thus, when conducting MDA on corpora containing short texts, such as the TEC, the meaningful collation of short texts (see 4.3.2.4) can help avoid zero counts causing undue influence on the resulting dimensions. Finally, it should also be acknowledged that a third reason why a text may appear to include zero occurrences of a particular feature may be a failure of the automatic tagger to identify the feature in question. This risk confirms the need to conduct thorough evaluations of the taggers that are used in MDAs, as discussed in 5.3.3.

We have seen that there are potentially several reasons why count matrices destined to be entered in MDAs may include zeros. For some of these reasons, mitigating steps have already been undertaken as part of the pre-processing of the corpus data. However, it may still be necessary to remove linguistic features that are too poorly distributed as a result of being entirely absent from a large proportion of the texts to be analysed. In the present analyses, features with zero occurrences in more than two thirds of texts were, whenever linguistically meaningful, merged with other features (e.g., *GET*-passives were merged with *BE*-passives) or else excluded from the analyses (see, e.g., Bohmann 2019: 72; Clarke 2020: Section 8.3.3 for similar procedures).

However, having removed features with high percentages of zero occurrences, the distributions of many of the remaining features nevertheless remained highly skewed. By way of illustration, the normalised frequencies of occurrence of five features across the TEC are plotted in Figure 6. A cursory look at these example histograms points to two potential issues. First, unsurprisingly, the ranges of rates of occurrence (plotted on the *y*-axes) vary considerably. These ranges depend (a) on how frequent a particular linguistic feature is (e.g., we would expect nouns [NN] to be generally much more frequent than split auxiliaries [SPLIT]) and (b) on each feature's normalisation basis (e.g., here, the normalised counts of nouns represent the number of nouns per 100 words, whereas progressives [PROG] and split auxiliaries are counted per 100 finite verbs). Second, it is obvious that at least three of these distributions are far from normal and, instead, appear to follow distributions sharing similarities with the Zipfian distribution that is very familiar to linguists (see, e.g., Brezina 2018: 44–46).

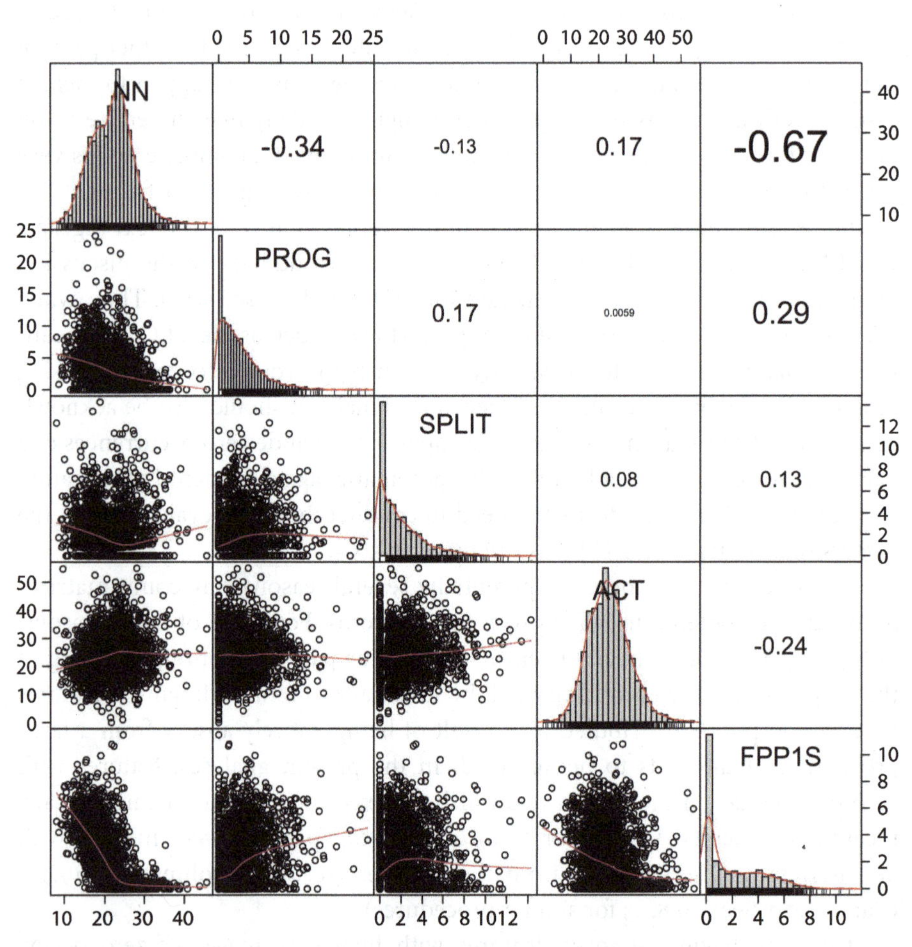

Figure 6. Distribution of normalised frequencies of five features across the TEC (histograms) and visualisations of their correlations (scatterplots)

Dealing with the first issue is relatively trivial: in such cases, it is common practice in multivariable analyses, and indeed in Biber's (1988: 94–95) MDA framework, to standardise variables to *z*-scores, i.e., to scale all frequencies to a mean of zero ($\mu = 0$) and a unit variance of one ($\sigma^2 = 1$). This *z*-transformation ensures that each feature makes the same overall contribution to the distances between the texts that will be explored in the following analyses (see 5.1 and Neumann & Evert 2017: 53). As for the second issue, Hair et al. (2019: 137) note on the assumptions of EFA that: "[f]rom a statistical standpoint, departures from normality, homoscedasticity, and linearity apply only to the extent that they diminish the observed correlations". In other words, factorial patterns may be harder to detect if variables are not normally distributed and if correlations are nonlinear (as shown in the scatterplots in Figure 6), but, if/when they *are* detected, there is no reason to assume that they are not real. Nonetheless, as pointed out at the beginning of this section, such skewed distributions run the risk of outliers exerting undue influence on the resulting models. Hence, following Neumann and Evert (2021), the standardised normalised counts were subjected to a signed log transformation[24] in order to (partially) deskew their distributions. Note that, whilst Neumann and Evert (2021) apply this transformation to deskew feature distributions as an alternative to removing very sparse features, the present methodology uses a combination of methods: removing any features that occur in fewer than a third of texts and transforming the remaining features' standardised normalised counts.

Overall, the factorability of the data depends on both the number and size of its variable intercorrelations. Bartlett's test of sphericity is often used to test whether variables are sufficiently intercorrelated to produce representative factors; however, it is a significance test of the hypothesis that the correlations in a correlation matrix are zero and, as such, is known to be overly sensitive and dependent on the sample size (Hair et al. 2019: 136) so that, in practice, it will always produce significant results in the context of MDAs carried out on sufficiently large corpora. As formulated in the null hypothesis that it is designed to test, Bartlett's test of sphericity merely indicates the presence of non-zero correlations, which is not to say that the pattern of these correlations is actually suitable for factor analysis (see also Hair et al. 2019: 168). In addition, the test assumes that the data is a sample from a multivariate normal population which is rarely, if ever, the case when dealing with linguistic data (Lee 2000: 178). Given that MDAs typically deal with many data points and variables with non-normal distributions, it is worth first examining the feature intercorrelations visually. Visualisation of correlation matrices can help to identify both extremely high correlations (collinear variables) and very low ones that can skew the results of the MDA and therefore ought to be excluded. In the present study, collinear features are defined as those correlating $>|0.95|$. Whenever this is the case, the less marked of the two

24. The following function was applied to the standardised normalised counts: signed.log <- function(x) {sign(x)*log(abs(x)+1)} (see Appendix E for details of the procedure)

collinear variables is excluded from the analysis. For example, in the MDA presented in Chapter 7, the present tense (VPRT) and past tense (VBD) variables correlated at 0.96, leading to VPRT being removed from the dataset. In addition, the Kaiser-Meyer-Olkin (KMO) index (1974: 112) is used to further explore the suitability of the feature intercorrelations for factor analysis. In the present study, this is achieved using the R *psych::KMO* function (Revelle 2020), which outputs an overall KMO Measure of Sampling Adequacy (MSA) as well as MSA scores for each individual feature. These can range from 0 (i.e., not in any way correlated with another feature) to 1 (indicating that this feature can be perfectly predicted by another feature) (Kaiser & Rice 1974). Following the procedure described in Hair et al. (2019: 136–37), the features' individual MSA values are examined and, if any feature has an MSA of ≤ 0.5, the feature with the lowest MSA is removed. The KMO index is then re-calculated and this process of omitting the variable with the lowest MSA value is continued until all features reach an MSA value of ≤ 0.5.

An additional step that is often taken to ensure that the results of factor analysis methods are robust consists in removing variables with low final communalities from the analysis (see, e.g., Hair et al. 2019: 173–81). Communality is measured as the sum of all the squared factor/component loadings for any one variable and therefore refers to the proportion of variance within a variable that is explained by the extracted factors. In other words, a low communality indicates that a substantial proportion of a variable's variance is not accounted for by the reduced solution. There are no hard and fast rules as to what constitutes a reasonable communality cut-off point because it very much depends on how much total variance a solution explains; however, in the context of MDA, Biber (1995: 138) recommends eliminating linguistic features with communalities ≤ 0.20. This is also the cut-off point that is used in the present study.

Once these various steps have been undertaken to eliminate very unevenly distributed features, those with overly high or particularly low correlations, and low communalities, the overall MSA can be re-calculated to evaluate the suitability of the dataset for this kind of analysis. The resulting overall KMO values may be interpreted following Kaiser and Rice's (1974: 112) (wonderfully flamboyant!) approximate scale:

≥.90 marvellous
≥.80 meritorious
≥.70 middling
≥.60 mediocre
≥.50 miserable
<.50 unacceptable

Arguably more meaningfully, KMO values may alternatively be compared to those of previous MDA studies. Unfortunately, few MDA studies report these: out of the 230 MDA studies that Goulart and Wood (2021: 124) surveyed, 26 claim to have checked the factorability of their data using KMO and 24 report overall KMO values. For these, Goulart and Wood (2021: 124) calculate a mean KMO value of 0.69 ($SD = 0.08$, min = 0.43, max = 0.86), which would suggest that correlation matrices typically entered in MDAs are only "mediocrely" to "middlingly" suitable for factor analysis. However, the measures outlined in this section (i.e., the transformation of particularly skewed distributions and the elimination of highly unevenly distributed features and those that have low MSA scores or low communalities) ought to contribute to higher overall KMO values and to correlation matrices that are more suitable for this kind of data-reduction analysis.

5.3.7 Computation of dimension scores

The MDA framework also foresees the computation of dimension scores (sometimes referred to as 'factor scores') for each text in the corpus under study. The dimension scores of texts in different (sub-)registers and/or other subgroups of the corpus can then be compared. As explained in 5.1, features with factor loadings below a pre-determined cut-off point (usually ±0.35 as in Biber 1988: 93) are typically excluded from the computation of their dimension scores. In addition, if a feature loads onto more than one factor with a loading above the chosen cut-off point, the feature is only counted for the factor on which it has the highest loading (though it can still be used in the qualitative analysis of the functional interpretation of the dimension). To calculate the dimension scores that correspond to a particular factor, the standardised normalised frequencies for each of the salient positive-loading features on that factor are added together whilst the salient negative-loading ones are subtracted.

MDA studies have sometimes been criticised for relying on an arbitrary cut-off point to determine the inclusion or exclusion of certain features from its dimension scores (e.g., Evert 2018: 12). There is, however, a valid rationale for removing low-loading features from dimension scores: they are likely to simply reflect noise in the data that is arguably best removed from models that aim to be representative of a larger population. As an alternative, statistical methods can be applied to exclude non-significant loadings, i.e., those that are likely to be the result of random patterns of variation in the data (Husson et al. 2018: 220). However, with large data sets such as those typically used in MDA studies, such significance tests are likely to return extremely low thresholds. In relying on a cut-off point of ±0.35, Biber (1988: 93) applied a slightly more conservative version of the common threshold in social sciences of ±0.30. It has the advantage of excluding loadings that, whilst perhaps statistically significant, may not have any practical relevance as they account for less than 12.25% ($=0.35^2$) of the shared variance (Lee 2000: 207).

Biber's (1988) exclusion of features contributing to more than one dimension has also been criticised. On the one hand, this procedure has the advantage of making the dimension scores "experimentally independent, as each feature contributes to only one dimension" (Lee 2000: 209; see also Biber 1988: 93). However, it clearly adds a degree of arbitrariness: for instance, in Biber's (1988) model, past participle WHIZ deletions contribute to Dimension 5 scores, but not to Dimension 1 scores, even though in Biber's rotated factor solution, past participle WHIZ deletions contributed to a very similar extent to Factor 1 (0.39) and Factor 5 (0.43). Biber (1988: 85) advocated for the use of oblique rotation because linguistic dimensions can reasonably be expected to intercorrelate given that "from a theoretical perspective, all aspects of language use appear to be interrelated to at least some extent" (Biber 1988: 85 fn.). It can be argued that this conceptualisation of language also suggests that individual linguistic features may make significant contributions to more than one dimension.

Finally, in most MDA studies, dimension scores have been calculated by dichotomising the feature loadings into positive and negative ones: all features that have absolute loadings above the cut-off point (while not contributing more to another factor) contribute equally to the dimension scores, whilst all those with loadings between zero and the cut-off point are do not contribute at all. The same principle applies to negative loading features. Hence, feature contributions are therefore equal to either one, minus one, or zero. This means that all loadings above the absolute cut-off point are considered equally important, even though they may have made substantially different contributions to the original factor solution. For example, in Biber's (1988) model, the standardised frequencies of past tense verbs and present participial clauses are treated as equally important contributors to Dimension 2 scores, even though their factor loadings are quite different (0.90 vs. 0.39). This approach can be argued to grant less salient linguistic features disproportionate significance. At the same time, however, such a dichotomous approach to calculating dimension scores is not without its advantages. In non-linguistic uses of factor analysis, discarding the relative importance of features has been shown to distort results only marginally (Gorsuch 2014: 275–276). In fact, dichotomisation may increase the chances that the resulting dimension scores can be replicated with a new sample of texts as it essentially removes some of the random noise inherent to small differences between factor loadings (Gorsuch 2014: 275–276). In what follows, the advantages and disadvantages of three distinct options are compared.

As mentioned in 5.3.5, with PCA, the component feature loadings are correlation coefficients between the observed features and the components and are therefore much simpler to interpret than the factor loadings computed in factor analyses. Nonetheless, the question still arises as to how much relevant information the exact feature loadings contribute to any component, whether a cut-off point is needed and, if so, which one. In effect, three solutions to calculate dimension scores can be envisaged. The first solution, the 'exact scoring method', simply consists in using the loadings as they are. In other words, on any one component, the standardised normalised feature frequencies of any one text are multiplied by their respective loadings on this component and these values are added to compute dimension scores. The second consists in applying a cut-off point to exclude low-loading features whilst retaining the other loadings as multiplying factors to calculate the dimension scores. Finally, the third solution is the one typically adopted in MDA studies: as explained above, it consists in dichotomising loadings according to a cut-off point. With a cut-off point of ±0.30, this would mean that to calculate dimension scores only the unweighted standardised normalised features with loadings of ≥ 0.30 or ≤ 0.30 are added (they are in effect multiplied by one, whilst those with loadings between 0.30 and 0.30 are multiplied by zero).

If the aim of an MDA is to produce a model of linguistic variation that is generalisable beyond the sample under study, as was presumably the case with Biber (1988), then solution three may indeed be the wisest. However, the potential issues it causes downstream should not be downplayed. For a start, the resulting dimension scores no longer correlate perfectly with the factors/components they purport to quantify. This is why Lee (2000: 211) argues that they should really be referred to as "estimates" rather than "scores" (see also Child 1990). Moreover, the reported R^2 values are no longer true. Hence, whilst Biber's (1988) Factor 1 accounts for 26.8% of the shared variance (Biber 1988: 82–83), this is not true of Dimension 1 that explains considerably less due to the loss of information caused by the dropping of low-loading features, the use of dichotomous loading weights (1 or 0) for the remaining features, and the exclusion of features with a higher loading on a different factor. On the other hand, the figure of 26.8% may represent an overfitted model.

Having considered the pros and cons, the present study adopts the first solution: the exact scoring method (as did Bohmann 2019: 91). This method allows linguistic features to contribute to more than one dimension. Whilst this may somewhat complicate the interpretability of the resulting dimension scores, it is in line with our understanding of communicative processes in which linguistic features are expected to intercorrelate in a multitude of ways. The chosen solution bears the advantage of not relying on an arbitrary cut-off point, maintains the true correlations of features to dimensions, and thus does not distort the PCA solution.

Since the loadings themselves act as factors in the computation of the dimension scores, the amount of noise added by low-loading features is assumed to be negligible (see also 5.3.10 for information on how the robustness of MDA models can be tested).

5.3.8 Comparison of dimension scores

To compare different registers on any one of Biber's (1988) dimensions, the mean dimension scores of all the texts of a register are usually compared to each other. Such comparisons have typically been quantified and tested for statistical significance using linear regression models (most often with just one predictor in the form of one-way ANOVAs) and their associated coefficients of determination (e.g., Berber Sardinha & Veirano Pinto 2019: 6; Biber 1988: 95; Kruger & van Rooy 2018: 244; Bohmann 2019: 188–190, 2021). The use of predictive Discriminant Function Analysis (DFA) as a post-hoc analysis method has also been proposed to verify the robustness of dimensions as predictors of register (e.g., Crossley, Allen & McNamara 2014; Crossley, Kyle & Römer 2019; Veirano Pinto 2019). However, a crucial assumption of such tests and models is that the data points be independent of each other (Gries 2015; Winter 2019: Chapter 14–15; on the consequences of using DFA on non-independent data, see Mundry & Sommer 2007). In the context of the present MDAs, and, indeed, in many, if not most, corpus linguistic studies, however, this assumption is not met. For example, in the case of the TEC, each textbook series (see 4.3.1.1) has largely been written by the same group of authors, following the same publisher guidelines. They are thus not independent. Similarly, the Youth Fiction and the Info Teens corpora consist of several samples from any one book or web domain (see 4.3.2.4–4.3.2.5) which means that not all of these texts can be said to be independent data points.

To account for variation inherent to the non-independence of some of the texts, linear mixed-effects models were computed for each dimension of the models presented in Chapters 6 and 7. In these models, the dimension scores are the outcome variable. In Chapter 6, which reports on intra-textbook variation, the models include 'by-series' random intercepts to account for the non-independence of texts coming from the same textbook series of the TEC. Register and textbook proficiency level are modelled as fixed-effect predictors. In addition, a two-way interaction term between these two variables is also fitted, since we can reasonably hypothesise that, as the proficiency of learners increases, the dimension scores of textbook texts within a register may move closer to their target language equivalents. For instance, fictional texts from upper-intermediate textbooks may be more like teenage or young adult fiction than a short story printed in a beginners' textbook. If this were true, we would expect dimension scores for some registers to increase as learners are expected to become more proficient, whilst they may decrease for other registers. Thus, on Biber's (1988) first dimension, advanced textbook dialogues may score higher than beginner ones, thereby more resembling naturally occurring conversation, whereas we may hypothesise that informative texts in advanced textbooks are likely to score lower on Dimension 1 than those targeted at beginner or intermediate learners.

For the comparative MDA of Textbook English vs. 'real-world' English (Chapter 7), a different random-effect variable was necessary as these comparisons involve not only the dimension scores of texts from the TEC, but also those from the three reference corpora (see 4.3.2). In these models, the random effect structure therefore involves varying 'by source' intercepts, where 'source' is a metadata categorical variable with nine levels corresponding to the series for the TEC, 300 book levels for the Youth Fiction corpus, 14 web domain levels for the Teens Info corpus, and one level for the Spoken BNC2014.[25] These levels have been chosen as the best-available proxies to capture the variation inherent to each (group of) author(s)/editor(s)/speaker(s). The fixed-effect variables entered in the models of Chapter 7 are Corpus type (Textbook vs. Target Language Reference) and Register (Conversation, Fiction, and Informative texts), as well as their two-way interactions.

All mixed-effects models were computed using the R package *lme4* (Bates et al. 2015). Details of the model selection procedure can be found in Le Foll (2022c: 215–17). The reported $R^2_{marginal}$-values summarise the predictive power of the fixed effects only, whilst $R^2_{conditional}$-values summarise those of both the fixed and random effects. The latter were computed using the R package *sjPlot* (Lüdecke 2020) on the basis of the procedure outlined in Nakagawa et al. (2017). The estimators of relative contrast effects between each category of interest were calculated using the default parameters of the *emmeans* package (Lenth 2020). Degrees-of-freedom (df) were computed using the Kenward-Roger method (Luke 2017). *P*-value adjustment followed the Tukey method (Rasch et al. 2014: 29–30) and the confidence level reported is 0.95.

Model diagnostic plots were inspected to check the assumptions of linearity, homogeneity of variance, and the normal distribution of residuals of the model. In addition, observed and estimated values were plotted for additional visual checks of the final model fits. Note that, for reasons of space, the results of the

25. This is motivated by the fact that, for the Spoken BNC2014, the unit of analysis is the conversation and that each conversation represents one text. However, this obscures the fact that some speakers contributed to several conversation recordings. Whilst most speakers do indeed only feature in one or at most two recordings (58%), it is worth bearing in mind that some speakers contributed considerably more recordings to the corpus (in one case: 78, accounting for 2.2% of all utterances or 2.4% of all tokens).

model comparisons and the diagnostic plots are not reported here, but they can be consulted and reproduced using the data and code provided in the Online Supplements on https://elenlefoll.github.io/TextbookMDA/.

5.3.9 Visualisation of the results

The results of MDAs are typically visualised by plotting the mean dimension score of (sub-)registers on a vertical line representing a dimension cline with the most negative-scoring text categories placed at the bottom of the line and the highest-scoring ones at the top. This is how Biber first visualised the results in his seminal 1988 MDA study (see Figure 3 for a reproduction of such a plot). Such plots provide effective and readily interpretable visual summaries of mean dimension scores. However, as these plots only visualise mean values, they conceal intra-category variability.[26] In other words, they give no indication of the range of dimension scores covered by a single category or the distribution of scores within a category. Whilst most MDA studies do report standard deviations alongside mean dimension score, this is usually only in tabular form, which makes it is very difficult to grasp how much overlap there is between different categories. For example, Gardner et al. (2019) present the results of an MDA study on learner academic writing with plots such as Figure 7. An improvement on the standard plot of dimension means used in MDA is that, in Figure 7, the number of texts that constitutes each category is printed in brackets; however, the plot nonetheless provides no indication of the distribution shape of dimension scores in each category. Furthermore, it is impossible to gauge whether any of the observed differences between the categories are likely to be statistically significant.

Given "the centrality of text in corpus-linguistic inquiries" (Biber 2021: n.p.) and the fact that the MDA framework applies a text-linguistic research design (Biber et al. 2016: 357), the plots represented in Chapters 6 and 7 display the position of each text, rather than only the mean dimension score of a text category. Moreover, as part of the qualitative analysis of the results, the positions of texts were plotted along several potentially relevant dimensions. This was achieved with facetted bidimensional plots (e.g., Figure 10) and interactive 3-D plots (Figure 9). This visualisation approach echoes Neumann and Evert's (2021) geometric multivariate analysis (GMA) which was, in turn, inspired by Biber's MDA framework. Linguistic differences between texts are analysed by examining the Euclidean distances between texts in this multi-dimensional feature space (for a similar approach using MCA, see Clarke 2020: Section 4.7.1).

---

26. Some studies (e.g., Lee 2000) have visualised the results of MDA using barplots of mean dimension scores, which is arguably even more misleading.

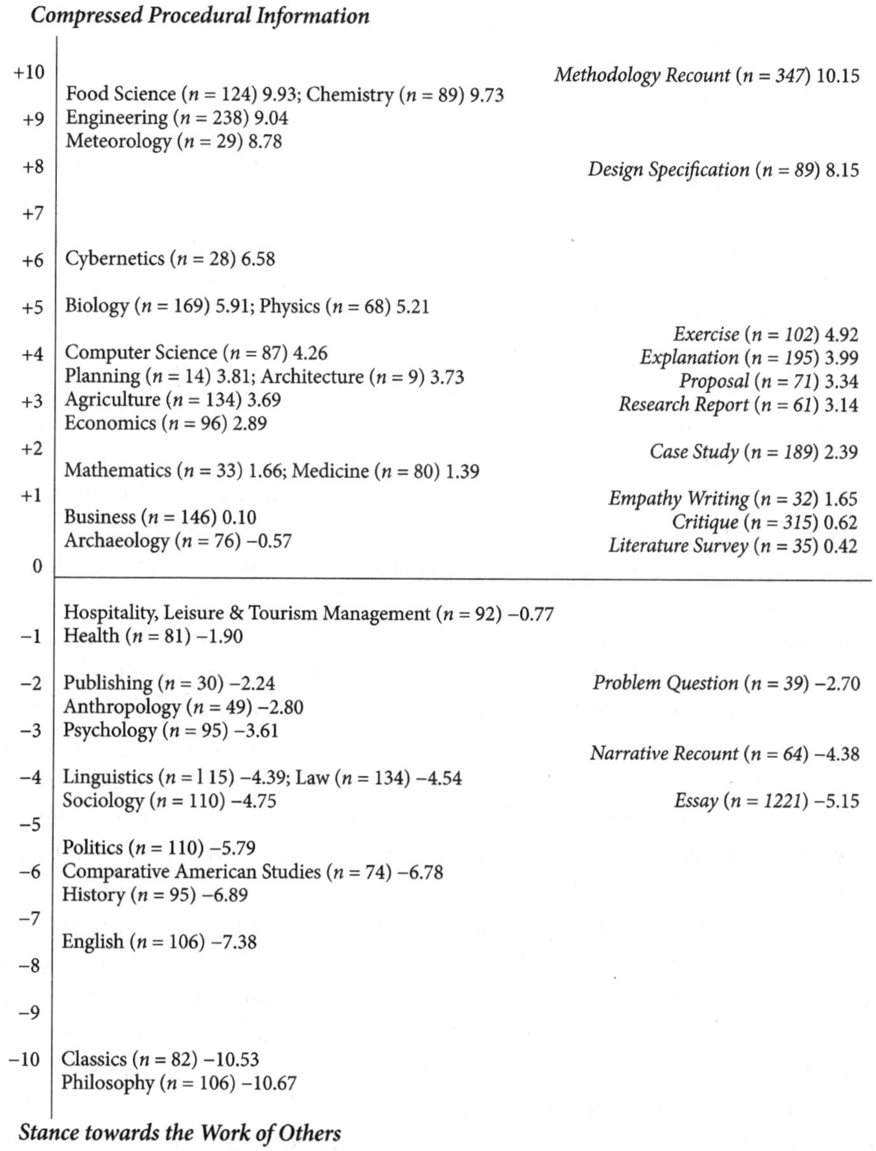

Compressed Procedural Information

+10 | *Methodology Recount* (n = 347) 10.15
Food Science (n = 124) 9.93; Chemistry (n = 89) 9.73
+9 | Engineering (n = 238) 9.04
Meteorology (n = 29) 8.78
+8 | *Design Specification* (n = 89) 8.15
+7
+6 | Cybernetics (n = 28) 6.58
+5 | Biology (n = 169) 5.91; Physics (n = 68) 5.21
Exercise (n = 102) 4.92
+4 | Computer Science (n = 87) 4.26 | *Explanation* (n = 195) 3.99
Planning (n = 14) 3.81; Architecture (n = 9) 3.73 | *Proposal* (n = 71) 3.34
+3 | Agriculture (n = 134) 3.69 | *Research Report* (n = 61) 3.14
Economics (n = 96) 2.89
+2 | *Case Study* (n = 189) 2.39
Mathematics (n = 33) 1.66; Medicine (n = 80) 1.39
+1 | *Empathy Writing* (n = 32) 1.65
Business (n = 146) 0.10 | *Critique* (n = 315) 0.62
Archaeology (n = 76) −0.57 | *Literature Survey* (n = 35) 0.42
0

Hospitality, Leisure & Tourism Management (n = 92) −0.77
−1 | Health (n = 81) −1.90
−2 | Publishing (n = 30) −2.24 | *Problem Question* (n = 39) −2.70
Anthropology (n = 49) −2.80
−3 | Psychology (n = 95) −3.61
Narrative Recount (n = 64) −4.38
−4 | Linguistics (n = 1 15) −4.39; Law (n = 134) −4.54
Sociology (n = 110) −4.75 | *Essay* (n = 1221) −5.15
−5
Politics (n = 110) −5.79
−6 | Comparative American Studies (n = 74) −6.78
History (n = 95) −6.89
−7
English (n = 106) −7.38
−8
−9
−10 | Classics (n = 82) −10.53
Philosophy (n = 106) −10.67

Stance towards the Work of Others

Figure 7. Dimension 1 mean scores for disciplines (left) and genre families (right) from Gardner et al. (2019: 655)

In addition, graphs of features (e.g., Figure 12) are used to visualise the linguistic features that contribute most to the position of texts on two-dimensional plots (more on how to interpret these in 6.2). These graphs illustrate the extent to which some (clusters of) features make salient contributions to more than one dimension. The exact loadings across all dimensions are printed in Tables 17 and 20. As these tables contain all the features entered in the MDAs, cell shading and font colours are used to highlight the most important contributions.

5.3.10 Reproducibility and replicability of the results

In line with the commitment to Open Science formulated in 4.2.2, the methodology employed in this study aims to be as reproducible as possible. The goal is to provide sufficient transparency for others to verify the results presented in the subsequent chapters, compare them to results obtained using different parameters and/or alternative methods, and encourage the replication of the findings on new data. Achieving this level of reproducibility is, however, particularly challenging given the complexity of MDA. In fact, replicability has been acknowledged as "something of a concern for the MD [multi-dimensional analysis] framework" (McEnery & Hardie 2011: 112; see also Le Foll 2023c; Le Foll & Brezina 2023). Many aspects must be considered. The most important ones are briefly discussed below.

First, to ensure the reproducibility of MDA, the source code of the computer programme(s) used to identify and count the linguistic features entered in an MDA must be accessible to other researchers. In many respects, Biber's (1988) Appendix II, which details the operationalisations of the algorithms used to identify the 67 features entered in his model, is a remarkable example of Open Science *avant la lettre*. That said, whilst the appendix explains the regular expressions used to count the features, their actual output largely depends on the POS-tagger used for the underlying layer of linguistic annotation. In a preliminary study (Le Foll 2021c), I relied on the MAT (Nini 2014, 2019) which, as an integrated tool, ensures greater reproducibility of the tagging and counting procedure. Its user-friendly GUI also means that studies relying on the MAT are more likely to be replicated by a range of researchers. However, whilst the source code of the MAT is available under a GNU General Public licence, its underlying algorithms are not directly accessible and cannot readily be adapted to specific use-cases. By contrast, the Multi-Feature Tagger of English (MFTE; Le Foll 2021d) used in the analyses of the present study (see 5.3.2–5.3.4) consists of a single Perl script whose regular expressions can readily be modified. It has been released under a GNU General Public licence and can therefore be scrutinised by the wider research community.[27]

27. To conduct new analyses, however, I recommend using the latest version of the MFTE Python, which is much easier to use and can tag many more features. All future developments of the MFTE will be made on the MFTE Python, which is also available as an open-source tool, see ⟨https://github.com/mshakirDr/MFTE⟩.

Second, when it is not possible to publish both the corpus data and the tagger used for the feature counts, it is essential that the matrix of frequencies entered in an MDA be included as supplementary data. For copyright reasons, the corpora used in the present study cannot be released publicly. However, the full tabular results of counts as output by the MFTE are included in the Online Supplements. They can be used to conduct new analyses on the data, e.g., to compare the results of the present MDAs to those produced by alternative multivariable analyses methods.

Third, as elucidated in this chapter, the MDA framework requires researchers to make numerous decisions regarding various parameters. As we have seen, these are often subjective and may even appear arbitrary. Consequently, it is imperative that each parameter choice be transparent so that the robustness of the results can be independently verified. However, due to limitations in word counts, methods sections in MDA studies are rarely detailed enough to cover all aspects of the methodology and very few include code as supplementary materials. This is clearly another barrier to the replicability of MDA (and, indeed, of many other quantitative linguistic methods, as this issue is pervasive in current linguistics research, see Bochynska et al. 2023). In alignment with the principles of Open Science, the Online Supplements to this study include all the code used to conduct the PCAs, the statistical tests, and models, as well as to produce all the plots and figures included in this publication.

Beyond replication, for the results of an MDA to be robust and generalisable, it is important that they also be replicable. There is currently no established procedure to test the replicability of MDAs (on replication and factor analysis more generally, see Costello & Osborne 2005; Osborne & Fitzpatrick 2005). One option is check whether approximately the same models are produced when the analysis is run multiple times across different configurations or sub-groups of the data (Biber 1990; Lee 2000: 393). In the present study, the robustness of the models presented in Chapters 6 and 7 was tested by comparing them to models conducted on multiple random subsets of two-thirds of the data. The results of these tests are summarised in 10.1.1. The code provided in the Online Supplements can be used to run additional tests on different subsamples.

CHAPTER 6

A model of intra-textbook linguistic variation

This chapter applies the modified MDA framework outlined in Chapter 5.3 to explore register variation *within* secondary school EFL textbooks along four dimensions of variation. In the following chapter, a second, PCA-based MDA is conducted to compare three key registers of Textbook English with comparable 'real-world' English registers, as used outside the EFL classroom.

6.1 A multi-feature/multi-dimensional model of Textbook English

The texts of the Textbook English Corpus (TEC) that were entered in this analysis (see 5.3.1) were all tagged with the Perl version of the MFTE (see 5.3.2–5.3.3). Of the tagger's three outputs, the 'mixed normalisation' table was used as the basis for all the PCAs conducted in the present study. Applying the feature exclusion procedure described in 5.3.6, the counts for the BE *(un)able to* construction (ABLE) were merged with the category of predicative adjectives (JJPR), whilst the counts for passive GET constructions (PGET) were added to the BE passive counts to create a more general passive category (PASS) as the two finer-grained passive categories were absent from more than two-thirds of texts. Other features which were also only observed in a third or fewer of TEC texts but could not be meaningfully subsumed with any other features were excluded from this intra-textbook MDA. These are: CONC, DWNT, ELAB, EMO, GTO, HGOT, HST, MDMM, PRP, QUTAG and URL (see Appendix C for the full table of features). The iterative process to arrive at individual feature MSA values of > 0.5 (as described in 5.3.6) led to the exclusion of one additional feature: MDWO. Finally, four features were removed due to low final communalities: STPR, MDNE, HDG and CAUSE. In addition, sixteen outlier texts were removed on the basis of some extremely high normalised feature counts (see code in Appendix E for details of the procedure; ⟨elenlefoll.github.io/TextbookMDA/AppendixE⟩).

The following intra-textbook PCA is therefore based on a matrix of 1,961 texts by 61 features, all *z*- and signed log-transformed (see 5.3.6), with a satisfactorily high overall KMO factor adequacy index of 0.88, or "meritorious" according to Kaiser and Rice (1974: 112). To determine the number of components to be considered in the analysis, a scree plot was first generated, see Figure 8. It shows the amount of variation each component captures from the TEC data. The "elbow" method (Jolliffe 2002: 115–118) is difficult to apply here because the plot can be said to feature several "breaking points". Following Biber's (1988: 84) advice to extract more rather than fewer components to start off with, the first six components were originally retained for further analysis. Together, these account for 50.88% of the total variance.[28]

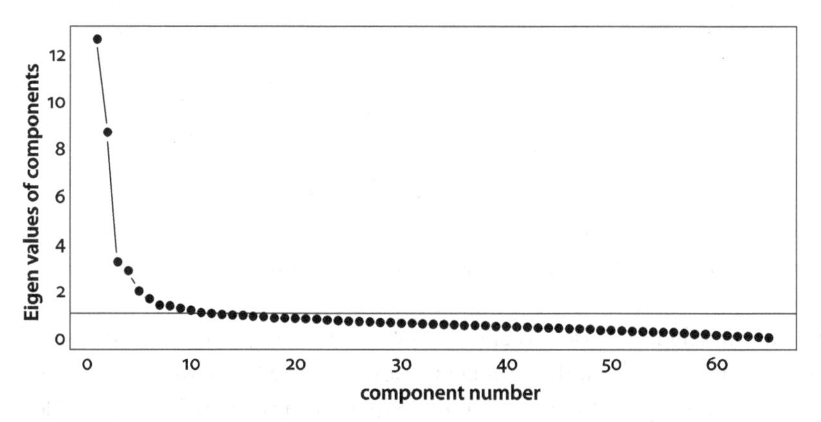

Figure 8. Scree plot of the eigenvalues of the principal components (PCs) for the TEC data

The distribution of the texts on the first three components was first explored interactively in a 3-D visualisation (see snapshots in Figure 9 and Appendix F; ⟨elenlefoll.github.io/TextbookMDA/AppendixF⟩. Here, and in all subsequent scatterplots, every data point represents a single text from the TEC. The closer points are, the more linguistic similarities they share. At first sight, the most striking aspect of the 3-D visualisation is that there are two clearly separated clusters of texts: one consisting of instructional language (in yellow) and the other of the remaining textbook registers. Within this second, much larger cluster of texts, we find that conversation is concentrated at one end (in red) and informative texts (blue) at the other, with fiction (green) and personal correspondence (purple) interspaced in between. The 3-D visualisation makes clear that all three components contribute to distinguishing register-based intra-textbook variation.

By contrast, the remaining three dimensions (PC4, PC5 and PC6) do not appear to distinguish between different textbook registers. This is illustrated in the biplot matrix of all combinations of the six retained dimensions in Figure 10. The

28. For reference, Biber's (1988) EFA solution of seven factors accounted for 51.9% of the shared variance (Biber 1988: 83).

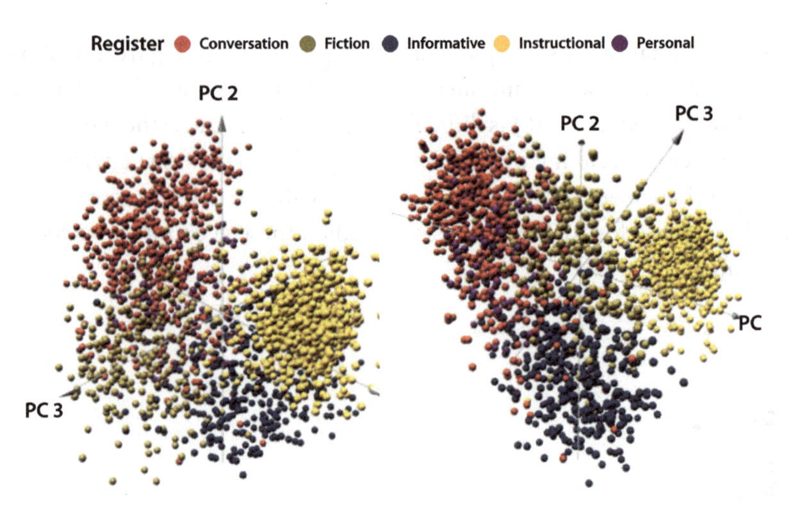

Figure 9. Snapshots from the 3-D visualisation of the first three dimensions of the multi-dimensional model of intra-textbook variation

same colour scheme is used to encode the different registers as in the 3-D visualisations and, in addition, the proficiency levels of the textbooks from which each text stems are represented by different shapes: beginner textbook texts (level A) are assigned the circle shape, while the texts from the most advanced textbooks in the TEC (level E) are represented by diamonds (see Appendix F for zoomable version of Figure 10).

Figure 11 is a more fine-grained projection of the texts of the TEC on the first two dimensions which, together, account for the greatest linguistic differences between the different registers of the TEC. The ellipses represent the 95% confidence intervals around each of the five textbook register centroids. As already observed in the 3-D plot, two clusters of texts are evident: to the right of the plot, instructional texts form a tight cluster whose ellipse does not overlap with any of the other four textbook registers. Thus, we can conclude that instructional language has a very characteristic linguistic profile which clearly sets this register apart. The linguistic features that contribute most to this very specific profile can be seen in the top right panel of Figure 12 (see also Table 17), in the area of the plot that corresponds to the area where the cluster of instructional texts can be found in Figure 12. They are, as illustrated in (16), imperatives (VIMP), verbs of communication (COMM), and verbs depicting mental processes (MENTAL).

(16) **Look** at the other groups' guides and **choose** which channel you would like to watch. **Use** the key phrases for making and **justifying** a choice. **Work** in pairs. **Answer** the questions. <TEC: Solutions pre-intermediate>

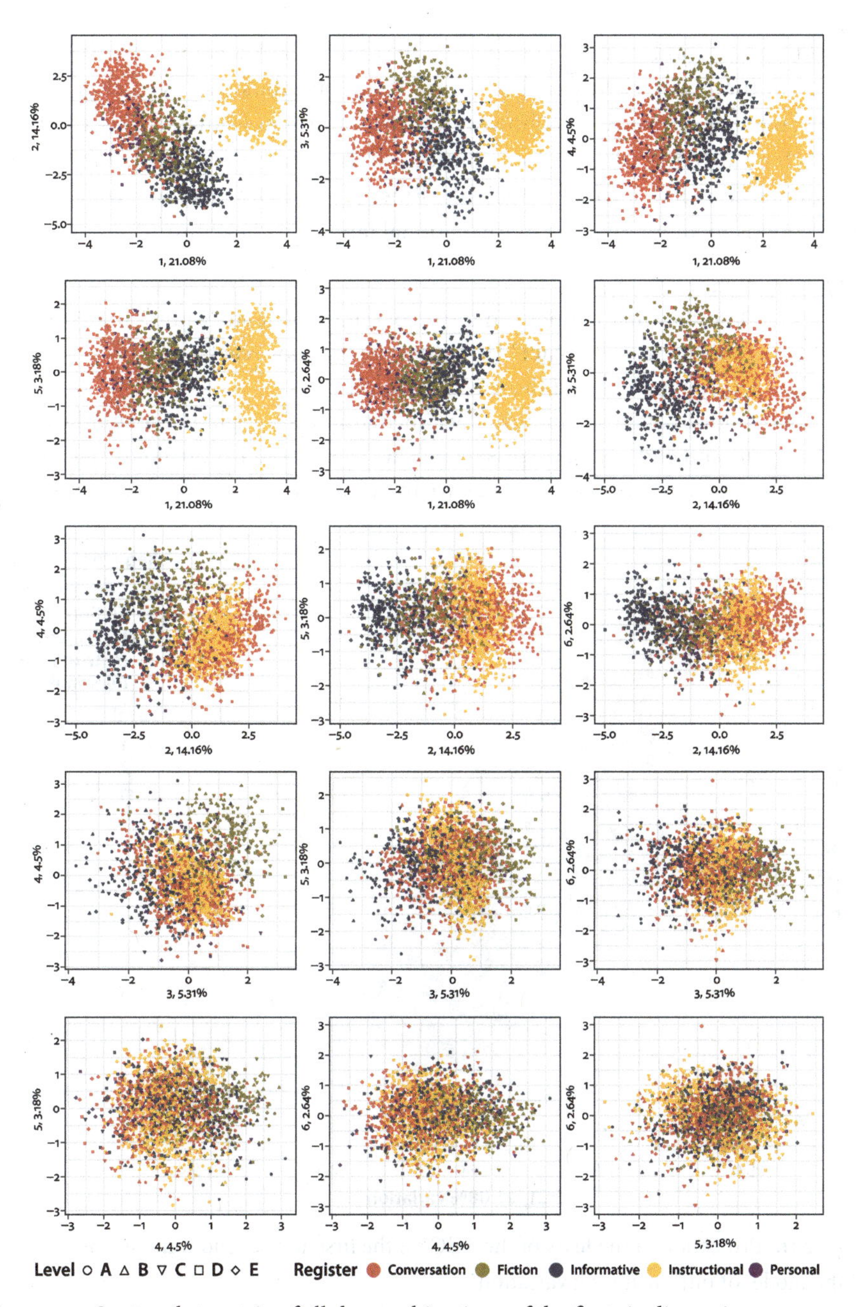

Figure 10. Scatterplot matrix of all the combinations of the first six dimensions of the model of intra-textbook variation (the number before the comma on each axis label shows which principal component is plotted on that axis; this is followed by the percentage of the total variance explained by that particular component)

In addition, second person referents (SPP2) and WH-questions (WHQU) also feature in the upper-right panel of Figure 12 and are thus very typical of instructional language, too, e.g., (17); however, these features are situated closer to the *y*-axis as they also make strong contributions to the positive end of the model's second dimension (PC2), which, much like Biber's (1988) Dimension 1 (see Figure 3), corresponds to an involved vs. informational language continuum.

(17) Reactions

a. Describe **what happens** in the second half of the story (after line 43). How **do** the customers **react**? How **does** the narrator **react**?

b. **Do** you **understand** the way they **react**?

Short stories often **start** unusually ("medias in res" – right in the middle of the action) **and end** with a surprise. Look at "Deportation at breakfast" again: find these elements **and** say **why** they **are** important here. <TEC: Green Line 5>

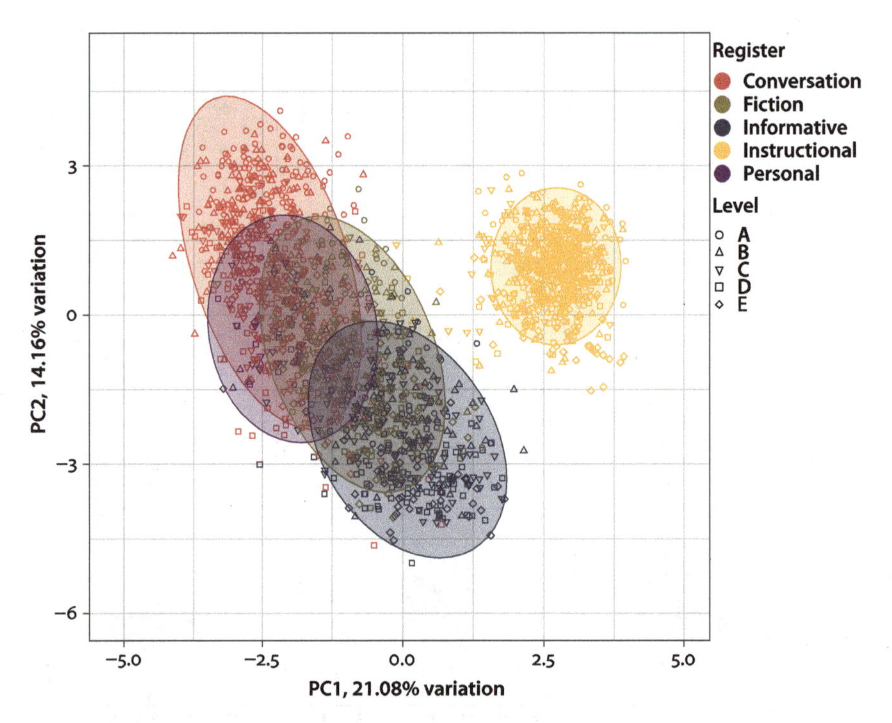

Figure 11. Projection of the texts of the TEC on the first and second dimensions of the model of intra-textbook variation

The second, larger cluster in Figure 11 reveals a clear register cline with textbook texts depicting conversations towards the top-left end of the cluster, fiction, and personal correspondence in the middle, whilst informative texts are concentrated at the bottom-right end of the cluster. The features that contribute most to

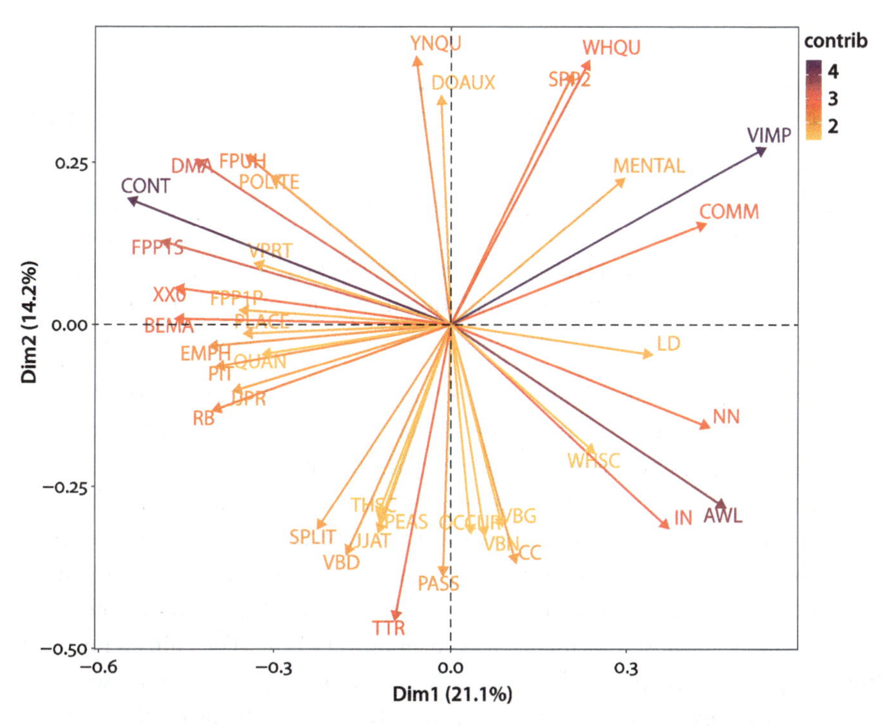

Figure 12. Graph of the features with the strongest contributions to the first and second dimensions of the model of intra-textbook variation (see also Table 17)

this distribution of registers can be seen in the graph of features in Figure 12. The advantage of this kind of biplot is that we can see that the features that are on or very close to one of the two axes contribute principally to just one of these first two dimensions, whilst those that draw diagonals contribute to both dimensions. Thus, Figure 12 shows that the upper end of the large, "non-instructional textbook English" cluster is characterised by high frequencies of fillers and interjections (FPUH), markers of politeness (POLITE), discourse markers (DMA), verbal contractions (CONT) and present tense verbs (VPRT), e.g., (18). By contrast, the lower end of the cluster features texts with longer words (AWL), high frequencies of nouns (NN), prepositions (IN) and subordinate WH-clauses (WHSC), e.g., (19). These two extremes echo the features with the highest estimated factor loadings on the two ends of Biber's (1988) 'Involved vs. Informational Production' dimension (see Table 10).

(18) Can I help **you?**
Yes, have you got the new 'Pets' magazine, **please**? I can'**t** find it.
It's there – next to the sports magazines.
Excuse me. Where can I try on this sweatshirt?

There, on the left.
Thanks. I **like** the colour, but the size **isn't** right.
No problem. We'**ve** got other sizes, too. <TEC: Green Line 1>

(19) The **Aboriginal Memorial** is an **installation of** 200 hollow **log coffins from Central Arnhem Land. Artists** made it to commemorate all the indigenous **people** who, since 1788, have lost their **lives** defending their **land. Visitors** can see it **in** the **National Gallery of Australia.** The **artists** said the **museum authorities** must locate this **installation in** a public **place** where they could preserve it **for** future **generations.** <TEC: New Missions 2[de]>

The large cluster's slanted shape in Figure 11 indicates that both the first (PC1) and second (PC2) dimension of this multi-dimensional model of intra-textbook variation capture important aspects of register-based variation. The biplot of the first two dimensions, Figure 11, clearly shows that many linguistic features (foremost those plotted in Figure 12) are distributed quite differently across at least three out of the five textbook registers under study: this is illustrated in Figure 11 by the fact that instructional language forms its own very distinct cluster, and the ellipses of the conversational and informative texts overlap very little. The ellipses for the fiction and personal correspondence texts, however, overlap much more, suggesting that these two textbook registers are not readily distinguishable on these first two dimensions. This brings us to the third and fourth dimensions.

Figure 13 displays the positions of the texts of the TEC on the third (PC3) and fourth dimensions (PC4). The intersection of these two dimensions highlights a distinctive linguistic profile for at least some of the fiction texts of the TEC. Indeed, part of the green ellipse is set apart from the rest of the texts. The features that contribute most to this characteristic linguistic profile can be found in the top right panel of corresponding graph of features in Figure 14. Just like on the narrative end of Biber's Dimension 2, the frequency of past tense verbs (VBD) and third-person referents (TPP3S) make the largest contributions to this characteristically 'narrative' cluster.

A closer look at the shapes of the points in this non-overlapping portion of the textbook fiction ellipse in the top-right panel of Figure 13 reveals that it is foremost composed of narrative texts from intermediate to advanced textbooks (levels C to E). To explore this further, Figure 15 displays the texts of the TEC on the same two dimensions as in Figure 13, but this time the colour scheme and the ellipses correspond to the proficiency levels of the textbooks from which the texts have been extracted, rather than the register of each text (which is, instead, coded by the shapes of the points). A comparison of the two biplots (Figure 13 and Figure 15) shows that, whilst register-based variation is greater, textbook proficiency level also makes some notable contributions to linguistic variation in Textbook English,

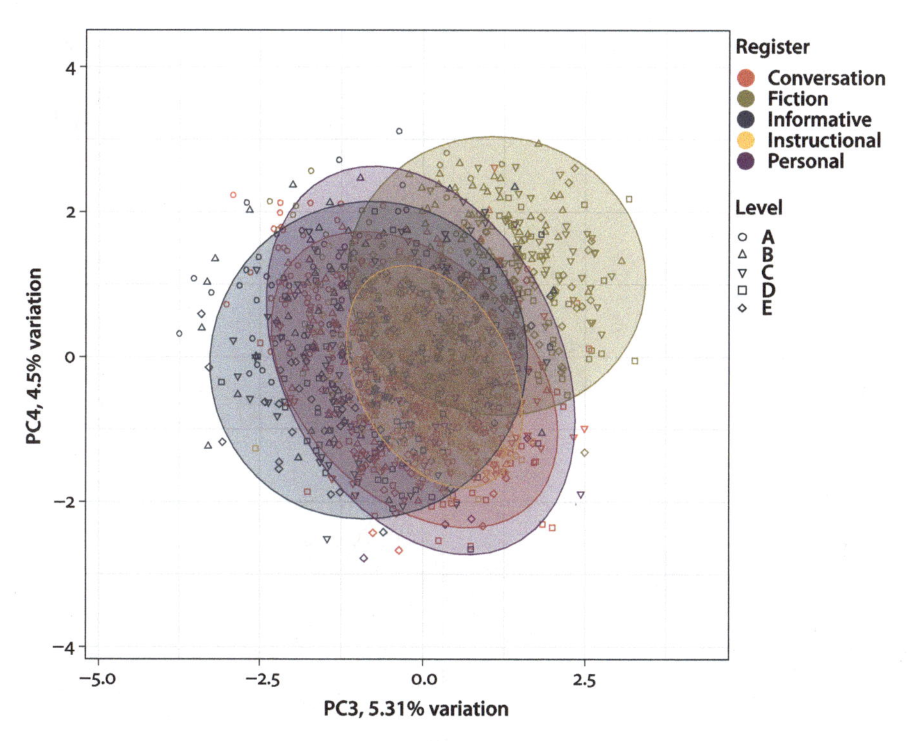

Figure 13. Projection of the texts of the TEC on the third and fourth dimensions of the model of intra-textbook variation

as evident on the third and fourth dimensions. These different factors contributing to linguistic variation in the TEC will be tested in more in-depth analyses of the first four dimensions in 6.2 to 6.5. The fifth and sixth dimensions (PC5 and PC6) will not be examined any further as they account for comparatively little of the total variance (PC5 = 3.18% and PC6 = 2.64%). Both the visualisations and the mixed-effects models conducted to explore these dimensions (see Appendix F) indicate that they contribute very little to differentiating between different text registers, proficiency levels, or textbook series.

In the following, the first four dimensions of this model of intra-textbook variation are functionally interpreted and examined in detail. Table 17 displays the full list of features and their loadings on these four dimensions. As explained in 5.3.7, in the present framework and unlike in a standard MDA (Biber 1988: 93), every linguistic feature entered in the analysis loads onto each dimension, as opposed to only on the dimension to which they contribute most. As a result, in this model, all 61 linguistic features contribute – to a greater or lesser (sometimes extremely minimal!) extent – to each dimension. Table 17 displays the feature loadings which shows the degree to which each feature correlates with each

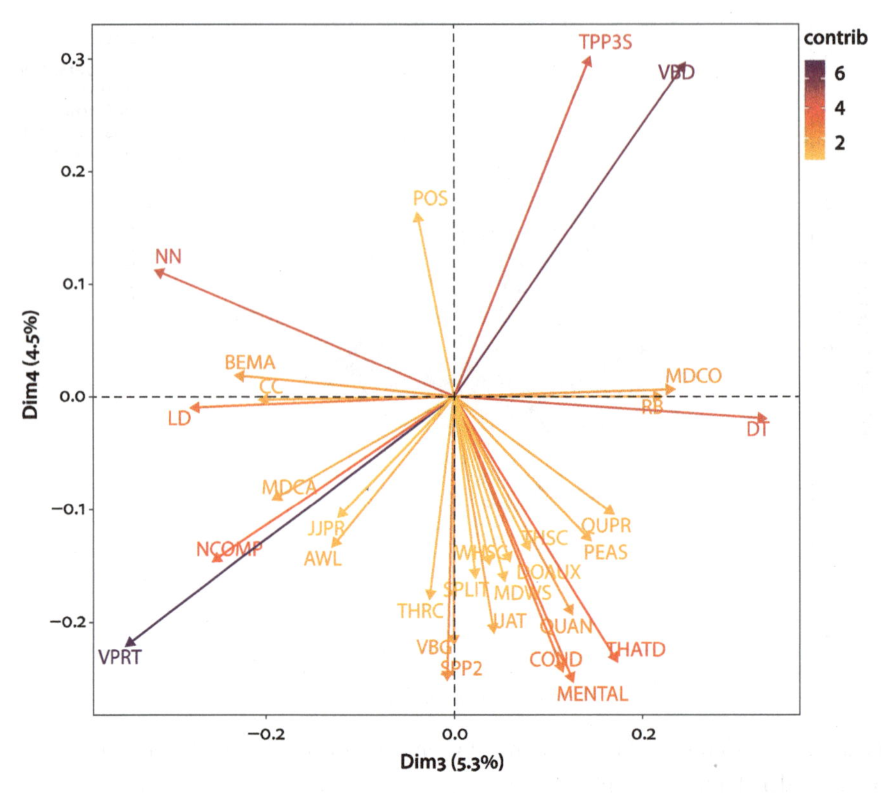

Figure 14. Graph of the features with the strongest contributions to the third and fourth dimensions of the model of intra-textbook variation

component. Positive values (in shades of yellow) contribute to high component scores, whilst negative ones (in shades of purple) contribute to low scores. These normalised weight values correspond to factor loadings in EFA: hence, to calculate a text's position along the first dimension (PC1), all the log *z*-scores of the 61 features of the text are multiplied by their corresponding PC1 loadings. Thus, if a text has a high average word length (AWL), its high (and positive) log *z*-score for AWL will be multiplied by 0.22, which will contribute to placing this text high on the PC1 dimension. Should this text also feature no or very few verbal contractions verbs (CONT), its low (and negative) log *z*-score for contractions will be multiplied by 0.25, thus contributing to an even higher overall PC1 score. By contrast, a text consisting of mostly short words and featuring many contractions will likely score low on PC1. Very low absolute loadings are printed in light grey to indicate that these feature contributions most likely only represent noise and are therefore not considered in the interpretation of these dimensions of linguistic variation. However, they are not entirely removed from the table as a reminder that no cut-off point was applied in the calculation of the component scores.

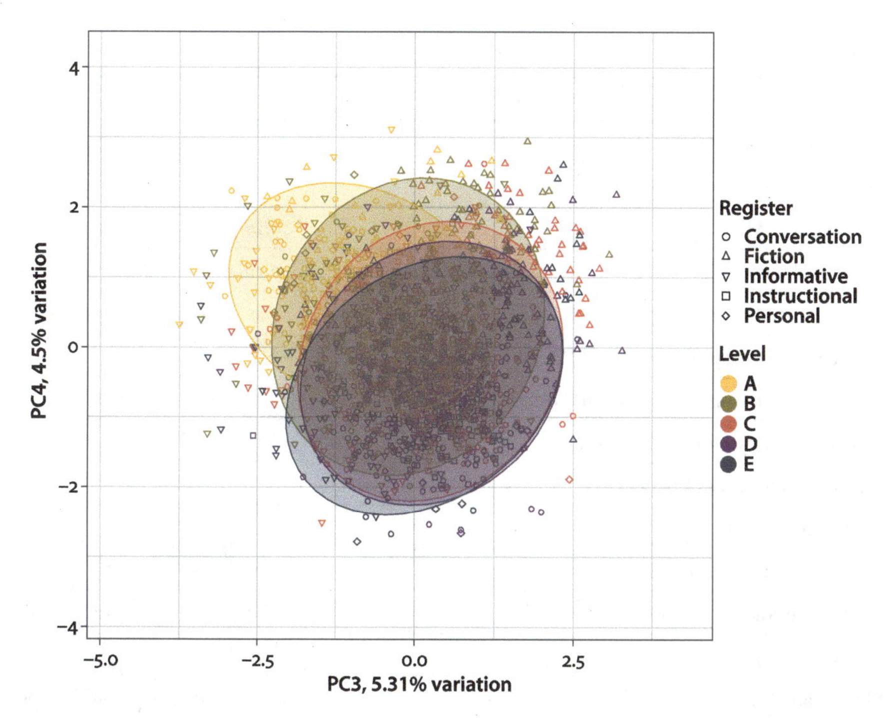

Figure 15. Projection of the texts of the TEC on the third and fourth dimensions with colours and ellipses indicating the proficiency level of the textbooks (as opposed to register as in Figure 13)

Table 17. Features entered in the intra-textbook MDA and their loadings on the four dimensions of interest

	PC1	PC2	PC3	PC4
Activity verbs (ACT)	0.08	−0.11	0.04	−0.10
Amplifiers (AMP)	−0.12	−0.10	−0.11	0.01
Aspectual verbs (ASPECT)	0.10	−0.05	0.14	−0.01
Average word length (AWL)	0.22	−0.16	−0.12	−0.13
BE as a main verb (BEMA)	−0.22	0.01	−0.22	0.02
Coordinating conjunctions (CC)	0.05	−0.21	−0.19	0.00
Communication verbs (COMM)	0.20	0.09	0.14	−0.04
Conditional conjunctions (COND)	−0.01	−0.02	0.11	−0.25
Verbal contractions (CONT)	−0.25	0.11	−0.03	−0.06
Causal conjunctions (CUZ)	−0.09	−0.13	−0.06	−0.02
Demonstratives (DEMO)	−0.12	0.08	0.03	−0.09
Discourse markers (DMA)	−0.20	0.14	−0.02	0.00

Table 17. *(continued)*

	PC1	PC2	PC3	PC4
DO as an auxiliary (DOAUX)	−0.01	0.20	0.06	−0.15
Determiners (DT)	0.12	0.00	0.31	−0.02
Emphatics (EMPH)	−0.19	−0.02	0.06	−0.14
Existential there (EX)	−0.10	−0.05	−0.12	0.05
Existential and relationship verbs (EXIST)	−0.02	−0.15	−0.09	−0.09
References of the speaker/writer (FPP1P)	−0.17	0.01	−0.07	0.00
References to the speaker/writer and others (FPP1S)	−0.23	0.07	0.08	−0.01
Fillers and interjections (FPUH)	−0.16	0.15	−0.09	0.07
Frequency references (FREQ)	−0.03	−0.05	0.01	−0.10
Prepositions (IN)	0.17	−0.18	0.02	−0.08
Attributive adjectives (JJAT)	−0.06	−0.18	0.04	−0.21
Predicative adjectives (JJPR)	−0.17	−0.06	−0.12	−0.11
Lexical density (LD)	0.16	−0.03	−0.26	−0.01
Modal can (MDCA)	−0.04	0.10	−0.18	−0.09
Modal could (MDCO)	−0.05	−0.10	0.22	0.01
Modals will and shall (MDWS)	−0.07	−0.01	0.05	−0.17
Mental verbs (MENTAL)	0.14	0.13	0.12	−0.25
Noun compounds (NCOMP)	0.04	−0.05	−0.23	−0.15
Nouns (NN)	0.20	−0.09	−0.29	0.11
Occurrence verbs (OCCUR)	0.02	−0.18	0.03	0.02
BE and GET passives (PASS)	−0.01	−0.22	−0.06	−0.06
Perfect aspect (PEAS)	−0.06	−0.17	0.13	−0.13
it pronoun references (PIT)	−0.19	−0.04	−0.06	−0.06
Place references (PLACE)	−0.16	−0.01	−0.07	0.09
Politeness markers (POLITE)	−0.14	0.13	−0.07	0.02
s-genitives (POS)	−0.01	0.03	−0.04	0.16
Progressive aspect (PROG)	−0.12	−0.02	0.11	0.00
Quantifiers (QUAN)	−0.15	−0.03	0.12	−0.19
Quantifying pronouns (QUPR)	−0.10	−0.05	0.16	−0.11
General adverbs (RB)	−0.19	−0.08	0.20	0.00
Verb particles (RP)	0.00	−0.09	0.14	0.02

Table 17. *(continued)*

	PC1	PC2	PC3	PC4
Split auxiliaries (SPLIT)	−0.11	−0.18	0.02	−0.16
Second-person references (SPP2)	0.10	0.22	−0.01	−0.25
that omission (THATD)	−0.05	0.04	0.16	−0.23
that-relative clauses (THRC)	0.02	−0.11	−0.02	−0.18
that-subordinate clauses (other than relatives) (THSC)	−0.06	−0.17	0.07	−0.14
Time references (TIME)	−0.13	−0.08	−0.01	0.06
References to more than one non- interactant (TPP3P)	−0.01	−0.16	−0.09	−0.02
References to one non-interactant (TPP3S)	−0.06	−0.11	0.13	0.30
Lexical diversity (TTR)	−0.04	−0.26	−0.05	−0.01
Past tense verbs (VBD)	−0.08	−0.20	0.23	0.30
Non-finite verb -ing forms (VBG)	0.04	−0.18	0.00	−0.22
Non-finite verb -ed forms (VBN)	0.03	−0.18	−0.07	−0.04
Imperatives (VIMP)	0.25	0.15	0.04	−0.08
Present-tense verbs (VPRT)	−0.16	0.05	−0.32	−0.22
WH-questions (WHQU)	0.11	0.23	0.00	−0.09
WH-subordinate clauses (WHSC)	0.11	−0.11	0.03	−0.15
Negated verb forms (XX0)	−0.22	0.03	0.06	−0.06
yes-no questions (YNQU)	−0.03	0.23	0.00	−0.08

6.2 Dimension 1: 'Overt instructions and explanations'

As we saw in Figures 9 to 11, the first dimension to emerge from this MDA of intra-textbook variation primarily separates instructional texts and explanations from the rest of the TEC data. Given that the negative end of the dimension does not imply any specific text quality other than being the least "instructional-like", interpreting the dimension with a bipolar label would potentially be misleading (see also Bohmann 2017:326); hence only the positive end of the dimension will be labelled: 'Overt instructions and explanations.'

As explained in 5.3.8, for each dimension, linear mixed-effects models were computed to quantify the extent to which register, textbook proficiency level and the individual styles of textbook authors and publishers (as very approximately captured by the textbook series variable) contribute to each textbook texts' location on each principal component. For the first dimension, 'Overt instructions and explanations', the model featuring only Register as a fixed effect already explains 88% of the total variance in PC1 scores. Adding the nine textbook series as random, varying intercepts only very marginally increases the R^2 value to 90%, thus indicating that register is a remarkably strong predictor of PC1 scores, whereas the textbook series variable does not make a significant contribution to PC1 scores (see also plots of random effects in the Appendix F). The ANOVA-based comparison of the PC1 models showed that modelling Register*Level interactions provides a marginally better fit (as measured using AIC): three interactions are significant at the level of $p < 0.01$. As shown in Table 18, these are: Instructional register with the textbook proficiency levels C, D, and E (see 4.3.1.2).

Detailed inspection of the mean log *z*-scores of the linguistic features with high absolute loadings on PC1 (see Figure 12 and Table 17) across the five textbook proficiency levels revealed that these significant Instructional*Level interactions are due to the number of imperative verbs (VIMP) featured in instructions and explanations progressively decreasing as textbook proficiency level increases, whilst the number of present tense verbs (VPRT) increases. Two reasons explain this. First, textbook instructions become more complex as textbook authors expect learners' proficiency in English to increase. This can be observed by comparing Extract (20), which stems from a level A textbook and scores high on PC1 with Extract (21), which was taken from a level E textbook and scores much lower on this dimension. Second, secondary school beginner textbooks tend to include far fewer explanations in English, preferring to explain, e.g., grammatical concepts in the students' L1/school language. This means that the level A and B instructional texts of the TEC include fewer explanations than levels C, D and E textbooks. That said, whilst these three Instructional*Level interaction terms are significant and interpretable, the estimated differences in PC1 scores remain small and the marginal R^2 value of 89% and conditional R^2 of 90.6% of the model summarised in Table 18 make clear that, as compared to the model that only included Register as a fixed effect and which already described 88% of the variance, the impact of textbook proficiency level on PC1 scores is only very marginal.

(20) **Identify** the people on the photograph. **Look** and **describe** what you can see. **Compare** the people. **Listen** and **describe** the characters' families. **Use** the genitive. <TEC: Piece of Cake 6e>

(21) Reactions
a. Describe what **happens** in the second half of the story (after line 43). How **do** the customers react? How **does** the narrator react?
b. **Do** you understand the way they **react**?
Short stories often **start** unusually ("medias in res" – right in the middle of the action) and **end** with a surprise. Look at "Deportation at breakfast" again: find these elements and say **why** they **are** important here. <TEC: Green Line 5>

Table 18. Summary of the model: lmer(PC1 ~ Register + Level + Level*Register + (1|Series))

Predictors	Estimates	CI	p-value
(Intercept) [Conversation, Level A]	−2.37	−2.59 – −2.15	**<0.001**
Register [Fiction]	1.61	1.36–1.87	**<0.001**
Register [Informative]	2.23	1.96–2.50	**<0.001**
Register [Instructional]	5.29	5.10–5.47	**<0.001**
Register [Personal]	0.48	0.08–0.88	**0.019**
Level [B]	−0.12	−0.30–0.05	0.167
Level [C]	0.12	−0.05–0.29	0.159
Level [D]	0.23	0.06–0.41	**0.01**
Level [E]	0.27	0.07–0.48	**0.01**
*Register [Fiction] * Level [B]*	0.18	−0.15–0.51	0.284
*Register [Informative] * Level [B]*	0.36	0.02–0.70	**0.038**
*Register [Instructional] * Level [B]*	−0.10	−0.35–0.15	0.434
*Register [Personal] * Level [B]*	0.11	−0.39–0.61	0.671
*Register [Fiction] * Level [C]*	−0.25	−0.58–0.07	0.13
*Register [Informative] * Level [C]*	0.00	−0.32–0.31	0.993
*Register [Instructional] * Level [C]*	−0.39	−0.62 – −0.15	**0.001**
*Register [Personal] * Level [C]*	−0.22	−0.72–0.28	0.381
*Register [Fiction] * Level [D]*	−0.05	−0.38–0.27	0.739
*Register [Informative] * Level [D]*	−0.01	−0.33–0.31	0.946
*Register [Instructional] * Level [D]*	−0.47	−0.72 – −0.23	**<0.001**
*Register [Personal] * Level [D]*	−0.07	−0.60–0.46	0.8
*Register [Fiction] * Level [E]*	−0.24	−0.58–0.10	0.173
*Register [Informative] * Level [E]*	0.06	−0.29–0.40	0.747
*Register [Instructional] * Level [E]*	−0.50	−0.77 – −0.22	**<0.001**
*Register [Personal] * Level [E]*	−0.18	−0.74–0.38	0.527
Random effects			
σ^2	0.45		
$\tau_{00\ Series}$	0.07		
ICC	0.14		
N_{Series}	9		
Observations	1961		
Marginal R^2 / Conditional R^2	0.890 / 0.906		

The lack of overlap in the confidence intervals in Figure 16 and the figures in Table 19 show that all of the register differences in estimated mean PC1 scores are significant, which confirms that PC1 distinguishes remarkably well between the different registers of the TEC data. Since PC1 accounts for 21.08% of the total variance in the TEC data, this confirms that much of the intra-textbook linguistic variation is register-driven.

Table 19. Estimated differences between mean PC1 scores for each TEC register pair (averaged across all textbook levels and series)

Contrast	Estimate	SE	df	*t*-ratio	*p*-value
Conversation – Fiction	−1.55	0.05	1962.95	−30.53	<.001
Conversation – Informative	−2.34	0.05	1960.92	−50.34	<.001
Conversation – Instructional	−4.99	0.04	1961.12	−125.14	<.001
Conversation – Personal Correspondence	−0.41	0.08	1958.34	−5.13	<.001
Fiction – Informative	−0.79	0.06	1962.12	−14.13	<.001
Fiction – Instructional	−3.44	0.05	1961.76	−69.17	<.001
Fiction – Personal Correspondence	1.15	0.08	1957.80	13.65	<.001
Informative – Instructional	−2.65	0.04	1956.92	−59.40	<.001
Informative – Personal Correspondence	1.93	0.08	1956.74	23.69	<.001
Instructional – Personal Correspondence	4.59	0.08	1956.63	58.82	<.001

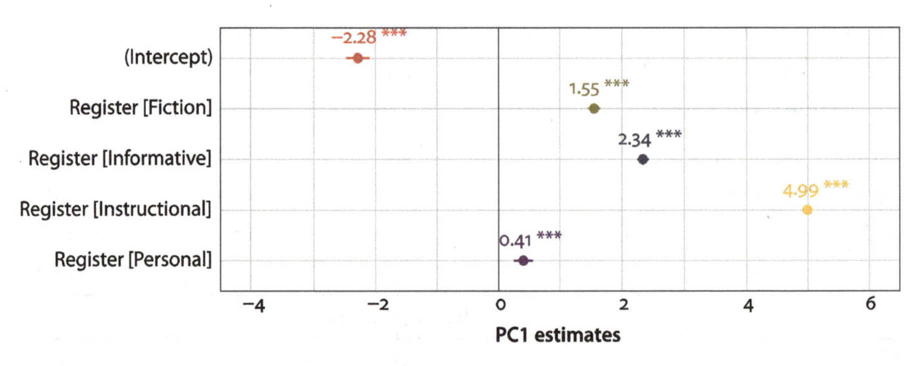

Figure 16. Coefficient estimates and 95% confidence intervals of the fixed effects in the model: lmer(PC1 ~ Register + (1|Series)) (the intercept corresponds to the reference level: Register [Conversation])

Let us now turn to the linguistic features that load onto PC1 to find out which linguistic features contribute the largest register-based differences in the TEC. The most important ones are visualised in Figure 12 (see also the first column of Table 17). Given that the upper end of the PC1 scale, roughly between 2 and 4, is entirely reserved for instructional texts (see Figures 9 and 11), we can expect the linguistic features that load positively on PC1 to be typical of textbook instructions and explanations. Indeed, these include imperative verbs (VIMP), the semantic categories of communication and mental verbs (COMM and MENTAL) and WH-questions (WHQU), e.g., Excerpt (16). Other features contributing to high PC1 scores, however, are more akin to the negative, 'informational' end of Biber's (1988) Dimension 1. These include longer words (AWL), nouns (NN), prepositions (IN), and a high ratio of content to function words (LDE), all of which are associated with impersonal and informational writing.

By contrast, the linguistic features with the most negative loadings on PC1 are associated with spontaneous, interactional production: e.g., contractions (CONT), first person singular referents (FFP1S) and *it* pronouns (PIT), negation (XX0), discourse markers (DMA), emphatics (EMPH), fillers and interjections (FPUH), and demonstrative pronouns (DEMO), e.g. (22). These features very much echo the upper, interactional, end of Biber's (1988) Dimension 1 (see Table 10).

(22) **Hi,** Amy.
Hi, you two.
Hello. What's so funny? Nothing – honestly. **Well,** what were you **talking** about? You'**ve** got big wide grins on your faces!
Oh, this and **that.** You **know, just chatting. We** were **talking** about thriller films. **We're thinking** of watching one. **Want** to join **us**?
Yeah, count **me** in. Sure. **I** have**n't** seen a good film for far too long. **Got** anything in mind?
Well, there was one film **we** were **thinking** about... But **I've** seen **it** – and **any-way, it'd** be far too scary for you two!
you **want** to bet? **There's** never been a horror film that **I** did**n't** watch all the way through.
Take **it** easy, Nick – **I** think she's **pulling** your leg!
Oh. Right. Sorry! <TEC: English in Mind 4>

6.3 Dimension 2: 'Involved vs. Informational Production'

The second dimension of variation in the TEC data (PC2) accounts for 14.16% of the total variance. As mentioned earlier, it shows a high degree of overlap with the linguistic features that contribute to both ends of Biber's (1988) Dimension 1 and will therefore also be labelled: 'Involved vs. Informational Production'. A first mixed-effects model with random intercepts for each textbook series and only Register as a fixed effect explained 56% of the variance in scores on this second dimension, whereas the full model adding Register*Level interactions explained

72%. This indicates that linguistic variation along this second dimension is driven by both register and the proficiency level of the textbooks. As with the first dimension, a comparison of the models showed that textbook series has no significant effect on the position of textbook texts along this dimension. As a result, only the estimated coefficients of the fixed effects of the full PC2 model are visualised in Figure 17. The colours correspond to the registers subcorpora of the TEC as in the previous biplots of texts. The intercept represents Textbook Conversation Level A texts, and the coefficients are interpreted just like in the model summary tables (e.g., Table 18).

The register cline on this second dimension bears strong similarities to Biber's (1988) Dimension 1, 'Involved vs. Informational Production' (see Figure 3), which, in various forms, has emerged as the strongest dimension of linguistic variation in many MDAs, across a wide range of domains and languages (Biber 2014). As shown in Figures 9 and 11, Textbook Conversation texts are mostly clustered at the upper end of the cline. In addition, Figure 17 indicates a clear proficiency-level effect – with more advanced textbook conversations scoring lower on average. The lower end of the register cline is dominated by Textbook Informative texts which all have negative PC2 scores. Personal correspondence and Fiction are, once again, situated in the middle. The overlapping confidence intervals in Figure 17 show that the two textbook registers cannot, on average, be reliably differentiated on this second dimension of linguistic variation.

As we would expect given that linguistic variation is multi-dimensional, some of the linguistic features with positive loadings on PC1 (see Figure 12 and Table 17) also contribute to positive values on PC2: these include imperatives, mental, and communication verbs – which are known to be particularly strongly associated with instructional texts, e.g., (16). In addition, we find WH- and *yes/no*-questions (WHQU and YNQU) and second-person referents (SPP2), which are also found in many textbook instructions and task descriptions. Consequently, many instructional texts score relatively high on PC2, e.g., (23). In contrast to the first dimension, on this second dimension these features are also associated with linguistic features typical of spontaneous conversation and interactional language, in particular with fillers and interjections (FPUH), discourse (DMA) and politeness markers (POLITE), the modal *can* (MDCA), and singular first-person referents (FPP1S). As a result, the highest PC2 scores are achieved by textbook dialogues such as (18), which comprise short turns. Some of the highest PC2 scores are found in textbook dialogues that model classroom interactions. These dialogues sometimes feature some of the instructions that accompany the textbooks' tasks and exercises verbatim, e.g., (23) and (24).

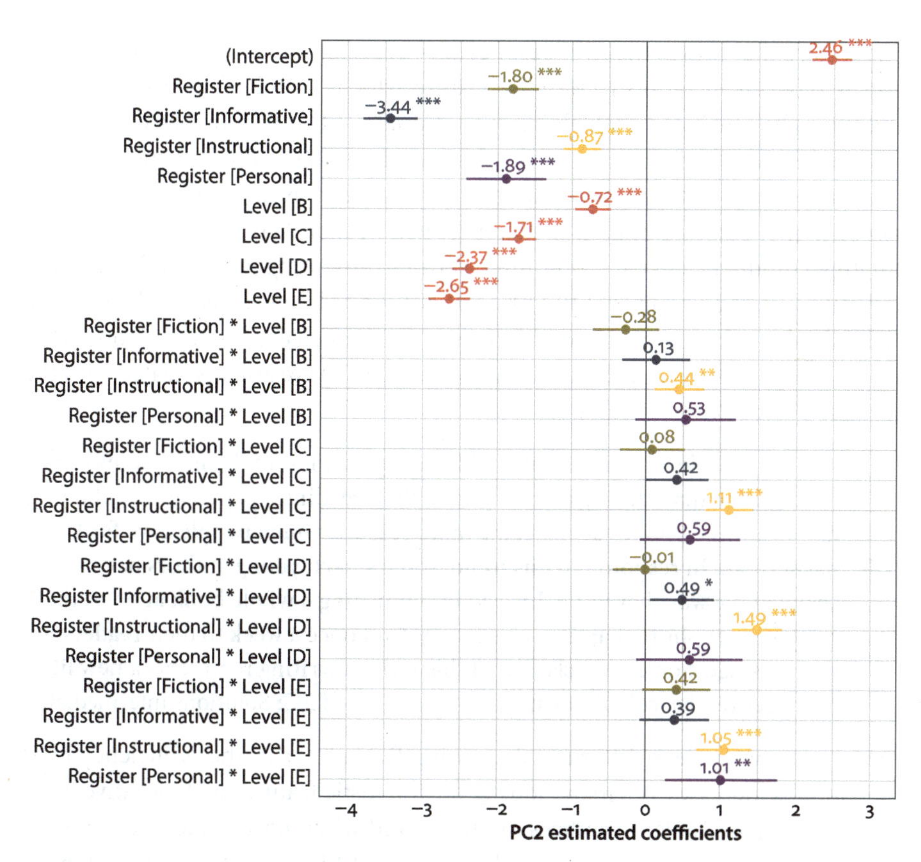

Figure 17. Coefficient estimates and 95% confidence intervals of the fixed effects in the model: lmer(PC2 ~ Register + Level + Register*Level + (1|Series)). The reference levels are Register [Conversation] and Level [A].

(23) Nadia is going on holiday A. **Read** her email to her friend. **Who** is going with her on holiday**? What does** she promise to do after her holiday?
(T) **Imagine you** are going on holiday. B. **Write** an email to an English-speaking friend and **tell** him/her what **you**'re going to do. **Use** the information and Nadia's email to help **you**. <TEC: English in Mind 2>

(24) Good morning, everyone! **Right, sit** down! Paul, **can you** show us where Scotland is?
OK, Miss.
Excellent. **Please take your** workbooks out. Now, **please open your** workbooks at page 12. Yes?
Sorry, Miss, my workbook is at home.
Can you work with Paul, **please**?
OK. <TEC: Access G 1>

The feature that makes the strongest negative contribution to this second dimension is type/token ratio (TTR)[29] – a feature which, in Biber's (1988) model, is also strongly associated with the 'informational' end of the 'Involved vs. Informational Production' dimension. In addition, the lower end of the dimension is characterised by further lexico-grammatical features typical of structurally more complex, meticulously drafted written production such as passives (PASS), coordinating conjunctions (CC), non-finite verb forms ending in *-ing* and *-ed* (VBG and VBN), split auxiliaries (SPLIT), and *that*-subordinate clauses (THSC), e.g., (25). Like the informational end of Biber's (1988) Dimension 1, prepositions (IN), longer words (AWL), and attributive adjectives (JJAT) are also associated with the negative end of PC2 (see Table 17).

(25) Although **books** are still popular **with** teenagers, most **of** them spend more of their **leisure time staring at** their **phone than reading** a paperback. And the more versatile **phones** become, the more **reasons young people** have **for looking at** them. **In response to** this **trend**, some **smart, young authors** have changed the **way** they write. **Instead of publishing** a **whole book at** once, they produce very **short chapters**, which they send once a **week to** their **readers by text message.** Some even claim **that** this **style of writing** represents a **new literary genre**: the '**cell phone novel**'. <TEC: Solutions intermediate>

Figure 17 shows a clear pattern of decreasing PC2 scores as the proficiency level of textbooks increases. A cursory look at the linguistic features with negative loadings on PC2 (see Table 17) suffices to understand why: most of these features are not introduced until the second or third year of EFL instruction. The extent to which these features are intrinsically linked to specific registers determines how large the shift to the negative end of the PC2 scale is, as learners are progressively introduced to these features in the more advanced textbooks.

Thus, we find that the median PC2 score for beginner textbook fiction texts is 1.09 (*MAD*=0.59) but, as soon as the past tense (VBD) is introduced in level B textbooks, the PC2 scores for fiction texts drop to a median of 0.06 (*MAD*=0.74) and then further to 0.82 (*MAD*=0.76) in level C fiction. The other features that make significant contributions to this negative shift include higher type/token ratio (TTR) and lexical density (LD), longer words (AWL), and higher normalised frequencies of the perfect aspect (PEAS), passives (PASS), *could* as a modal (MDCO), occurrence and existential verbs (OCCUR and EXIST), prepo-

29. Following (Biber 1988: 238–239), type/token ratio (TTR) is calculated on the basis of the first 400 words of each text. It has long been established that type/token ratios must be calculated on the basis of text samples of equal text length as this lexical diversity measure is highly sensitive to text length (e.g., Brezina 2018: 58). Whilst recognising that more robust measures of lexical diversity exist, TTR was chosen here for its transparency and ease of interpretation.

sitions (IN), attributive adjectives (JJAT), and *that*-subordinate clauses (THSC), e.g., (26). Figure 18, however, suggests that, on average, the linguistic features that contribute to PC2 are used to a similar extent in level D and E fiction texts. Indeed, apart from type/token ratio, which can be expected to continue to grow as learners become more proficient in English, all the aforementioned features that contribute to the negative end of PC2, e.g., perfect aspect, passives, *could*, can be expected to have been taught by the fourth year of secondary school EFL instruction.

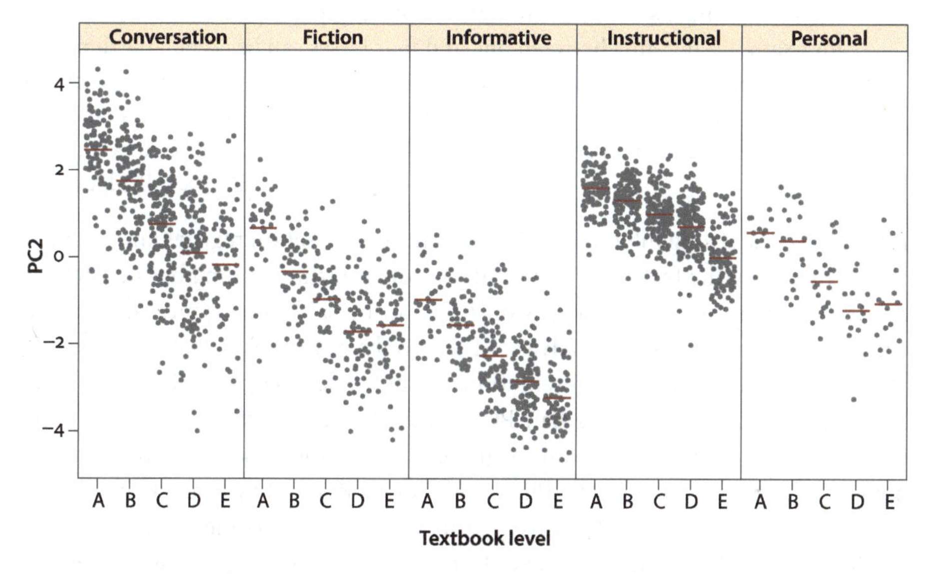

Figure 18. Estimated PC2 scores across each register and the five textbook proficiency levels

(26) "If I just **had** that knife **in** my hand, I **could** ..." Suddenly a smile **lit** up his face as he **thought of** a plan. He **took** hold **of** his fishing line. The pole **was** still **in** the canoe so he **could** pull the boat **towards** him, get the knife, cut the roots and get free. Carefully, he **began to** pull **on** the line and **felt** the canoe start **to** move. Then, just as he **started to** so hope **that** his plan might be working, he **heard** a **quiet** splash as his fishing pole **fell** out **of** the canoe **into** the water. The canoe **stopped** moving. [...] **While** he **had watched** the alligator, his canoe **had drifted** up **behind** him and **hit** him **in** the back. <TEC: Access G 4>

For the informative and conversation texts, the shift towards the negative end of the PC2 scale from level A to E is more or less linear (see Figure 18). This pattern is to be expected for informative texts: as for the narrative texts, textbook authors are necessarily restricted in their choice of grammatical features given that learners have only been introduced to a limited number of grammatical features and basic vocabulary. Many of the negative loading features on PC2 are typical of informational writing so that it comes as no surprise that, on average, the informative texts of the more advanced textbooks score lowest on this dimension, e.g., (27):

(27) A kiss is ambiguous **at** the best **of** times, **signifying** anything **from** friendliness **to** desire, deference **to** insult. Kissing – **on** the lips, originally – **was, in fact,** a common form **of** social greeting **in** Britain **from** Roman times **at least until** the 1700s, **when** the potential **for** misinterpretation **led to** its disappearance. Abroad, of course, they'**ve never really abandoned** the gesture, **although** the rules **governing** its use **are sometimes exceedingly complicated. In** France, **for example,** anything **between** one **and** four kisses can be acceptable **depending on** who you are, who you're kissing, how well the two **of** you know each other **and** exactly where you both happen **to** be **in** France. There are so many variables **that** even French people **within** the same region confess **to being** confused. <TEC: New Bridges 2[de]>

By contrast, the strong interactions between the conversation register and the proficiency levels of the textbooks constitute a more puzzling finding because few of the features with negative loadings on PC2 can be said to be typical of real-life conversation; yet, on average, advanced textbooks nevertheless feature considerably more of these in their representations of spoken language than beginner textbooks (see Figure 18). The median PC2 value of level A textbook conversations is 2.60 ($MAD=0.76$), with many beginner conversations scoring considerably higher, e.g., (18) and (24) with PC2 scores of 4.08 and 3.53 respectively. However, median PC2 scores progressively drop as textbooks become more advanced, reaching −0.16 ($MAD=1.33$) for level E textbook conversations. This echoes the results of the additive MDA based on Biber's (1988) Dimension 1 (Le Foll 2021c, 2022c: Chapter 6). Advanced textbook dialogues with low PC2 scores tend to feature much higher type/token ratios, longer words, more passives, past tense and perfect verbs, split auxiliaries, coordinating conjunctions, nouns, prepositions, and subordinate clauses, e.g., (28) and (29).

(28) We're here **at** the **BBC Radio**'s annual **Teen Awards at Wembley. As** I'm sure many **of** our **listeners** know, the **prizes are awarded to** the **year's** best **vloggers, sport and music stars and to teenage heroes who have inspired** everyone! Best **of** all, they **have been voted for by Britain's teenagers!** So let's find out **what** the **fans** here **thought of** the **show.** OK, what **did** you think **was** the best **moment of** the **afternoon?**
Well, **for** me, it has to be **when Jack G got** his **award for** standing up **to** bullying. If I'**d been** him, I wouldn't **have had** the **courage to** start a **campaign against** the **bullies in** my **school,** so I really admire him **for** doing that.
<TEC: Solutions intermediate plus>

(29) The **state** is **also** very active **in** limiting **air pollution. But** what **about traffic in** places like L.A.?
Yes, the **traffic in Los Angeles** is a huge problem **which has existed since** the **arrival of** the **automobile in** the late 1800s. **Until then people were transported in L.A. by** streetcar. **Once** the **automobile arrived, people came** to love the **freedom** it **offered.** It **allowed** them **to** move far **from** the **center of L.A. and still** be able **to** reach **downtown** – something the **streetcars** couldn't offer.
<TEC: Green Line New 5>

The pattern observed in the instructional register in Figure 18 is in line with that observed in the previous section on the first dimension. Linguistically, it is driven by more complex sentence structures in the explanations of more advanced textbooks which are characterised by higher frequencies of subordinate clauses (THSC and WHSC) and coordinating conjunctions (CC) – three features which contribute to lower PC2 scores. This leads to the modest, but nevertheless significant, interaction effects between the instructional register and textbook proficiency level reported in the mixed-effects model of PC2 scores (see Figures 17 and 18 and Appendix F for the full results of the model).

6.4 Dimension 3: 'Narrative vs. Factual discourse'

The third dimension that emerges from this intra-textbook MDA accounts for just 5.31% of the variance. As illustrated by Figures 13 and 15, this dimension of variation appears to involve both register-based and proficiency level-based linguistic variation. This visual observation was confirmed in the mixed-effects models computed to model PC2 scores: a comparison of models for this dimension shows that register alone explains 27% of the variance in PC3 scores; the proficiency level variable alone accounts for 12%, but by modelling the interactions between the two variables 44% of the variance in PC3 can be explained. The fixed effects coefficient estimates of the full model that includes these interactions are displayed in Figure 19.

The effects of the interactions are also visualised in Figure 20. Across all five registers, the largest jump in PC3 scores is observed between Level A and Level B textbook texts. It is largely driven by the near absence of past tense verbs in Level A textbooks (e.g., (30) which scores very low on this third dimension) contrasted by the highly frequent use of the past in Levels B and C textbooks as learners are taught to comprehend and produce this grammatical feature (e.g., (31) which scores very high). Other features with salient on PC3 whose frequencies are also strongly mediated by the proficiency level of the textbooks include the

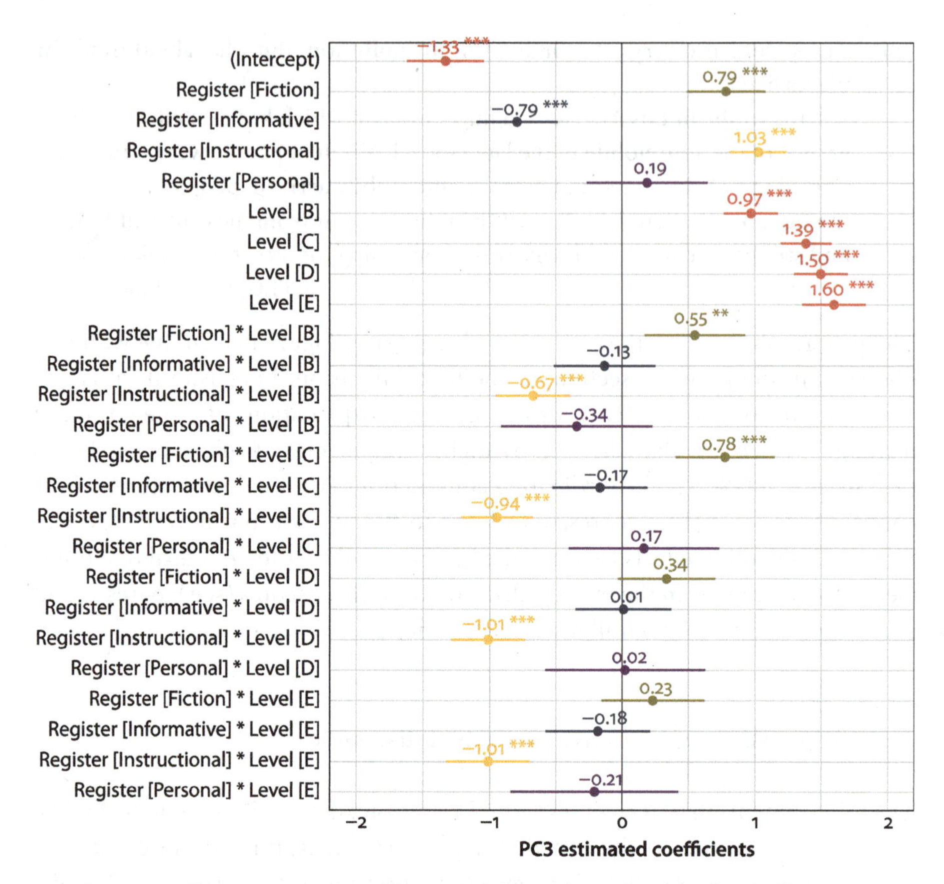

Figure 19. Coefficient estimates and 95% confidence intervals of the fixed effects in the model: lmer(PC3 ~ Register + Level + Register*Level + (1|Series). The intercept corresponds to the reference levels Register [Conversation] and Level [A].

perfect aspect (PEAS), the modal *could* (MDCO), and conditional subordination (COND) – all three of which make positive contributions to PC3 scores.

(30) Harry Potter **is** ten years old and he'**s** very unhappy. His mother and father **are** dead and he **lives** with his aunt and uncle. Harry **doesn't** like them or their son Dudley at all. One day, Harry **gets** a letter from Hogwards, a school for wizards! At Hogwards, Harry **is** famous and popular. He **learns** magic and **plays** a game called 'Quidditch'. Harry'**s** very happy there.

<TEC: English in Mind Starter>

(31) The person who **has taught** me the most about life is my grandmother. My parents **did** a lot of travelling when I **was** younger so I **spent** most of my school holidays with her. [...] She **knew** how much I **missed** my parents so she did everything she **could** to make me feel at home. She **was** also really imaginative

> and **spent** hours telling me stories that she **had made** up. I'm sure it **was** because of her that I **became** a writer. But as well as keeping a young boy entertained, she **taught** me so many important things. I **was** very impatient when I **was** a child and she **taught** me that good things **happened if** you **could** wait for them. <English in Mind 3>

Interestingly, aside from the present tense variable (VPRT), the frequencies of all the other strong contributors to the negative end of this dimension are not correlated with textbook proficiency and hence do not contribute to the effects visualised in Figure 20. Instead, this cluster of negative-loading features – which includes the total frequency of nouns (NN), lexical density (LD) and noun-noun compounds (NCOMP) – describes the nominal, factual style of the negative end of this dimension. The interaction of register and proficiency effects at play in this dimension make it difficult to interpret solely from a functional point of view but, for now, this dimension is tentatively labelled as 'Narrative vs. Factual discourse'.

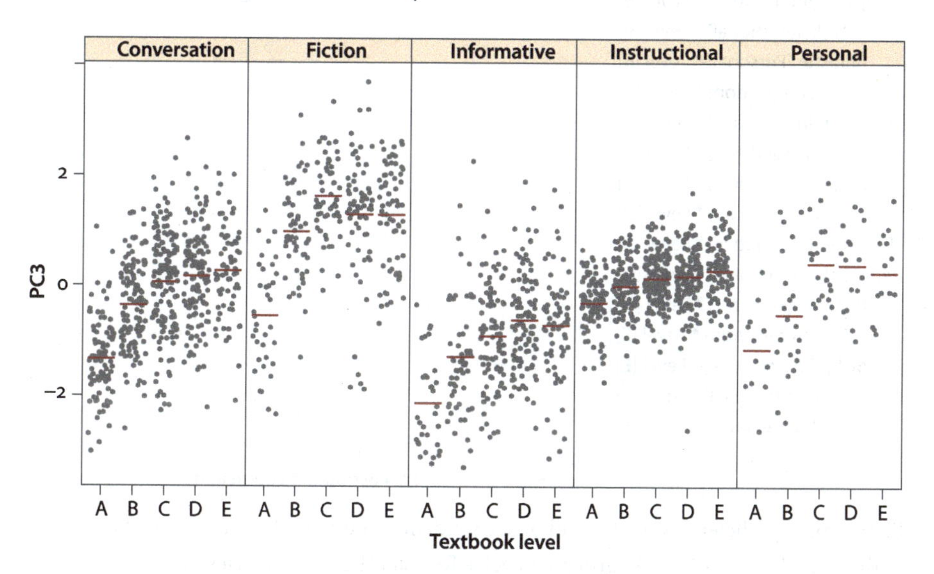

Figure 20. Estimated PC3 scores across each register and the five textbook proficiency levels

6.5 Dimension 4: 'Informational compression vs. Elaboration'

Similarly to PC3, the fourth dimension that emerges from this intra-textbook MDA only accounts for 4.50% of the variance in the texts of the TEC. It, too, captures both register- and proficiency-level-based variation – this time to almost equal degrees: register alone explains 20% of the variance in PC3 scores, whilst the five levels of the proficiency level variable account for 19%. The full mixed-effects model involving the interactions between the register and proficiency levels, however, explains a total of 43% of the variance in PC4 scores. The estimated coefficients of the fixed effects of this model are plotted in Figure 21.

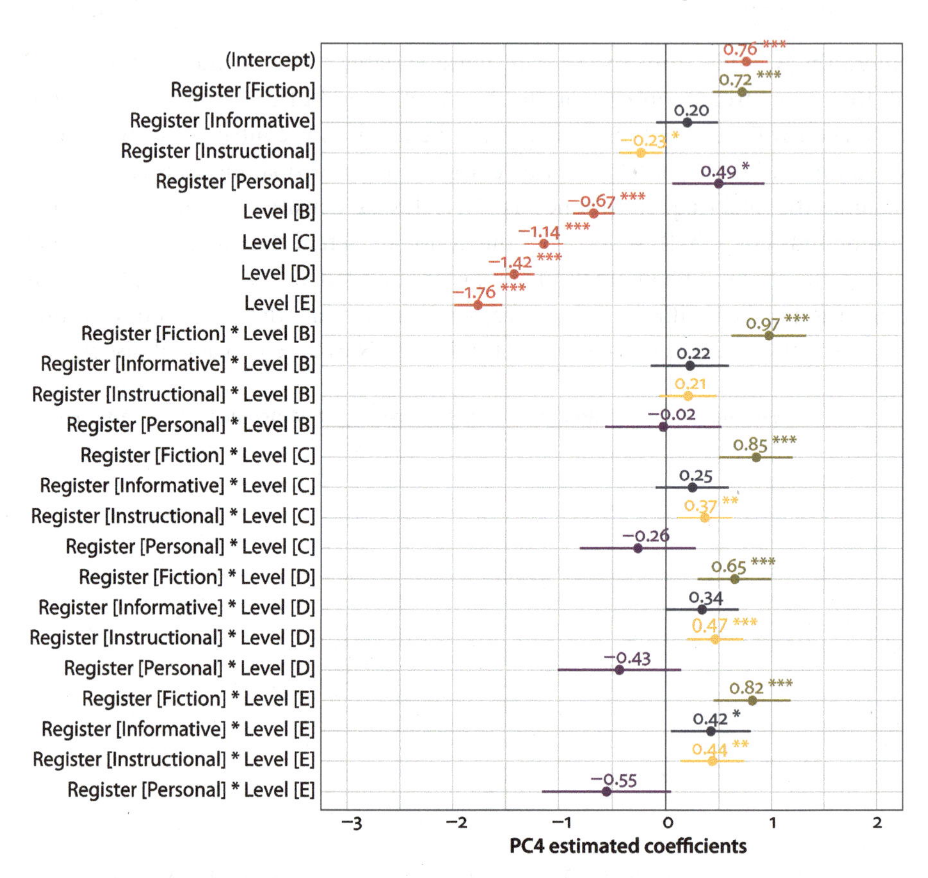

Figure 21. Coefficient estimates and 95% confidence intervals of the fixed effects in the model: lmer(PC4 ~ Register + Level + Register*Level + (1|Series)). The reference levels are Register [Conversation] and Level [A].

At first glance, the highest loading features on this fourth dimension might suggest a second 'narrative' dimension since some of these features (e.g., past tense verbs and third-person reference) are shared with the positive-loading features of the third dimension (see Figure 14). However, this dimension appears to be much more driven by the interaction effects of proficiency level and register. These effects, predicted by the model summarised in Figure 21, are illustrated in Figure 22. Their direction is somewhat surprising given that the second highest loading feature on PC4 is past tense verbs (VBD, see Table 17) and, whilst we have seen in 6.3 that the occurrence of past tense verbs drastically increases from level B textbook onwards, Figure 22 show that PC4 scores actually decrease as the proficiency level of the textbook increases.

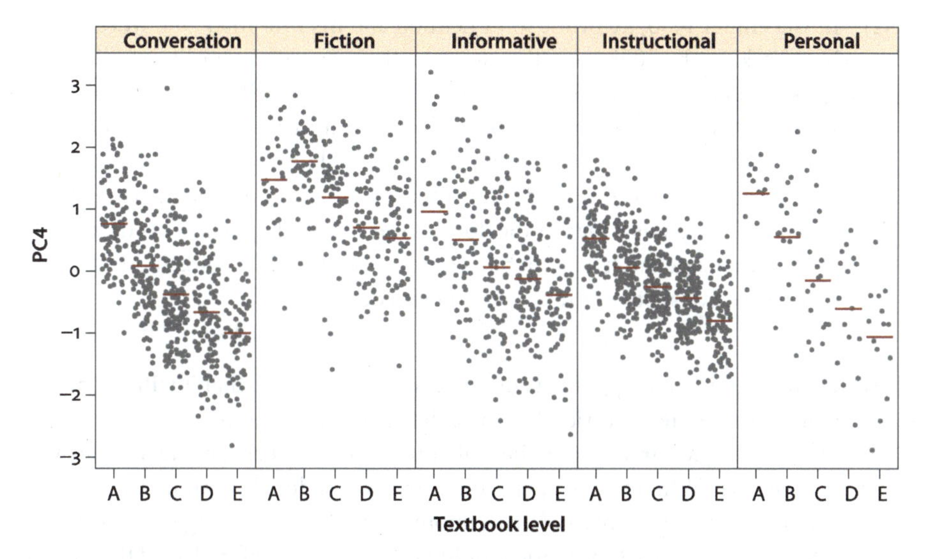

Figure 22. Estimated PC4 scores across each register and the five textbook proficiency levels

Consequently, this proficiency-level-based effect must be driven by other lexico-grammatical phenomena that contribute to negative scores on this dimension and which are gradually introduced in the later years of secondary school EFL teaching. These include *if*-conditionals that lead to an increase in conditional subordinators (COND) and the modals *will* and *should* (MDWS), as in Extract (33). Furthermore, this dimension points to linguistic variation that, at the positive end, is characterised by narrative past-tense discourse that relies foremost on individual words for brief descriptions. As illustrated in (32), these include references to time and place, and the frequent use of the *there is/are* construction. By contrast, the negative end of this fourth dimension is characterised by more complex clausal structures that, in fiction, allow for more detailed descriptive passages and in conversation, personal correspondence, instructional, and informative texts, convey more elaborate explanations, opinions, or arguments, as attested by the negative loadings of features such as COND, THATD, VBG, THRC, WHSC and THSC in Table 17 and Figure 14 (see also, Extract (33)). Hence, this dimension can be interpreted as representing a complexity cline with the simplest constructions clustering at the upper end of the dimension and the most complex, elaborate ones at the bottom. For this fourth dimension, the label 'Informational compression vs. Elaboration' was therefore chosen. As exemplified in (33), informational elaboration is also characterised by high frequencies of attributive adjectives (JJAT) and quantifiers (QUAN) per noun.

(32) In **December 1980**, ex-Beatle John Lennon and **his** wife Yoko Ono **were** in New York. **In the afternoon**, they **were** on their way to a recording studio to work on a new song. **There was** an American called Mark Chapman in the street. In **his** hand, **there was** a piece of paper and a pen. 'Mr Lennon,' **he said.** 'Can I have your autograph?' John Lennon **signed his** name and Chapman **went** away. **In the evening**, John and Yoko **were** in front of their apartment building. **There was** a man at the door. It **was** Mark Chapman. This time, **there wasn't** a pen in **his** hand, but a gun. 'Mr Lennon!' he **said.** Suddenly, **there were** five shots and John Lennon **was** dead.
<TEC: English in Mind Starter>

(33) On the other hand, opponents of **nuclear** weapons argue **that** it **will** not be long **before some** countries develop a defence system **that** makes them immune to **nuclear** attack, **while** still **being** able to launch a **nuclear** offensive of their own. **When** this happens, the world **will** suddenly become an extremely **dangerous** place. Furthermore, they point to the **huge** cost of the weapons and say **that** the world **would** be a **better** and **safer** place **if** the money were spent on health and education. <TEC: Solutions Intermediate plus>

CHAPTER 7

A comparative model of Textbook English vs. 'real-world' English

This chapter presents the results of a second PCA-based MDA aimed at describing the similarities and differences between the texts of the Conversation, Fiction, and Informative subcorpora of the TEC (see 4.3.1.3) and the three corresponding reference corpora: the Spoken BNC2014 (see 4.3.2.1), the Youth Fiction Corpus (see 4.3.2.4) and the Informative Texts for Teenagers Corpus (hereafter referred to as Teens Info, see 4.3.2.5). It first describes the four dimensions of the model, before proceeding with in-depth comparisons of the three pairs of textbook and reference registers (Conversation, Fiction, and Informative writing) along these four dimensions to provide answers to RQ3: "To what extent is the language of current EFL textbooks used in secondary schools in France, Germany, and Spain representative of 'real-world' English as used by native/proficient English speakers in similar communicative situations? To what extent are some registers more faithfully represented than others?"

7.1 A multi-feature/multi-dimensional model of Textbook English vs. 'real-world' English

Following the same data preparation steps as in the previous chapter (see also 5.3.6), the exclusion of linguistic features that are absent from more than two-thirds of the texts of the TEC and reference corpora together led to the merging of the ABLE and JJPR categories and the PGET and PASS, as well as the removal of the EMO, HST, PRP and URL features (see Appendix C for details). Due to otherwise very low final communalities, the singular third-person (TPP3S) and the plural third-person referent categories (TPP3P) were merged into a single TPP3 category. For the same reason, the adverbs of frequency (FREQ) and time (TIME) were also combined into a more general 'adverbs of frequency and time' (FQTI) category. The normalised counts of all the features were then standardised before plotting their distributions. Next, 115 outlier texts (=2.28% of the texts) were identified based on excessively high *z*-scores. The majority of these outlier texts ($n=74$) stem from the Info Teens corpus. Many of these outliers are articles composed of bullet point lists featuring very few finite verbs, leading to improbably high counts of some of the linguistic features normalised per finite verb phrase (FVP) (see 5.3.4). These texts were therefore removed from the dataset to be entered in the following PCAs to avoid them exerting undue influence on the model and inflating or distorting differences between texts (see, e.g., Le Foll 2021a: 110–113 on the consequences of leaving such texts in such analyses). Here, too, signed log transformation was applied to tame some of the highly skewed feature distributions. The dataset was checked for collinearities and excessive correlations (see Appendix G for details of these procedures; ⟨elenlefoll.github.io/TextbookMDA/AppendixG⟩. This led to the exclusion of the present tense feature (VPRT) because, with a correlation of 0.97, its normalised counts per FVP are almost the perfect mirror image of past tense counts per FVP (which, given that finite verbs can either be tagged as past tense, present tense, or modal does not come as a surprise).

As a result of the above steps, none of the remaining features returned individual MSA values < 0.5 or final communalities of < 0.2 so that the final data matrix consisted of the signed log transformed standardised normalised counts of 70 features in 4,980 texts. An overall KMO value of 0.95 suggests that the data matrix is "marvellously" suitable for factor analysis (Kaiser & Rice 1974: 112). The scree plot of eigenvalues suggested a four-component solution (see Figure 23). The cumulative proportion of variance explained by these four principal components is 47.15%.

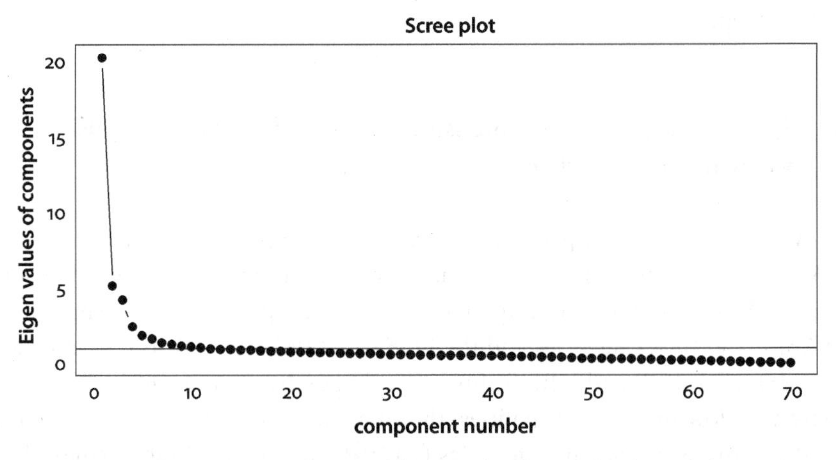

Figure 23. Scree plot of the eigenvalues of the PCs for the Textbook English vs. 'real-world' English PCA

As with the analysis of intra-textbook linguistic variation in the previous chapter, the retained components were first explored with 3-D projections of the position of the texts. The projection of the first three principal components (see Figure 24) shows three very well-defined clusters for the three reference corpora (in red, bright green, and dark blue) – with hardly any overlap. By contrast, the three TEC subcorpora cluster across much larger areas of the 3-D plot, including around the intercept of the plot, which is an area in which hardly any of the reference texts are found.

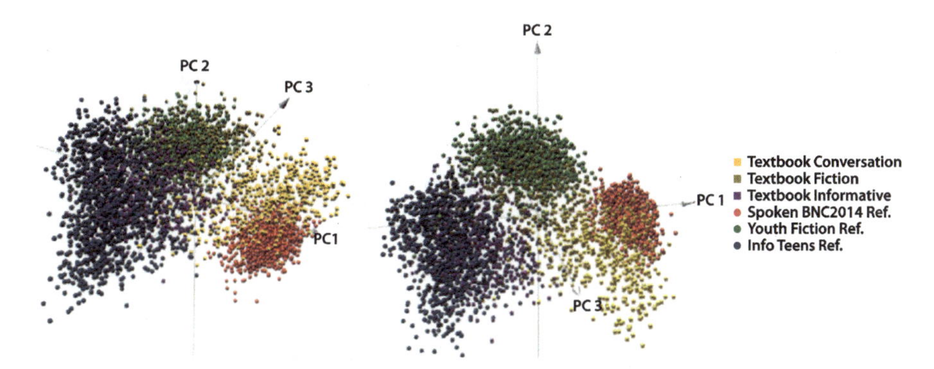

Figure 24. Snapshots from the 3-D representation of texts along PC1–PC3

This pattern can also be observed in the scatterplot matrix of all combinations of the four dimensions in Figure 25. At first sight, the Textbook Fiction texts appear, on all dimensions, to share many similarities with those of the Youth Fiction corpus. This is in stark contrast to the Textbook Conversation and Spoken BNC2014 clusters which overlap very little on all four dimensions. In addition, Figure 25 indicates that there is a lot of internal variation within the Info Teens corpus.

Together, the first two principal components explain 37.85% of the total variance. As shown in more detail in Figure 26, both these dimensions of linguistic variation appear to capture differences between the three textbook registers and their corresponding reference corpora. The corresponding graph of features (Figure 27) shows that these first two dimensions share many similarities with Biber's (1988) first two dimensions.

The first dimension (PC1) places highly interactional, spontaneous speech at the upper end, whilst informationally dense, edited texts score lowest. It will therefore be labelled 'Spontaneous interactional vs. Edited informational'. On both ends of the dimension, many of the strongest contributing features overlap with those that also have the highest absolute loadings on Biber's (1988) Dimension 1, e.g., verbal contractions (CONT) and discourse markers (DMA) at the positive pole and nouns (NN), longer average word length (AWL), prepositions (IN), and higher type/token ratio (TTR) at the negative pole.

The second dimension (illustrated on the *y*-axes of Figures 26 and 27) is also very comparable to Biber's (1988) Dimension 2 and will therefore be labelled: 'Narrative vs. Non-narrative'. The highest loading features are the same even though different normalisation units are used: past tense verbs (VBD) and third-person ref-

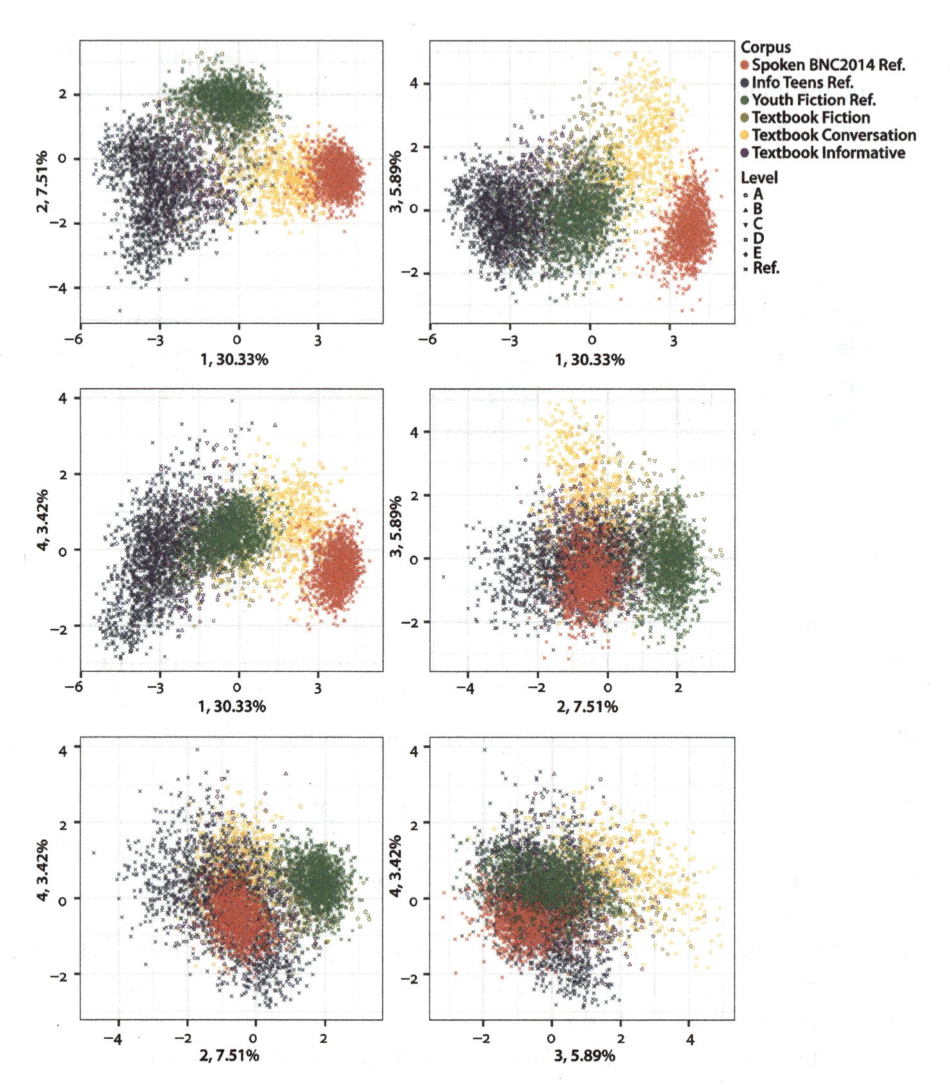

Figure 25. Scatterplot matrix of combinations of the four dimensions of the model of Textbook English vs. 'real-world' English (the number before the comma on each axis label shows which principal component is plotted on that axis; this is followed by the percentage of the total variance explained by that particular component)

erents (TPP3). The perfect aspect (PEAS), which is the third highest-loading feature on Biber's Dimension 2, ranks eighth on PC2 (see Table 20), whilst public verbs (e.g., EXPLAIN, SAY, TELL), the fourth most important positive contributor to Biber's Dimension 2, corresponds broadly to the high contribution of verbs of communication (COMM) on PC2. However, unlike Biber's (1988) Dimension 2, the 'Narrative vs. Non-narrative' dimension that emerges from the present MDA involves several significantly loading features with negative contributions to the dimension. These include noun compounds (NCOMP), BE as a main verb (BEMA), and the modal *can* (MDCA).

The three ellipses of the TEC registers are noticeably "shifted" towards the middle of the biplot depicting texts on the first and second dimensions (Figure 26). The following sections explore the reason for this "shift" towards the middle of the biplot. To this end, both the full table of feature loadings (Table 20) and graphs of variables such as Figure 27 are examined to understand the linguistic specificities of these three textbook registers. Linear mixed-effects models were also computed for each principal component but, for reasons of space, only the most salient findings are reported in this chapter. All the models, tables, and plots that were examined in these analyses are in Appendix H ⟨elenlefoll.github.io/TextbookMDA/AppendixH⟩.

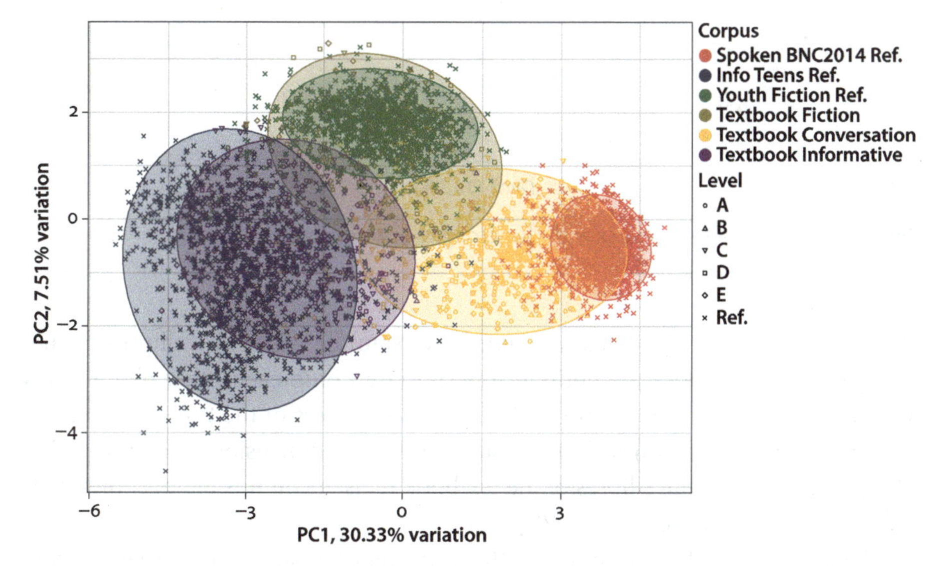

Figure 26. Projection of the texts of the three subcorpora of the TEC and the reference corpora on PC1 and PC2

Given that the first two dimensions appear to be functionally and linguistically analogous to Biber's (1988) dimensions, we can expect that many of the similarities and differences between Textbook English registers and situationally comparable, reference registers observed in Le Foll (2021c, 2022c: Chapter 6) using additive MDA will be confirmed in the present analysis. The third dimension (PC3), however, is not represented in Biber's (1988) model. Indeed, Figure 28 shows that this third dimension appears to directly model some specificities of Textbook English as opposed to non-textbook, naturally occurring English. It was

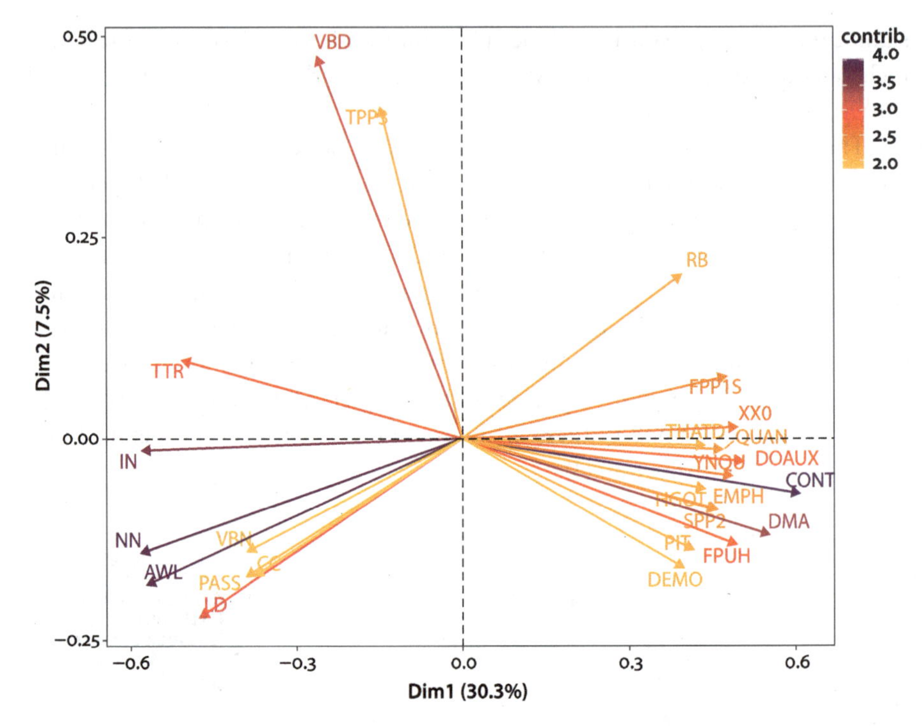

Figure 27. Graph of the features with the strongest contributions to the first and second dimensions

therefore labelled 'Pedagogically adapted vs. Natural'. Whilst the ellipses of the three reference corpora are entirely superimposed onto each other along PC3, with centroids around zero on the PC3 axis, the ellipses of the three TEC registers are notably shifted towards the positive end of the dimension. In addition, the elongated shapes of the ellipses of the textbook registers on this biplot shows that these texts cover a wide range of PC3 scores.

Figure 29 indicates that much of this intra-register variation is driven by the proficiency levels of the textbooks: it displays the texts on PC3 and PC4 in exactly the same position as in Figure 28 but, in Figure 29, the ellipses correspond to the Level variable rather than, as in Figure 28, the (Sub)Corpus variable. These ellipses show that, on average, level A textbook texts score highest on this third dimension and that, as the proficiency level of the textbooks increases, PC3 scores decrease.

This effect is confirmed in the summary of the linear mixed-effects model computed to predict scores on this third 'Pedagogically adapted vs. Natural' dimension (Table 21). Note that, in this and all other models explored in the following sections, the reference level is the Reference (Ref.) Conversation data, i.e.,

Table 20. List of feature loadings (eigenvectors) in the Textbook English vs. 'real-world' English MDA model

	PC1	PC2	PC3	PC4
Activity verbs (ACT)	−0.10	0.01	−0.01	0.12
Amplifiers (AMP)	0.00	−0.05	−0.05	0.09
Aspectual verbs (ASPECT)	−0.08	0.10	−0.01	0.00
Average word length (AWL)	−0.21	−0.13	−0.06	−0.01
BE as a main verb (BEMA)	0.08	−0.24	0.06	−0.02
Causative verbs (CAUSE)	−0.08	−0.12	0.06	0.14
Coordinating conjunctions (CC)	−0.14	−0.13	−0.09	−0.09
Communication verbs (COMM)	−0.03	0.19	0.03	0.20
Concessive conjunctions (CONC)	−0.03	−0.03	−0.18	−0.06
Conditional conjunctions (COND)	0.08	−0.02	−0.17	0.23
Verbal contractions (CONT)	0.22	−0.05	0.03	0.00
Causal conjunctions (CUZ)	0.10	−0.14	−0.20	−0.18
Demonstratives (DEMO)	0.15	−0.12	−0.08	−0.04
Discourse markers (DMA)	0.20	−0.09	−0.04	−0.16
DO as an auxiliary (DOAUX)	0.18	−0.02	0.06	0.00
Determiners (DT)	0.08	0.16	−0.24	−0.03
Downtoners (DWNT)	−0.04	0.10	−0.12	0.09
Elaborating conjunctions (ELAB)	−0.07	−0.17	−0.04	0.07
Emphatics (EMPH)	0.17	−0.07	−0.09	−0.03
Existential *there* (EX)	0.06	−0.02	−0.04	0.00
Existential and relationship verbs (EXIST)	−0.13	−0.09	−0.05	0.00
References of the speaker/writer (FPP1P)	0.08	−0.02	0.09	0.19
References to the speaker/writer and others (FPP1S)	0.17	0.06	0.06	0.08
Fillers and interjections (FPUH)	0.18	−0.10	−0.05	−0.19
Time and frequency references (FQTI)	−0.07	0.03	0.01	0.14
Going to constructions (GTO)	0.14	0.00	−0.04	0.00
Hedges (HDG)	0.10	−0.07	−0.14	−0.12
HAVE *got* constructions	0.16	−0.05	−0.01	−0.11
Prepositions (IN)	−0.21	−0.01	−0.08	0.01
Attributive adjectives (JJAT)	−0.05	−0.13	−0.25	0.07

Table 20. *(continued)*

	PC1	PC2	PC3	PC4
Predicative adjectives (JJPR)	−0.03	−0.17	−0.03	0.21
Lexical density (LD)	−0.17	−0.16	0.13	−0.04
Modal *can* (MDCA)	0.05	−0.21	0.11	0.22
Modal *could* (MDCO)	0.00	0.19	−0.15	0.10
Modals *may* and *might* (MDMM)	−0.02	−0.10	−0.14	0.17
Modals of necessity (MDNE)	0.06	−0.02	−0.06	0.22
Modal *would*	0.07	0.11	−0.18	0.04
Modals *will* and *shall* (MDWS)	0.06	−0.02	−0.01	0.25
Mental verbs (MENTAL)	0.11	−0.02	−0.05	0.16
Noun compounds (NCOMP)	0.00	−0.27	−0.05	0.03
Nouns (NN)	−0.21	−0.10	0.10	−0.07
Occurrence verbs (OCCUR)	−0.13	−0.02	−0.05	−0.06
BE and GET passives (PASS)	−0.14	−0.13	−0.09	−0.10
Perfect aspect (PEAS)	−0.06	0.12	−0.19	0.12
it pronoun references (PIT)	0.15	−0.10	−0.15	−0.07
Place references (PLACE)	0.02	0.09	0.09	0.07
Politeness markers (POLITE)	0.09	0.00	0.20	0.11
s-genitives (POS)	0.02	0.09	0.04	−0.05
Progressive aspect (PROG)	0.09	0.08	−0.04	0.15
Quantifiers (QUAN)	0.17	−0.01	−0.16	0.01
Quantifying pronouns (QUPR)	0.08	0.11	−0.12	0.21
Question tags (QUTAG)	0.15	−0.04	−0.07	−0.15
General adverbs (RB)	0.14	0.15	−0.18	0.07
Verb particles (RP)	−0.01	0.22	−0.09	0.15
Split auxiliaries (SPLIT)	−0.03	−0.11	−0.21	0.08
Second-person references (SPP2)	0.17	−0.07	0.10	0.16
Stranded prepositions (STPR)	0.10	0.01	0.01	−0.04
that omission (THATD)	0.16	−0.01	−0.14	−0.02
that-relative clauses (THRC)	−0.05	−0.17	−0.15	−0.02
that-subordinate clauses (other than relatives) (THSC)	−0.02	−0.08	−0.27	0.07

Table 20. *(continued)*

	PC1	PC2	PC3	PC4
References to non- interactant(s) (TPP3)	−0.05	0.30	−0.04	−0.15
Lexical diversity (TTR)	−0.19	0.07	−0.02	0.16
Past tense verbs (VBD)	−0.10	0.35	−0.05	−0.20
Non-finite verb *-ing* forms (VBG)	−0.14	−0.02	−0.14	0.12
Non-finite verb *-ed* forms (VBN)	−0.14	−0.10	−0.08	−0.07
Imperatives (VIMP)	0.01	−0.07	0.21	0.21
WH-questions (WHQU)	0.13	−0.02	0.20	0.07
WH-subordinate clauses (WHSC)	−0.09	−0.10	−0.20	0.05
Negated verb forms (XX0)	0.18	0.01	−0.06	0.06
yes-no questions (YNQU)	0.18	−0.03	0.14	−0.02

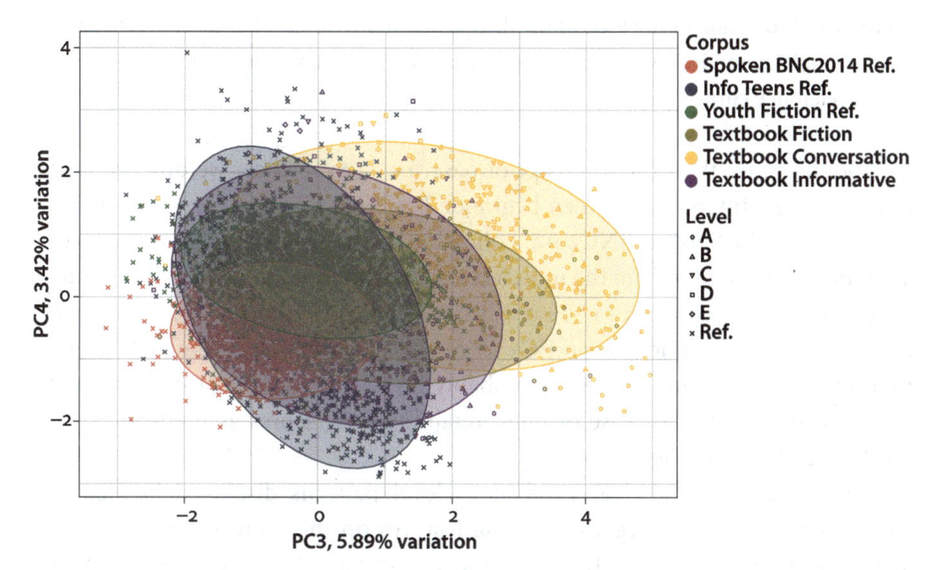

Figure 28. Projection of the texts of the three subcorpora of the TEC and the reference corpora on PC3 and PC4

the Spoken BNC2014. As opposed to the MDA model of intra-textbook variation discussed in Chapter 6, only three registers are now modelled: Conversation, Fiction, and Informative. In addition, the Level variable now includes a sixth level for the Ref. corpora alongside the (by now, familiar) proficiency levels of the TEC (A to E; see Table 3). This means that, on this third dimension, Table 21 shows us that Textbook Conversation texts from beginner (level A) textbooks score, on average,

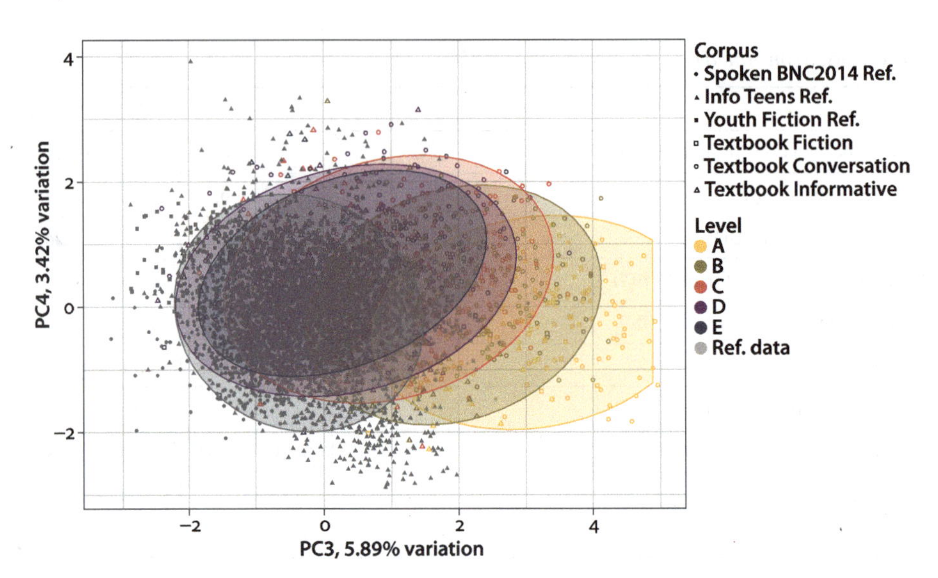

Figure 29. Projection of the texts of the three subcorpora of the TEC and the reference corpora on PC3 and PC4 with ellipses representing the five textbook proficiency levels vs. the reference corpora

4.25 points more than the intercept of 0.64, i.e., 3.61. Hence, we observe a particularly large difference between beginner Textbook Conversation texts and the transcripts of the Spoken BNC2014. Following the same logic, Table 21 shows that Textbook Fiction texts from the most advanced textbooks in the TEC have a mean PC3 score of 0.05 (=0.64+1.29+0.43+1.03), which, by contrast, is remarkably close to the Youth Fiction mean PC3 score of 0.21 (=0.64+0.43), which suggests that, on this dimension, there are probably no meaningful linguistic differences between these texts. For ease of interpretability, PC3 scores as predicted by the model are plotted in Figure 30.

At first glance, the clear proficiency level patterns displayed in Figure 30 would suggest that the negative loading features on this third dimension are all advanced linguistic features that are typically not taught until after learners have been acquainted with more basic lexico-grammatical phenomena. Looking at Figure 31 and Table 20, however, we find that the linguistic features that make the greatest negative contributions to PC3 scores include subordinate clauses (THSC and WHSC) and causative subordinators (CUZ) per 100 finite verb phrases, as well as the frequency of attributive adjectives (JJAT) and determiners (DT) per 100 nouns – which are all features that are introduced early in the curricula fleshed out by the textbooks included in the TEC. Only split auxiliaries (SPLIT) and the perfect aspect (PEAS) further down the list are unambiguous examples of features not usually introduced until the third year of secondary EFL instructions.

Table 21. Summary of the model: lmer(PC3 ~ 1 + Level + Register + Level*Register + (1|Source))

Predictors	**Estimates**	**95% CI**	***p*-value**
(Intercept) [Conversation] [Ref.]	−0.64	−1.99–0.71	0.354
Level [A]	4.25	2.82–5.69	**<0.001**
Level [B]	3.09	1.66–4.52	**<0.001**
Level [C]	2.12	0.69–3.55	**0.004**
Level [D]	1.64	0.21–3.07	**0.024**
Level [E]	1.29	−0.15–2.73	0.078
Register [Fiction]	0.43	−0.92–1.79	0.533
Register [Informative]	0.43	−0.96–1.83	0.544
Level [A] * Register [Fiction]	−1.5	−2.89–−0.12	**0.033**
Level [B] * Register [Fiction]	−1.39	−2.76–−0.01	**0.048**
Level [C] * Register [Fiction]	−1.34	−2.71–0.03	0.056
Level [D] * Register [Fiction]	−1.35	−2.72–0.03	0.055
Level [E] * Register [Fiction]	−1.03	−2.41–0.35	0.142
Level [A] * Register [Informative]	−1.92	−3.35–−0.49	**0.008**
Level [B] * Register [Informative]	−1.45	−2.86–−0.03	**0.045**
Level [C] * Register [Informative]	−1.36	−2.77–0.05	0.058
Level [D] * Register [Informative]	−1.43	−2.84–−0.02	**0.047**
Level [E] * Register [Informative]	−1.53	−2.95–−0.11	**0.034**
	Random effects		
σ^2	0.52		
$\tau_{00\ Source}$	0.48		
ICC	0.48		
N_{Source}	325		
Observations	4980		
Marginal R^2 / *Conditional* R^2	0.425 / 0.700		

Some of the features that characterise the positive end of the third dimension are reminiscent of the instructional end of the first dimension of the intra-textbook model (see 6.2): e.g., imperative verbs (VIMP), WH-questions (WHQU), and second-person referents (SPP2). Indeed, many of the texts that score particularly high on the present third dimension model classroom dialogues. Such dialogues also include high frequencies of the modal verb *can* (MDCA), *yes/no* questions (YNQU), and politeness markers (POLITE) which also contribute to high PC3 scores, e.g.:

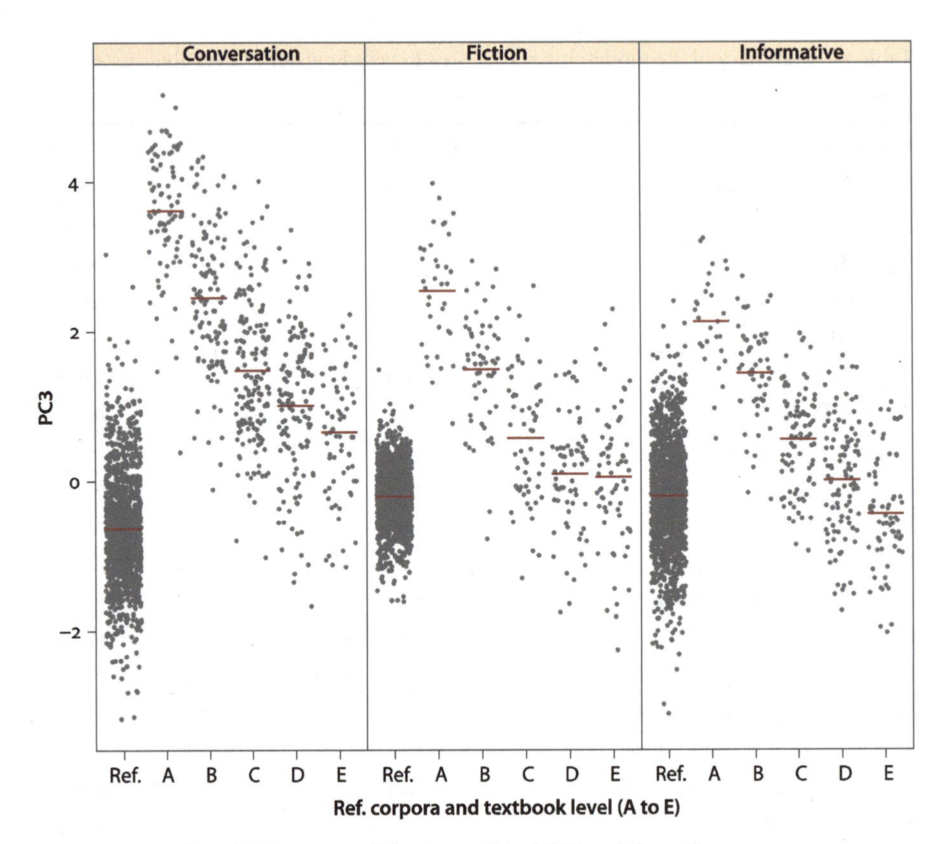

Figure 30. Predicted PC3 scores of the texts of the TEC and the reference corpora

(34) **What's your** name young man?
I'm Chad, Sir, Chad O'Malley. Well I'm Mr Lloyd, the headmaster. **Remember** my name. Now, **act** your age and **stop** chatting! Patrick, **can you** open the window, **please? Sorry** Mrs Preston, I'm late. **Can** I come in? It's alright for today Scarlett, but don't **forget** the room number next time. Well, children, let's start. Let's talk about kings and queens! **Can you** give me the name of...the Queen of England? Queen Elizabeth! Well. That's easy. More difficult... **Can you** give me the name of a Norman king... Tom! **Can you** repeat the question? ... a Norman king! William the Conqueror! Congratulations Scarlett! Wow! And now [a] question for the champions. **Can you** tell me who this man is? He had six wives. His first wife was Catherine of Aragon, his second wife was Ann Boleyn and... Miss... Miss... I know! I know! Yes Patrick? It's King George. No, it isn't. Scarlett! **Can you** answer? Henry VIII. Brilliant! **Join** the school history club! She's incredible!
<TEC: Join the Team 6e>

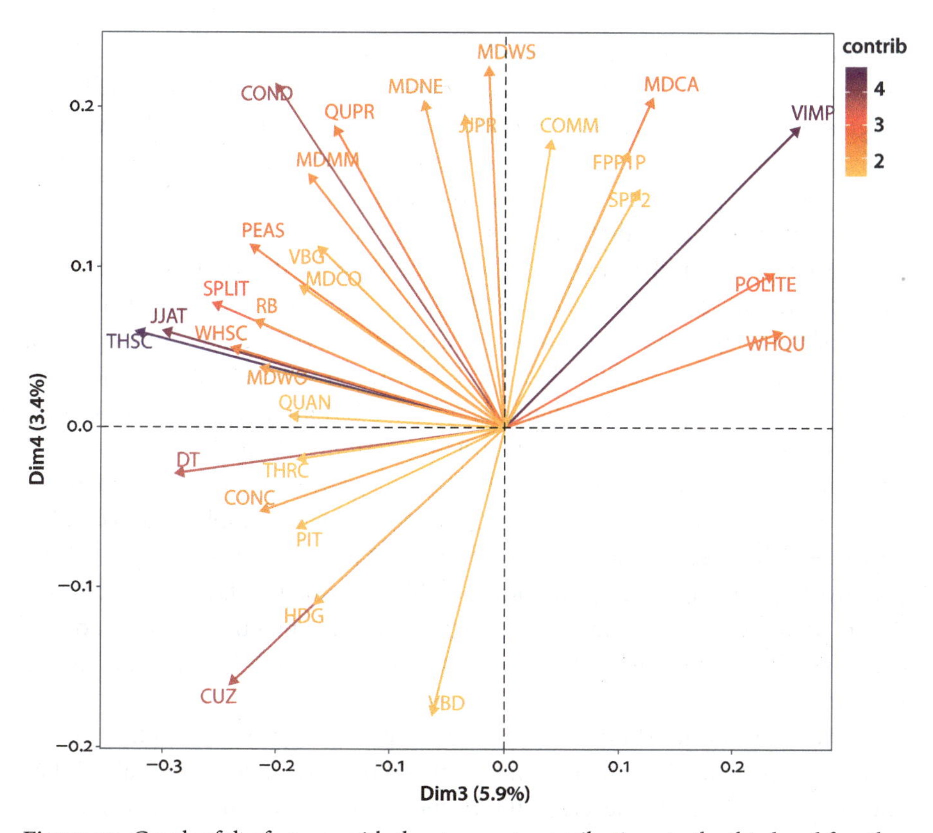

Figure 31. Graph of the features with the strongest contributions to the third and fourth dimensions

In general, this third dimension indicates that, as opposed to non-textbook language, Textbook English is characterised by high lexical density (LD) and, in particular, a high frequency of nouns (NN). Encouragingly, Figure 30 shows that, on this 'Pedagogically adapted vs. Natural' dimension, texts from more advanced textbooks tend to score most like their corresponding reference corpora, although the gap between Level E textbook dialogues and the Spoken BNC2014 remains alarmingly wide.

The fourth dimension to emerge from this 'Textbook English vs. real-world English' PCA accounts for just 3.42% of the total variance. However, it is considered of relevance in the present study because it further contributes to identifying aspects of Textbook Conversation that distinguish this text variety from naturally occurring conversation. Whilst the ellipses of the other two TEC ellipses largely overlap with those of their corresponding reference corpora, it is clear from Figure 28 that most Textbook Conversation texts score higher on this dimension than those of the Spoken BNC2014. As shown in Figure 31, the features that characterise its positive pole include conditional clauses (COND), the (semi)modals *must* and *need* (MDNE), *will* and *shall* (MDWS), *may* and *might* (MDMM), the progressive (PROG) and perfect aspects (PEAS), and imperative verbs (VIMP), whilst its negative end is associated with causative subordinators (CUZ), hedges (HDG), and the past tense (VBD). The texts that score highest on this dimension are informative texts that dispense advice (e.g., many texts from the teenkidsnews.com and teenvogue.com subcorpora of the Info Teens corpus) whilst those that score lowest are factual texts reporting on historical events (e.g., many of the texts of the factmonster.com, and historyforkids.net subcorpora of the Info Teens corpus). This could hint at a 'Factual vs. Speculative' dimension, were it not for the fact that hedging devices (HDG) are a major contributor of the positive, 'factual', end of the dimension. Truth be told, this dimension does not lend itself well to a purely functional interpretation: it primarily differentiates between texts with simple verb forms and those with complex ones (modals, perfect and progressive aspects, etc.). The result is that a register that generally employs high rates of simple verb forms per FVP, e.g., natural face-to-face conversation, scores low on this dimension whilst textbooks' synthetic representations of conversation are characterised by many more complex verb forms and therefore score higher.

Given that this fourth dimension (at least partly) captures verb phrase complexity, it is not surprising that, as in the third dimension, it is considerably influenced by the proficiency levels of the textbooks. On this fourth dimension, the proficiency level effects are evidently driven by the fact that many of the aforementioned positive-loading features representing more complex verb forms are not introduced until the second or third year of secondary school EFL tuition. The results of the mixed-effects model computed for PC4 scores indicate that the proficiency level of a textbook affects dimension scores differently depending on the register under study. These effects are visualised in Figure 32. Thus, we observe that, as the proficiency level of the textbooks increases, the dimension scores of the Fiction and Informative textbook subcorpora converge to that of their corresponding reference corpora whereas, curiously, the opposite pattern emerges for Textbook Conversation. The driving forces behind this effect will be examined in the following section (7.2), which delves into the linguistic differences between the texts of the Textbook Conversation subcorpus and those of the Spoken BNC2014.

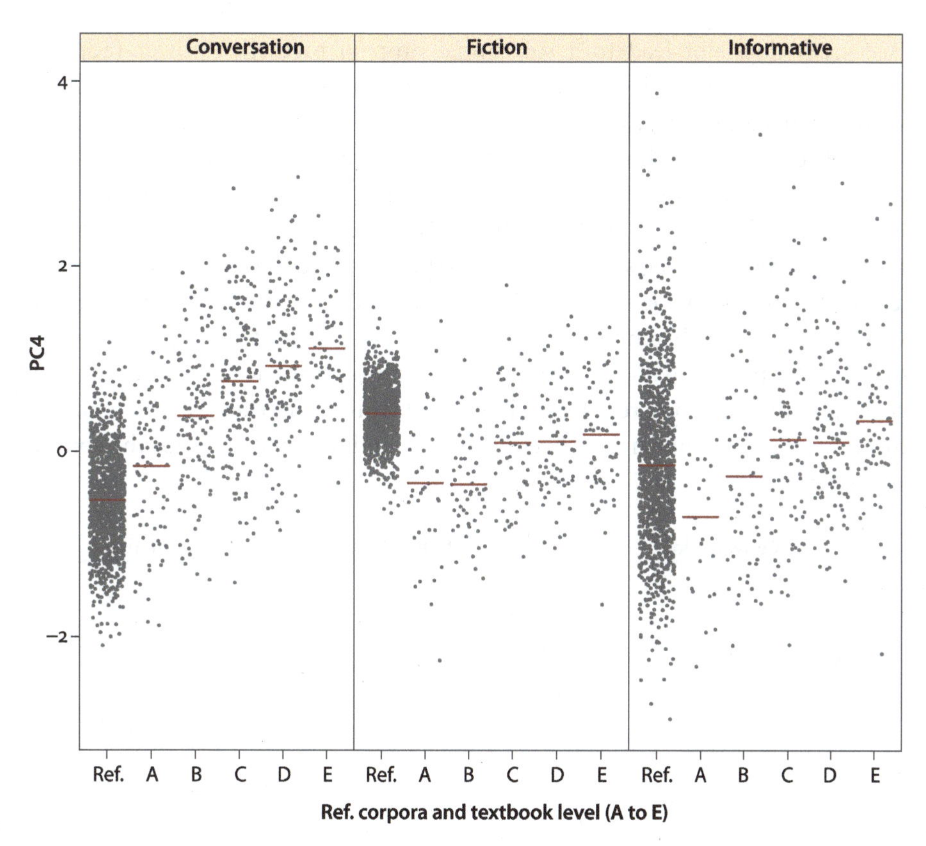

Figure 32. Predicted PC4 scores of the texts of the TEC and the reference corpora

7.2 Textbook conversation vs. the Spoken BNC2014

As seen in Figure 33, most Textbook Conversation texts differ quite substantially from the texts of the Spoken BNC2014 on the first, 'Spontaneous interactional vs. Edited informational' dimension, which explains nearly a third of the total variance in the full data matrix. The projection of texts in Figure 33 also shows that, whilst the reference conversation data forms a relatively tight cluster of texts (*mean* = 3.74, *SD* = 0.49), the ellipse of the conversation subcorpus of the TEC (*mean* = 1.56, *SD* = 1.25) spreads across a much larger area. On this first dimension, therefore, Textbook Conversation texts vary considerably more than the texts of the Spoken BNC2014 that resemble each other much more.

To explore this variation further, PC1 scores were modelled by entering Register, Level, and their interactions in a mixed-effects model. The full model (see summary in Table 22) explains 92% of variation in PC1 scores (conditional R^2). Removing the random slopes and intercepts accounting for different text sources (see 5.3.8) does not lead to a substantial drop in predictive power (adjusted $R^2 = 87\%$). Table 22 confirms that Textbook Conversation at all proficiency levels scores significantly lower on PC1 than the Spoken BNC2014 (here, the reference level). The results also show that the proficiency levels of the textbooks do interact significantly with scores on this first dimension but, as already observed on Biber's (1988) Dimension 1 in the additive MDA (Le Foll 2021c, 2022c: Chapter 6), for the conversation register, not in the expected direction: the more advanced textbooks present dialogues that are even less similar to naturally occurring conversation than the beginner textbooks. This is illustrated in Figure 33, which displays the predicted PC1 scores across the three reference corpora and their corresponding textbook registers subdivided by proficiency levels. The modelled mean PC1 scores confirm that this unexpected finding is only true for the conversation register.

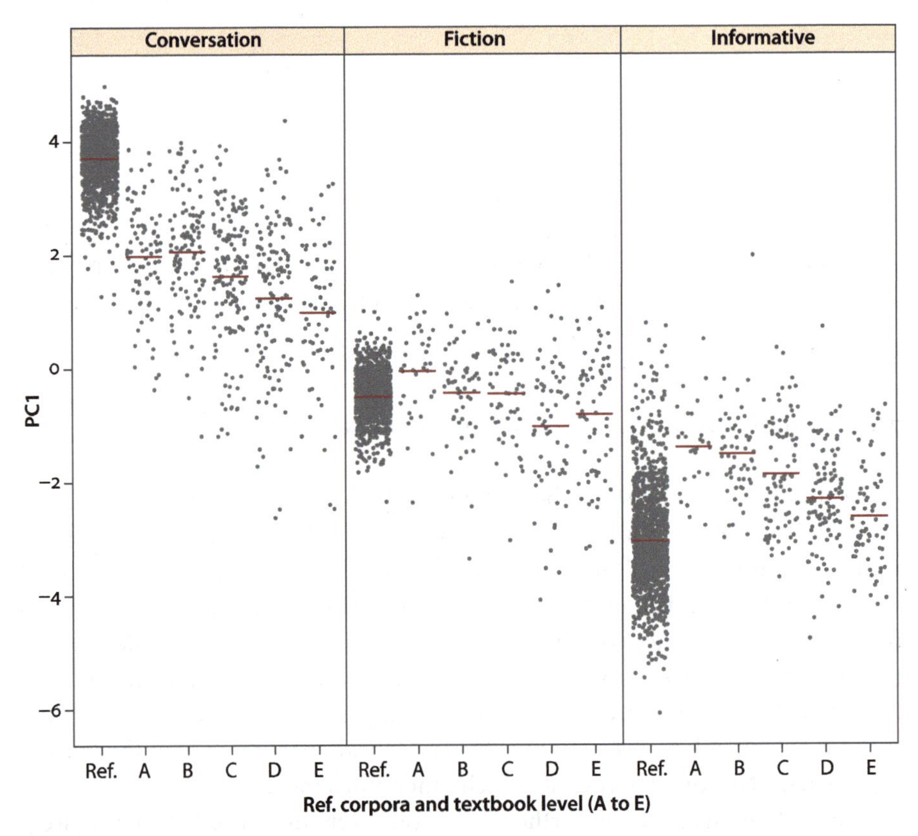

Figure 33. Predicted PC1 scores of the texts of the TEC and the reference corpora

Table 22. Summary of the model: lmer(PC1 ~ 1 + Level + Register + Level*Register + (Register|Source))

Predictors	Estimates	95% CI	*p*-value
(Intercept) [Conversation] [Ref.]	3.71	2.46–4.96	<0.001
Level [A]	−1.73	−3.06–−0.40	0.011
Level [B]	−1.65	−2.97–−0.32	0.015
Level [C]	−2.08	−3.40–−0.76	0.002
Level [D]	−2.47	−3.80–−1.15	<0.001
Level [E]	−2.73	−4.06–−1.40	<0.001
Register [Fiction]	−4.20	−5.45–−2.95	<0.001
Register [Informative]	−6.75	−8.03–−5.47	<0.001
*Level [A] * Register [Fiction]*	2.18	0.86–3.49	0.001
*Level [B] * Register [Fiction]*	1.71	0.41–3.01	0.01
*Level [C] * Register [Fiction]*	2.12	0.83–3.42	0.001
*Level [D] * Register [Fiction]*	1.93	0.64–3.23	0.003
*Level [E] * Register [Fiction]*	2.41	1.10–3.71	<0.001
*Level [A] * Register [Informative]*	3.37	2.01–4.73	<0.001
*Level [B] * Register [Informative]*	3.17	1.83–4.51	<0.001
*Level [C] * Register [Informative]*	3.24	1.90–4.57	<0.001
*Level [D] * Register [Informative]*	3.20	1.87–4.53	<0.001
*Level [E] * Register [Informative]*	3.14	1.80–4.48	<0.001
	Random effects		
σ^2	0.59		
τ_{00} *Source*	0.41		
τ_{11} *Source.RegisterFiction*	0.12		
τ_{11} *Source.RegisterInformative*	0.20		
ρ_{01}	−0.05		
	−0.48		
ICC	0.41		
N *Source*	325		
Marginal R^2 / Conditional R^2	0.870 / 0.923		

We have already noted that the first dimension to emerge from the present MDA bears many similarities to Biber's (1988) Dimension 1. As shown in Figure 26 and Table 20, many of the features with particularly high and low loadings are shared. In particular, the upper end of the dimension is dominated by texts that contain high frequencies of many features of unplanned speech, e.g., discourse markers (DMA), fillers and interjections (FPUH), and causative subordinators (CUZ), as well as features typical of social interaction, e.g., questions and question tags (YNQU, WHQU, QUTAG), first-person and second-person referents (FPP1S, FPP1P, SPP2), as in Extract (35). All of these features are less frequent in Textbook Conversation than in the Spoken BNC2014, which is one of the reasons why, on average, the dialogues of the TEC score significantly lower on PC1 than the transcripts of the Spoken BNC2014, e.g., (36). This is likely because, in their carefully crafted, scripted dialogues, textbook authors very rarely model any disfluencies in spoken interactions, e.g., in the form of hesitations, interruptions, backtracking, or repair. In addition, many Textbook Conversation texts are much more like series of short monologues than genuine interactions. On average, turns are much longer and feature far fewer signs of unplanned speech, e.g., (37).

(35) **yeah well** there's a few things **I** need to do in **um** town
mum was thinking of dropping **me** off at Zumba and then going
yeah well I need to pay **those** cheques in
can **you** pay **my** cheque in? and get some money out for the rent. can **you** pay **my** cheque in?
yeah
thanks
pay your cheque in and anything else **we** need in town?
I can't think but **we**'re gonna have to get up early
what? How early's early?
well I well not too early **we** just leave at nine **we** have to be ready and **I** have to have **my** breakfast before then so **I** can
okay <BNC2014: SWU3>

(36) What are **you** up to at the weekend, Toby?
I'm going to go for a bike ride on Saturday. Do **you** fancy coming too?
I can't, I'm afraid. I'm going to help **my** dad with some gardening. **We**'re going to do some work for a neighbour.
That doesn't sound like the best way to spend **your** weekend. Gardening is hard work! And according to the forecast, the weather isn't going to be good.
I know. But the neighbour is going to pay **us** for **it**. And **my** dad's a gardener so he's got all the right tools.

Really? I'll come and help **you. I mean**, if that's OK with **you** and **your** dad... <TEC: Solutions Intermediate>

(37) **That's right.** This passion for having a perfect body is definitely a negative product of Hollywood. There seems to be an unwritten rule that in order to make it in the movies you must be beautiful. Your looks are almost like your business card and are often the only way to make a good first impression. But things get dangerous when they're taken to extremes. Examples of this are the body builders at Venice Beach, like in this picture, or people who spend tens of thousands of dollars a year on taking care of their looks and on plastic surgery – and they're not just celebrities. But is taking care of your body all bad?
As June said, it's when things are taken to extremes that they're harmful. There's also a very positive side to this Californian symbol. A lot of new kinds of sports were invented in California – here are some examples – and a lot of Californians lead very active and healthy lifestyles. In addition, California is often the country's leader when it comes to making public health laws. The Golden State was the first to ban smoking in workplaces, bars and restaurants in 1998 and now about half of the states in the US have similar laws. The state is also very active in limiting air pollution. But **what about** traffic in places like L.A.? <TEC: Green Line New 5>

Another factor that contributes to lower PC1 scores is the fact that some of the features with high loadings on PC1 are more likely to be used by language users who are physically in the same space, e.g., demonstratives (DEMO) and the pronoun *it* (PIT). It therefore comes as no surprise that these are less frequent in the written and audio (as opposed to audio-visual) materials which make up the largest proportion of the Conversation subcorpus of the TEC. By virtue of sharing a common environment, the speakers of the Spoken BNC2014 can also afford to resort to much vaguer language. This difference is also captured on this first dimension: in addition to the extensive use of demonstratives and the pronoun *it*, it is observable in the considerably more frequent use of quantifiers (QUAN), quantifying pronouns (QUPR), and hedges (HDG) than in Textbook Conversation (38).

(38) oh right so you **sort of** get so you **sort of** get things that **kind of** yeah I guess localised
yeah so you you got a potential for these vast metropolises filled with **loads of like** diverse em cultures and backgrounds **and stuff** but you end up getting **these** close communities em so I wanted to explore **that** idea and and in the video at the end when asked how what what would be the role of an artist em to to explore **this** idea or to confront **it** and em he suggested that

perhaps the artist could expand em **sort of** enlarge the the garden gnome to the size of the statue of liberty **or something** just just poke fun of out of **it** and em so so that that was part of the reasoning for **this** first art project that I was going to do <BNC2014: SCJL>

Since the positive- and negative-loading features that contribute to each dimension are complementary, it is important to not only consider which positive high-loading features are absent from or less frequent in the Conversation subcorpus of the TEC to understand the nature of Textbook Conversation, but also which negative-loading ones are markedly more frequent in the Conversation subcorpus of the TEC than in the reference Spoken BNC2014. These include nouns (NN), prepositions (IN), longer words (AWL), a higher lexical density (LD), and lexical diversity (TTR). In other words, on average, Textbook Conversation is considerably more nominal than naturally occurring conversation. The fact that dialogues from more advanced textbooks score even lower than beginner textbooks on PC1 is due to higher *z*-scores of these features. Excerpts (28), (29), and (37) constitute examples of particularly low-scoring texts from advanced textbooks (level E). By contrast, Excerpt (39) stems from a second-year secondary school textbook and, on this dimension, is situated in the same region as the majority of the Spoken BNC2014 texts. Note that it also features much shorter turns than the average textbook dialogue.

(39) **This** is lovely.
Isn't **it** lovely?
What is **it** exactly?
It's a coffee machine.
Oh, yes. Of course. Is **it** battery powered?
No, it's mains powered.
Look, the cable's here, under the base. If **you** press **this** button, the plug appears.
That's clever. **I** love **it. It's** perfect for my kitchen at home. **I'll** come back later today and buy **it.**
Would **you** like to try a cup before **you** go?
I'm sorry?
A cup of coffee?
Oh, no thanks. **I** never drink coffee. Horrible stuff.
<TEC: Solutions Pre intermediate>

The distribution of texts along the third dimension (PC3) confirms that, as opposed to real-life conversation, Textbook Conversation tends to feature exclusively well-formed polite interactions, with very few disfluencies. Whilst the dialogues of the more advanced textbooks of the TEC score closest to the reference Spoken BNC2014 texts (see Figure 33), a noticeable distance can nevertheless be observed between the two varieties. On this third 'Pedagogically adapted vs. Natural' dimension, it is mostly driven by the high nominal content of Textbook Conversation leading to high noun counts (NN), high lexical density (LD), and proportionally fewer of those nouns being qualified by an attributive adjective (JJAT), as well as generally fewer causative subordinators (CUZ), subordinate clauses per finite verb phrases (THSC and WHSC), and general adverbs (RB). In addition, the modals *could* and *would* and phrasal verbs (as imperfectly captured by the RP variable, see Appendix C) are, across all proficiency levels, less frequent in Textbook Conversation than in the Spoken BNC2014, e.g., (40). These three features also contribute to negative PC3 scores.

(40) I **would** like something to extract all the vegetable
I don't know I I like the idea of eating **very** little meat I **really** love molluscs and they can't and no one else even likes them why can't I have them?
I I doubt they're the worst I mean
do you think should I investigate **whether** the fishing practices **that** get molluscs are harmful to the environment?
yes I also think just reducing the amount you **would** eat **would** be doing a favour to the animals in some ways
but you should also look at erm **who** was involved with the farming industry problem okay? there might be [...]
there might be people treated **badly**
mm mm but that's almost in everything and once you **really** get **down** to it
exactly
like you you **basically**
it's terrifying
stop eating
so that's **probably** so that's why I was a bit like well I **couldn't** commit myself to this erm
no no
lab meat thing **cos** there'll be cruelty somewhere
yeah and
cos there's cruelty in everything there's **probably** cruelty in this potato.
<BNC2014: SFC2>

On the fourth dimension, more advanced Textbook Conversation texts are situated further away from the reference Spoken BNC2014 than beginner and intermediate ones (see Figure 32). One of the driving factors behind this, at first sight, surprising finding is that textbook authors use printed dialogues and audio and video materials to introduce new vocabulary and "recycle" previously introduced lexical items, leading to higher type/token ratios in more advanced textbooks, even though real-life conversations tend not to be characterised by particularly high lexical diversity, e.g., compare (40) and (41).

(41) Good morning Mr. **Stone**. Good morning. So, first, could you tell us more about the **movie**?
Sure, well… As a **historian, Modern Times** seems **particularly interesting** to me because **Chaplin** showed the **effect** of **mechanization** on the **lives** of **people** in the **modern industrialized world**. The **film** is about the **hardship** of an **ordinary** man who **struggles** to **survive** in the **depressed economy** of 1930s **America**. The **factory scene** is just **brilliant**! It is exactly what **modernity** was about at that time: the **assembly line**, the **division** of **labour, mass production** and the **daily grind** of many **industrial workers**. They were **exploited** by their **bosses**, who made them work from **dawn** to **dusk** in very **tough conditions**. The film shows the **workers' repetitive labour** and how some of them went **crazy** as they **repeated** the **same task** over and over again, **tightening bolts** for **instance**. […] <TEC: Piece of Cake 4[e]>

7.3 Textbook Fiction vs. the Youth Fiction corpus

Of the three TEC registers that were compared to target language reference corpora, Textbook Fiction is most similar to its corresponding target reference corpus: the Youth Fiction corpus. This confirms one of the key findings of a preliminary additive MDA (Le Foll 2021c, 2022c: Chapter 6). Where differences are observed, they are mostly due to beginner textbooks having not yet introduced more advanced grammatical features. Indeed, the strong proficiency level effects observed along the second 'Narrative vs. Non-narrative' dimension (see Table 23) are largely driven by the absence of the past tense in Level A textbooks. Other high positive-loading features on PC2 that are almost entirely absent from Levels A and B textbooks include the modals *could* and *would* (MDCO and MDWO), and the perfect aspect (PEAS). In addition, the PC2 scores of Level A Textbook Fiction texts are lower due to a strong over-representation of two features with some of the largest negative-loading weights on this second dimension (see Table 20): the modal *can* (MDCA) (median = 6.25 per 100 FVPs) as compared to Youth Fiction (median = 1.65 per 100 FVPs) and BE as a main verb (BEMA) (19.2 per 100 FVPs compared to 14.2).

It is, however, important to remember that there are relatively few Level A texts in the Fiction subcorpus of the TEC so that these figures must be interpreted

Table 23. Summary of the model: lmer(PC2 ~ 1+Level+Register+Level*Register+(1|Source))

Predictors	Estimates	95% CI	*p*-value
(Intercept) [Conversation] [Ref.]	−0.52	−1.27–0.24	0.183
Level [A]	−0.54	−1.35–0.28	0.195
Level [B]	−0.15	−0.96–0.66	0.721
Level [C]	0.08	−0.72–0.89	0.842
Level [D]	0.04	−0.76–0.85	0.915
Level [E]	0.07	−0.75–0.89	0.866
Register [Fiction]	2.27	1.51–3.03	<0.001
Register [Informative]	−0.46	−1.24–0.32	0.25
*Level [A] * Register [Fiction]*	−1.01	−1.82–−0.21	0.014
*Level [B] * Register [Fiction]*	−0.25	−1.04–0.54	0.532
*Level [C] * Register [Fiction]*	−0.21	−1.00–0.58	0.602
*Level [D] * Register [Fiction]*	−0.41	−1.20–0.38	0.307
*Level [E] * Register [Fiction]*	−0.47	−1.26–0.32	0.246
*Level [A] * Register [Informative]*	0.49	−0.34–1.33	0.246
*Level [B] * Register [Informative]*	0.59	−0.22–1.40	0.154
*Level [C] * Register [Informative]*	0.26	−0.54–1.06	0.524
*Level [D] * Register [Informative]*	0.55	−0.26–1.35	0.183
*Level [E] * Register [Informative]*	0.33	−0.49–1.14	0.431
	Random effects		
σ^2	0.45		
$\tau_{00\ Source}$	0.15		
ICC	0.25		
N_{Source}	325		
Observations	4980		
Marginal R^2 / *Conditional* R^2	0.671 / 0.753		

with caution. Nonetheless, Excerpt (42) constitutes a representative example of a narrative text from a beginner EFL textbook: it relies on present tense narration and features high frequencies of BE as a main verb and the modal *can*.

(42) B) Holly **is** at home with her two guinea pigs, Mr Fluff and Honey. They live in the kitchen. But they **aren't** in the kitchen now. They**'re** in Holly's room.

It's fun for the guinea pigs on the floor. They **can** explore – everywhere in the room! C) Ding-dong! Who's at the door? It's Holly's best friend Olivia..
<TEC: Green Line New 1>

Textbook Fiction texts that score within the range of the Youth Fiction corpus on the second dimension are characterised by high frequencies of past tense (VBD) and perfect aspect (PEAS) verbs, third-person referents (TPP3), and verbs of communication (COMM), but also *could* (MDCO), phrasal verbs (RP), and general adverbs (RB), see (43). That said, the latter two features are key contributors to the slightly lower average scores of intermediate and advanced Textbook Fiction texts compared to the Youth Fiction corpus (see Table 23 and Figure 34). Contrary to expectations, type/token ratio (TTR) or average word length (AWL) do not contribute to the observed minor differences between the more advanced Textbook Fiction texts and the reference Youth Fiction corpus.

(43) **He ran back** to Bill. On the way **he picked up** a stick. As **he came** over the hill, **he ran** at the boar, hitting it again and again. It **turned** to face Colm. There **was** blood on its tusks. Bill **tried** to pull himself away, leaving a trail of blood behind **him.** Colm raised the stick high and brought it **down** on the boar's head. The boar **snorted**, but instead of running at Colm, it **turned back** to Bill. Colm **threw** the stick **down** and **grabbed** Bill's gun. **He was** shaking as **he raised** the gun to **his** shoulder. Colm **knew** that if **he shot** the animal in the back, it would only make it wild. **He let** out a scream, a long, loud scream. The boar **turned round.** <TEC: Access G 5>

Figure 34 clearly shows that, aside from Level A Textbook Fiction, the narrative texts of the TEC are, on average, largely comparable to those of the Youth Fiction on this second dimension. Encouragingly, the Register*Level effect plots in Figures 30 and 32 show that this is also true on the third and fourth dimensions. It is, however, worth noting that there is a great deal more variation within the Textbook Fiction subcorpus than there is across the much larger Youth Fiction corpus, as evident from the large range of predicted dimension scores on all dimensions and across all proficiency levels (see, e.g., Figure 26). The Textbook Fiction subcorpus being relatively small (285 texts, ca. 241,500 words) and narrative texts being rather rare in the three French textbook series (see 4.3.1.3), further data from additional textbooks would be needed to confirm the trends concerning Textbook Fiction reported in this and the previous chapter.

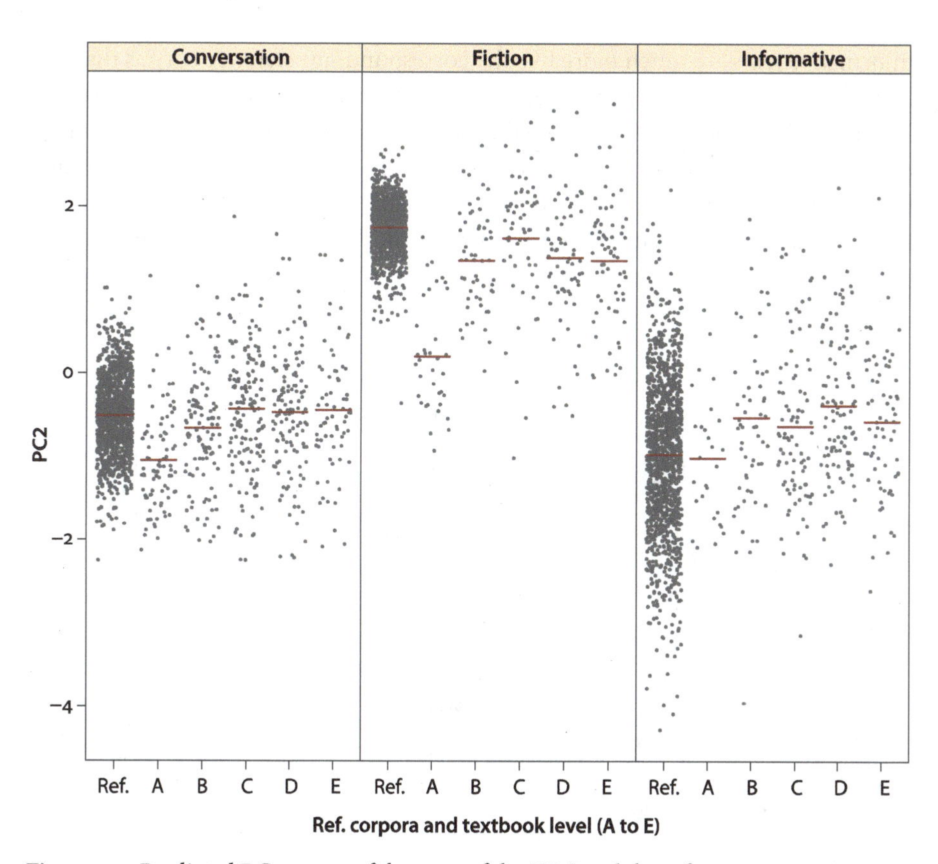

Figure 34. Predicted PC2 scores of the texts of the TEC and the reference corpora

7.4 Textbook Informative vs. the Info Teens corpus

The most striking differences between the Textbook Informative subcorpus and the Info Teens reference corpus can be observed on the first dimension. Echoing the results of the additive MDA reported in Le Foll (2021c, 2022c: Chapter 6), Figures 25 and 26 indicate that some of the Textbook Informative texts are closer to the interactional, "oral-like" end of the dimension than the Info Teens reference corpus. Figure 26 also shows some overlap between the ellipses of the Textbook Informative and the Textbook Fiction subcorpora. Thus, we find that a proportion of textbook texts blur the otherwise well-defined register-based distinctions between the three reference corpora that emerge from the combination of the first and second dimension in Figure 26. As confirmed by the model summarised in Table 22 and visualised in Figure 33, however, many of the Textbook Informative texts that are not within the ellipse of the Info Teens corpus stem from beginner textbooks. In fact, on the first, third, and fourth dimensions, the more advanced informative texts are much more like the corresponding reference corpus than the less advanced ones. These proficiency level patterns have already been explored in the previous chapter on intra-textbook variation. Interestingly, the differences observed between the texts of the beginner Textbook Informative subcorpus and those of the Info Teens corpus are only partially due to more complex linguistic features not being introduced until after the first few years of EFL tuition.

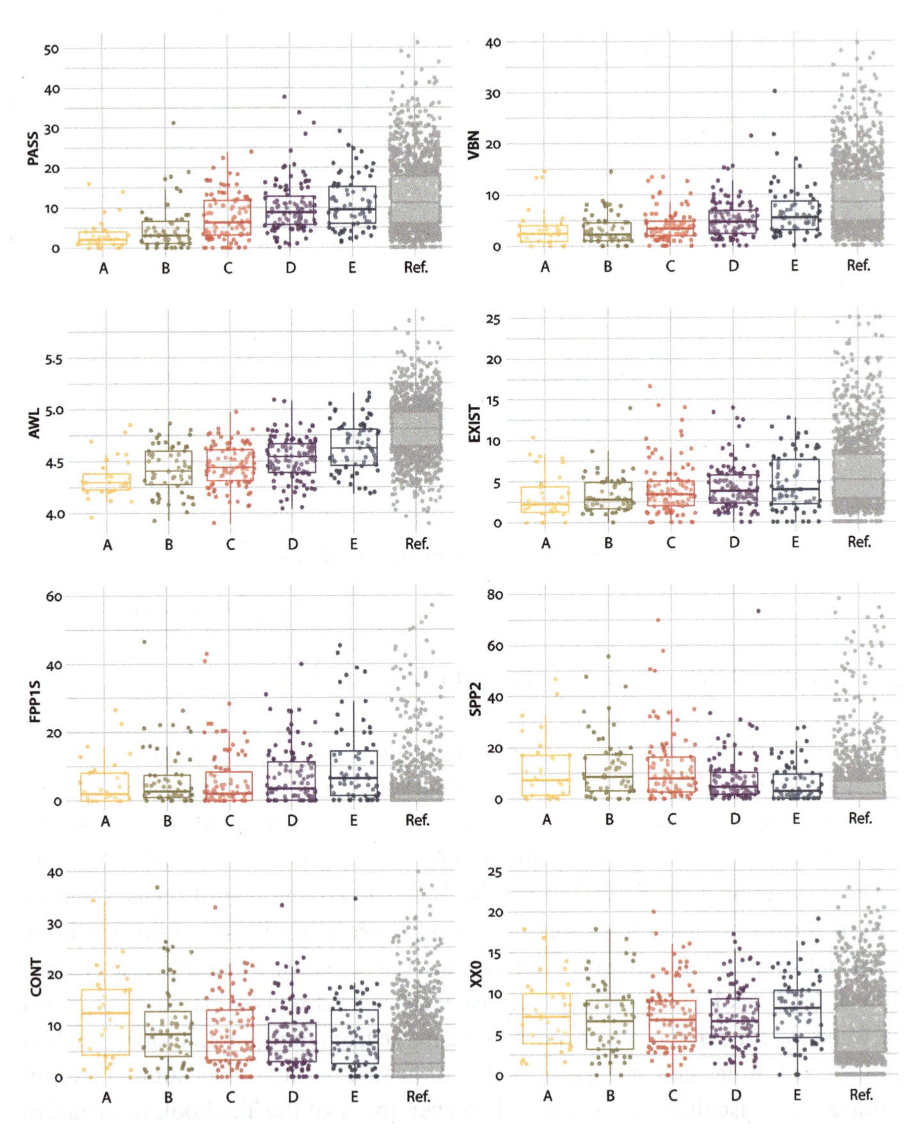

Figure 35. Normalised counts of selected features with salient loadings on PC1 in the Textbook Informative subcorpus (Levels A to E) and the reference Info Teens corpus (Ref.). Outliers have been removed for greater legibility (see Appendix G for details).

Figure 35 displays normalised counts for a sample of features with high absolute loadings on PC1 that most contribute to the differences observed between textbook and non-textbook informative texts.

Three groups of features can be identified in Figure 35. The first group consists of complex grammatical features such as passive constructions (PASS) and non-finite present participial constructions (VBN) which, as expected, are very infrequent in beginner informative texts but, as Figure 35 makes clear, whose frequencies progressively increase as learners are expected to progress. Second, we find features such as average word length (AWL) and existential verbs (EXIST) which also have considerably lower rates in beginner textbooks than in more advanced ones, but whose rates in Level E textbooks do not, on average, reach rates quite as high as those observed in the Info Teens corpus. Finally, the third group of interest consists of features that are, across all proficiency levels, more frequent in the Textbook Informative subcorpus than in the reference Info Teens. As these features have high positive-loading weights on PC1, they contribute to the observed shift of Textbook Informative texts towards the middle of the plots in Figures 24 and 26. They include singular first- and second-person referents (FPP1S and SPP2), verbal contractions (CONT), and negation (XX0), which on average are considerably rarer in the texts of the Info Teens corpus than in Textbook Informative writing. These differences are exemplified in Excerpts (44) and (45). In (44), the highlighted words correspond to negative-loading features that are, on average, rare in Textbook Informative texts yet typical of the Info, whilst the words in bold in (45) correspond to positive-loading features that contribute to Textbook Informative texts scoring higher on the first dimension than those of the Info Teens reference corpus.

(44) Tennyson was the son of an intelligent but unstable clergyman in Lincolnshire. His early literary attempts **included** a play, The Devil and the Lady, **composed** at 14, and poems **written** with his brothers Frederick and Charles but **entitled** Poems by Two Brothers (1827). [...] His volume Poems (1832) **included** some of his most famous pieces, such as "The Lotus-Eaters," "A Dream of Fair Women," and "The Lady of Shalott." In 1833 he **was overwhelmed** by the sudden death of Hallam. [...] Tennyson passed his last years in comfort. In 1883 he **was created** a peer and occupied a seat in the House of Lords. Throughout much of his life he was a popular as well as critical success and **was venerated** by the general public. Ignored early in the 20th century, Tennyson has since **been recognized** as a great poet, notable for his mastery of technique, his superb use of sensuous language, and his profundity of thought. ⟨Info Teens: factmonster.com⟩

(45) **You** might be surprised at the number of rather unusual sports that exist around the world. Mostly, they are little known outside the areas where they were invented – though occasionally they have gained international recognition. Here are some examples – but, if **you're** interested, have a look on the web. **You** may find other, even crazier, ones!
Sandboarding
Of course there **can't** be many people who **don't** know what snowboarding is, but how about sandboarding? The basic principle behind the two sports is the same; start at the top of a slope and use a board to get **you** to the bottom. [...] It's popular in many countries, including Australia, Namibia and South Africa. The quickest way of getting to the bottom involves standing with both feet on a board and weaving from side to side while trying not to fall off. If this sounds a little bit adventurous **you** could always just get on **your** stomach and slide down. Either way, it's a lot of fun! However, **don't** forget to keep **your** mouth closed. <TEC: English in Mind 4>

The less pronounced differences observed between the texts of the Info Teens and those of the Textbook Informative subcorpus on the second 'Narrative vs. Non-narrative' dimension (see Figure 34) are largely driven by past tense verbs: we know that they are largely absent from Level A textbooks, but, as soon as this tense and, to a lesser extent, the perfect aspect are introduced, textbooks from Level B onwards tend to feature more past and perfect aspect verbs in informative texts than are generally found in the texts of the Info Teens corpus. This explains the small overlap between the Textbook Informative ellipse (purple) and the ellipses of the two fiction corpora (light and dark green) on Figure 26.

CHAPTER 8

Discussion

What is Textbook English?

Chapters 6 and 7 presented two multi-feature/multi-dimensional models of Textbook English. The first depicted linguistic variation within secondary school EFL textbook series, whilst the second presented a comparative model highlighting the similarities and differences between Textbook English and situationally similar texts from outside the EFL classroom. The first model showed that Textbook English cannot be adequately described without considering register- and proficiency-level-based variation. It also highlighted the clusters of linguistic features that most contribute to this intra-textbook linguistic variation. In Chapter 7, the comparative model of Textbook English vs. 'real-world' English explored the key linguistic differences that set textbook-like texts apart from those found outside the EFL classroom. It also described how these differences are mediated by the effects of both register and proficiency level, as well as their interactions on three dimensions of variation. This chapter summarise and discusses the key findings that emerged from these two models by revisiting the four sets of research questions formulated in Chapter 4.

8.1 RQ1: How homogenous is Textbook English as a variety of English? Which factors mediate intra-textbook linguistic variation?

The results of the present study have confirmed that Textbook English cannot be conceptualised as a homogenous variety of English. Indeed, we have seen that a much larger proportion of intra-textbook variation can be attributed to register differences than to proficiency levels, country of use, or of any potential idiosyncrasies of specific groups of authors or editorial policies (as captured by the textbook series variable). In particular, the first few dimensions of the model of intra-textbook variation in Chapter 6 revealed distinct clusters for the Conversation, Instructional, and Informative register subcorpora of the TEC (see Figures 9 and 10).

The linguistic interpretation of the loadings of the 61 lexico-grammatical and semantic features entered in the model of intra-textbook variation highlighted the defining characteristics of these different registers that are frequently featured in secondary school EFL textbooks. While the two models also demonstrated clear examples of proficiency level effects, register-driven variation was far more substantial. In addition, we also noted some significant interactions between register- and proficiency-level-based variation. The most notable such interaction occurred with the fiction register and was due to the near absence of the past tense and perfect aspect in beginner textbooks. However, these effects were limited in scope when compared with the extent of register-driven variation.

8.2 RQ2: To what extent are French, German, and Spanish secondary school pupils confronted with varying English input via their textbooks?

Given that the textbooks examined as part of this project were designed for very different educational contexts, it was hypothesised that there would be noticeable differences in the nature of the language input that students learning English in France, Spain, and Germany are exposed to via their textbooks. In answer to this second research question, however, no statistically significant, systematic differences could be discerned between the language of textbooks used in these three European countries. Similarly, when comparing the nine textbook series of the TEC, very little of the observed intra-textbook linguistic variation could be attributed to the authors or editorial policies of individual textbook series. We can therefore conclude that the variety of English that French, German, and Spanish secondary school pupils are confronted with via their textbooks is, in fact, remarkably similar, despite different academic traditions, school systems, and textbook publishing structures.

That being said, it is worth remembering that the present study focused on the *qualitative* nature of the English input delivered via secondary school EFL textbooks. There are, however, major differences in terms of the *quantity* of English texts that learners in France, Germany, and Spain are (potentially) exposed to via their textbooks. Indeed, of the three "national" subcorpora of the TEC, the French subcorpus is the smallest (see Figure 1 in 4.3.1.3). This is because the French textbooks of the TEC contain fewer, shorter texts and a much higher proportion of non-English input than the textbooks used in Germany and Spain. Of course, it goes without saying that not all secondary school pupils in Germany or Spain will engage with every single text featured in their coursebooks. It is perfectly conceivable that some teachers use textbooks more as "sourcebooks" from which to pick and choose the texts and activities they believe to be most suitable for their students (see, e.g., Möller 2016; Schaer 2007). Equally, we can expect many teachers, in France and elsewhere, to supplement the textbook contents with additional (textbook or non-textbook) materials. Nonetheless, future research focusing on teachers' and learners' perceptions of EFL textbooks and/or their pedagogical effectiveness ought to consider both the *quantity* and *quality* of textbook-based language input given that both factors are likely to impact learners' development of linguistic competences.

8.3 RQ3: To what extent is the language of current EFL textbooks used in secondary schools in France, Germany, and Spain representative of 'real-world' English as used by native/proficient English speakers in similar communicative situations? To what extent are some registers more faithfully represented than others?

The second MDA conducted in Chapter 7 aimed to model three major registers of Textbook English in relation to the three corresponding target learner language reference corpora: the Spoken BNC2014 (4.3.2.1), Info Teens (4.3.2.4) and Youth Fiction (4.3.2.5). The results clearly show that, whilst register-based differences within textbooks do exist, they are considerably less pronounced than in 'authentic', 'real-world' English. The similarities and differences between these three textbook registers and comparable 'real-world' registers were examined on four dimensions of linguistic variation.

Except for the rare few narrative texts in beginner textbooks which rely on present-tense narration and understandably feature very limited vocabulary, the results suggest that Fiction is the most faithfully represented register in school EFL textbooks. This is demonstrated by the large overlaps between the Textbook Fiction and the Youth Fiction ellipses on the bi-dimensional projections of texts in Figures 26 and 28. We also noted considerable overlaps in the Informative register. By contrast, on all multi-dimensional projections of texts, only a small proportion of the Textbook Conversation texts are situated within the ellipses of the Spoken BNC2014, thus pointing to major differences between natural speech and textbook representations thereof. These findings confirm the trends observed in two comparative case studies on representations of the progressive (Le Foll 2022a, 2022c: Chapter 4) and the verb MAKE (Le Foll 2022b, 2022c: Chapter 5) in the Conversation and Fiction subcorpora of the TEC.

8.3.1 Representations of spoken, conversational English in school EFL textbooks

Section 7.2 brought to light the constellation of features that make most textbook dialogues fundamentally different from naturally occurring conversation (as captured by the Spoken BNC2014). These include low frequencies of many features that are typical of spontaneous speech, including fillers and interjections, discourse markers and causative subordinators, markers of interactional discourse such as tag questions, WH-questions, pronouns, as well as hedges and demonstratives in communicative situations in which interlocutors share a common environment and/or common knowledge (see also Figure 27).

Furthermore, we saw that Textbook Conversation is characterised by a highly nominal style. The dialogues of textbooks are defined by high lexical density and diversity. Hence, they display considerably more diverse and often complex vocabulary than everyday, 'real-world' conversation. At the same time, however, they feature far fewer syntactic structures that are characteristic of more complex utterances, e.g., *that* and WH-subordinate clauses and causative subordination (see Figure 31). Confirming an earlier analysis on the verb MAKE with the same data (Le Foll 2022b: 173–175), phrasal verbs were also found to be conspicuously rare in textbook dialogues, including those featured in the more advanced textbook volumes of the TEC. Section 9.1 is devoted to the potential implications of these inauthentic representations of conversational English in pedagogical EFL materials. It is followed by recommendations as to how the results of this study can be used to make textbook representations of spoken interactions more natural in 9.2.

8.3.2 Representations of informative texts in school EFL textbooks

The results also pointed to some consequential differences between the texts of the Informative subcorpus of the TEC and those of the Info Teens corpus (see 7.4). However, we noted that the location of Textbook Informative texts on several dimensions of variation is strongly mediated by interaction effects by the proficiency levels of the textbooks. Reassuringly, informative texts in the more advanced textbooks of the TEC share more similarities with the texts of the Info Teens corpus than differences.

Nonetheless, the Informative subcorpus of the TEC is characterised, on the one hand, by shorter words and fewer verbs belonging to the semantic category of existential/relationship verbs (e.g., *INVOLVE, IMPLY, REPRESENT, SEEM*) and, on the other, by higher relative frequencies of first-person singular and second-person referents, contracted and negated verbs. Together with the results of the intra-textbook analysis, these observations suggest that some of the informative texts of the TEC can be considered to represent hybrid registers: their linguistic characteristics frequently cross the line between factual and impersonal informative writing, narrative explanations, and involved, interactional communication. Potential pedagogical consequences of this lack of register coherence are discussed in Chapter 9.

8.3.3 Representations of fiction in school EFL textbooks

Excluding the texts from beginner textbooks, Textbook Fiction was found to be closest to its corresponding reference corpus on all dimensions of variation examined. This finding is easily explained: unlike dialogues and informative texts which are mostly crafted especially for pedagogical purposes, many of the narrative texts featured in school EFL textbooks are extracts of 'authentic', published, popular novels and short stories – samples of which may even feature in the Youth Fiction corpus. That said, a couple of caveats also deserve mention.

First, Textbook Fiction is one of the smallest register subcorpora of the TEC, meaning that the sample may not be representative of this register within Textbook English as a whole (see Table 6). Of the 42 textbook volumes of the TEC, some include no or very few fiction texts (see Figure 1). In particular, the three French textbook series hardly feature any fiction texts. This is worth highlighting because, when (very minor) differences across textbook series *were* observed, these almost always concerned the French textbook series (see also Le Foll 2018a).

8.4 RQ4: What are the defining linguistic features that characterise Textbook English registers as compared to these target language registers? To what extent are these defining features stable across entire textbook series? To what extent are some specific to certain proficiency levels?

Whilst the comparative model presented in Chapter 7 shows that many Conversation, Fiction, and Informative texts featured in school EFL textbooks are, at least on the first two dimensions of linguistic variation, very akin to or sometimes even practically indistinguishable from situationally similar real-world texts, the ellipses of the three TEC registers are nonetheless noticeably shifted towards the middle of the plot as compared to those of the corresponding reference corpora (see Figure 26). These register-specific differences were discussed in the previous section.

By contrast, the third dimension, 'Pedagogically adapted vs. Natural', that emerged from the comparative MDA of Textbook English revealed a gap between textbook and non-textbook language that appears to transcend register-specific variation. As shown in Figure 41, regardless of their register, the texts of the TEC tend to be shifted towards the positive end of this dimension.

In sum, the most prototypical exemplar texts of Textbook English are likely to be located around zero on the 'Spontaneous interactional vs. Edited informational' and 'Narrative vs. Non-narrative' dimensions (i.e., in the intercept of Figure 26) and towards the 'adapted' end of the 'Pedagogically adapted vs. Natural' dimension (i.e., in the right-hand side panel of Figure 41). In the following, we will examine Excerpts (46) to (48), which are examples of such texts and can thus be said to be most "prototypically textbook-like". They are stylistically remarkably similar even though (46) corresponds to an interview, (47) to an informative text, and (48) represents fiction. Moreover, they are taken from three different textbook series. Yet, they share many linguistic features: an abundance of nominal phrases, high lexical density, high relative frequencies of *yes/no* and WH-questions, a strong preference for the modal *can* over other modal verbs, and BE as a main verb over other lexical verbs, to mention but a few. In other words, these texts are written in an informal style that, in many ways, appears to emulate some aspects of casual conversation yet, as seen in all the comparisons with the Spoken BNC2014 in 7.2, these texts nonetheless lack many of the defining features of natural, spontaneous conversation.

Excerpt (46) constitutes a representative example of a typical textbook dialogue in that, whilst it attempts to model some natural disfluencies in the form of hesitations and the occasional paralinguistic filler or discourse marker (*mmm, well*), it remains first and foremost a vehicle for vocabulary teaching. Hence, the dialogue is built around words, phrases, and idioms that are to be acquired by the learners. In Excerpt (46), these include *playground, kangaroo, palm tree, suit sb. down to the ground, kookaburra, sailing boat, bush*, and *rollers*. In such texts, the textbook authors clearly prioritise the placement of these vocabulary items over the naturalness of the dialogue. This observation does not imply that such a focus cannot be pedagogically well-founded. Potential issues only arise if learners are expected to acquire the necessary linguistic and pragmatic competences to interact with others in spontaneous conversation *solely* on the basis of such highly unnatural models of spoken interaction (more on this in Chapter 9).

(46) Now, **what** about you, **Charlene**? **What** it is like to live here?
Well, it's really great! We have a vast **garden**. And it's a great **playground** for **Joey**, our two-year-old **kangaroo**. The **garden**'s full of **palm trees** and exotic **plants**. There's **kookaburras** and other **birds** that sing all **day** long.

It's really wonderful! Our **house is** typically Australian, which suits me down to the **ground.** And the **view** from the front **porch is** fabulous! We **can** see **sailing boats** everywhere in the **summer.**
Now, tell us about your **everyday life. What** do you do here in **Sydney?**
On **Sundays,** we usually go walking in the **bush** with the whole **family.** And we also go shopping at the **Rocks** or on **Circular Quay.** And if we've got **time,** we go for a **walk** in **Hyde Park.**
Charlene?
We often go on **visits** to the **Aquarium, Darling Harbour** and **Taronga Zoo** with **friends.** We go to **Bondi beach.** Mmm... there's great **rollers** there for **surfing.** <TEC: New Bridges 2de>

Another prototypical textbook text that blurs register differences can be seen text (47). Although it is cast as an informative text in the form of a short article, it is much more spoken-like than the majority of informative texts found in the Info Teens corpus: it features rhetorical questions, many second-person referents, and a number of discourse markers typical of speech.

(47) The British **soap opera Coronation Street** started in 1960 and **is** still on TV today. Other popular **soaps are Neighbours, Emmerdale** and **EastEnders.** All the **soaps** try to be realistic about **life** with its happy **times,** its **problems** and some **violence.** The **name** "**soap opera**", or just "**soap**", goes back to **radio dramas** in the 1930s – the **commercials were** for **housewives,** and they advertised **soap,** and other cleaning **products.** Want to be a **star?** Want to be discovered? Not so fast! Before you **can** get anywhere, the **programme** has to "cast" you first. Have you ever been invited to do a **casting?** You haven't? Well, **TEENBUZZ** tells you all about it. **Matt Stirling** from **East-Enders can** give you a few **tips,** too. First, you talk to an **agent** and give him or her your **photo.** Then one day the **agent** is phoned by a **Casting Director** who is looking for a special **character** for a **soap.** She tells the **agent** who she needs. Let's call him "**Justin**". So the **agent** looks through his **files** and finds a **photo** of – you! Your **photo** is sent to the **Casting Director,** who looks at hundreds of **photos** for the right "**Justin**". She likes your **face!**
<TEC: Green Line 3>

Excerpt (48) is a representative example of a fictional text from a textbook targeted at learners in their second year of English classes at secondary school. It is narrated in the present tense and features more contracted verbs and occurrences of BE as a main verb per finite verb phrase than the average novel targeted at teenagers and young adults. However, it would be inappropriate to conclude that it is 'unnatural' or 'inauthentic' simply by virtue of being situated among the clusters of 'prototypically textbook-like' texts on Figures 40 and 41. The fact that such texts are amongst the most stereotypically textbook-like texts located in the middle of Figures 26 and 41 and towards the positive end of Dimension 3 (see also Figure 28) merely points to the narrative nature of prototypical textbook texts, regardless of the register they intend to portray, as illustrated in (46) and (47).

(48) "There **are** good ideas and bad **ideas,**" thinks **Ruby.** "And this **is** a bad **idea.**" On **Saturdays, Ruby** usually reads or paints at **home.** She often goes out and takes unusual **photos** of **things** in her **town.** Sometimes she even makes short **films** and uploads them onto her **website.** But today, on this cold, sunny **Saturday** in **April, Ruby** is running up a **mountain.** OK, it**'s** a very small **mountain.** But **Ruby doesn't** like **mountains.** And she hates **running. Ruby** and her **friends** are raising **money** for a **charity.** They want to help **schools** in **Africa** buy new **computers.** And yes, **Ruby** knows it**'s** a good **idea** to raise **money** for **charity.** But **running**? Up a **mountain**? That **is** simply terrible. **Ruby** stops, closes her **eyes** and holds her **head** in her **hands.** She feels terrible. She **is** out of **breath,** her **chest** is burning and her **legs** hurt.
<TEC: Achievers A2>

Whilst the defining characteristics of Textbook English captured on the pedagogical end of the 'Pedagogically adapted vs. Natural' dimension are common to all three textbook registers entered in this analysis (Conversation, Fiction, and Informative texts), they are strongly mediated by textbooks' intended proficiency levels. This means that texts intended for beginner EFL learners are much more likely to be situated high on the 'Pedagogically adapted' end of the dimension, whereas texts intended for more advanced learners are usually located on the 'Natural' end.

Though to a much lesser extent, we also saw that, on the first ('Spontaneous interactional vs. Edited informational') and second ('Narrative vs. Non-narrative') dimensions of the comparative model presented in Chapter 7, proficiency level effects interact with the degree of linguistic similarity observed between the texts featured in EFL textbooks and those of the reference corpora. Given the obvious relationship between the language of foreign language textbooks and textbook users' target proficiency levels, the presence of such proficiency level effects does not come as a surprise. As in the third, 'Pedagogically adapted vs. Natural' dimension, we expected that, on the first and second dimensions that explain the most linguistic variation, more advanced textbooks texts of all registers would score closer to those of their corresponding reference corpora than those aimed at less proficient learners. However, the observed interaction effects between register-based and proficiency-level-based variation did not always match these expectations. In particular, the proficiency level trends observed for Textbook Conversation on the

'Spontaneous interactional vs. Edited informational' dimension follow the opposite direction to what common sense would have predicted: Conversation texts from the most advanced textbooks of the TEC are, on average, the ones that are most different to the transcripts of the Spoken BNC2014 (see 7.2).

In sum, we have seen that Textbook English differs considerably from English as used outside the EFL classroom and that not all the differences observed can meaningfully be attributed to textbook language being adapted to meet the needs of learners of different proficiency levels. In the following chapter, we discuss the potential pedagogical implications of the study's main findings.

CHAPTER 9

Pedagogical implications and recommendations

This chapter considers the potential impact of Textbook English as a distinct variety of English on secondary school EFL learners. On this basis, a series of recommendations are then made. These are illustrated by concrete examples for practitioners involved in foreign language teaching, teacher training, and materials design.

Before doing so, however, it is worth remembering that the analyses presented in this study are, by nature, descriptive. The aim of the study was decisively not to investigate the *effectiveness* of Textbook English or the extent to which prototypically textbook-like language may or may not support EFL learners in their English acquisition processes. That said, it has provided the first comprehensive account of how the language of lower secondary school textbooks used in three European countries differs from the kind of English learners can be expected to interact with outside the EFL classroom and, as such, can help point to potentially problematic areas where improvements could be made.

Moreover, it should be stressed that the proficiency level effects that were found to mediate linguistic variation within Textbook English suggest that some of the identified defining characteristics of Textbook English are pedagogically well-founded, or, at the very least, intended by the textbook authors and editors. Of course, it would not make pedagogical sense to expose learners to the same kind of language in their first year of learning English as in their fifth. At the same time, however, we have seen that some of the distinctive features of Textbook English are common to textbooks targeted at a range of proficiency levels.

Thus, this chapter first considers the potential consequences of exclusively teaching 'Textbook English' to secondary school EFL learners (9.1), before making concrete suggestions as to how corpora can be used to improve representations of conversational, spoken English (9.2), on the one hand and informative, written English, on the other (9.3). Having concluded that English cannot, even at lower secondary school level, be conceptualised as a monolithic entity, Section 9.4 argues that it is high time we shifted towards a *register approach* to teaching languages. The chapter concludes with a discussion of the implications of such an approach both for teacher education (9.4.1) and materials design (9.4.2).

9.1 Unpacking the role and impact of Textbook English

When Segermann (2000: 339) asserted that foreign language textbook texts represent a text type "*sui generis*", she probably had the kind of texts situated in the middle of Figure 26 in mind, see also Excerpts (46), (47), and (48). These texts epitomise the type of contrived language which has been meticulously crafted by textbook authors to fulfil very specific pedagogical criteria. Constraints on textbook authors are multiple. In many cases, these texts are predominently determined by the lexis and grammar of the stringent learning progressions that are enshrined in the textbooks' tables of contents and which are, in turn, devised on the basis of the curricula and syllabi in force (see Burton 2023). It is not uncommon for textbook authors and teachers to believe that this particular type of contrived text is – at least in the first few years of language learning – indispensable because learners are only to be exposed to "controllable portions" of language (Segermann 2000; see also Thornbury's [2000] infamous "grammar McNuggets").

This belief can be traced back to Pienemann's (1984) 'teachability hypothesis' that postulates that, when acquiring new morpho-syntactic structures, L2 learners follow a natural developmental sequence which means that they can only acquire a new structure once they have mastered the structures that precede it in this developmental sequence (see also Krashen 1982, 1985 on the related notion of "comprehensible input"). The hypothesis of universal developmental sequences has been, to some extent, confirmed in empirical studies (e.g., Ellis 1989; Spada & Lightbown 1999). What has been refuted, however, is the accompanying hypothesis that teaching a structure for which learners are not yet "developmentally ready" will not only fail to result in learning, but also have a detrimental effect on learning outcomes (e.g., Larsen-Freeman 2006, 2018; Spada & Lightbown 1999; Ur 2011: 513). Yet, this underlying belief that learning a foreign language is a linear process and that a text is only accessible to learners if they are already familiar with every aspect of its lexis and grammar remains widespread (see, e.g., Phakiti & Plonsky 2018).

Given that these pedagogically contrived texts (and, again, it is worth reiterating that these do not, by any means, represent *all* textbook texts!) are created, first and foremost, to meet very restrictive criteria, they cannot be expected to "sound natural" or to be perceived by learners as such:

> Von ihr [dieser Textsorte *sui generis*] zu verlangen, dass sie von einem Schüler wie ein normaler Text rezipiert wird (mit normaler Erwartungshaltung, Eigeninteresse und entsprechender Bereitschaft zur selbsttätigen Sinngebung), hieße, ihre Funktion zu verkennen und die Quadratur des Kreises zu verlangen. [To expect that it [this kind of textbook text *sui generis*] be perceived by pupils as a normal text (with normal expectations, intrinsic interest and hence the willingness to make sense of it by themselves) would be to misjudge its function and to demand the squaring of the circle.]
> (Segermann 2000: n.p.)

Indeed, if textbook dialogues are often the butt of *Brian-is-in-the-kitchen*-type jokes (see Chapter 1), it is precisely because learners (and their parents) are well aware that many of these dialogues are anything but natural-sounding. This is exemplified in the following extract from a focus group interview conducted with secondary school pupils in Germany:

M: (...) Wenn irgendwie so ne englische Sendung ist im Fernsehen, da versteht man nicht jedes Wort, weil die umgangssprachlich reden und wir lernen in der Schule ja ein anderes Englisch. Wir lernen eher so das Englisch, äh, so

M: normales Schulenglisch

M: normal

M: Schulenglisch

M: Schulenglisch, und das ist anderes Englisch was die reden. Das ist umgangssprachlich, die haben andere Wörter

M: da ist das auch viel schneller, unverständlicher
[M: (...) When, like, in an English programme on TV, you don't understand every word, because they use colloquial language and in school we learn a different English. We kind of learn the English, ahm, like

M: normal school English

M: normal

M: school English

M: school English, and this is different from the one they use. It's colloquial, they use different words

M: it's a lot faster, and not so easy to understand]

(Grau 2009: 170, 173; translation Grau)

In German, the widely-used term *Schulenglisch* [school English] is mostly used in a pejorative sense to describe "a form of English that marks its users as having acquired the language in school" (Grau 2009: 170; see also Le Foll 2024a). It is considered different from the English used by competent English speakers in extracurricular contexts. In the following extract of an interview, a Spanish L1 English L2 speaker refers to the same phenomenon as *inglés de libro* [(text)book English]:

> Yo cuando llegué aquí [en Inglaterra] por primera vez es que hablaba un inglés de libro y me sentía fatal. O sea, no tenía esos recursos de conversación más informal, más de registro. Pues sí, con amigos, con familia. Me faltaba ese vocabulario y digo llevo años estudiando inglés y era muy artificial.
> [When I arrived here [in England] for the first time, I spoke textbook English and I felt awful. Like, I didn't have those resources for more informal conversation, [that are more appropriate] for that register. Well, that is, with friends, with fam-

ily. I lacked that vocabulary and, I mean, I'd been studying English for years and it was so fake.] (Pérez-Paredes & Abad forthcoming)

Here, too, an English L2 learner describes textbook-based EFL instruction as inadequate in terms of teaching spoken communicative skills. The layperson's perception that representations of spoken English in EFL textbooks are particularly inauthentic has indeed been confirmed in the present study. On all dimensions of linguistic variation examined in Chapter 7, Textbook Conversation was consistently found to be the least natural sounding of textbook registers. This is why, in turning to the practical implications of the present study, the following section begins with the potential pedagogical implications of these unnatural representations of spoken English in secondary school EFL textbooks. Having pointed to what makes these dialogues potentially problematic, it goes on to suggest solutions to improve the naturalness of EFL materials intended to model conversational English.

9.2 Improving representations of conversational English

By far the greatest gap between Textbook English and natural English that learners are expected to encounter outside the EFL classroom was found in the Conversation register. To begin, however, it is worth highlighting that not all textbook dialogues were found to be strikingly different from naturally occurring conversation. Excerpt (49), for instance, is situated within the ellipses of the Spoken BNC2014 on all projections of texts visualised in Chapter 7. This is because, among other factors, it features relatively high frequencies of fillers and interjections, discourse markers, the modal *could*, contracted verbs, negation, and an abundance of first and second-person referents.

(49) **Amy:** **Hi**, Nick.

Nick: **Hi**, Amy. Amy, **is** this **your** backpack on the floor?

Amy: That's right.

Nick: **Well, could you perhaps** put **it** somewhere else? **It's kind of** in the way.

Amy: **No, it's not. It's** where **I** always **leave it.**

Nick: **Yes, I know you** always **leave it** there. **And it's** always in the way. This **is** a pretty small place, Amy. **So perhaps just** for once **you could** put **your** backpack somewhere where **it isn't** in the way, **hmm**?

Amy: **You don't own** this place, Nick. **So don't try** and **tell me** what to do. **I** came in early to get some things done. **I** put **my** backpack on the floor. **You deal** with **it**! <TEC: English in Mind 4>

Thus, it would be a grossly misleading simplification but to claim that all textbook dialogues are poor representations of spontaneous spoken language. That said, the majority of the texts of the Textbook Conversation subcorpus did score much lower than (49) and the texts of the Spoken BNC2014 on the 'Spontaneous interactional vs. Edited informational' dimension (see Chapter 7). Most worryingly from a pedagogical point of view, the statistical analyses of the 'Textbook English vs. 'real-world' English' model showed that the dialogues of the most advanced textbooks of the TEC are, on average, the least representative of natural conversation (see 7.2).

Depending on the learning objectives associated with these texts, sound pedagogical reasons may well justify the unnaturalness of some of these dialogues. If a textbook dialogue's primary aim is to teach a pre-defined list of nouns, it may make sense to construct the text around these nouns. If, however, the primary purpose of these texts is to develop learners' oral competences (i.e., their receptive and/or productive skills), then such low scores on an oral–literate dimension of variation are a cause for concern. Excerpt (50), for example, is an extract of a textbook dialogue for the fifth year of secondary EFL instruction that is situated closer to the edited/informational end of the 'Spontaneous interactional vs. Edited informational' dimension than any of the conversation transcripts of the Spoken BNC2014. In fact, it is linguistically far removed from natural conversation on all dimensions of variation explored in the present study. This is due to its considerably higher type/token ratio and longer average word length than most real-life conversations, as well as the fact that it features many complex nominal phrases, which, in turn, lead to high relative frequencies of prepositions and attributive adjectives.

(50) **Journalist:** This is **Sally Gordon** here in **Leicester Square, London.** I'm right **in** the **middle** of **sports fans.** Excuse me, Sir. Who is your **favourite sports hero**?

Dwayne: Definitely, **Chris Hoy**, the **British track cyclist** – won two **gold medals.** He represents **strength** and **courage**, he never gave up.

Journalist: What about you? Who is the **best representative of** your **country**?

Donna: Kobe Bryant for sure. I'm American and we are very patriotic when it comes **to sport**. He has shown the **world** we remain the **dominant leaders in basketball,** no doubt. And **Michael Phelps** of course.

Journalist: Why?

Donna: Why? He has just won four **golds** and two **silver medals** and he is a **record holder**. The **dream** came true. Incredible. That's why he is nicknamed "the **Baltimore Bullet**". He **symbolises determination, generosity, hope... great values.** You see, he's a **role model**! He will be remembered forever.

<TEC: New Mission 2de>

Hence, whilst textbook dialogues such as (49) expose learners to interactional, genuinely conversation-like language that they are likely to encounter outside the classroom, texts such as (50) cannot be considered to be realistic models for EFL learners to acquire spontaneous spoken language comprehension and/or production skills. As mentioned above, such texts can be argued to serve other pedagogical purposes, e.g., the high lexical diversity of Excerpt (50) may be specifically aimed at increasing learners' receptive vocabulary range by introducing learners to many nouns from a single semantic field (e.g., *strength, courage, determination, generosity, hope*).

Given that such dialogues represent the norm rather than the exception in secondary school EFL textbooks, textbook authors and teachers ought to carefully consider the primary pedagogical purpose of such highly unnatural-sounding dialogues. If they are destined to model and enhance learners' conversational skills, they should consider replacing them with authentic materials. If no suitable authentic materials can be sourced, corpus data or the results of corpus-based studies may be used to revise them. The following paragraphs illustrate these various options on the basis of Excerpt (50).

Given the now widespread availability of corpora and corpus tools, there is no longer a need for textbook authors to systematically craft their textbook dialogues from scratch (for a list of freely available English corpora and corpus tools, see Le Foll 2021b: Appendix). Of course, this is not to suggest that the transcripts of spoken corpora such as the Spoken BNC2014 can or should be printed *verbatim*, as in (51), in coursebooks. However, if learners are to be expected to develop real-life conversational skills, the kind of natural interaction that is captured in such transcripts ought to be featured in at least some of the audio-visual materials that accompany EFL coursebooks. For instance, in a conversation about meeting a sports hero from the Spoken BNC2014, Excerpt (51) demonstrates how speakers frequently interrupt each other, ask for clarification when things are unclear (e.g., *who is who is it?*) and manifest their interest in the conversation with laughter, other paralinguistic sounds, and various interjections (e.g., *yeah, uhu, mm, oh cool*).

(51) I met my hero didn't I? I text you remember?
yeah
who did you meet?
Hans no way Rey
you were[?]
who is who is it?
he's talking about a famous mountain climber
famous bike rider
oh okay
he's astonishing I went well I wasn't very old I think maybe I was employed to drive maybe I was just starting to drive

uhu
and there was like a big there used to be a big like erm biking event in <anon type="place"/>
mm
and he was in like a a show and the things he did honestly cos bikes were crap in those days but he was
<unclear/>
amazing and he had the stereo going in the background and he like had these picnic tables and he was like hopping onto them and jumping between them
oh cool
yeah he had all quite
<vocal desc="laugh"/>
people would lie on the floor and he was like jumping over them and he'd get his front wheel and then he'd put the front wheel onto there and <unclear/> it was <trunc>am</trunc> a show like <BNC214: SBKN>

As demonstrated by the complex turn structure in (51), faithfully scripting such dialogues is no mean feat. For "cleaner", less "chaotic", yet linguistically accurate representations of spoken language textbook authors and teachers may want to turn to film and TV series (see, e.g., Quaglio 2009; Werner 2021 on the relationship between the language of scripted telecinematic language and face-to-face conversation) for more readily usable materials. Indeed, screenwriters are professionals in imitating natural speech. Often such materials can be adapted for classroom use relatively easily. Excerpt (52), for instance, was sourced from the freely accessible TV Movie Corpus hosted on the online corpus platform english-corpora.org (Davies 2019) by searching for the target phrase *gold MEDAL*[30] featured in the original textbook dialogue (50). It could be used with beginner learners of English without any modification.

(52) Hey, Smoochie, come here.
I have something pretty special to show you. Come here, bub, do you want to see a video of one of the best gymnasts in the entire world? It's not just me saying that. She won an actual **gold medal**. Her name is Simone Biles, that's her right there.
Oh, Simone Biles, she is amazing.
Right? Here, watch this. [Crowd_Noises_On_Laptop]
Wow, she is very flexible.
[...]
There we go, look at this, look at this.

30. On english-corpora.org, words can be capitalised to search for all forms of a lemma (i.e., here *medal* and *medals*).

Whoa!
Whoo! Whoo, she's so good, did you like that?
It was really good.
I know, right? <TV Movie Corpus: I'm Sorry (2017)>

In staying with the topic covered in textbook Excerpt (50), a quick query for the phrase *sports* HERO in the TV/MOVIES subcorpus of the *Corpus of Contemporary American English* (COCA; also available on english-corpora.org; Davies 2010) returned several snippets of conversation which could also be integrated in an EFL lesson with hardly any need to 'doctor the text'. One of these is re-printed below in (53).

(53) **The point is**, we're both trying to teach you the same thing, to be a winner, not a Rosie Ruiz.
A Rosie Who-now?
Okay, Goldfarb.
One last lesson before I go... That lesson was about Rosie Ruiz, a world-class runner in the' 80s, famous for winning the Boston Marathon by **taking the subway**. [...]
This woman cheated to win the Boston Marathon?
And no one noticed?
Nope. Everybody **was too caught up in the excitement** that an unfit woman who knew nothing about the sport didn't even **break a sweat** while **shattering a world record.**
Wow. That is so wrong.
Yeah.
She **took the subway**?
The subway!
Everyone has a **sports hero**, and Rosie Ruiz is mine.
Controversial, but okay.
That's why during the mile run, I'll jump into your car, and you can drive me to the **finish line**?
Aw, kiddo. I... I can't help you.
Cause cheating is wrong?
No!
Cheating's that rush that **keeps me ticking.**
I can't help you 'cause I don't have a license. <COCA: The Goldbergs (2019)>

At this stage, it is worth noting that drawing on conversational language from films and TV series would not necessarily lead to a lexico-grammatical impoverishment of the language input students are exposed to – on the contrary. Excerpt (53), for example, features numerous idiomatic collocations to which materials designers and teachers would do well to draw learners' attention, e.g., *take the subway, be caught up in the excitement, break a sweat, shatter a world record.* It is worth noting that in contrast to the vocabulary conveyed in Excerpt (50) which consists foremost of individual nouns, Excerpt (53) features many high-frequency verb + noun collocations (see also Barlow 2003: 7). This is crucial as much research has shown that the acquisition of such patterns of co-occurrence (e.g., collocations, chunks, lexical bundles) is essential to developing both fluency and accuracy in a foreign language (see, among others, Altenberg & Granger 2001; Cowie 1998; Herbst 1996; Hoey 2005; Hunston & Francis 2000; Langacker 2001; Nesselhauf 2005). Following a usage-based L2 instruction paradigm (see 2.3), these patterns of co-occurrence are conceptualised as constructions. The comparison of Excerpts (50) and (53) illustrates the scarcity of constructions in stereotypically textbook-like texts. This is highly problematic because, as eloquently put by Herbst (2016: 77):

> If "it's constructions all the way down" (Goldberg 2006: 18) and language learning consists of the learning of constructions, then language teaching should consist of the teaching of constructions.

Unfortunately, however, the pervasiveness of constructions in language has yet to be fully grasped by many involved in L2 teaching (Ellis, Römer & O'Donnell 2016; Pérez-Paredes, Mark & O'Keeffe 2020; Tyler et al. 2018). In particular, excerpts such as (50) suggest that textbook authors seemingly continue to be tasked with the artificial insertion of many individual nouns in textbook representations of spontaneous, spoken English, e.g., in (50), *strength, courage, determination, generosity, hope*, etc., at the detriment of frequent and idiomatic collocations.

Returning to Excerpt (53), it can also be hypothesised that, from a motivational point of view, students are more likely to learn and remember the term *driving license* if they first came across it in a text such as (53) in which there is a genuine communicative need to understand that, here, *license* refers to *driving license* to make sense of the conversation. More generally, students are more likely to be intrinsically motivated when asked to engage with materials that they, themselves, recognise as "authentic" and "real" (Gilmore 2011). In advocating for the inclusion of corpus-informed spoken grammar in ELT, Carter & McCarthy (1996: 370) question whether deciding that learners need not be exposed to certain kinds of natural English might "not ignore a psychological reality in that all of us as language learners and teachers are intrigued by real discourse and by what native speakers do with it". The authors go on to convincingly argue that only offering contrived, simplified models of English in ELT materials amounts to holding back information which ultimately disempowers learners. Given that a large body of (corpus) linguistic research has now demonstrated and extensively documented pedagogically relevant lexico-grammatical differences between different registers of English (e.g., Biber et al. 2021; Carter 2014; Carter & McCarthy 2017, 2006b), continuing to offer learners models of conversational English that are evidently based on written norms no longer seems tenable.

Although calls to rely more on authentic data and corpus tools in ELT materials design now go back two or more decades (e.g., Conrad 2000; McEnery & Xiao 2011; Mindt 1996; Prowse 1998; Römer 2004b, 2006; Sinclair 1991, 2004, to mention but a few), up until recently, textbook authors could be forgiven for lacking the skills and knowledge to source and/or adapt authentic materials. Today, however, the availability of a wealth of suitable resources and ease of use of free, online corpus tools (e.g., corpora.lancs.ac.uk/bnclab/, english-corpora.org, yohasebe.com/tcse/, see Le Foll 2021b: Appendix for many more) considerably facilitate the task. In addition to spoken corpora and film/TV series, podcasts and videocasts, televised talk shows, radio discussions and interviews can also make for suitable sources of natural spoken English. An example from a broadcast discussion on the topic of sports heroes is printed as (54). It comes from a radio interview and shows that, whilst many aspects of interaction can only be meaningfully conveyed in video materials, authentic audio materials can also be meaningfully integrated in the EFL classroom. Their transcripts typically lend themselves better to be printed as textbook dialogues than those of spoken conversation corpora like the Spoken BNC2014.

(54) **MARTIN:** **Well**, Jimi, what do you think?

Mr-IZRAEL: I think it's the end of the baseball hero. **I mean, it's been coming for some time.** But I think, **again, you know**, as L. Spence says, **you know**, this is kind of **a nail in the coffin. I mean, you know**, our kids should be **looking up to sports heroes anyway** but now we know that they can for sure, **you know**. And Howard, **you know**, I was curious, do you think he should **be in the Hall of Fame** after this?

Mr-WITT: No, I don't see how. **I mean, you know**. Michel said **the question comes down to whether** he knew he was taking **a banned substance**. The question is what was he taking anything for, **you know? I mean**, how are you supposed to explain to your kids, **well**, he might have been taking something but it was, **you know**, might have been okay. **I mean**, that's **shades of gray** there that just shouldn't even exist, **you know**, taken after...

Dr-SPENCE: You **take pills** for headaches, don't you, Howard?

Mr-WITT: What's that?

Dr-SPENCE: Don't you **take pills** for headaches?

Mr-WITT: **Well**, I do **take pills** for headaches.

Mr-IFTIKAR: **Yeah**, you don't **take pills** to make your head grow, though.

<COCA: Tell Me More (NPR, 2007)>

Note that, in addition to an abundance of discourse markers (*well, I mean, you know, anyway*), Excerpt (54) also features a number of frequent idioms and chunks with high communicative value (e.g., *it's been coming for some time, the final nail in the coffin, the question comes down to whether*). Going beyond its pure linguistic value, a text such as (54) also has the potential to trigger genuinely meaningful discussions among students, e.g., on who deserves to be considered a sports hero, whether athletes are role models for young people, or how doping is influencing professional sport.

As discussed in 7.2, textbook conversations not only tend to display neat and predictable turn-taking with no hesitations or misunderstandings of any kind, they almost exclusively consist of "referential discourse" (Blyth 2009:196). Their primary function is "transactional" (Gilmore 2007:102) or "informational-cognitive" (Blyth 2003:63, 68). As such, they overwhelmingly neglect the "psychosocial functions of language, such as the creation of solidarity or the display of aggression" (Blyth 2009:196; see also Cook 2000). This means that such pedagogical materials largely fail to represent the more interactional, relationship-building, or psychosocial functions of conversations that may involve "controversial and imaginary content, or emotionally charged interaction" (Cook 2000:158). Unsurprisingly, it is exactly these kinds of situations that instructed L2 learners often struggle to navigate (Gilmore 2007). This observation ties in with the well-known fact that commercial constraints can lead textbook publishers to avoid contentious topics. This is particularly true of the global EFL/ESL textbook market: textbook authors are often explicitly required to abstain from any mention of "PARSNIP topics" (Politics, Alcohol, Religion, Sex, Narcotics, *-Isms*, and Pork; Gray 2010:119; see also Dinh & Siregar 2021; Smith 2020:21–22), thus contributing to the kind of bland and banal textbook dialogues that are typically associated with EFL textbooks (see also Le Foll 2022b:173). Though European school textbook publishers face slightly different constraints, textbook dialogues depicting difficult relationships are few and far between (see, however, Excerpt (49) for an exception).

Some may counter that authentic listening materials – e.g., those drawn from film, TV or radio as discussed above, as well as from podcasts or social media such as YouTube – are inappropriate for lower secondary school EFL teaching because natural delivery rates are too fast for non-proficient speakers of English. Indeed, this is likely one of the reasons why many textbook publishers prefer to feature scripted dialogues which are then performed by professional actors at prescribed delivery rates deemed more appropriate for beginners. This belief, however, is not supported by the conclusions of empirical research on the effect of delivery rates on EFL learners' listening comprehension: it has repeatedly been shown that lower-than-average speech rates are not beneficiary to or, indeed, preferred by language learners (e.g., Blau 1990; Derwing 1990, 2001; Derwing et al. 2012; Griffiths 1990, 1991; Munro & Derwing 1998; Révész & Brunfaut 2013).

Despite all the aforementioned advantages of using non-scripted conversational materials, in some cases, it might not be feasible or practical to source suitable, authentic spoken materials. In such cases, textbook authors would do well to draw on corpus data or, failing this, on the findings of corpus research to arrive at a more realistic portrayal of conversational English. For instance, unnatural-sounding excerpts could be improved by consulting a corpus such as the Spoken BNC2014 (freely accessible on cqpweb.lancs.ac.uk) and to research the way in which some of the frequent lexico-grammatical features of spontaneous, interactional speech with high loadings on the 'Spontaneous interactional vs. Edited informational' dimension are used in context. This approach was exemplified in Le Foll (2021c: 238–239) with a revised version of the textbook dialogue printed at the beginning of this section as (50). This revised version is re-printed here as Excerpt (55). It features more 'mental' verbs (e.g. THINK, FORGET), *that* omissions (marked [THATD]), contracted and negated verbs, present tense verbs, first- and second-person referents, emphatics (*definitely, really*), causative subordination (*because)*, discourse and pragmatic markers (*well, you know, if you know what I mean, what I'm saying is*), hedges (*kind of*), fillers and interjections (*erm, oh, yeah*), the modal *would*, demonstrative pronouns, and 'stranded' prepositions (e.g., *let's see who can talk to*) than the original textbook dialogue (50). As Example (55) shows, such additions will also naturally lead to revised dialogues with lower type/token ratios, shorter average word lengths and, in particular, lower noun/verb ratios, which all contribute to higher scores on the first 'Spontaneous interactional vs. Edited informational' dimension, too.

(55) **Journalist: I'm** Sally Gordon, reporting from Leicester Square in London and the place **is** full of sports fans. **Let's** see **who we** can talk **to. Excuse me**, Sir. Can **I** ask **you who's your** sports hero?

Dwayne: Erm, for **me, it'd definitely** have to be Chris Hoy, **you know**, the British track cyclist **who** won two gold medals. **I think** [THATD] he **really stands** for strength and and **I really admire** his courage **because, well,** he **just** never **gives** up.

Journalist: Sure. And erm what about **you? Who would you** say **is your** national hero?

Donna: Erm, actually, I'm American **so** Kobe Bryant, **for sure. We're kind of** very patriotic, **especially** when **it** comes to sports, **if you know what I mean.**

Journalist: And would you say [THATD] basketball is **your** sport **then**?

Donna: Yeah I am into basketball and that and, **you know, I think** [THATD] he**'s really** shown the world **we're** still the best at **it**!

Journalist: Mm.

Donna: Oh and **I** shouldn**'t forget** Michael Phelps, **of course.**

Journalist: Uhu. What makes you say that?

Donna: You kidding? I mean, he's **just** won **like** four gold medals and two silver.

Journalist: Right, he did, **didn't he?**

Donna: And he's a record holder! **I guess** what **I'm saying is** the the dream came true.

Journalist: Right.

Donna: Yeah, he's **just** incredible. **I mean that's** why **we** call him "the Baltimore Bullet" **because** he's **all** about determination, generosity, hope... he's **all** about **all these really** great values. **You see,** he's he's a role model! And **we'll** never **forget** him, **that's for sure.**

Though it was not the object of this study to investigate the pedagogical efficacy of the language of school EFL textbooks, there is ground to believe that textbook dialogues with high Dimension 1 scores are better models for EFL learners to acquire the necessary skills to navigate real-life conversational situations (O'Keeffe, McCarthy & Carter 2007: 21). This includes the competent use of a variety of fluency-enhancing strategies to overcome planning phases and manage turn-taking. Interestingly, learner corpus research has shown that EFL learners significantly underuse discourse and vagueness markers as compared to native speakers and tend to rely more on filled and unfilled pauses and/or on a very limited set of such markers, instead (e.g., Müller 2005; Götz 2013; Gilquin 2016; Dumont 2018). Wolk, Götz and Jäschke (2021: 4) have suggested that this frequently observed underuse of discourse markers in learner speech "might stem from the fact that an explicit teaching of discourse markers as a fluency-enhancing strategy has not been systematically integrated into EFL textbooks" (see also Gilquin 2016). Though these studies were conducted on diverse learner populations who will have learnt with a variety of textbook and non-textbook materials, the results of the present study nevertheless lend support to this hypothesis – especially given that, in this respect, representations of conversation in Textbook English are relatively homogenous: all nine textbook series of the TEC were found to generally misrepresent natural conversation in very similar ways.

9.3 Improving representations of informative texts

Although the results of Chapters 7 and 8 showed that, on the whole, the informative texts of the more advanced textbooks of the TEC are linguistically quite similar to informative texts aimed at teenagers, some texts stood out as being more prototypically "textbook-like" than representative of this register. An example of such a text was already presented in 8.3.2: Excerpt (47), about soap operas, was written in the style of a teenager magazine and, indeed, close inspection of the random effects associated with the Teen Vogue subcorpus of the Info Teens corpus (see 4.3.2.5) in the 'Textbook English vs. real-world English' model presented in Chapter 7 suggests that, on both the 'Spontaneous interactional vs. Edited informational' and the 'Narrative vs. Non-narrative' dimensions of the model, Teen Vogue texts are closer to Textbook Informative texts than the rest of the reference Info Teens corpus of informative texts targeted at English-speaking teenagers.

Whilst this type of informative writing certainly has its place in secondary school EFL textbooks, some of the informative texts that also score high on the 'Spontaneous interactional vs. Edited informational' dimension make for rather unlikely candidate articles in such publication outlets. Text (56), for instance, is an informative text from a French textbook used in the fourth year of secondary English tuition that scores considerably higher than most texts of the reference Info Teens corpus on both the 'Spontaneous interactional vs. Edited informational' and the 'Pedagogically adapted vs. Natural' dimensions.

(56) Iwokrama, in what is called the Guiana shield, is a tropical rainforest reserve. **Because** there are only three other rainforest ecosystems like this in the world, Iwokrama is invaluable. It**'s a part of** "the lungs of the earth".
Moreover, it's in a pristine state: it is **as if it had been untouched by humans. As though nobody had ever cut a tree**! But **indigenous people have lived there**: they have just done **so very** discreetly, leaving their natural environment **pretty much** intact.
Guyana's landscapes and wildlife are not only protected, they are also stunning: the Kaieteur Falls are majestic and it**'s** as if animals and plants were all "giant"! **You can** meet giant anteaters, giant water lilies, giant leaf frogs and giant otters!
Because this is such a unique place, Iwokrama has been made into an official reserve. The priority is the preservation of the rainforest. **But** this does not mean that Guyana refuses to make money out of the forest: it **just** has to be done sustainably so, with income for the communities that live there rather than gains for investors on the other side of the world. <TEC: Piece of Cake 3[e]>

The interactive web-based version of the textbook gives the impression that this is an authentic text and claims that it was "Adapted from Iwokrama.org." ⟨https://www.lelivrescolaire.fr/page/16871655⟩ (27 March 2024) – the official website of the *Iwokrama International Centre for Rain Forest Conservation and Development.* However, no text resembling the one featured in the textbook could be found on this informative website. In fact, text (56) has several tell-tale signs of a pedagogically doctored text. It hovers between different degrees of formality (e.g., *moreover* vs. *pretty much*) and, as such, sits rather uncomfortably between different registers (for similar issues in English L2 academic writing, see Gilquin & Paquot 2008). In this particular case, there is no doubt that the text was constructed around a pre-defined grammatical syllabus: the second paragraph features two conditional sentences (*as if it had been* and *as though nobody had ever*) and the textbook unit in which it is embedded includes several exercises on *as if/though* constructions (see (57) and (58)). In both cases, the use of the past perfect in these two conditional sentences is clearly contrived: the present perfect would have sufficed. Moreover, whilst BE *untouched* is attested in corpora of naturally occurring English, the collocation REMAIN *untouched* is considerably more frequent and would have been a more idiomatic choice. It would also have helped address the fact that, across all registers, Textbook English features more occurrences of BE as a main verb per finite verb phrase (FVP) than in 'real-world' English as used outside the EFL classroom.

(57) **Exercise 3: An incredible reserve**

1. Imagine yourself in Guyana and describe it to a friend. Use *as if.*
   [Text box for students to type their answer]
2. Imagine how the Makushi could make money from the forest without destroying it.
   [Text box for students to type their answer]

⟨https://www.lelivrescolaire.fr/page/16871655⟩ (14 February 2022)

(58) **As if... / As though...**

Observe: It is as if nobody had ever touched the forest! It is as though nobody had ever cut a tree!

Think: Are we discussing real actions / facts here? Two tenses are used in each sentence: what are they?

Practise: Make 5 assumptions about the Amazon.

[Text box for students to type their answer]

⟨https://www.lelivrescolaire.fr/page/16871655⟩ (14 February 2022)

A cursory look at the Iwokrama centre's website suffices to spot engaging materials which could be integrated with very few modifications into such a unit on the preservation of tropical rainforests for this proficiency level, e.g., (59). As an aside, it is also worth noting that Excerpt (56) is potentially misleading in that the phrase "*have lived there*" without a temporal marker implies that indigenous people no longer live in the Iwokrama Forest. The reader will notice that Excerpt (59), taken from the iwokrama.org website, does not involve such ambiguity.

(59) DID YOU KNOW?
The Iwokrama Forest is located in central Guyana, approximately 300 km south of Georgetown, the capital. The area encompasses about 371,000 hectares and is covered in lush, intact lowland tropical forest. The wide range of intact habitats in the Iwokrama Forest supports a diverse flora and fauna with an estimated 1,500–2,000 higher plant species, 420 species of fish, 150 species of snakes, lizards and frogs, 500 species of birds and 180 species of mammals. [...]
VIEWING TIPS!
Most mammals are secretive and can be hard to see. Since many mammals are nocturnal, a good way to see them is at night with the help of a headlamp. Fruiting trees are also a good place to see mammals as they congregate to feed. And always keep an eye on the ground for signs – especially tracks in the wet mud on the edge of pools. [...]
DID YOU KNOW?
The Iwokrama Forest is in the homeland of the Makushi people, **who have lived in and used the forest for thousands of years**. People are a critical part of the ecosystem and the success of Iwokrama relies on the combined skills of specialists and its community partners.
⟨https://iwokrama.org/wp-content/uploads/2018/01/Iwokrama-Mammal-Guide-2017-Web.pdf⟩ (14 February 2022>

Drawing on real-world resources to source ELT materials such as (59) affords learners valuable opportunities to acquire English in naturally occurring contexts. In a usage-based L2 instruction paradigm, context is known to be paramount to supporting language comprehension and pattern abstraction. That said, it can also "be a stressor that introduces noise, complexity, and cognitive overload" (Tyler & Ortega 2018: 17–18). Hence, in some cases, it may make pedagogical sense to adapt authentic texts for specific proficiency levels and/or learner groups. Should textbook authors or teachers be worried that a text such as (59) – i.e., one drawn from a resource not especially targeted at L2 learners – could feature vocabulary that may be too demanding for their target learner group, user-friendly corpus-based tools can be used to identify potentially problematic lexical items. For instance, the text analysis tool from english-corpora.org can be used to highlight the least frequent words based on frequency data from the COCA (Figure 36).

Some of these low-frequency words (highlighted in yellow in Figure 36) can also be found in the textbook Excerpt (56) (e.g., *ecosystem, frog*). Others could

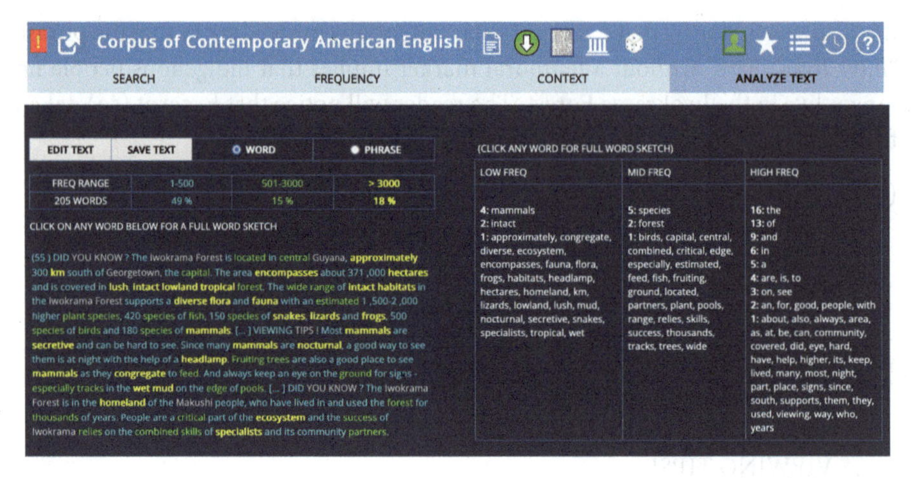

Figure 36. Word frequency analysis conducted with english-corpora.org (on the basis of COCA data) of Excerpt (59)

easily be replaced by more frequent alternatives without compromising on the style of writing (e.g., *flora and fauna* → *plants and animals*). In choosing which low-frequency words to potentially replace, teachers and textbook authors would do well to focus on isotopy, i.e., on the lexical items that involve semantic redundance, rather than on those that involve strong collocational associations or make important contributions to a text's overall coherence (Hausmann 2005). For example, consider *lush, intact* and *tropical* in the first paragraph of Excerpt (59). These are three low-frequency and semantically closely related words that are used to describe the *forest*. They need not all be included. Alternatively, clicking on any of the coloured words in the text analysis tool (see Figure 38) redirects the user to the corresponding 'word profile' page. Figure 37 is an excerpt of the word profile page for the word *lush*. It shows a list of topics associated with the word, its most strongly associated collocates and makes suggestions for (potential) synonyms – all derived from the COCA. Based on this information, teachers and materials designers may decide to replace *lush* with a higher-frequency word that learners are expected to already be familiar with, e.g., *beautiful* or *green*. In addition, learners' previous knowledge can be drawn on to make pedagogically informed adjustments to authentic texts. In the context of secondary EFL instruction, this also means taking account of which lexical items are cognates in the learners' L1 or school language. Thus, given that Excerpt (56) is from a French EFL textbook, the adjectives *intact* and *tropical* should not pose a problem and can therefore be left unmodified. By the same token, with French L1 speakers as the target readership, *fertile* (see Figure 37) could be chosen as an alternative to the word *lush* in the context of this informative text.

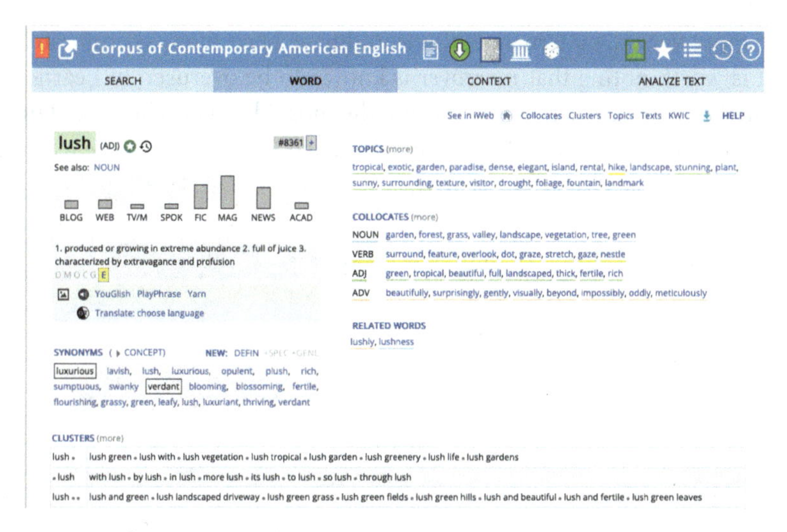

Figure 37. Part of the 'word profile' page of the word *lush* as generated on english-corpora.org/coca

Note that, as shown on Figure 38, and perhaps contrary to teachers' expectations, it is not the case that text (56), crafted specifically for pedagogical purposes, contains fewer low-frequency words than the one taken verbatim from Iwokrama.org.

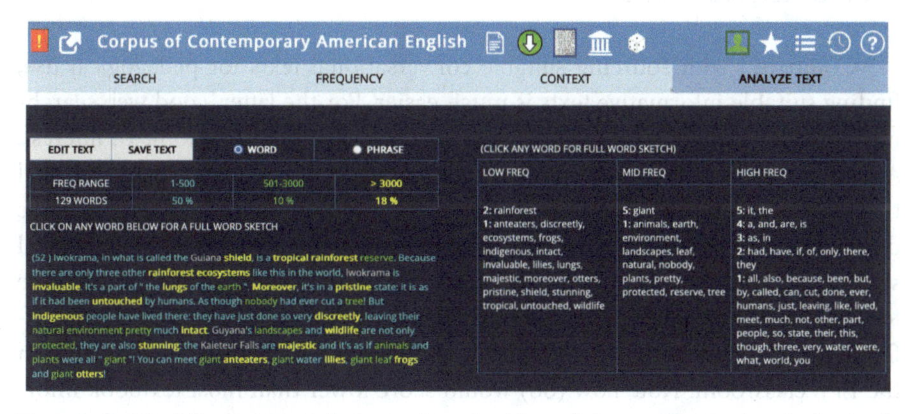

Figure 38. Word frequency analysis conducted with english-corpora.org (on the basis of the COCA) of Excerpt (56)

Corpus tools can also be used to check whether a chosen alternative is suitable for any given register. For example, the 'word profile' page of *moreover* (see Figure 39 for an extract) shows that *moreover* is typical of academic writing but comparatively rare in news reports. Thus, in the context of (56), there is no doubt that the more versatile alternative *also* would have been more appropriate. As an aside, it is worth noting that *moreover* is known to be overused in Learner Englishes, including in registers where it is not the most idiomatic choice and that this overuse has been particularly noted among French L1 speakers (see, e.g., Granger & Tyson 1996: 21–22; Waibel 2005: 163).

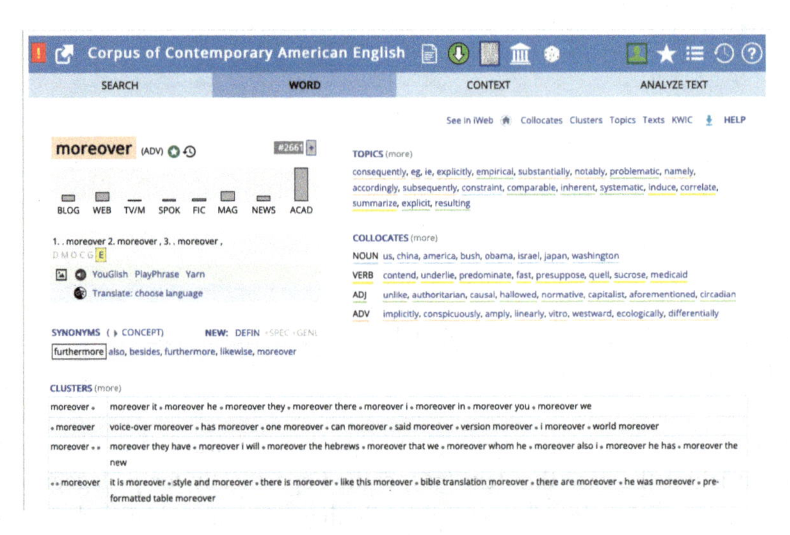

Figure 39. Part of the "word profile" page of the word *moreover* on english-corpora.org/coca

Compared with sourcing suitable conversational texts for pedagogical use, finding suitable informative texts is much easier. For the latter, good web searching strategies should suffice to find suitable texts on almost any topic of interest. A broad range of different text registers are readily available. However, it is crucial that textbook authors, editors, and teachers be aware of register-driven linguistic differences in order to avoid creating patchwork texts that result in unnatural sounding texts such as (56). Excerpts (60) and (61), which are both on the same topic yet clearly fulfil very different functions and are therefore written in very different styles, illustrate two such registers. Both could easily be adapted for use in the EFL classroom. Note how (60) would score lower than most textbook informative texts on the 'Spontaneous interactional vs. Edited informational' dimension as a result of its high frequency of passive constructions, coordinating conjunctions, and non-finite *-ed* and *-ing* verb forms, among other features. It also includes numerous useful collocations and constructions of the kind often missing from pedagogically adapted textbook texts (e.g., *SEEK to do sth., BOAST a wide range of, MAKE sth. An ideal sth., over the years, the likes of*).

(60) The Iwokrama International Centre for Rainforest Conservation is an autonomous, non-profit institution which **was set up** to manage the Iwokrama forest, **as** a "living laboratory".
The aim of the centre is to show how tropical forests can **be conserved** and sustainably **used** for ecological, social and economic benefits to local national and international communities. [...]
The Iwokrama forest is in the homeland of the Makushi people who have lived and used the forest for thousands of years. **As such**, the Centre got its name Iwokrama from the range of mountains and **according to** the indigenous peoples, Iwokrama means 'place of refuge'.
Since its creation, Iwokrama has sought to **advance best practices** in the sustainable management of the world's remaining rain forests. It currently **boasts a wide range** of diverse flora and fauna **making it an ideal location** for bird-watching lovers, students, scientists, volunteers and interns **interested in seeing** and **experiencing** the untouched, lush rain forest. And, **over the years**, the Centre has attracted **the likes of** His Royal Highness Prince Charles; Prince Harry; President David Granger and First Lady Sandra Granger, Ministers of government, **among others.**
⟨https://guyanachronicle.com/2019/03/24/iwokrama-30-years-on⟩
(27 March 2024)

As a marketing text with many imperatives, contracted verbs, and first-person referents, Excerpt (61) would score higher than (60) on the 'Spontaneous interactional vs. Edited informational' dimension. It is very representative of its genre and, on the website from which it was sourced, is illustrated with several photos (e.g., of the *canopy walk*) that could support students' comprehension of the text without (systematically) resorting to translation.

(61) **If you're considering** travel to South America, **step outside the box** of typical Brazil **beach vacations** or Colombian coffee tours. Here, **we introduce you to** the beautiful country of Guyana, which will **feel like** an authentic slice of the "real" South America, from its **pristine rainforest** to its **welcoming villages**. Nature and wildlife lovers **are at home** here, where **first-hand exploration** of the **untrammeled countryside** is encouraged. There's an unmistakable pride in Guyana's people, as they **open their doors and hearts** to **curious travelers** seeking eco-friendly vacations, cultural immersion and a Lost World vibe. **Get** to Guyana now, before the crowds arrive. [...]
In a country that is 80 percent covered with **virgin tropical rainforest, it makes sense that** one of its top tourist attractions is a center focused on its conservation. **Feel as one with** the jungle as **you** tackle the canopy walk in the middle of the reserve – the birdwatching at this vantage point is unbelievable. The jaguar lives here – South America's largest cat – and while **we can't**

> **promise you a glimpse of** this elusive feline, **we** can almost guarantee that **you'll** meet ocelots, river turtles, otters, anteaters, caimans and more. **You** may even see a Goliath bird-eating spider as large as **your** fist!
> ⟨https://navsumo.com/top-11-sights-to-see-in-guyana⟩ (27 March 2024)

9.4 Towards a register approach to teaching EFL

In sum, the two preceding sections have demonstrated that, if the language to be taught in EFL textbooks is to be genuinely relevant to students' present and future lives, textbook materials must acknowledge that English is not a "monolithic block" (Rühlemann 2008: 681); but rather that, like all languages, it varies across different situational contexts of use. A large body of corpus linguistic research has demonstrated that various extralinguistic, socio-functional aspects of register have a direct impact on the linguistic features that characterise them (Crystal 2018: 490). Indeed, modern corpus-informed grammars of English no longer present "Standard English" as a single, homogenous language variety (as did, e.g., Quirk et al. 1985) but rather show how grammar varies across modes (e.g., in the *Cambridge Grammar of English*; Carter & McCarthy 2006a) and/or major registers (e.g., in the *Longman Grammar of Spoken and Written English*; Biber et al. 1999, 2021). This is necessary because vocabulary and grammar vary according to sociocultural, situational, and functional contexts.

The model of intra-textbook variation presented in Chapter 6 shows that a certain amount of situational/functional variation is already (almost exclusively implicitly) present across the texts featured in secondary school EFL textbooks. However, as explained in Chapter 7, the continued prevalence of pedagogically adapted, artificial texts results in considerably less register-based linguistic variation than across situationally similar registers that EFL learners can be expected to encounter outside the classroom. In particular, most textbook representations of conversation remain very close to written norms. The grammatical phenomena that continue to form the backbone of textbook progressions (see Burton 2023) are, for the most part, still presented as universally valid across all registers. Thus, it is fair to say that Conrad's (2000) optimistic prediction at the start of the millennium that corpus linguistics could "revolutionise the teaching of grammar" and that, among other consequences, "[m]onolithic descriptions of English grammar [would] be replaced by register-specific descriptions" (Conrad 2000: 549) has not yet been fulfilled.

As the examples of the previous sections have shown, a register-sensitive approach to teaching English goes well beyond grammar. It involves all elements of the lexico-grammatical continuum. In fact, this study has repeatedly hinted at the fact that it also entails a re-appraisal of the semantic and pragmatic content of some textbook texts as modern school EFL materials largely continue to avoid potentially contentious topics (see also Timmis 2016: 5). They almost exclusively model harmonious, largely transactional interactions between proficient English users (see 9.2).

It is with similar concerns in mind that Rühlemann (2008) proposed a "register approach to teaching conversation". He convincingly argued that:

> the mismatch between school English and spoken English amounts to a mismatch between the end and the means deployed to reach it: SE-based [Standard English-based] school English fails to support learners in reaching their goal – to approximate to authentic English. (Rühlemann 2008: 688)

The present study has shown that – although the gap between textbook dialogues and real-life English conversation is certainly the most disconcerting – this issue in fact concerns all registers. Adopting a register approach would certainly entail several long-term changes that cannot be expected to happen overnight. In many ways, however, it is quite surprising that register is still not firmly anchored in ELT, especially given that European school EFL curricula are now all aligned with the CEFR and that many of the *can-do* statements of the CEFR very much imply a register approach, e.g.:

> **B1** Can scan through straightforward, **factual texts in magazines, brochures** or on the **web**, identify what they are about and decide whether they contain information that might be of practical use. Can find and understand relevant information in everyday material, such as **letters, brochures** and **short official documents.** Can pick out important information about preparation and usage on the **labels on foodstuff** and **medicine.** Can assess whether an **article, report** or **review** is on the required topic. Can understand the important information in simple, clearly drafted **adverts** in **newspapers** or **magazines**, provided there are not too many abbreviations.
> (CEFR "Reading for orientation"; Council of Europe 2020: 56 emphases added)

This is true of all four categories of communicative language activities described in the CEFR: reception, production, interaction, and mediation. For instance, for oral interaction, the CEFR (Council of Europe 2020: 71) mentions a range of linguistically quite distinct registers:

- interpersonal: "Conversation";
- evaluative: "Informal discussion (with friends)"; "Formal discussion (meetings)", "Goal-oriented collaboration";
- transactional: "Information exchange", "Obtaining goods and services", "Interviewing and being interviewed", and "Using telecommunications".

The present study has demonstrated that modern secondary school EFL textbooks very rarely model realistic "interpersonal" and "evaluative oral interactions" (see 9.4.1). Given the current state of affairs, we may therefore question how EFL textbooks currently support learners in achieving descriptors such as:

> **B2** Can establish a relationship with interlocutors through sympathetic questioning and expressions of agreement plus, if appropriate, comments about third parties or shared conditions. Can indicate reservations and reluctance, state conditions when agreeing to requests or granting permission, and ask for understanding of their own position. Can engage in extended conversation on most general topics in a clearly participatory fashion, even in a noisy environment. Can sustain relationships with users of the target language without unintentionally amusing or irritating them or requiring them to behave other than they would with another proficient language user. Can convey degrees of emotion and highlight the personal significance of events and experiences.
>
> (Council of Europe 2020: 73)

Not only is a monolithic understanding of English not compatible with the CEFR and the many school curricula which are based on the framework, it is also not in line with a task-based language teaching (TBLT) approach (see, e.g., Crawford & Zhang 2021). Indeed, in TBLT, learners are pushed to acquire language skills through real-world communicative situations which, as a large body of corpus linguistic research has shown, will naturally have specific situational characteristics that, in turn, call for register-specific patterns of language use. Decades after the so-called 'communicative turn' to foreign language teaching, it is somewhat perplexing that learners are still only rarely encouraged to communicate in differentiated ways depending on the situational context. In effect, students are left to deduce this by themselves. As exemplified by the interview excerpts quoted at the beginning of the chapter, many learners are aware that the kind of English they engage with outside the classroom is different from the kind of "Textbook English", "*Schulenglisch*" or "*inglés de libro*" that they learn at school.

We also noted in 2.5 that a large proportion of teenagers in Germany regularly engage with media in English (Feierabend et al. 2020: 48) and we can expect this trend to be on the rise throughout Europe and beyond. What is striking is that, at least in Germany, there appears to be a genuine disconnect between students', sometimes quite extensive, contact with English outside the classroom and their English teachers' estimates of the quantity, quality, and pedagogical value of that input (see, e.g., the results of a survey and focus group interviews with Year 9 students and their teachers in Grau 2009; for a more recent assessment of the situation and its underlying causes, see Blume 2020). A resolute commitment to a register approach and to raising learners' sociolinguistic awareness (see also

Geeslin 2014: 255–75) could help to bridge this gap by helping learners and their teachers to understand the value of extracurricular English input whilst highlighting important linguistic differences between the various registers that learners encounter both *in* and *outside* the EFL classroom (see also Roberts & Cooke 2009). A register approach may therefore contribute to bringing together what Grau (2009: 161) refers to as "English from above" and "English from below", i.e., English as it is taught in the EFL classroom and English as it is "playfully taken up by German youths [or any other English L2 learners] and integrated into their own language" (Grau 2009: 163). In a similar vein, Willis' claim (2009: 224) that "[r]eal language provides a refreshing link between the classroom and the world outside" ties in with the need to do away with artificial, 'register-neutral' textbook language. In short, by raising sociolinguistic awareness and adopting a register-sensitive approach, EFL teachers can acknowledge and validate learners' extracurricular exposure to English, whilst highlighting relevant register-driven differences in frequent, and therefore contextually appropriate, language use.

Although it is in line with the curricula of the educational systems examined in the present study (see 2.1) and the CEFR (see above), adopting a comprehensive register approach to secondary school EFL teaching undoubtedly entails a major overhaul in how English is taught. It carries far-reaching implications for EFL teachers and all those involved in pre- and in-service teacher education, as well as textbook authors, editors, and publishers. Implications for teacher training will first be sketched out in 9.4.1. This will be followed by some thoughts as to how the textbook publishing industry could contribute to such a shift in perspective in 9.4.2.

9.4.1 Implications for teacher education

The introduction of a register approach to secondary EFL instruction can only succeed if several prerequisites are met. The first, perhaps obvious, but by no means trivial, prerequisite is that (future) English teachers be aware of and knowledgeable about register-driven variation. A recent survey of 80 English schoolteachers from Sweden and Germany suggests that this is not yet common knowledge: in their answers on target language norms, many of the surveyed teachers appear to perceive standard target varieties of English as stable and homogenous entities (Forsberg, Mohr & Jansen 2019; Mohr, Jansen & Forsberg 2019). This is also the author's impression having worked with pre-service teachers of English at a German university for the past eight years (see Le Foll forthcoming). Whilst student teachers are familiar with some of the differences between regional (mostly inner-circle) varieties of English (especially lexical and pronunciation differences between British and American English), on the whole, they are largely oblivious to register-based linguistic variation. In fact, they frequently react with scepticism at any suggestion that lexico-grammar be subject to any form of situational variation (see also, more broadly, Wiese et al. 2017 regarding teachers' attitudes towards linguistic diversity in Germany; and Hall et al. 2017 for a report of similar teacher beliefs in the context of ELT in China). This does not come as a surprise since these pre-service teachers have themselves learnt English (and other foreign languages) in educational systems that do not foresee such variation.

Hence, the first implication for teacher education resides in the content of future EFL teachers' (English) linguistics classes which, at least in Germany, are usually limited to an introductory lecture followed by one or two elective seminars on more specialised topics (Jansen, Mohr & Forsberg 2021: 67–69). Bridges between (socio)linguistics as an academic discipline and student teachers' future careers are not always made explicit and many students fail to grasp the connection between what they are expected to learn in these courses and their future professional roles (see, e.g., Diehr 2018, 2020; Siepmann 2018b; Sommer 2020). In fact, in many cases, the practical English language classes they attend at university continue to propagate the myth of 'proper', 'Standard English' as a homogenous, register-neutral entity. Often, the only exception made is for Academic English – though, here too, it is not infrequent for the language of lectures, conference presentations, and journal articles to be considered as one register and taught as such – resulting in some students confusing spoken and written academic discourse. Student teachers' university-level language practice classes therefore also have a crucial role to play in paving the way for a register-sensitive approach to EFL teaching.

At this stage, it is worth remembering that the development of register-sensitive language skills is a "universal process" that both L1 and L2 users develop over time (Gray & Egbert 2021: 177). Jansen et al. (2021) suggest that EFL student teachers may need to first reflect on the sociolinguistic implications of standard varieties in their L1(s) before they can begin to question Standard English ideologies and their implications in the EFL classroom. The same principle may also apply to register awareness: it may be beneficial to elucidate how language varies across different registers in students' L1 before transferring this sociolinguistic awareness to English.

Increased sociolinguistic knowledge, alone, however, will not suffice to bring about any meaningful change in the EFL classroom. The second, essential prerequisite to the successful introduction of a register approach in ELT entails a fundamental change in teachers' attitudes. This is something that should be addressed in pre-service English/foreign language education classes. On the introduction of conversational grammar in the EFL classroom, Rühlemann (2008: 682) notes that:

> many teachers are likely to perceive the advent of conversational grammar as a threat to dearly held habits and convictions. To them, conversational grammar may simply be 'bad grammar' and, hence, not worth teaching.

In many cases, a register-sensitive approach will entail abandoning the conveniently simplistic dichotomy of 'correct' vs. 'incorrect' across all situations of use. Instead, it calls on notions of frequency and 'appropriateness' within specific contexts of use. Thus, rather than being able to apply a single rule:

> in a register approach, what is appropriate depends on the register and the specific set of conditions in that register constraining the use of the form in question. (Rühlemann 2008: 682)

Resistance to long-held teacher beliefs and socially entrenched expectations that particular lexico-grammatical structures are either 'right' or 'wrong' is to be expected – though it remains to add that this is hardly a radically new idea, either (see, e.g., the concepts of 'appropriateness' and 'conformity' in traditional stylistics Crystal & Davy 1969: 4–7, 149–50).

Beyond gaining the necessary sociolinguistic knowledge and developing the willingness to apply this knowledge in the classroom, Rühlemann (2008: 682) emphasises that practical concerns will also need to be addressed:

> [t]he problem arising is less that correctness may be a dearly held notion that is hard to dispense with than rather that appropriateness is more difficult to handle.

This issue of added complexity is also acknowledged by Koch and Oesterreicher (2011: 276):

> Der Unterricht wird freilich durch die Berücksichtigung konzeptioneller Varianz für den Schüler keineswegs leichter. Dieser muss nunmehr alternative Regeln erlernen und in der Lage sein, sie situationsadäquat anzuwenden [However, by no means does taking contextual variation into account make learning any easier for students. They must now learn alternative rules and be able to apply them appropriately according to the situation].

The truth is, whether we like it or not, no language is monolithic. Corpus linguistics and, in particular, corpus-based register analysis has provided ample quantitative evidence supporting "the reality of underlying functional dimensions of language use" (Egbert & Biber 2018: 271). In fact, even young learners appreciate that the kind of English they engage with outside the classroom, e.g., on social media, is different from what they are expected to produce in an academic essay. In other words, rather than complicating teachers' jobs, a register approach can instead help foreign language teachers explain, on the one hand, why some structures may be "grammatically acceptable" yet not appropriate in specific contexts of use and, on the other, why other structures may be widely attested and therefore idiomatic in some registers, yet very rare and therefore inappropriate in other situational contexts. Of course, this is also true in learners' L1/school language; thus, it may be beneficial to first raise awareness and illustrate the principle of register-specific patterns of language use in students' L1/school language before applying it to students' L2.

Ultimately, if the foremost aim of school foreign language teaching is to develop learners' communicative competence, language learning cannot be detached from the situational contexts in which this communication is to take place. This is not to say that all aspects of the English lexico-grammatical system ought to be subdivided into an array of registers from the very first stages of language acquisition. Like all aspects of language acquisition, the process will necessarily be gradual. Learners will need to be encouraged, over time, to develop register awareness and to vary their language use according to different situational contexts. It probably makes sense to begin with key distinctions between the two poles of a broad oral/informal/immediate vs. literate/formal/distant continuum of English variation (see also Chafe 1982; Koch & Oesterreicher 1985, 2011) before moving to more fine-grained distinctions as learners develop their language skills and expand the repertoire of communicative situations they are expected to master in English.

As shown in 9.2 and 9.3, even basic corpus literacy can go a long way in helping teachers to source and adapt suitable teaching materials. The need to systematically integrate corpus literacy in the curricula of English teacher training study programmes is thus the third implication for teacher education (see, among others, Boulton & Tyne 2015; Farr & Leńko-Szymańska 2023; Callies 2019; Leńko-Szymańska 2017; Le Foll 2023a). Corpus linguistics can, to begin with, be used as an "eye-opener" for pre- and in-service teachers to understand why the doctrinal correct vs. incorrect dichotomy is not only unhelpful, but also often inaccurate in light of real language data. It is not within the scope of the present chapter to describe the kinds of corpus-based data-driven learning activities that may be used to introduce pre- and in-service teachers to register-based variation in English, but the evaluation of a project-based seminar (Le Foll 2020a, 2023a) suggests that activities that encourage students to debunk normative linguistic myths are particularly effective (see also the "surprise-the-teacher" modules suggested by Mukherjee 2004; as well as numerous books with suggestions for activities, e.g.: Bennett 2010; Crosthwaite 2020; Friginal 2018; Le Foll 2021b; O'Keeffe, McCarthy & Carter 2007; Pérez-Paredes & Mark 2021; Timmis 2015; Viana 2023).

In this context, corpus literacy is to be understood as a subset of skills belonging, more broadly, to teachers' professional (critical) digital literacy and competence (Le Foll forthcoming). Even pre-COVID-19, studies had shown that, whilst many teachers were interested in using more digital tools and media in their instruction, many were also acutely aware of their limited knowledge and competence in this area (e.g., Diz-Otero et al. 2022; Rohleder 2019). The pressing need for professional development opportunities in this domain was made all the more evident during the COVID-19 pandemic when teachers were forced to shift to online teaching with little to no preparation and, in many cases, suitable devices and/or infrastructure (see, e.g., Kerres 2020; Starkey et al. 2021; van de Werfhorst, Kessenich & Geven 2020). Reflecting on the situation in Germany, Blume (2020: 890) suggest that teachers often lack both the necessary theoretical and practical knowledge to develop their own materials and make meaningful use of web-based tools and materials. Studies suggest that the situation is likely comparable in France, Spain and across Europe (see, e.g., Fominykh et al. 2021). Few teachers appear to be aware of high-quality resources other than those proposed by the handful of textbook publishers that dominate each domestic market. Thus, in addition to raising awareness of what constitutes Textbook English from a linguistic point of view and reflecting, more generally, on the advantages and limitations of commercially published materials, teacher education in the 21st century also ought to focus on 'Technological Pedagogical Content Knowledge' (Mishra & Koehler 2006) and aim to develop future teachers' critical digital literacy and competence. Such courses would likely need to begin with relatively basic, general professional skills such as effective web searching strategies before moving to more complex, subject-specific competences such as ELT materials design and adaptation. The aforementioned project demonstrated the potential and impact of project-based seminars in which student teachers engage in creating, adapting and reusing Open Educational Resources (OER) in ways that can create bridges not only between theory and practice, but also between pre-service teacher education, in-service teacher training, and continuous professional development (Le Foll 2021b, 2023a; see also Kosmas et al. 2021; Vyatkina 2020).

Although 9.2 and 9.3 explained how teachers can easily find and, if necessary, adapt authentic texts to create pedagogical materials for their students, this is not to suggest that, at least at lower secondary school level, we do away with foreign language textbooks altogether. For a start, teachers' workloads in most European school systems simply do not allow enough time for this to be feasible. But even if time were not a constraint, the reality is that most teacher education programmes currently do not adequately prepare teachers for this task. In fact, it has been argued that commercially published textbooks – together with their handy multimodal packages consisting of texts, tasks, and exercises, teacher handbooks, assessment materials, additional worksheets, games, songs, videos, etc. – play a crucial role in supporting (inexperienced) teachers. Schäfer (2003: 305) goes as far as to claim:

> Wer die Abschaffung des Lehrbuchs fordert, sollte gute Alternativen zu bieten haben. Immerhin bietet es Halteseile für den unsicheren Lehrer und schützt den Schüler vor dem schlechten Lehrer [Those who claim we should do away with textbooks ought to propose good alternative offers. After all, textbooks act as safety lines for insecure teachers and protect pupils from incompetent teachers].

The metaphor of "*Halteseile* [safety lines]" may seem like an exaggeration to some but, even if there is only a semblance of truth in the statement, it points to an alarming situation. For a start, it begs the question as to why teachers are placed in such a perilous situation that "safety lines" are necessary in the first place. It also places a disproportionate amount of responsibility on the textbook industry that appears to be effectively tasked with filling glaring gaps in initial teacher education with bite-size on-the-job training materials. Hence, a final yet crucial implication for teacher education consists in a much stronger emphasis, in pre- and in-service training, on the selection and use of pedagogical materials, including the considered and deliberate use of commercially-published textbook materials – many of which, it is worth stressing, are of excellent quality. At the end of the day, textbooks are not categorically 'good' or 'bad', 'suitable' or 'unsuitable'; however, the way they are exploited in the classroom may be effective or not. It is very much a case of: "Coursebooks don't kill learning, bad teachers kill learning" (Chong 2012). Thus, teacher education programmes would also do well to emphasise that:

> Kein Lehrwerk passt von selber zu jeder Lernsituation – und schon gar nicht gleichermaßen zu den Bedürfnissen eines jeden Lerners in einer größeren Lerngruppe: Lehrwerke sind vom Prinzip her auf aktive Interpretation angelegt [No textbook will, in and of itself, suit every learning situation – and can certainly not be expected to fulfil the needs of every learner in larger learning groups: textbooks are fundamentally designed to be actively interpreted].
>
> (Vielau 2005: n.p.; see also, e.g., Nold 1998)

In sum, this section has made clear that teacher education – at all stages of teachers' careers – has a paramount role to play in addressing teachers' gaps in knowledge, competence, attitudes, and beliefs on a range of issues relevant to successfully implementing a register approach in the secondary EFL classroom. In addition to raising awareness of the variety of English typically taught in EFL textbooks, such an approach must challenge the status of the textbook as "*the* authorised/legitimated educational medium for language learning" (Canale 2021: 1; emphasis original) on all language-related matters and as the best or "safest" way to implement the curriculum. It also involves developing teachers' own register awareness, both in their L1(s) and L2(s), by placing a stronger emphasis on the acquisition of sociolinguistic knowledge in pre-service teacher education (see also Geeslin 2014). Furthermore, it entails a shift away from register-neutral dichotomies of *right* or *wrong* towards situationally dependent notions of *frequency, idiomaticity* and *appropriateness* in specific contexts of use. Finally, this section has also pointed to the need for teacher education curricula to systematically integrate the development of both theoretical knowledge and practical skills in ELT materials design, including sourcing suitable authentic texts from online resources, adapting them to learners' needs, making competent use of corpora and the basic functions of corpus tools, and formulating clear and concise task instructions.

9.4.2 Implications for materials design

As we have seen, at lower secondary school level, foreign language textbooks are considered "indispensable" (Leroy 2012: 62) and, for a whole host of reasons, are unlikely to become obsolete any time soon. Hence, it goes without saying that this paradigm shift towards a register approach to ELT cannot happen without the involvement of the textbook publishing industry.

Of the three major textbook registers compared to equivalent 'real-world' registers from outside the EFL classroom in Chapter 7, we saw that Textbook Fiction is the closest to its corresponding reference corpus. We concluded that this finding is not particularly surprising given that many of these fictional texts are excerpts of published novels and short stories. Furthermore, those that are not have been shown to be either practically indistinguishable from texts originally written as novels or short stories (thus, demonstrating that, on the whole, textbook authors appear to have an excellent command of this register) or to have been convincingly written with low proficiency level learners in mind (e.g., using present-tense narration and low lexical diversity for beginner learners). However, the same cannot be said of representations of the informative and, in particular, spoken conversation texts featured in the textbooks of the TEC. In contrast to many of the fictional texts featured in EFL textbooks, most of these texts are crafted by textbook authors.

Adopting a register approach would require textbook authors and editors to systematically account for register-driven linguistic variation when selecting, adapting, and drafting textbook texts. How this could be achieved using corpus data and tools has already been exemplified in 9.2 and 9.3. These suggestions and recommendations are by no means new or particularly innovative. More than three decades ago, Sinclair (1991: 39–51) already explained why lexicographers and other applied linguists would do well to rely less on a combination of existing descriptions of languages and (native-speaker) introspection and more on attested language data in the form of large corpora. Yet, whilst it is true that corpora have since revolutionised the development of (learner) dictionaries and (many) reference grammars (see 2.7), textbook publishers have seemingly been much slower to follow this trend. That so few textbook publishers have latched onto the potential of corpus linguistics over the past three decades may seem particularly surprising given that corpora and corpus tools are more accessible than ever. However, Nelson (2022) notes that corpora are scarcely mentioned in reviews of ELT materials development such as Tomlinson (2008, 2012, 2013a) and Garton and Graves (2014; Graves & Garton 2019). By the same token, Meunier and Reppen's (2015: 501) encouraging report that "there has been a significant increase in corpus-informed teaching materials" cannot be confirmed for the European pre-tertiary EFL textbook industry. Whilst some of the large Anglo-Saxon publishing houses operating on the global (mostly adult) EFL/ESL market have invested in their own corpus resources and expertise and now advertise many of their products as "corpus-informed" (see 2.7), only one series of the TEC (*English in Mind for Spanish Speakers*, Cambridge University Press) explicitly states that it incorporates insights from (in this case, learner) corpus data:

> 'Get it right!' section based on information from the unique Cambridge Learner Corpus tackle problem areas common to learners of each level.
> ⟨https://www.cambridge.org/us/cambridgeenglish/catalog/secondary/english-mind-2nd-edition⟩ (25 January 2022)

From the earliest prophesies that corpora had the potential to revolutionize language teaching, it was clear that materials designers had a crucial role to play in this "corpus revolution" (see, e.g., Conrad 2000: 557). However, as we have seen, in secondary school EFL materials design, this revolution has yet to materialise in any significant way. As briefly outlined in 2.6, the school EFL textbook industry operates under very (national and regional) specific constraints and is known to be particularly resistant to change.

In advocating for the use of corpora in materials design, there is sometimes a misconception that corpus linguists believe that frequency of use should override all other considerations. This assumption is misguided on several grounds. For a start, corpus linguistics necessarily involves a combination of quantitative and qualitative analyses (see, e.g., Bennett 2010: 7). Hence, when selecting the items to be included in pedagogical materials, textbook authors and editors cannot rely on frequency as the sole criterion. They will also need to consider additional factors such as salience, contingency, range, teachability, learnability, etc. (see, e.g., Ellis 2002, 2006, 2008). In other words, whilst corpora can provide valuable frequency-based information that is not accessible to (even native speaker) intuition, these quantitative statistical results need to be complemented with qualitative analyses. Making the same argument, McCarthy and Carter (2001: 338) assert that: "corpora can afford considerable benefits for classroom teaching, but the pedagogic process should be informed by the corpus, not driven or controlled by it." Nonetheless, Biber and Conrad (2001: 335) convincingly argue that:

> [i]n the absence of other compelling factors (e.g., learnability at a given stage or basic knowledge required as a building block for later instruction), [...] dramatic differences in frequency should be among the most important factors influencing pedagogical decisions.

In the context of secondary school textbooks designed for national markets, factors that are specific to certain L1s (i.e., 'learnability') can arguably best be teased out on the basis of learner corpus data (see, e.g., Granger 2015) and/or of contrastive analyses of L1 and L2 corpus data (see, e.g., Valero Garcés 1998). The textbook series of the TEC were specifically targeted at learners with a common L1/school language. Yet, echoing Granger's (2015: 494) observations that learner corpora's impact on textbooks has so far been more "more nominal than real", remarkably little contrastive metalinguistic information was provided by these textbooks. This seems like a missed opportunity since much research has shown that progress in L2 learning involves complex interactions between general language developmental processes and L1 constraints (e.g., Madlener 2018; Spada & Lightbown 1999). Corpus-based contrastive L1–L2 research and the findings of learner corpus research can provide textbook authors and editors with "information essential to producing customised syllabi applicable to teaching L2 learners of specific mother tongues" (Liu & Shaw 2001: 189). For instance, Winter and Le Foll (2022: 61–63) sketch out ideas for such corpus-informed, register-sensitive and L1-specific "customised syllabi" with respect to the teaching of *if*-conditionals at lower secondary school level.

In sum, materials development can be both directly informed by the results of corpus queries formulated by the materials designers themselves and indirectly by incorporating the results of corpus linguistic research into the design process. Meunier and Reppen (2015: 501; see also Friginal & Roberts 2022) list the following ways in which corpora can inform materials design:

- in helping select the linguistic target features (e.g. vocabulary, lexicogrammar; grammar);
- the amount of space in the text devoted to the features;
- in the sequencing of materials;
- through the inclusion of actual corpus data (e.g. lists of vocabulary or common lexico-grammar patterns);
- through the inclusion of information on register differences (e.g. conversation and academic prose);
- in the selection of the texts used in examples (e.g. do the texts accurately reflect the use of the target feature?).

Note that the penultimate bullet point refers specifically to the kind of register approach advocated for in 9.4, thus reiterating the major role that corpora and corpus tools can play in helping materials developers to promote register awareness in EFL teaching and learning.

Another idea, not touched upon in Meunier and Reppen's (2015: 501) summary, goes beyond the language featured in textbooks. It concerns the learning activities that textbooks propose. Though calls to incorporate corpus-based data-driven learning activities in the EFL/ESL classroom date back to the 1980s (e.g., Johns 1986), in secondary school contexts in particular, they remain an absolute exception (see, e.g., Chambers 2019; Boulton & Vyatkina 2021). The norm, as we have seen in 2.6, is for lower secondary school EFL teachers to largely follow the structure and activities of the textbook and since very few publishing houses have yet dared to include hands-on data-driven learning activities in their materials, only very few students (presumably those with particularly dedicated teachers who have attended at least one university seminar or continuous professional development course on corpus linguistics) benefit from these kinds of activities. Given that we know that learners already use an array of online resources to support them in their language learning processes, it would be wise for textbooks to include activities that guide students towards more trustworthy sources than they currently tend to choose (including – but not limited to – web-based corpus tools), teach them efficient and effective querying methods, as well as the necessary interpretative skills to make the best use of these resources (see, e.g., Gilquin & Laporte 2021; Le Foll 2018b).

CHAPTER 10

Methodological reflections

Having considered the study's potential pedagogical implications in the previous chapter, this chapter reflects on the strengths (10.1) and limitations (10.2) of the methodology. Although firmly anchored within the decade-long tradition of MDA, the method applied involved numerous modifications to the standard MDA framework (5.3). These were implemented in response to challenges specific to the study of Textbook English (as a variety of English that brings about particular methodological issues), as well as to more general concerns about the reproducibility, replicability, and robustness of MDA. These are not to be understood as definite solutions to these challenges, but rather as suggestions that ought to be explored further in future studies.

The modified MDA framework was applied to describe the language of secondary school EFL textbooks along several dimensions of variation. In Chapter 6, we saw that the methodological framework provided an effective way of disentangling the various sources of intra-textbook variation and their interactions. In Chapter 7, it allowed for the bottom-up comparison of Textbook English to naturally occurring, 'real-world' English along multiple dimensions of linguistic variation. The present chapter considers the strengths and limitations of this modified MDA framework in the context of studying Textbook English and beyond it. Indeed, many of the adjustments made to the standard MDA approach may be of interest to linguists examining a broad range of language registers and varieties to answer very diverse research questions.

10.1 Strengths and methodological contributions

This section explores how the modified MDA framework can potentially contribute to addressing three primary concerns associated with MDA. First, Section 10.1.1 addresses concerns pertaining to the replicability and robustness of MDA results. Sections 5.3.2 to 5.3.10 of the methodology chapter outlined the steps undertaken to mitigate these concerns. The outcomes of the robustness tests conducted as part of this study are summarised and briefly discussed in 10.1.1. The second concern centres around the undeniable complexity inherent to MDA. Indeed, in summarising criticisms of MDA, McEnery and Hardie (2011: 111) content that, in addition to the aforementioned replicability concerns, "[i]t is almost certainly this complexity that has inhibited the widespread uptake of what appears to be a useful technique". This is admittedly less true now that several book chapters detailing the implementation of all the steps of the standard MDA framework in widely used software and programming languages have been published (e.g., Brezina 2018: 160–182; Egbert & Staples 2019; Friginal & Hardy 2014). Moreover, in response to this complexity concern, it can be argued that language being a highly complex phenomenon, it should come as no surprise that empirical methods to describe it are likely to be complex, too. Nonetheless, it is important to acknowledge that complexity has likely restricted the number of linguists choosing to work within the MDA framework[31] and, at the same time, the range of applications and potential for methodological innovations. Section 10.1.2 discusses the complexity of the modified MDA framework and the measures undertaken to, if not reduce it, at least render this complexity as transparent as possible. Transparency also closely ties into the third concern, which revolves around the reproducibility of MDA studies. A brief discussion of this crucial aspect concludes this chapter.

10.1.1 Replicability and robustness

Given that the modified MDA framework presented in 5.3 involves many novel aspects, it was particularly important to ensure that the results it yielded are robust. As recommended by Lee (2000: 393; see also Biber 1990; Clarke 2020: Section 4.8 for similar approaches), the two models presented in Chapters 6 and 7 were therefore replicated on random subsets of the data to test the stability and robustness of the results. The reader is invited to use the data and R code provided in the Online Supplements to re-run these analyses and/or carry out additional replications on new sub-samples.

For reasons of space, not all these replications can be presented here. Instead, this section focuses on the results of a single replication of the comparative model of Textbook English vs. 'real-world' English presented in Chapter 7. Figures 40

31. Of the 210 unique studies examined in a recent synthesis of MDA studies, 33 were authored or co-authored by Biber and a further 73 studies were authored or co-authored by at least one of Biber's graduate students or direct affiliates (Goulart & Wood 2021: 6). There are, of course, many reasons for this but the (perceived) complexity of the method is likely to be one of them. Another reason worth mentioning is also certainly the non-availability of the Biber tagger to the wider research community. Indeed, the release of an open-source replication of the 1988 version of the Biber tagger (the MAT; Nini 2019) coincides with a rise in the popularity of MDA outside of Northern Arizona University (although other factors, including the publication of step-by-step instructions to conduct MDAs have likely also played an important role, e.g., Brezina 2018: 160–169; Egbert & Staples 2019; Friginal & Hardy 2014).

and 41 display the first model replication run on a random subset of two-thirds of the data (see Appendix H for details of the procedure). The plots can be compared to Figures 26 and 28 from Chapter 7 that were computed on the basis of the full dataset. With only marginal differences, the patterns of variation observed in Chapter 7 and further discussed in Chapter 8 are clearly identifiable on both these figures. In fact, aside from the inversion of the negative and positive poles of some of the components (which, in PCA, are entirely arbitrary), the results proved to be very stable across the six attempted replications of each model, attesting to the robustness of the results.

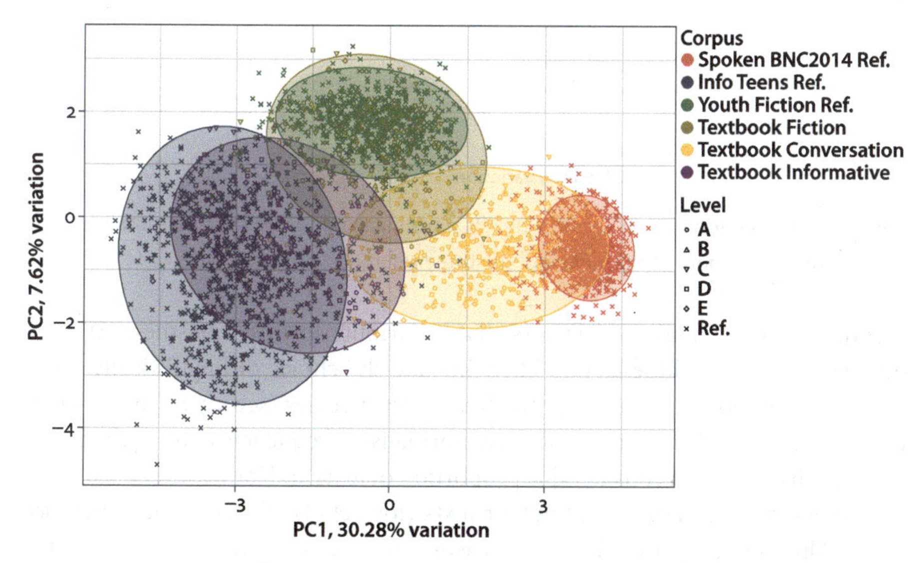

Figure 40. Projection of texts on PC1 and PC2 from a random 2/3 split-data analysis of the three subcorpora of the TEC and the three reference corpora

In addition to these randomised subset analyses, for each of the two models presented in this study, three additional PCAs were conducted using only the texts stemming from (1) the French, (2) the German (see also Le Foll 2024a), and (3) the Spanish subcorpora of the TEC. Again, only minor differences in the ranking of the feature loadings were observed. We can therefore conclude that the observations and trends discussed in Chapter 8 are stable across all three "national" subcorpora of the TEC. This confirms the finding that the language of lower secondary school EFL textbooks is very comparable across the nine series used in France, Germany, and Spain that constitute the TEC (see 8.2).

The fact that the results could be successfully replicated over various (random and non-random) subsets of the data testifies to the robustness of the modified MDA framework. However, it is not within the scope of the present study to

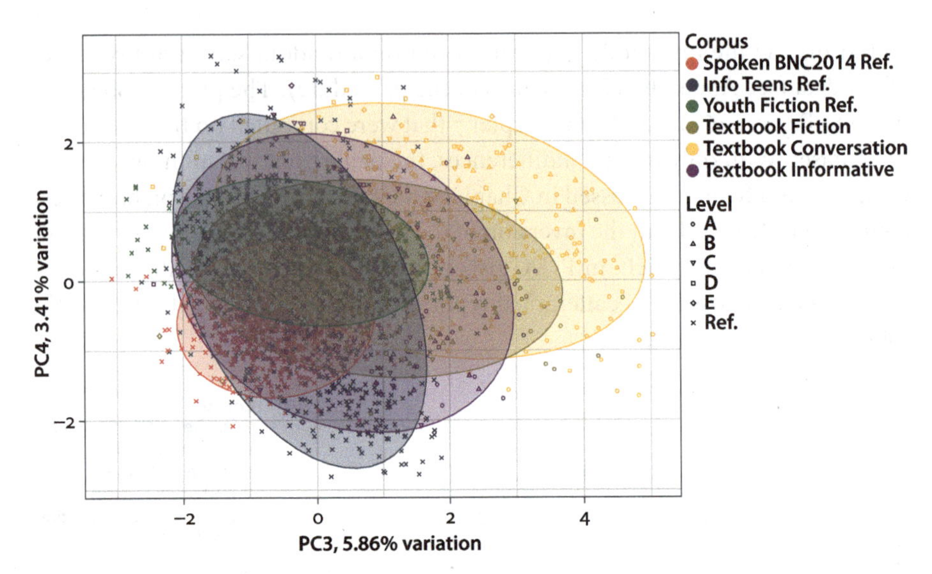

Figure 41. Projection of texts on PC3 and PC4 from a random 2/3 split-data analysis of the three subcorpora of the TEC and the three reference corpora

identify the combination of factors that contribute to this robustness. We can only speculate that these factors likely include the choice of linguistically motivated normalisation baselines for the feature frequencies (see 5.3.4), the (partial) deskewing of the distributions of these normalised frequencies, the exclusion of features absent from a considerable proportion of texts and/or with very low communalities, and the removal of outlier texts (for details of these procedures, see 5.3.6). Although they are often – for reasons of space or otherwise – not explicitly stated in the methods chapters of MDA studies, it is worth noting that many of these steps are already frequently implemented by researchers applying 'standard' MDA, too (see, e.g., Brezina 2018: 160–182; Egbert & Staples 2019; Friginal & Hardy 2014).

10.1.2 Complexity

Although this study did not set out to reduce this complexity, in some respects, the modified MDA framework can be said to be easier to implement than the standard one. For instance, using PCA rather than EFA as the underlying dimensionality-reduction method means that the number of dimensions to be extracted can be linguistically and/or pragmatically motivated without fear of influencing the results of the entire model (see 5.3.5). In addition, not only can doing away with any cut-off points to calculate dimension scores be theoretically motivated (see 5.3.7), it also means that the output of the standard PCA functions offered in most statistical software can be interpreted without any additional manipulations. Finally, many open-source statistical packages for PCA also include multi-dimensional plotting functions (e.g., Blighe & Lun 2020; Lê, Josse & Husson 2008). Thus, visualising the results of PCA-based MDAs across several dimensions is comparatively easy and, as we have seen, visualisation is key to identifying more subtle patterns of variation (see 5.3.9 and Neumann & Evert 2021).

At the same time, the multi-dimensional visualisations explored as part of the modified MDA framework can be criticised for adding complexity. The same can be said of the use of linear mixed-effects models as a means of describing the variance in dimension scores across and within different text types. There is no denying that these models are complex. However, it is hoped that this study has shown that, together with visualisations that display the full breadth of variation within each text category, they can constitute a valuable addition to the standard MDA framework, as they can help us to disentangle the various factors (and potentially their interactions) that contribute to observed differences in dimension scores.

Furthermore, some may argue that interpreting the feature loadings of the models presented in this study is more complex given that the feature frequencies entered in the PCAs represent signed logged-transformed standardised frequencies (see 5.3.6) that have been normalised to different baselines (see 5.3.4). However, it is important to note that the feature frequencies entered in standard MDAs are not immediately interpretable either: they represent standardised *z*-scores (see 5.1). As for the different normalisation baselines, it was argued that the linguistic motivation for opting for different normalisation baselines is considerably stronger than any interpretability arguments – especially given that the currently preferred alternative (i.e., using word-based baselines) is almost certain to lead to intricate interpretation issues. In 5.3.4, we saw that, for example, if the relative frequencies of features such as contractions, negation, and present tense per 1,000 words all contribute to one pole of a dimension, whilst the frequencies of nouns and prepositions per 1,000 words contribute to the opposite end, there is a risk that the dimension in question largely represents the proportion of verbs to nouns. In other words, relying on word-based normalisation baselines potentially adds a considerable amount of uncontrolled variation to the relative frequencies entered in the analysis. This, in turn, may impact the reproducibility of the results (Wallis 2020: 74).

10.1.3 Reproducibility

In and of itself, warranted complexity is not an issue. However, where complexity results in methodological opacity, it can become a concern for the reproducibility of the results. This is why, in line with the principles of Open Science (see 4.2.2), considerable efforts were deployed to ensure that the modified MDA framework applied in the present study is as transparent and accessible as possible. To this end, it was important to rely on an open-source tagger (the MFTE; Le Foll 2021a, 2021d). In addition, the Online Supplements to this study includes the full analysis code to (a) select the features to be entered in a PCA, (b) conduct the PCA, (c) produce (multi-dimensional) visualisations of the results, and (d) perform the statistical modelling of the dimension scores. All of these procedures are implemented in the open-source programming environment R (R Core Team 2022) which is now widely used among quantitative (corpus) linguists (Anthony 2020:187; Mizumoto & Plonsky 2016).

The publication of the full code and data used to run the analyses presented in this study not only allows for the full computational reproducibility of the results, but also for additional, independent replications (see 10.1.1). Regrettably, such Open Science practices are currently far from the norm in (corpus) linguistics (see 4.2.2). It is therefore also hoped that this study may serve as a showcase for future research by exemplifying how quantitative corpus-linguistic methods can be made more transparent, reproducible, and replicable (see also Le Foll 2024b; Schweinberger 2020).

10.2 Limitations of the study

While the modified MDA framework proved well-aligned with the research questions of the present study in that it yielded both interesting and robust findings, a few important caveats nonetheless apply.

First, as with most corpus-based studies, arguably the most fundamental limitation of the present study concerns the representativeness of the corpus data from which we drew our conclusions (see, e.g., Egbert 2019). In other words, it lies within the design of the corpora themselves. The decision-making processes that informed the design and compilation of both the TEC and the reference corpora were outlined in 4.3. As explained in 4.3.1.1, stringent criteria were established to ensure that the selection of textbooks included in the TEC would be as representative as possible of the body of EFL textbooks used at lower secondary school level in France, Germany, and Spain at the time of data collection between December 2016 and September 2017. Similarly, considerable efforts were made to ensure that the three reference corpora used for comparisons with the Conversation, Fiction, and Informative subcorpora of the TEC were carefully chosen/compiled to reflect as accurately as possible the kind of target language with which teenage EFL learners can be expected to aspire to interact (see 4.3.2). However, given the lack of publicly available textbook sales figures and considering other practical constraints, some convenience choices had to be made (see 4.3.1.1).

Hence, as with all corpus studies, generalisability of the results beyond the corpus sample(s) analysed should not be assumed. For now, we cannot tell whether the results of the present study will generalise to other secondary school EFL textbooks used in France, Germany, and Spain, let alone to textbooks designed for entirely different education systems and/or produced by very different textbook publishing cultures. That said, the TEC is one of the largest and most diverse corpus of contemporary secondary school EFL textbooks to date.

In fairness to the authors and editors of the textbooks featured in the TEC, some of the differences observed between Textbook Conversation and natural spoken conversation (as represented in the Spoken BNC2014) may be due to what is arguably an overly simplistic textbook register classification scheme (see 4.3.1.3). Indeed, as shown in some of the excerpts featured in the previous chapters, the Conversation subcorpus of the TEC also includes radio and TV interviews which are situationally quite different from the informal everyday conversations among friends and relatives that constitute most of the texts of the Spoken BNC2014 (see 4.3.2.1). It is, however, worth stressing that the Conversation subcorpus of the TEC only includes texts presented in the textbooks as supposedly spontaneous, non-scripted representations of speech (see 4.3.1.3). That said, future annotators of textbook corpora may consider subdividing the Conversation register category into 'private' and 'public' (e.g., broadcast) situational contexts. This would allow for additional comparisons with a reference corpus of TV and radio language for the 'public conversation' register, whilst the Spoken BNC2014 would only be used as a comparison benchmark for 'private conversation'. Though we might reasonably hypothesise this new analysis would likely considerably reduce the observed gap between how spoken English is portrayed in EFL textbooks and how it is spoken outside the EFL classroom, I would nonetheless expect the trends described in the present study to remain largely the same. This prediction is motivated by the results of a preliminary study (Le Foll 2017) which was conducted before the Spoken BNC2014 was made available to the wider research community and, instead, relied on a corpus of TV captions and subtitles (a subset of the BBC corpus used in Fankhauser forthcoming). This study, which only included the German and French subcorpora of the TEC, also reported a wide gap between Textbook Conversation and (pseudo)spoken language as observed in TV news, shows and series (Le Foll 2017).

In addition, future textbook corpus annotators may want to consider making a distinction between written textbook dialogues and transcripts of textbooks' accompanying audio and audio-visual materials. Whilst many textbook dialogues are featured both in written form within a textbook unit and within its accompanying audio or audio-visual materials, a hypothesis worth testing would be whether those that are only featured in audio-/audio-visual materials share more similarities with natural speech than those that are exclusively 'written-to-be-read(-out-loud)'.

Future compilers of textbook corpora could also consider including XML tags (see, e.g., Hardie 2014) that reflect the internal structure and layout of the textbooks. The simple mark-up scheme devised for the TEC only included a header with metadata on each textbook volume (see 4.3.1.2). Whilst this proved sufficient for this study, it may also be worthwhile adding mark-up tags defining each textbook page, lesson unit, and chapter – provided there are enough resources for this additional manual annotation workload. For the present study, this would have facilitated the process of collating short textbook texts into meaningful units (see 5.3.1). In future projects, it would allow for more fine-grained evaluations of textbooks' intended progressive development of learners' language competences.

Another limitation inherent to all quantitative corpus studies that rely on automated corpus annotation resides in the fact that taggers are never 100% accurate. Reliability issues at this initial level of the analysis should not be underestimated (see, e.g., Picoral, Staples & Reppen 2021). In the case of MDA studies that rely on dozens of features in hundreds of texts, manual checks are simply not feasible. The advantage of the present study is that it includes a formal evaluation of the accuracy of the output of the MFTE on the TEC and the reference corpus data (see 5.3.3). This procedure led to the exclusion or merging of some features. It also means that it is possible to check that the results of the two MDA models presented in Chapters 6 and 7 were not unduly influenced by some of the less reliably tagged features (as confirmed by the random sub-sample replications presented in 10.1.3).

Finally, construct validity may also be considered a weakness. Following standard practice in MDA interpretative labels were assigned to describe the functional, communicative functions captured by each dimension (Friginal & Hardy 2019). Some may disagree with the labels assigned to the dimensions of the two models presented in this study. Indeed, whilst the co-occurrence patterns underlying each dimension are empirically determined, their interpretation remains subjective. The present labels are, however, the result of rigorous analyses of the patterns of linguistic co-occurrences inherent to each dimension involving much back-and-forth between the plots of dimension scores, graphs of features and, most importantly, the texts themselves. Full disclosure of the data and code allows for alternative and/or complementary interpretations.

CHAPTER 11

Conclusions

The preceding chapters detailed the study's potential pedagogical implications (Chapter 9) and the strengths and limitations of its methodological approach (Chapter 10). This concluding final chapter provides a synthesis of the study, before outlining future research desiderata and potential directions.

11.1 Synthesis

This study has provided a systematic, empirical account of the kind of English that secondary school EFL learners interact with via their textbooks as compared to the kind of English that they can be expected to encounter outside the EFL classroom. This new understanding of Textbook English is important because textbooks constitute one of the major, if not the most important, vector of English language input that EFL learners encounter in the first four to five years of their secondary education. Although it is popular knowledge that the language portrayed in EFL textbooks somehow "feels" different from how English is generally used outside the classroom, this study is the first to attempt to model the nature of these linguistic peculiarities across different registers and textbook proficiency levels by accounting for a broad range of linguistic features and their co-occurrences. Specifically, it set out to describe the language that secondary school pupils in France, Germany, and Spain are exposed to via their coursebooks and their accompanying audio and audio-visual materials.

To this end, the Textbook English Corpus (TEC) was compiled. It comprises nine series of secondary school EFL textbooks (42 textbook volumes) used at lower secondary level in France, Germany, and Spain and was manually annotated for register. Three reference corpora (Spoken BNC2014, Info Teens, and Youth Fiction) were used as baselines for comparisons between the language of the TEC and the kind of naturally occurring English that learners can be expected to encounter, engage with, and produce themselves outside the EFL classroom.

From the literature review (Chapter 3), we concluded that, to date, a multitude of studies have focused on the representations of *individual* linguistic features in EFL and ESL textbooks. Some of these studies were described as 'intra-textbook analyses' because they seek to explore and describe the language of textbooks without relying on any comparison benchmarks. By contrast, 'comparative textbook language analyses' draw on reference corpora or corpus-driven lists to infer what is special about the language of textbooks. In this second paradigm, we identified three recurrent issues. First, previous research has failed to consider interactions between the individual linguistic features examined. Thus, whilst some influential studies have helped us to understand how English learners can be misled by their textbooks into making unidiomatic use of specific lexico-grammatical features (e.g., progressive aspect; Römer 2005), we concluded that only a multivariable approach can paint the full picture as to how Textbook English – as a whole – differs from the English that language learners are likely to encounter outside the EFL classroom. Second, we saw that prior scholarship has mostly ignored register differences between the various types of texts typically included in school foreign language textbooks. Given that school EFL textbooks frequently feature, for example, extracts from short stories, dialogues, instructions, and exercises on a single double page, we argued that a meaningful analysis of Textbook English requires a register-based approach. Third, previous quantitative corpus-based studies have usually been undertaken at the corpus level, e.g., comparing the occurrences of a linguistic feature across an entire textbook corpus with those from a reference corpus, and have therefore often failed to account for the effects of varying textbook proficiency levels or the potential idiosyncrasies of individual textbook authors, editors, or publishers. Thus, prior to the present study, much textbook language research had (often implicitly) assumed that Textbook English constitutes a homogenous variety of English with no (systematic) sources of internal variation.

This study set out to test this assumption and uncover the linguistic specificities of Textbook English. Specifically, it examined the extent to which the language of current EFL textbooks used in secondary schools in France, Germany, and Spain is representative of 'real-world' English as used by native/proficient English speakers in similar communicative situations. It asked whether some textbook registers are more faithfully represented than others and whether textbooks' portrayal of different registers becomes more natural-like as the textbooks' targeted proficiency level increases. Finally, the study also sought to identify the clusters of linguistic features that characterise Textbook English across different registers and learner proficiency levels.

To answer these research questions, Biber's (1988, 1995) multi-feature/multi-dimensional analysis (MDA) framework was chosen as a method capable of summarising the patterns of co-occurrences of many linguistic features across different groups of texts. In a preliminary study, the texts of the TEC were compared against the dimensions of Biber's (1988) seminal model of variation in general spoken and written registers of English (Le Foll 2021c, 2022c: Chapter 6). On this basis, the present study identified a number of potential methodological issues linked to both the use of Biber's (1988) model as a baseline and the MDA framework as it is traditionally applied. Consequently, a modified MDA framework was developed and implemented for the present study. This modified framework relies on a stringent selection of linguistic features, the normalisation of feature counts to linguistically informed baselines, the application of a computationally stable dimension reduction method (Principal Component Analysis; PCA), the use of mixed-effects linear regression modelling to tease out the potential mediating effects of various variables, and the interpretation of the results using multi-dimensional graphs that expose, rather than obscure, the full breadth of linguistic variation.

In applying the modified MDA framework, the results of the study have convincingly debunked the long-held assumption that the language of school EFL textbooks can meaningfully be considered a homogenous variety of English. Mode and register emerge as significant drivers of intra-textbook linguistic variation, making it impossible to adequately describe Textbook English without considering situationally determined, functional variation. Despite few significant differences between the language of EFL textbooks used in France, Germany, and Spain or between the nine different textbook series of the TEC, this study did uncover noteworthy interactions between the different text registers and target proficiency levels. The clusters responsible for these interactions underwent close examination. The study also explains and illustrates the key linguistic differences that distinguish stereotypically textbook-like texts from situationally similar 'real-world' texts.

Corroborating the findings of previous Textbook English studies, notably Mindt (1987, 1992, 1995b) and Römer (2004a, 2005), the present study identified a wide gap between conversational English as it is presented in contemporary secondary school EFL textbooks and 'real-world' conversation that learners can be expected to be involved in outside the EFL classroom. Whilst we are not claiming that *all* textbook dialogues should resemble the everyday, casual conversations of English L1 speakers (as represented, e.g., in the reference Spoken BNC2014 corpus), it is somewhat disconcerting that, across all nine textbook series of the TEC, textbooks' representations of conversational spoken English become less authentic as learners are expected to become more proficient in English.

By contrast, and more reassuringly, as the target proficiency levels of the textbooks increased, so did the observed similarities between the informative and fiction subcorpora of the TEC and their respective reference corpora. This latter trend likely points to well-intended pedagogical progressions aimed at scaffolding the development of learners' linguistic competences. Despite this general trend towards more authentic informative texts as the textbooks' target proficiency level increases, the results also highlighted potentially problematic textbook texts, even at the highest proficiency levels represented in the TEC (B2). We concluded that some informative texts featured in B2 textbooks were characterised by a lack of register coherence, e.g., pairing words and phrases typical of formal, written English with others more commonly found in informal, (pseudo-)spoken registers. Although this descriptive study makes no claim as to any potential causal links between Textbook English and EFL learners' production, we did note that a lack of register awareness is an issue that has also been observed in learner corpus research (e.g., Gilquin & Paquot 2008).

We acknowledged that not all textbook texts are designed to reflect naturally occurring English. However, when it *is* the aim, the results of the present study, along with the use of corpus tools, can be used to adapt or create textbook texts that better reflect the kind of English learners can expect to encounter outside the EFL classroom. The results of the present study support the adoption of a "register approach" to ELT, which entails exposing learners to lexico-grammatical patterns of use in the form of situationally contextualised, meaningful constructions and texts, as proposed by Rühlemann (2008). In terms of pedagogical implications, Section 9.4 spelt out the wide-reaching implications of such a register approach for teacher education and materials design.

Although it was originally conceived with the analysis of Textbook English in mind, it is hoped that many of the changes implemented in the modified MDA framework (see 5.3) will be of interest to corpus linguists working on a wide range of research questions and language varieties. Indeed, many of the issues raised in Chapter 5 are not by any means confined to the analysis of textbook language. For instance, the solutions proposed in 5.3.1 to overcome issues such as the comparison of texts of radically different lengths, the lack of punctuation in transcriptions of spoken language (see 5.3.2), and the non-independence of texts/text samples from the same textbook series, web domain or novel (see 5.3.8) are relevant to many other research areas. These include the study of many e-language registers (e.g., social media posts, blogs, forums, product reviews) and texts produced by young L1 users and L2 learners of all ages and proficiency levels.

Whilst by no means claiming to be fail-safe, the publication of the full code and data used to perform the analyses presented in this study is intended to allow for the computational reproducibility of the results. Crucially, it also allows for additional, independent replications. The Online Supplements exemplify how quantitative (corpus)linguistic methods can, with relatively simple means, be made more transparent, robust, and replicable. Thus, it is hoped that this study may serve as a springboard for further methodological innovations in the multivariate analysis of linguistic data.

11.2 Future directions

The present study is descriptive and exploratory in nature. As such, it opens many avenues for future research. It has contributed some methodological innovations to the MDA framework that may be further explored and tested in future MDA studies on diverse language varieties and registers. Regarding the analysis of school EFL textbooks, it has shown how Textbook English can be examined across a broad range of linguistic features both as a variety of English in its own right, and in comparison to various target reference varieties. Future studies could apply the method to study the language of different EFL, ESL and ESP textbooks and other pedagogical materials (e.g., online e learning courses) used in different educational systems and/or at different proficiency levels.

Another avenue to be explored concerns the quality and quantity of the lexical input provided by EFL textbooks. For each textbook volume and series, the word and phraseme types can be extracted and their rates of repetition across each textbook volume and series can be calculated. The lexical input of the 42 textbook volumes and nine textbook series of the TEC could then be compared to examine the extent to which they share a common core EFL lexical syllabus. In addition, the textbooks' lexical range may be compared to corpus-based lists such as the new General Service List (Brezina & Gablasova 2015) and the PHRASE List (Martinez & Schmitt 2012). Given the TEC's register annotation, it would also be possible to compare the words and phrasemes of an individual textbook register, e.g., the Conversation subcorpus of the TEC with corpus-derived lists of the most frequent words and phrasemes in spoken English (e.g., Fankhauser in preparation).

The modified MDA framework could also be applied to analyses of secondary school textbooks of other languages. Indeed, it would be most interesting to compare the present multi-feature/multi-dimensional models of Textbook English with those of other "textbook languages". Such comparisons may reveal that, cross-linguistically, some of the observed characteristics of Textbook English are in fact universal features of foreign language textbooks – representative of what we might then call: '(School) Textbook Language'.

It is important to stress that, on the basis of the present study, we can only speculate as to the impact of Textbook English in and outside the EFL classroom. As vividly put by Cook (2002: 268),

> [i]t may be better to teach people how to draw with idealised squares and triangles than with idiosyncratic human faces. Or it may not. The job of applied linguists is to present evidence to demonstrate the learning basis for their claims [...].

Whilst a large body of evidence from usage-based linguistic studies and related disciplines has consistently highlighted the strong connection between input exposure and L2 learners' developmental patterns (e.g., Achard & Niemeier 2004; Pérez-Paredes, Mark & O'Keeffe 2020; Tyler 2012; Tyler et al. 2018), it still remains unclear the extent to which "bring[ing] textbooks for teaching English as a foreign language into closer correspondence with actual English" (Mindt 1996: 247) will facilitate or hamper learners' progress. Crucially, we must remember that, as insightful as these multi-dimensional descriptions of Textbook English have been, textbooks do not exist in a vacuum. Yet surprisingly few empirical studies have looked into how textbooks – i.e., not only their language, but also their structures, tasks, and activities – mediate classroom interactions and learning outcomes (Rösler & Schart 2016: 490). In addition, much research remains to be done on how teachers and students actually use textbooks in the classroom. Empirical data on the *status quo* in secondary EFL classrooms is urgently needed to (a) understand the real impact of textbooks and (b) develop research-informed recommendations for materials designers and new pre- and in-service teacher training courses that genuinely address current problems and meet teachers' and learners' needs.

In addition to classroom-based investigations into textbook use and learning outcome, the results of the present study and follow-up corpus-based textbook language studies may be triangulated with findings from learner corpora to gain new insights into L2 learning processes. Such research could test McEnery and Kifle's (1998) hypothesis that "[w]here textbooks are included in an exploration of L2 learning, they can explain differences between NS [native speaker] and NNS [non-native speaker] usage" (as cited in Tono 2004: 52). In such endeavours, robust models of textbook language are potentially very useful because few large-scale research projects will realistically be able to investigate both the language of the textbooks that learners use and the language production of these same learners (though see Möller 2020 for such a research design in the context of Content and Language Integrated Learning). The hope is that, if the models of Textbook English elaborated in the present study are shown to be generalisable to further EFL textbooks, they may be used as a means of better understanding certain usage patterns that are more frequent in the language of instructed EFL learners than in that of naturalistic ESL learners (for first attempts in this direction, see Winter & Le Foll 2022 on EFL learners' use of *if*-conditionals; and Le Foll 2023b on periphrastic causative constructions).

In sum, there is still much to be learnt from "pedagogically-driven corpus-based research" (Gabrielatos 2006: 1). In this study, we have even seen how MDA can be applied to describe the language of textbooks on multiple dimensions of variation and to point to potential pedagogical issues. These corpus-based findings highlight the need for greater consideration of register in language teaching and learning. The findings were used to point to the benefits of using freely available corpora and tools to create more meaningful, content-rich learning contexts. In other words, this study has not only demonstrated how multivariable corpus-linguistic methods can be used to analyse Textbook English, but it has also outlined ways in which corpora and corpus tools can be used to boost the representativeness of 'real-world' language use in school EFL textbooks. As such, this pedagogically-driven corpus-based study can be said to have "corpused" full circle.

References

Abello-Contesse, Christián & López-Jiménez, María Dolores. 2010. The treatment of lexical collocations in EFL textbooks. In *Exploring New Paths in Language Pedagogy: Lexis and Corpus-based Language Teaching* [Equinox English Linguistics and ELT], María Moreno Jaén, Fernando Serrano & María Calzada Pérez (eds), 95–109. London: Equinox.

doi Achard, Michel & Niemeier, Susanne (eds). 2004. *Cognitive Linguistics, Second Language Acquisition, and Foreign Language Teaching* [Studies on Language Acquisition 18]. Berlin: De Gruyter.

doi Ahmad, Hamdi & Millar, Robert McColl. 2020. Review of Text Authenticity Relationship with Language Learner Motivation and Communicative Competence. *International Journal of English Linguistics* 10(5): 89.

doi Alejo González, Rafael, Piquer Píriz, Ana & Reveriego Sierra, Guadalupe. 2010. Phrasal verbs in EFL course books. In *Fostering Language Teaching Efficiency through Cognitive Linguistics* [Applications of Cognitive Linguistics 17], Sabine De Knop, Frank Boers & Antoon De Rycker (eds), 59–78. Berlin: De Gruyter.

Alemi, Minoo & Isavi, Ebrahim. 2012. Evaluation of interactional metadiscourse in EFL textbooks. *Advances in Asian Social Science* 2(1): 422–430.

doi Al-Hoorie, Ali H. & Marsden, Emma. 2024. Open scholarship and transparency in applied linguistics research. *OSF.*

doi Altenberg, Bengt. 1989. Review of Douglas Biber (1988) Variation across speech and writing. *Studia Linguistica* 43(2). 167–174.

doi Altenberg, Bengt & Granger, Sylviane. 2001. The grammatical and lexical patterning of MAKE in native and non-native student writing. *Applied Linguistics* 22(2): 173–195.

doi Anthony, Laurence. 2020. Programming for corpus linguistics. In *A Practical Handbook of Corpus Linguistics*, Magali Paquot & Stefan Th. Gries (eds), 181–207. Cham: Springer.

Anton, Daniela. 2017. Inter- und transkulturelles Lernen im Englischunterricht: Eine didaktische Analyse einschlägiger Lehrbücher [Anglistische Forschungen 456]. Heidelberg: Universitätsverlag Winter.

doi Argamon, Shlomo. 2019. Register in computational language research. *Register Studies* 1(1): 100–135.

doi Atkins, Sue, Clear, Jeremy & Ostler, Nicholas. 1992. Corpus design criteria. *Literary and Linguistic Computing* 7(1): 1–16.

Ballier, Nicolas, Díaz Negrillo, Ana & Thompson, Paul (eds). 2013. *Automatic Treatment and Analysis of Learner Corpus Data* [Studies in Corpus Linguistics 59]. Amsterdam: John Benjamins.

doi Barbieri, Federica. 2005. Quotative use in American English: A corpus-based, cross-register comparison. *Journal of English Linguistics* 33(3): 222–256.

doi Barbieri, Federica & Eckhardt, Suzanne E. B. 2007. Applying corpus-based findings to form-focused instruction: The case of reported speech. *Language Teaching Research* 11(3): 319–346.

Barlow, Michael. 2003. Corpora and language teaching. *KATE Forum* 27(1): 6–9.

Barlow, Michael & Kemmer, Suzanne (eds). 2000. *Usage-Based Models of Language*. Stanford, CA: CSLI.

doi Baroni, Marco & Bernardini, Silvia. 2005. A new approach to the study of translationese: Machine-learning the difference between original and translated text. *Literary and Linguistic Computing* 21(3): 259–274.

doi Baroni, Marco & Evert, Stephanie. 2009. Statistical methods for corpus exploitation. In *Corpus Linguistics: An International Handbook*, Merja Kytö & Anke Lüdeling (eds), Ch. 36, 777–803. Berlin: De Gruyter.

Baroni, Marco, Kilgarriff, Adam, Pomikálek, Jan & Rychlý, Pavel. 2006. WebBootCaT: A web tool for instant corpora. In Elisa Corino, Carla Marello & Onesti Cristina (eds), *Proceedings of the 12th Euralex International Congress*, 123–132. Torino: European Association for Lexicography.

doi Bates, Douglas, Mächler, Martin, Bolker, Ben & Walker, Steve. 2015. Fitting linear mixed-effects models using lme4. *Journal of Statistical Software* 67(1): 1–48.

Bausch, Karl-Richard (ed.). 2005. *Bildungsstandards für den Fremdsprachenunterricht auf dem Prüfstand: Arbeitspapiere der 25. Frühjahrskonferenz zur Erforschung des Fremdsprachenunterrichts* [Giessener Beiträge Zur Fremdsprachendidaktik]. Tübingen: Gunter Narr.

doi Behrens, Heike. 2006. The input–output relationship in first language acquisition. *Language and Cognitive Processes* 21(1–3): 2–24.

doi Bell, Jan & Gower, Roger. 2011. Writing course materials for the world: A great compromise. In *Materials Development in Language Teaching*, Brian Tomlinson (ed.), 135–150. Cambridge: CUP.

doi Belz, Anya, Agarwal, Shubham, Shimorina, Anastasia & Reiter, Ehud. 2021. A systematic review of reproducibility research in natural language processing. *arXiv:2103.07929 [cs]*. ⟨http://arxiv.org/abs/2103.07929⟩ (26 July 2021).

Bendix, Regina. 1997. *In Search of Authenticity: The Formation of Folklore Studies*. Madison WI: University of Wisconsin Press.

Benhamou, Émile & Dominique, Philippe. *Speak English : 6ᵉ série verte*. Paris: Fernand Nathan.

doi Bennett, Gena. 2010. *Using Corpora in the Language Learning Classroom: Corpus Linguistics for Teachers*. Ann Arbor, MI: University of Michigan Press.

doi Berber Sardinha, Tony & Veirano Pinto, Marcia (eds). 2014. *Multi-Dimensional Analysis, 25 Years on: A Tribute to Douglas Biber* [Studies in Corpus Linguistics 60]. Amsterdam: John Benjamins.

doi Berber Sardinha, Tony & Veirano Pinto, Marcia (eds). 2019. *Multi-Dimensional Analysis: Research Methods and Current Issues*. London: Bloomsbury Academic.

doi Berber Sardinha, Tony, Veirano Pinto, Marcia, Mayer, Cristina, Zuppardi, Maria Carolina & Kauffmann, Carlos Henrique. 2019. Adding registers to a previous multi-dimensional analysis. In *Multi-Dimensional Analysis: Research Methods and Current Issues*, Tony Berber Sardinha & Marcia Veirano Pinto (eds), 165–188. London: Bloomsbury.

doi Berez-Kroeker, Andrea L., Gawne, Lauren, Kung, Susan Smythe, Kelly, Barbara F., Heston, Tyler, Holton, Gary, Pulsifer, Peter, et al. 2018. Reproducible research in linguistics: A position statement on data citation and attribution in our field. *Linguistics* 56(1): 1–18.

doi Berns, Margie S., de Bot, Kees & Hasebrink, Uwe (eds). 2007. *In the Presence of English: Media and European Youth* [Language Policy 7]. New York, NY: Springer.

doi Bezemer, Jeff & Kress, Gunther. 2016. The textbook in a changing multimodal landscape. In *Handbuch Sprache im multimodalen Kontext*, Nina-Maria Klug & Hartmut Stöckl (eds), 476–498. Berlin: De Gruyter.

Biber, Douglas. 1984. A Model of Textual Relations within the Written and Spoken Modes. PhD dissertation, University of Southern California.

doi Biber, Douglas. 1988. *Variation across Speech and Writing*. Cambridge: CUP.

doi Biber, Douglas. 1990. Methodological issues regarding corpus-based analyses of linguistic variation. *Literary and Linguistic Computing* 5(4): 257–269.

doi Biber, Douglas. 1995. *Dimensions of Register Variation*. Cambridge: CUP.

doi Biber, Douglas. 2006. *University Language: A Corpus-Based Study of Spoken and Written Registers* [Studies in Corpus Linguistics 23]. Amsterdam: John Benjamins.

doi Biber, Douglas. 2012. Register as a predictor of linguistic variation. *Corpus Linguistics and Linguistic Theory* 8(1): 9–37.

doi Biber, Douglas. 2014. Using multi-dimensional analysis to explore cross-linguistic universals of register variation. *Languages in Contrast* 14(1): 7–34.

doi Biber, Douglas. 2019. Multi-dimensional analysis: A historical synopsis. In *Multi-Dimensional Analysis: Research Methods and Current Issues*, Tony Berber Sardinha & Marcia Veirano Pinto (eds), 11–26. London: Bloomsbury Academic.

Biber, Douglas. 2021. Corpus linguistics is for text-lovers. *Linguistics with a Corpus* (blog), 22 December 2021. ⟨https://linguisticswithacorpus.wordpress.com/2021/12/22/corpus-linguistics-is-for-text-lovers%EF%BF%BC/⟩ (28 December 2021).

doi Biber, Douglas & Barbieri, Federica. 2007. Lexical bundles in university spoken and written registers. *English for Specific Purposes* 26(3): 263–286.

doi Biber, Douglas & Conrad, Susan. 2001. Quantitative corpus-based research: Much more than bean counting. *TESOL Quarterly* 35(2): 331–336.

Biber, Douglas & Conrad, Susan. 2010. Corpus Linguistics and Grammar Teaching. *Pearson Longman Education*. http://longmanhomeusa.com/content/pl_biber_conrad_monograph5_lo.pdf. (7 March, 2017).

doi Biber, Douglas & Conrad, Susan. 2019. *Register, Genre, and Style*, 2nd edn. Cambridge: CUP.

doi Biber, Douglas, Conrad, Susan, Reppen, Randi, Byrd, Pat & Helt, Marie. 2002. Speaking and writing in the university: A multidimensional comparison. *TESOL Quarterly* 36(1): 9.

Biber, Douglas, Conrad, Susan, Reppen, Randi, Byrd, Pat, Helt, Marie, Clark, Victoria, Cortes, Viviana, Csomay, Eniko & Urzua, Alfredo. 2004. *Representing Language Use in the University: Analysis of the TOEFFL 2000 Spoken and Written Academic Language Corpus* [TOEFL Monograph Series]. Princeton, NJ: Educational Testing Service.

doi Biber, Douglas & Egbert, Jesse. 2016. Register variation on the searchable web: A multi-dimensional analysis. *Journal of English Linguistics* 44(2): 95–137.

doi Biber, Douglas & Egbert, Jesse. 2018. *Register Variation Online*. Cambridge: CUP.

doi Biber, Douglas, Egbert, Jesse, Gray, Bethany, Oppliger, Rahel & Szmrecsanyi, Benedikt. 2016. Variationist versus text-linguistic approaches to grammatical change in English: Nominal modifiers of head nouns. In *The Cambridge Handbook of English Historical Linguistics*, Merja Kyto & Paivi Pahta (eds), 351–375. Cambridge: CUP.

doi Biber, Douglas & Finegan, Edward. 1994. *Sociolinguistic Perspectives on Register*. Oxford: OUP.

doi Biber, Douglas & Gray, Bethany. 2013. Discourse characteristics of writing and speaking task types on the TOEFL IBT test: A lexico-grammatical analysis. *ETS Research Report Series* 2013(1).

doi Biber, Douglas & Gray, Bethany. 2015. *Grammatical Complexity in Academic English: Linguistic Change in Writing* [Studies in English Language]. Cambridge: CUP.

Biber, Douglas, Johansson, Stig, Leech, Geoffrey, Conrad, Susan & Finegan, Edward. 1999. *Longman Grammar of Spoken and Written English*. Harlow: Longman.

doi Biber, Douglas, Johansson, Stig, Leech, Geoffrey N., Conrad, Susan & Finegan, Edward. 2021. *Grammar of Spoken and Written English*. Amsterdam: John Benjamins.

Biber, Douglas & Quirk, Randolph (eds). 2012. *Longman Grammar of Spoken and Written English*, 10th edn. Harlow: Longman.

doi Biber, Douglas & Reppen, Randi. 2002. What does frequency have to do with grammar teaching? *Studies in Second Language Acquisition* 24(2): 199–208.

Biebighäuser, Katrin, Zibelius, Marja & Schmidt, Torben. 2012. *Aufgaben 2.0: Konzepte, Materialien und Methoden für das Fremdsprachenlehren und -lernen mit digitalen Medien*. BoD – Books on Demand.

doi Bieswanger, Markus. 2008. Varieties of English in current English language teaching. *Stellenbosch Papers in Linguistics* 38: 22–47.

Birkland, Annie, Block, Adeli, Craft, Justin, Sedarous, Yourdanis, Wang, Sky, Gou, Wu & Namboodiripad, Savithry. 2022. Problematizing the "native speaker" in linguistic research: History of the term and ways forward. Presented at the Linguistic Society of America, January 8, ⟨https://osf.io/jufmg/⟩ (16 January 2022).

doi Blau, Eileen K. 1990. The effect of syntax, speed, and pauses on listening comprehension. *TESOL Quarterly* 24(4): 746.

Blighe, Kevin & Lun, Aaron. 2020. PCAtools: Everything principal components analysis, ⟨https://github.com/kevinblighe/PCAtools⟩ (22 April 2021).

doi Blume, Carolyn. 2020. German teachers' digital habitus and their pandemic pedagogy. *Postdigital Science and Education* 2(3): 879–905.

doi Blumenthal-Dramé, Alice. 2012. *Entrenchment in Usage-based Theories: What Corpus Eata do and do not Reveal about the Mind* [Topics in English Linguistics 83]. Berlin: Mouton De Gruyter.

Blyth, Carl. 2003. Playing games with literacy: The poetic function in the age of communicative language teaching. In *Reading between the Lines: Perspectives on Foreign Language Literacy* [Yale Language Series], Peter Charles Patrikis (ed.), 60–73. New Haven, CT: Yale University Press.

Blyth, Carl. 2009. From textbook to online materials: The changing ecology of foreign language publishing in the era of ICT. In *Foreign Language Learning with Digital Technology*, Michael J. Evans (ed.), 174–202. London: Continuum.

BNC Consortium. 2007. The British National Corpus. *Oxford Text Archive*, ⟨http://www.natcorp.ox.ac.uk/corpus/⟩ (28 August 2023).

doi Bochynska, Agata, Keeble, Liam, Halfacre, Caitlin, Casillas, Joseph V., Champagne, Irys-Amélie, Chen, Kaidi, Röthlisberger, Melanie, Buchanan, Erin M. & Roettger, Timo B. 2023. Reproducible research practices and transparency across linguistics. *Glossa Psycholinguistics* 2(1).

Bohmann, Axel. 2017. Variation in English World-wide: Varieties and Genres in a Quantitative Perspective. PhD dissertation, University of Texas, Austin.

doi Bohmann, Axel. 2019. *Variation in English Worldwide: Registers and Global Varieties.* Cambridge: CUP.

doi Bohmann, Axel. 2021. Register in World Englishes research. In *Bloomsbury World Englishes, Vol. 1: Paradigms*, Britta Schneider, Theresa Heyd & Mario Saraceni (eds), 80–96. London: Bloomsbury Academic.

doi Boulton, Alex & Cobb, Tom. 2017. Corpus use in language learning: A meta-analysis. *Language Learning* 67(2): 348–393.

Boulton, Alex & Tyne, Henry. 2015. Corpus-based study of language and teacher education. In *The Routledge Handbook of Educational Linguistics*, Martha Bigelow & Johanna Ennser-Kananen (eds), 301–312. New York, NY: Routledge.

Boulton, Alex & Vyatkina, Nina. 2021. Thirty years of data-driven learning: Taking stock and charting new directions over time. *Language Learning* 25(3): 66–89.

Bragger, Jeannette D. & Rice, Donald B. 2000. Foreign language materials: Yesterday, today, and tomorrow. In *Agents of Change in a Changing Age*, Robert M. Terry (ed.), 107–40. Lincolnwood, IL: National Textbook Company.

doi Brezina, Vaclav. 2018. *Statistics in Corpus Linguistics: A Practical Guide.* Cambridge: CUP.

doi Brezina, Vaclav & Gablasova, Dona. 2015. Is there a core general vocabulary? Introducing the new general service list. *Applied Linguistics* 36(1): 1–22.

doi Brezina, Vaclav, Hawtin, Abi & McEnery, Tony. 2021. The Written British National Corpus 2014 – Design and comparability. *Text & Talk* 41(5–6): 595–615.

Brown, Dale. 2014. The power and authority of materials in the classroom ecology. *The Modern Language Journal* 98(2): 658–661.

Bruyn, Bert Le & Paquot, Magali. 2021. *Learner Corpus Research Meets Second Language Acquisition.* Cambridge: CUP.

Burnard, Lou (ed.). 2007. *Reference Guide for the British National Corpus*, XML edn. ⟨http://www.natcorp.ox.ac.uk/XMLedition/URG/⟩ (17 September 2021).

Burnard, Lou & Bauman, Syd. 2021. *TEI P5: Guidelines for electronic text encoding and interchange v. 4.3.0.* TEI consortium. ⟨https://tei-c.org/Guidelines/P5/⟩ (2 January 2022).

doi Burton, Graham. 2012. Corpora and coursebooks: Destined to be strangers forever? *Corpora* 7(1).

Burton, Graham. 2019. The Canon of Pedagogical Grammar for ELT: A Mixed Methods Study of its Evolution, Development and Comparison with Evidence on Learner Output. PhD dissertation, University of Limerick.

doi Burton, Graham. 2020. Grammar. *ELT Journal* 74(2): 198–201.

doi Burton, Graham. 2023. *Grammar in ELT and ELT Materials.* Multilingual Matters.

doi Bybee, Joan. 2007. *Frequency of Use and the Organization of Language.* Oxford: OUP.

doi Bybee, Joan & Hopper, Paul (eds). 2001. *Frequency and the Emergence of Linguistic Structure* [Typological Studies in Language 45]. Amsterdam: John Benjamins.

doi Callies, Marcus. 2019. Integrating corpus literacy into language teacher education: The case of learner corpora. In *Learner Corpora and Language Teaching* [Studies in Corpus Linguistics 92], Sandra Götz & Joybrato Mukherjee (eds), 245–63. Amsterdam: John Benjamins.

doi Canale, Germán. 2021. The language textbook: Representation, interaction & learning: Conclusions. *Language, Culture and Curriculum* 34(2): 199–206.

doi Carrie, Erin. 2017. "British is professional, American is urban": Attitudes towards English reference accents in Spain. *International Journal of Applied Linguistics* 27(2): 427–447.

doi Carter, Ronald & McCarthy, Michael 1996. Correspondence. *ELT Journal* 50(4): 369–371.

Carter, Ronald. 2014. Grammar and spoken English. In *Applying English Grammar: Corpus and Functional Approaches*, Caroline Coffin, Ann Hewings & Kieran O'Halloran (eds), 25–39. Oxon: Routledge.

Carter, Ronald, Hughes, Rebecca & McCarthy, Michael. 1998. Telling tails: Grammar, the spoken language and materials development. In *Materials Development in Language Teaching*, Brian Tomlinson (ed.), 67–86. Cambridge: CUP.

doi Carter, Ronald & McCarthy, Michael. 1995. Grammar and the spoken language. *Applied linguistics* 16(2): 141–158.

Carter, Ronald & McCarthy, Michael. 2006a. *Cambridge Grammar of English: A Comprehensive Guide: Spoken and Written English Grammar and Usage*. Cambridge: CUP.

Carter, Ronald & McCarthy, Michael. 2006b. *Cambridge Grammar of English: A Comprehensive Guide: Spoken and Written English Grammar and Usage*. Cambridge: CUP.

doi Carter, Ronald & McCarthy, Michael. 2017. Spoken grammar: Where are we and where are we going? *Applied Linguistics* 38(1): 1–20.

Catalán, Rosa Maria Jiménez & Mancebo Francisco, Rocío. 2008. Vocabulary input in EFL textbooks. *Revista Española de Lingüística Aplicada (RESLA)* 21: 147–166.

Chafe, Wallace. 1982. Integration and involvement in speaking, writing, and oral literature. In *Spoken and Written Language: Exploring Orality and Literacy* [Advances in Discourse Processes 9], Deborah Tannen (ed.), 35–54. Norwood, NJ: Ablex.

doi Chambers, Angela. 2019. Towards the corpus revolution? Bridging the research–practice gap. *Language Teaching* 52(4): 460–475.

doi Chapelle, Carol A. 2010. The spread of computer-assisted language learning. *Language Teaching* 43(1): 66–74.

doi Chen, Alvin Cheng-Hsien. 2016. A critical evaluation of text difficulty development in ELT textbook series: A corpus-based approach using variability neighbor clustering. *System* 58: 64–81.

Chen, Alvin Cheng-Hsien. 2017. Assessing text difficulty development in ELT textbooks series using n-gram language models based on BNC. Presented at the Corpus Linguistics Conference 2017, Birmingham. ⟨https://www.birmingham.ac.uk/Documents/college-artslaw/corpus/conference-archives/2017/general/paper137.pdf⟩ (21 January 2019).

Chen, Lin. 2010. An investigation of lexical bundles in ESP textbooks and electrical engineering introductory textbooks. In *Perspectives on Formulaic Language: Acquisition and Communication*, David Wood (ed.), 107–125. London: Continuum.

Cheng, Winnie. 2007. Sorry to interrupt, but...: Pedagogical implications of a spoken corpus. In *Spoken Corpora in Applied Linguistics* [Linguistic Insights 51], Mari Carmen Campoy & María José Luzón (eds), 199–216. Bern: Peter Lang.

Cheng, Winnie, Greaves, Christopher & Warren, Martin. 2005. The creation of a prosodically transcribed intercultural corpus: The Hong Kong Corpus of Spoken English (prosodic). *ICAME journal* 29: 47–68.

Cheng, Winnie & Warren, Martin. 2005. // → Well I Have a DIFferent // ↘ THINking You Know //: A corpus-driven study of disagreement in Hong Kong business discourse. In *Asian Business Discourse(s)*, Francesca Bargiela-Chiappini & Maurizio Gotti (eds), 241–70. Frankfurt: Peter Lang.

Cheng, Winnie & Warren, Martin. 2006. I would say be very careful of...: Opine markers in an intercultural business corpus of spoken English. In *Managing Interaction in Professional Discourse: Intercultural and Interdiscoursal Perspectives*, Julia Bamford & Marina Bondi (eds), 46–57. Rome: Officina Edizioni.

doi Cheng, Winnie & Warren, Martin. 2007. Checking understandings: Comparing textbooks and a corpus of spoken English in Hong Kong. *Language Awareness* 16(3): 190–207.

Chien, Chu Ying & Young, Kathie. 2007. The centrality of textbooks in teachers' work: Perceptions and use of textbooks in a Hong Kong primary school. *The Asia-Pacific Education Researcher* 16(2): 155–163.

doi Chomsky, Noam. 1995. Language and nature. *Mind* 104(413): 1–61.

doi Chomsky, Noam. 2002. *On Nature and Language*, ed. by Adriana Belletti & Luigi Rizzi. Cambridge: CUP.

Chong, Chia Suan. 2012. The teach-off – My reaction to coursebooks & uncount nouns. *chiasuanchong.com* (blog), 26 April 2012, ⟨https://chiasuanchong.com/2012/04/26/the-teach-off-my-reaction-to-coursebooks-uncountable-nouns/⟩ (17 September 2020).

Clark, Eve V. & Casillas, Marisa. 2016. First language acquisition. In *The Routledge Handbook of Linguistics*, Keith Allan (ed.), 311–28. New York, NY: Routledge.

doi Clarke, Isobelle. 2019. Functional linguistic variation in Twitter trolling. *International Journal of Speech Language and the Law* 26(1): 57–84.

Clarke, Isobelle. 2020. Linguistic Variation across Twitter and Twitter Trolling. PhD dissertation, University of Birmingham. ⟨http://etheses.bham.ac.uk/id/eprint/10009⟩

doi Clarke, Isobelle. 2022. A multi-dimensional analysis of English tweets. *Language and Literature: International Journal of Stylistics* 31(2): 124–149.

doi Clarke, Isobelle & Grieve, Jack. 2017. Dimensions of abusive language on Twitter. In *Proceedings of the First Workshop on Abusive Language Online*, 1–10, ⟨https://www.aclweb.org/anthology/W17-3001.pdf⟩ (11 February 2021).

doi Coats, Steven. 2016. Grammatical feature frequencies of English on Twitter in Finland. In *English in Computer-Mediated Communication*, Lauren Squires (ed.), 179–210. Berlin: De Gruyter.

Cohen, Henri & Lefebvre, Claire. 2017. *Handbook of Categorization in Cognitive Science*, 2nd edn. Amsterdam: Elsevier.

doi Condon, Nora. 2008. How cognitive linguistic motivations influence the learning of phrasal verbs. In *Cognitive Linguistic Approaches to Teaching Vocabulary and Phraseology*, Frank Boers & Seth Lindstromberg (eds), 133–58. Berlin: De Gruyter Mouton.

doi Conrad, Susan. 2000. Will corpus linguistics revolutionize grammar teaching in the 21st century? *TESOL Quarterly* 34(3): 548–560.

doi Conrad, Susan. 2004. Corpus variety: Corpus linguistics, language variation, and language teaching. In *How to Use Corpora in Language Teaching* [Studies in Corpus Linguistics 12], John McH. Sinclair (ed.), 67–85. Amsterdam: John Benjamins.

Conrad, Susan & Biber, Douglas (eds). (2001) 2013. *Variation in English: Multi-Dimensional Studies* [Studies in Language and Linguistics]. New York, NY: Routledge.

Conrad, Susan, Biber, Douglas & Leech, Geoffrey N. 2011. *Longman Student Grammar of Spoken and Written English. Workbook.* Harlow: Longman.

Conseil supérieur des programmes. 2015. Projet de programme de cycle 4. ⟨https://www.education.gouv.fr/media/18161/download⟩ (1 January 2018).

Consejería de Educación, Juventud y Deporte de Madrid. 2015. Decreto 48/2015 Curriculo de educación secundaria obligatoria. *Boletín Oficial de la Comunidad de Madrid.* ⟨www.bocm.es⟩ (12 January 2022).

Cook, Guy. 2000. *Language Play, Language Learning.* Oxford: OUP.

doi Cook, Vivian. 2002. The functions of invented sentences: A reply to Guy Cook. *Applied Linguistics* 23(2): 262–269.

Cools, Dorien & Sercu, Lies. 2006. Die Beurteilung von Lehrwerken an Hand des Gemeinsamen Europäischen Referenzrahmens für Sprachen: Eine empirische Untersuchung von zwei kürzlich erschienenen Lehrwerken für Deutsch als Fremdsprache. *Zeitschrift für interkulturellen Fremdsprachenunterricht* 11(3): 1–20.

doi Costello, Anna B. & Osborne, Jason. 2005. Best practices in exploratory factor analysis: four recommendations for getting the most from your analysis. *Practical Assessment, Research, and Evaluation* 10(7): 1–9.

Council of Europe (ed.). 2001. *Common European Framework of Reference for Languages: Learning, Teaching, Assessment (CEFR).* Modern Languages Division, Strasbourg. Cambridge: CUP.

Council of Europe (ed.). 2020. *Common European Framework of Reference for Languages: Learning, Teaching, Assessment. Companion Volume.* Strasbourg: Council of Europe Publishing, ⟨https://rm.coe.int/common-european-framework-of-reference-for-languages-learning-teaching/16809ea0d4⟩ (6 February 2022).

doi Cowie, Anthony P. (ed.). 1998. *Phraseology: Theory, Analysis, and Applications* [Oxford Studies in Lexicography and Lexicology]. Oxford: OUP.

doi Crawford, William J. & Zhang, Meixiu. 2021. How can register analysis inform task-based language teaching? *Register Studies* 3(2): 180–206.

doi Croft, William & Cruse, D. Alan. 2004. *Cognitive Linguistics.* Cambridge: CUP.

doi Crossley, Scott, Allen, Laura & McNamara, Danielle. 2014. A multi-dimensional analysis of essay writing: What linguistic features tell us about situational parameters and the effects of language functions on judgments of quality. In *Multi-Dimensional Analysis, 25 Years on: A Tribute to Douglas Biber* [Studies in Corpus Linguistics 60], Tony Berber Sardinha & Marcia Veirano Pinto (eds), 197–238. Amsterdam: John Benjamins.

doi Crossley, Scott, Kyle, Kristopher & Römer, Ute. 2019. Examining lexical and cohesion differences in discipline-specific writing using multi-dimensional analysis. In *Multi-Dimensional Analysis: Research Methods and Current Issues*, Tony Berber Sardinha & Marcia Veirano Pinto (eds), 189–216. Bloomsbury Academic.

Crosthwaite, Peter (ed.). 2020. *Data-driven Learning for the next Generation: Corpora and DDL for Pre-tertiary Learners*. London: Routledge.

Crowley, Tony. 2003. *Standard English and the Politics of Language*, 2nd edn. Houndmills: Palgrave Macmillan.

Crystal, David. 2018. *The Cambridge Encyclopedia of the English Language*. Cambridge: CUP.

Crystal, David & Davy, Derek. 1969. *Investigating English Style* [English Language Series 1]. Harlow: Longman.

Cullen, Richard & Kuo, I-Chun (Vicky). 2007. Spoken grammar and ELT course materials: A missing link? *TESOL Quarterly* 41(2): 361–386.

Curry, Niall, Love, Robbie & Goodman, Olivia. 2022. Adverbs on the move: Investigating publisher application of corpus research on recent language change to ELT coursebook development. *Corpora* 17(1): 1–38.

Dat, Bao. 2008. ELT materials used in Southeast Asia. In *English Language Learning Materials: A Critical Review*, Brian Tomlinson (ed.), 263–280. London: Continuum.

Dat, Bao. 2013. Developing materials for speaking skills. In *Developing Materials for Language Teaching*, 2nd edn, 407–428. London: Bloomsbury.

Davies, Mark. 2009. The 385+ million word *Corpus of Contemporary American English* (1990–2008+): Design, architecture, and linguistic insights. *International Journal of Corpus Linguistics* 14(2): 159–190.

Davies, Mark. 2010. The Corpus of Contemporary American English as the first reliable monitor corpus of English. *Literary and Linguistic Computing* 25(4): 447–464.

Davies, Mark. 2019. The Movie Corpus. ⟨https://www.english-corpora.org/movies/⟩ (28 February 2022).

Day, Richard R. & Bamford, Julian. 1998. *Extensive Reading in the Second Language Classroom*. Cambridge: CUP.

de Bot, Kees, Lowie, Wander & Verspoor, Marjolijn. 2007. A dynamic systems theory approach to second language acquisition. *Bilingualism: Language and Cognition* 10(1): 7–21.

De Knop, Sabine & Gilquin, Gaëtanelle. 2016. *Applied Construction Grammar*. Berlin: De Gruyter Mouton.

Derwing, T. 2001. What speaking rates do non-native listeners prefer? *Applied Linguistics* 22(3): 324–337.

Derwing, Tracey M. 1990. Speech rate is no simple matter: Rate adjustment and NS–NNS communicative success. *Studies in Second Language Acquisition* 12(3): 303–313.

Derwing, Tracey M., Thomson, Ron I., Foote, Jennifer A. & Munro, Murray J. 2012. A longitudinal study of listening perception in adult learners of English: Implications for teachers. *The Canadian Modern Language Review* 68(3): 247–266.

Diehr, Bärbel (ed.). 2018. *Universitäre Englischlehrerbildung: Wege zu mehr Kohärenz im Studium und Korrespondenz mit der Praxis*. Berlin: Peter Lang.

Diehr, Bärbel. 2020. Kohärenz und Korrespondenz: Die fachdidaktische Perspektive auf die universitäre Englischlehrerbildung. In *Die Stimmen der Fächer hören: Fachprofil und Bildungsanspruch in der Lehrerbildung*, Michaela Heer & Ulrich Heinen (eds), 325–342. Paderborn: Ferdinand Schöningh.

Diepenbroek, Lori G. & Derwing, Tracey M. 2014. To what extent do popular ESL textbooks incorporate oral fluency and pragmatic development. *TESL Canada Journal* 30(7): 1.

doi Dinh, Thuy Ngoc & Siregar, Fenty Lidya. 2021. Intercultural competence and parsnip: Voices from teachers of English in Australia. In *Intercultural Competence Past, Present and Future: Respecting the Past, Problems in the Present and Forging the Future* [Intercultural Communication and Language Education], María Dolores López-Jiménez & Jorge Sánchez-Torres (eds), 255–274. Singapore: Springer.

doi Dirven, René. 1990. Pedagogical grammar. *Language Teaching* 23(1): 1.

doi Diwersy, Sascha, Evert, Stephanie & Neumann, Stella. 2014. A weakly supervised multivariate approach to the study of language variation. In *Aggregating Dialectology, Typology, and Register Analysis: Linguistic Variation in Text and Speech*, Benedikt Szmrecsanyi & Bernhard Wälchli (eds), 174–204. Berlin: De Gruyter.

doi Diz-Otero, Mario, Portela-Pino, Iago, Domínguez-Lloria, Sara & Pino-Juste, Margarita. 2022. Digital competence in secondary education teachers during the COVID-19-derived pandemic: Comparative analysis. *Education + Training* 65(2): 181–192.

doi Dörnyei, Zoltán, Durow, Valerie & Zahran, Khawla. 2004. Individual differences and their effects on formulaic sequence acquisition. In *Formulaic Sequences: Acquisition, Processing, and Use* [Language Learning and Language Teaching 9], Norbert Schmitt (ed.), 87–106. Amsterdam: John Benjamins.

Duffley, Patrick J. 2006. *The English Gerund-Participle: A Comparison with the Infinitive* [Berkeley Insights in Linguistics and Semiotics 61]. Frankfurt: Peter Lang.

Dumont, Amandine. 2018. Fluency and Disfluency: A Corpus Study of Non-native and Native Cpeaker (dis)Fluency Profiles. PhD dissertation, Université catholique de Louvain. ⟨http://hdl.handle.net/2078.1/198393⟩ (12 April 2024).

doi Eckhardt, Suzanne. 2001. *Reported Speech: Empirical Corpus Findings Compared with EFL/ESL Textbook Presentations.* MA thesis, Iowa State University, Ames.

doi Edwards, Alison. 2016. *English in the Netherlands: Functions, Forms and Attitudes* [Varieties of English Around the World G56]. Amsterdam: John Benjamins.

doi Egbert, Jesse. 2019. Corpus design and representativeness. In *Multi-Dimensional Analysis: Research Methods and Current Issues*, Tony Berber Sardinha & Marcia Veirano Pinto (eds), 27–42. London: Bloomsbury Academic.

doi Egbert, Jesse & Biber, Douglas. 2018. Do all roads lead to Rome? Modeling register variation with factor analysis and discriminant analysis. *Corpus Linguistics and Linguistic Theory* 14(2): 233–273.

doi Egbert, Jesse, Biber, Douglas & Davies, Mark. 2015. Developing a bottom-up, user-based method of web register classification. *Journal of the Association for Information Science and Technology* 66(9): 1817–1831.

doi Egbert, Jesse, Biber, Douglas & Gray, Bethany. 2022. *Designing and Evaluating Language Corpora: A Practical Framework for Corpus Representativeness.* Cambridge: CUP.

doi Egbert, Jesse, Larsson, Tove & Biber, Douglas. 2020. *Doing Linguistics with a Corpus: Methodological Considerations for the Everyday User.* Cambridge: CUP.

doi Egbert, Jesse & Mahlberg, Michaela. 2020. Fiction – One register or two? Speech and narration in novels. *Register Studies* 2(1): 72–101.

doi Egbert, Jesse & Staples, Shelley. 2019. Doing multi-dimensional analysis in SPSS, SAS, and R. In *Multi-Dimensional Analysis: Research Methods and Current Issues*, Tony Berber Sardinha & Marcia Veirano Pinto (eds), 125–144. Bloomsbury Academic.

Elio, Renee & Anderson, John R. 1981. The effects of category generalizations and instance similarity on schema abstraction. *Journal of Experimental Psychology: Human Learning & Memory* 7(6): 397–417.

doi Elio, Renee & Anderson, John R. 1984. The effects of information order and learning mode on schema abstraction. *Memory & Cognition* 12(1): 20–30.

doi Ellis, Nick C. 1998. Emergentism, connectionism and language learning. *Language Learning* 48(4): 631–664.

doi Ellis, Nick C. 2002. Frequency effects in language processing. *Studies in Second Language Acquisition* 24(2): 143–188.

doi Ellis, Nick C. 2006. Language acquisition as rational contingency learning. *Applied Linguistics* 27(1): 1–24.

Ellis, Nick C. 2008. Usage-based and form-focused language acquisition: The associative learning of constructions, learned attention, and the limited L2 endstate. In *Handbook of Cognitive Linguistics and Second Language Acquisition*, Peter Robinson & Nick C. Ellis (eds), 372–405. London: Routledge.

doi Ellis, Nick C. 2019. Essentials of a theory of language cognition. *The Modern Language Journal* 103(S1): 39–60.

doi Ellis, Nick C. & Ferreira-Junior, Fernando. 2009a. Constructions and their acquisition: Islands and the distinctiveness of their occupancy. *Annual Review of Cognitive Linguistics* 7(1): 188–221.

doi Ellis, Nick C. & Ferreira-Junior, Fernando. 2009b. Construction learning as a function of frequency, frequency distribution, and function. *The Modern Language Journal* 93(3): 370–385.

doi Ellis, Nick C. & Larsen-Freeman, D. 2006. Language emergence: Implications for applied linguistics--Introduction to the special issue. *Applied Linguistics* 27(4): 558–589.

doi Ellis, Nick C. & Larsen-Freeman, Diane. 2009. Constructing a second language: Analyses and computational simulations of the emergence of linguistic constructions from usage. *Language Learning* 59: 90–125.

Ellis, Nick C., Römer, Ute & O'Donnell, Matthew Brook. 2016. *Usage-based Approaches to Language Acquisition and Processing: Cognitive and Corpus Investigations of Construction Grammar* [Language Learning Monograph Series]. Malden, MA: Wiley-Blackwell.

doi Ellis, Rod. 1989. Are classroom and naturalistic acquisition the same? A study of the classroom acquisition of German word order rules. *Studies in second language Acquisition* 11(3): 305–328.

doi Ellis, Rod. 1997. The empirical evaluation of language teaching materials. *ELT Journal* 51(1): 36–42.

Elman, Jeffrey L., Bates, Elizabeth A., Johnson, Mark H., Karmiloff-Smith, Annette, Parisi, Domenico & Plunkett, Kim. 1996. *Rethinking Innateness: A Connectionist Perspective on Development.* Cambridge, MA: The MIT Press.

European Commission, EACEA, & Eurydice. 2017. *Key data on teaching languages at school in Europe: Eurydice Report.* Luxemburg: Publications Office of the European Union. ⟨http://data.europa.eu/doi/10.2797/839825⟩ (15 October 2018).

Evert, Stephanie. 2018. Statistics for linguists with R – A SIGIL course: Unit 7: A multivariate approach to linguistic variation. *FAU Erlangen-Nürnberg*, September. ⟨http://www.stephanie-evert.de/SIGIL/sigil_R/⟩ (4 November 2021).

Fankhauser, Anna. In preparation. *Formulaic language in the EFL classroom: A corpus-based study of phraseological items in British English and American English conversation with implications for EFL teaching*. Osnabrück University.

Fankhauser, Anna. Forthcoming. Suggestions for a new model of functional phraseme categorization for applied purposes. In *Recent Advances in Multiword Units in Machine Translation and Translation Technology*, Johanna Monti, Ruslan Mitkov & Gloria Corpas Pastor (eds). Amsterdam: John Benjamins.

doi Farr, Fiona & Leńko-Szymańska, Agnieszka. 2023. Corpora in English language teacher education: Research, integration, and resources. *TESOL Quarterly*.

Feierabend, Sabine, Rathgeb, Thomas, Kheredmand, Hediye & Glöckler, Stephan. 2020. JIM-Studie 2020: Jugend, Information, Medien. Basisuntersuchung zum Medienumgang 12- bis 19-Jähriger. Medienpädagogischer Forschungs- verbund Südwest (mpfs). ⟨https://www.mpfs.de/fileadmin/files/Studien/JIM/2020/JIM-Studie-2020_Web_final.pdf⟩ (20 January 2022).

doi Fogal, Gary G. & Verspoor, Marjolijn H. (eds). 2020. *Complex Dynamic Systems Theory and L2 Writing Development* [Language Learning & Language Teaching 54]. Amsterdam: John Benjamins.

doi Fominykh, Mikhail, Shikhova, Elizaveta, Soule, Maria Victoria, Perifanou, Maria & Zhukova, Daria. 2021. Digital competence assessment survey for language teachers. In *Learning and Collaboration Technologies: New Challenges and Learning Experiences*, Panayiotis Zaphiris & Andri Ioannou (eds), 264–282. Cham: Springer.

doi Forsberg, Julia, Mohr, Susanne & Jansen, Sandra. 2019. "The goal is to enable students to communicate": Communicative competence and target varieties in TEFL practices in Sweden and Germany. *European Journal of Applied Linguistics* 7(1): 31–60.

forum discussions on neoprofs.org. 2016. [Anglais] La question des manuels: Les utilisez-vous? Vous appuyez-vous sur celui de votre établissement? ⟨https://www.neoprofs.org/t103210-anglais-la-question-des-manuels-les-utilisez-vous-vous-appuyez-vous-sur-celui-de-votre-etablissement⟩ (6 January 2022).

Fournier, Yann, Gaudry-Lachet, Anne & DEPP-MIREI. 2017. *L'apprentissage des langues vivantes étrangères dans l'Union européenne: Parcours des élèves. Note d'information N° 17.15*. Ministère de l'Education Nationale. ⟨https://www.education.gouv.fr/l-apprentissage-des-langues-vivantes-etrangeres-dans-l-union-europeenne-parcours-des-eleves-2588⟩ (1 August 2018).

doi Frazier, Stefan. 2003. A corpus analysis of would-clauses without adjacent if-clauses. *TESOL Quarterly* 37(3): 443–466.

Freeman, David & Holden, Susan. 1986. Authentic listening materials. *Techniques of Teaching*, 67–69. London: Modern English Publications.

Freudenstein, Reinhold. 2002. Was morgen geschah... Schulischer Fremdsprachenunterricht gestern, heute – und in Zukunft? In *Perspektiven für die zukünftige Fremdsprachendidaktik*, Christiane Neveling (ed.), 45–62. Tübingen: Gunter Narr.

doi Friederici, Luisa. 2019. Vorschlag für eine pluriperspektivische Analyse der Zielgruppe zur Auswahl eines neuen Lehrwerks oder: Vergesst die Lehrer nicht! *Pandaemonium Germanicum* 22: 281–301.

doi Friginal, Eric. 2018. *Corpus Linguistics for English Teachers: New Tools, Online Resources, and Classroom Activities*. New York, NY: Routledge.

doi Friginal, Eric & Hardy, Jack. 2019. From factors to dimensions: Interpreting linguistic co-occurrence patterns. In *Multi-Dimensional Analysis: Research Methods and Current Issues*, Tony Berber Sardinha & Marcia Veirano Pinto (eds), 145–64. London: Bloomsbury Academic.

doi Friginal, Eric & Hardy, Jack A. 2014. Conducting multi-dimensional analysis using SPSS. In *Multi-Dimensional Analysis, 25 Years on: A Tribute to Douglas Biber* [Studies in Corpus Linguistics 60], Tony Berber Sardinha & Marcia Veirano Pinto (eds), 297–316. Amsterdam: John Benjamins.

doi Friginal, Eric & Roberts, Jennifer. 2022. Corpora for materials design. In *The Routledge Handbook of Corpora and English Language Teaching and Learning*, Reka R. Jablonkai & Eniko Csomay (eds), 131–46. London: Routledge.

doi Friginal, Eric & Weigle, Sara. 2014. Exploring multiple profiles of L2 writing using multi-dimensional analysis. *Journal of Second Language Writing* 26: 80–95.

Fujimoto, Kazuko. 2017. Do English textbooks reflect the actual use of English? The present perfect and temporal adverbials. Presented at the The 9th International Corpus Linguistics Conference, University of Birmingham, July 25. ⟨https://www.birmingham.ac.uk/Documents/college-artslaw/corpus/conference-archives/2017/general/paper117.pdf⟩ (9 January 2017).

Gabrielatos, Costas. 1994. Collocations: Pedagogical Implications, and Their Treatment in Pedagogical Materials. PhD dissertation, Research Centre for English and Applied Linguistics, Cambridge University, UK. ⟨https://www.researchgate.net/publication/261708736_Collocations_Pedagogical_implications_and_their_treatment_in_pedagogical_materials⟩ (12 April 2024).

Gabrielatos, Costas. 2003. Conditional sentences: ELT typology and corpus evidence. Presented at the BAAL 36th Annual Meeting. ⟨https://www.researchgate.net/publication/261708834_Conditional_Sentences_ELT_typology_and_corpus_evidence⟩ (12 April 2024).

Gabrielatos, Costas. 2006. Corpus-based analysis of pedagogical materials: If-conditionals in ELT coursebooks and the BNC. Presented at the 7th Teaching and Language Corpora Conference. ⟨https://www.researchgate.net/publication/228880683_Corpus-based_evaluation_of_pedagogical_materials_If-conditionals_in_ELT_coursebooks_and_the_BNC⟩ (6 February 2020).

Gabrielatos, Costas. 2013. *If*-conditionals in ICLE and the BNC: A success story for teaching or learning? In *Twenty Years of Learner Corpus Research: Looking Back, Moving Ahead*, Sylviane Granger, Gaëtanelle Gilquin & Fanny Meunier (eds), 155–166. Louvain-la-Neuve: Presses Universitaires de Louvain.

doi Gabrielatos, Costas. 2019. *If*-Conditionals and modality: Frequency patterns and theoretical explanations. *Journal of English Linguistics* 47(4): 301–334.

doi Gardner, Dee & Davies, Mark. 2007. Pointing out frequent phrasal verbs: A corpus-based analysis. *TESOL Quarterly* 41(2): 339–359.

doi Gardner, Sheena, Nesi, Hilary & Biber, Douglas. 2019. Discipline, level, genre: Integrating situational perspectives in a new MD analysis of university student writing. *Applied Linguistics* 40(4): 646–674.

Garinger, Dawn. 2002. Textbook selection for the ESL classroom. *Center for Applied Linguistics Digest.* ⟨http://www.mcael.org/uploads/File/provider_library/Textbook_Eval_CAL.pdf⟩ (12 January 2017).

doi Garton, Sue & Graves, Kathleen (eds). 2014. *International Perspectives on Materials in ELT.* London: Palgrave Macmillan.

Gass, Susan M. 1997. *Input, Interaction, and the Second Language Learner.* New York, NY: Routledge.

doi Geeraerts, Dirk. 2006. *Cognitive Linguistics: Basic Readings.* Berlin: Walter de Gruyter.

doi Geeslin, Kimberly L. 2014. *Sociolinguistics and Second Language Acquisition: Learning to Use Language in Context.* New York, NY: Routledge.

Gehring, Wolfgang. 2013. Can't judge a book by its cover: An analytical approach to textbook innovations. In *Basic Issues in EFL Teaching and Learning*, Maria Eisenmann & Theresa Summer (eds), 2nd edn, 357–370. Heidelberg: Winter.

doi Ghanbari, Nasim, Esmaili, Fatemeh & Shamsaddini, Mohammad Reza. 2015. The effect of using authentic materials on Iranian EFL learners' vocabulary learning. *Theory and Practice in Language Studies* 5(12): 2459–2468.

Ghosn, Irma K. 2013. Talking like texts and talking about texts: How some primary school coursebook tasks are realized in the classroom. In *Developing Materials for Language Teaching*, 2nd edn, 291–305. London: Bloomsbury.

doi Gilmore, Alex. 2004. A comparison of textbook and authentic interactions. *ELT Journal* 58(4): 363–374.

doi Gilmore, Alex. 2007. Authentic materials and authenticity in foreign language learning. *Language Teaching* 40(2): 97.

doi Gilmore, Alex. 2011. "I prefer not text": Developing Japanese learners' communicative competence with authentic materials. *Language Learning* 61(3): 786–819.

doi Gilmore, Alex. 2019. Materials and authenticity in language teaching. In *The Routledge Handbook of English Language Teacher Education*, Steve Walsh & Steve Mann (eds), 1st edn, 299–318. London: Routledge.

doi Gilquin, Gaëtanelle. 2016. Discourse markers in L2 English: From classroom to naturalistic input. In *New Approaches to English Linguistics: Building Bridges* [Studies in Language Companion Series 177], Olga Timofeeva, Anne-Christine Gardner, Alpo Honkapohja & Sarah Chevalier (eds), 213–249. Amsterdam: John Benjamins.

doi Gilquin, Gaëtanelle. 2018. American and/or British influence on L2 Englishes – Does context tip the scale(s)? In *Varieties of English Around the World* [Varieties of English Around the World G61], Sandra C. Deshors (ed.), 187–216. Amsterdam: John Benjamins.

doi Gilquin, Gaëtanelle & Laporte, Samantha. 2021. The use of online writing tools by learners of English: Evidence from a process corpus. *International Journal of Lexicography* 34(4): 472–492.

doi Gilquin, Gaëtanelle & Paquot, Magali. 2008. Too chatty: Learner academic writing and register variation. *English Text Construction* 1(1): 41–61.

Gnutzmann, Claus & Intemann, Frauke (eds). 2008. *The Globalisation of English and the English Language Classroom.* Tübingen: Narr Francke.

Goldberg, Adele E. 1995. *Constructions: A Construction Grammar Approach to Argument Structure.* Chicago, IL: The University of Chicago Press.

Goldberg, Adele E. 2006. *Constructions at Work: The Nature of Generalization in Language*. Oxford: OUP.

doi Goldberg, Adele E., Casenhiser, Devin M. & Sethuraman, Nitya. 2004. Learning argument structure generalizations. *Cognitive Linguistics* 15(3): 289–316.

doi Gomes, Dylan G. E., Pottier, Patrice, Crystal-Ornelas, Robert, Hudgins, Emma J., Foroughirad, Vivienne, Sánchez-Reyes, Luna L., Turba, Rachel, et al. 2022. Why don't we share data and code? Perceived barriers and benefits to public archiving practices. *Proceedings of the Royal Society B: Biological Sciences* 289(1987): 20221113.

doi Goretzko, David. 2022. Factor retention in exploratory factor analysis with missing data. *Educational and Psychological Measurement* 82(3): 444–464.

doi Gorsuch, Richard L. 2014. *Factor Analysis*, 2nd edn. Hillsdale, NJ: Lawrence Erlbaum Associates.

doi Götz, Sandra. 2013. *Fluency in Native And Nonnative English Speech* [Studies in Corpus Linguistics 53]. Amsterdam: John Benjamins.

doi Goulart, Larissa, Gray, Bethany, Staples, Shelley, Black, Amanda, Shelton, Aisha, Biber, Douglas, Egbert, Jesse & Wizner, Stacey. 2020. Linguistic perspectives on register. *Annual Review of Linguistics* 6(1): 435–455.

doi Goulart, Larissa & Wood, Margaret. 2021. Methodological synthesis of research using multi-dimensional analysis. *Journal of Research Design and Statistics in Linguistics and Communication Science* 6(2): 107–137.

doi Gouverneur, Céline. 2008. The phraseological patterns of high-frequency verbs in advanced English for general purposes: A corpus-driven approach to EFL textbook analysis. In *Phraseology in Foreign Language Learning and Teaching*, Fanny Meunier & Sylviane Granger (eds), 223–243. Amsterdam: John Benjamins.

doi Grabowski, Łukasz. 2015. Keywords and lexical bundles within English pharmaceutical discourse: A corpus-driven description. *English for Specific Purposes* 38: 23–33.

Granger, Sylviane. 1998. The computer learner corpus: A versatile new source of data for SLA research. In *Learner English on Computer* [Studies in Language and Linguistics], Sylviane Granger (ed.), 3–18. London: Longman.

doi Granger, Sylviane. 2004. Computer learner corpus research: Current status and future prospects. *Language and Computers* 52(1): 123–145.

doi Granger, Sylviane. 2015. The contribution of learner corpora to reference and instructional materials design. In *The Cambridge Handbook of Learner Corpus Research*, Sylviane Granger, Gaetanelle Gilquin & Fanny Meunier (eds), 485–510. Cambridge: CUP.

doi Granger, Sylviane. 2018. Has lexicography reaped the full benefit of the (learner) corpus revolution? In *Proceedings of the XVIII EURALEX International Congress: Lexicography in Global Contexts*, Simon Krek, Jaka Čibej, Vojko Gorjanc & Iztok Kosem (eds), 17–24. Ljubljana: University of Ljubljana.

doi Granger, Sylviane, Hung, Joseph & Petch-Tyson, Stephanie (eds). 2002. *Computer Learner Corpora, Second Language Acquisition, and Foreign Language Teaching* [Language Learning & Language Teaching 6]. Amsterdam: John Benjamins.

doi Granger, Sylviane & Tyson, Stephanie. 1996. Connector usage in the English essay writing of native and non-native EFL speakers of English. *World Englishes* 15(1): 17–27.

doi Grau, Maike. 2009. Worlds apart? English in German youth cultures and in educational settings. *World Englishes* 28(2): 160–174.

doi Graves, Kathleen & Garton, Sue. 2019. Materials use and development. In *The Routledge Handbook of English Language Teacher Education*, Steve Walsh & Steve Mann (eds), 417–431. London: Routledge.

doi Gray, Bethany. 2015. *Linguistic Variation in Research Articles: When Discipline Tells Only Part of the Story* [Studies in Corpus Linguistics 71]. Amsterdam: John Benjamins.

doi Gray, Bethany. 2019. Tagging and counting linguistic features for multi-dimensional analysis. In *Multi-Dimensional Analysis: Research Methods and Current Issues*, Tony Berber Sardinha & Marcia Veirano Pinto (eds), 43–66. London: Bloomsbury Academic.

doi Gray, Bethany & Egbert, Jesse. 2019. Editorial: Register and register variation. *Register Studies* 1(1): 1–9.

doi Gray, Bethany & Egbert, Jesse. 2021. Register in L1 and L2 language development. *Register Studies* 3(2): 177–179.

doi Gray, John. 2000. The ELT coursebook as cultural artefact: How teachers censor and adapt. *ELT Journal* 54(3): 274–283.

Gray, John. 2002. The global coursebook in English language teaching. In *Globalization and Language Teaching*, David Block & Deborah Cameron (eds), 151–167. London: Routledge.

doi Gray, John. 2010. *The Construction of English: Culture, Consumerism and Promotion in the Elt Global Coursebook*. Houndmills: Palgrave Macmillan.

doi Gries, Stefan Th. 2005. Null-hypothesis significance testing of word frequencies: A follow-up on Kilgarriff. *Corpus Linguistics and Linguistic Theory* 1(2).

doi Gries, Stefan Th. 2013. Statistical tests for the analysis of learner corpus data. In *Automatic Treatment and Analysis of Learner Corpus Data* [Studies in Corpus Linguistics 59], Ana Díaz-Negrillo, Nicolas Ballier & Paul Thompson (eds), 287–310. Amsterdam: John Benjamins.

doi Gries, Stefan Th. 2015. The most under-used statistical method in corpus linguistics: Multi-level (and mixed-effects) models. *Corpora* 10(1): 95–125.

doi Gries, Stefan Th. 2018. On over- and underuse in learner corpus research and multifactoriality in corpus linguistics more generally. *Journal of Second Language Studies* 1(2): 276–308.

doi Gries, Stefan Th. & Deshors, Sandra C. 2020. Statistical analyses of learner corpus data. In *Routledge Handbook of SLA and Corpora*, Nancy Tracy-Ventura & Magali Paquot (eds), 119–132. New York, NY: Routledge.

doi Grieve-Smith, Angus B. 2007. The envelope of variation in multidimensional register and genre analyses. In *Corpus Linguistics Beyond the Word: Corpus Research from Phrase to Discourse*, Eileen Fitzpatrick (ed.), 21–42. Amsterdam: Rodopi.

doi Griffiths, Roger. 1990. Speech rate and NNS comprehension: A preliminary study in time-benefit analysis. *Language Learning* 40(3): 311–336.

doi Griffiths, Roger. 1991. Language classroom speech rates: A descriptive study. *TESOL Quarterly* 25(1): 189.

doi Gurzynski-Weiss, Laura, Geeslin, Kimberly L., Daidone, Danielle, Linford, Bret, Long, Avizia Yim, Michalski, Ian & Solon, Megan. 2018. Examining multifaceted sources of input. Variationist and usage-based approaches to understanding the L2 classroom. In *Usage-Inspired L2 Instruction: Researched Pedagogy* [Language Learning & Language Teaching 49], Andrea E. Tyler, Lourdes Ortega, Mariko Uno & Hae In Park, 291–311. Amsterdam: John Benjamins.

Hair, Joseph F., Black, William C., Babin, Barry J. & Anderson, Rolph E. 2019. *Multivariate Data Analysis*, 8th edn. Andover, Hampshire: Cengage.

doi Hall, Christopher J., Wicaksono Rachel, Liu Shu, Qian Yuan & Xu Xiaoqing. 2017. Exploring teachers' ontologies of English: Monolithic conceptions of grammar in a group of Chinese teachers. *International Journal of Applied Linguistics* 27(1): 87–109.

Hallet, Wolfgang & Legutke, Michael K. 2013. Task-approaches revisited: New orientations, new perspectives. *The European Journal of Applied Linguistics and TEFL* 2(2): 139–159.

Halliday, Michael A. K. 1988. On the language of physical science. In *Registers of written English: Situational Factors and Linguistic Features*, Mohsen Ghadessy (ed.), 162–172. London: Pinter.

doi Hardie, Andrew. 2014. Modest XML for corpora: Not a standard, but a suggestion. *ICAME Journal* 38(1): 73–103.

Harel, Idit & Papert, Seymour. 1991. *Constructionism: Research Reports and Essays, 1985–1990*. Norwood, NJ: Ablex.

doi Harwood, Nigel. 2005. What do we want EAP teaching materials for? *Journal of English for Academic Purposes* 4(2): 149–161.

doi Hausmann, Franz Josef. 2005. Isotopie, scénario, collocation et exemple lexicographique. In *L'exemple lexicographique dans les dictionnaires français contemporains*, Michaela Heinz (ed.), 283–292. Berlin: De Gruyter.

doi Henry, Alastair. 2014. Swedish students' beliefs about learning English in and outside of school. In *Motivation and Foreign Language Learning: From theory to practice* [Language Learning & Language Teaching 40], David Lasagabaster, Aintzane Doiz & Juan Manuel Sierra (eds), 93–116. Amsterdam: John Benjamins.

doi Henson, Robin K. & Roberts, J. Kyle. 2006. Use of exploratory factor analysis in published research: Common errors and some comment on improved practice. *Educational and Psychological Measurement* 66(3): 393–416.

doi Herbst, Thomas. 1996. What are collocations: Sandy beaches or false teeth? *English Studies* 77(4): 379–393.

doi Herbst, Thomas. 2016. Foreign language learning is construction learning–What else? Moving towards Pedagogical Construction Grammar. In *Applied Construction Grammar*, Sabine De Knop & Gaëtanelle Gilquin (eds), 32:56–96. Berlin: De Gruyter Mouton.

doi Herbst, Thomas, Schmid, Hans-Jörg & Faulhaber, Susen (eds). 2014. *Constructions Collocations Patterns* [Trends in Linguistics. Studies and Monographs 282]. Berlin: Walter De Gruyter.

Hermes, Liesel. 2009. "Reading can be fun if...": Lektüren in der Sekundarstufe I. In *Literaturdidaktik und Literaturvermittlung im Englischunterricht der Sekundarstufe*, I, Jan Hollm (ed.), 7–22. Trier: Wissenschaftlicher Verlag Trier.

Hessisches Kultusministerium. 2010. Lehrplan Englisch – Gymnasialer Bildungsgang – Jahrgangsstufen 5G bis 9G. ⟨https://kultusministerium.hessen.de/sites/kultusministerium.hessen.de/files/2021-06/g8-englisch.pdf⟩ (6 February 2022).

Hoey, Michael. 2005. *Lexical Priming: A New Theory of Words and Language*. London: Routledge.

Holliday, Adrian. 2005. *The Struggle to Teach English as an International Language*. Oxford: OUP.

doi Holmes, Janet. 1988. Doubt and certainty in ESL textbooks. *Applied Linguistics* 9(1): 21–44.

doi Hu, Chieh-Fang & Maechtle, Cheyenne. 2021. Construction learning by child learners of foreign language: Input distribution and learner factors. *The Modern Language Journal* 105(1): 335–354.

doi Huang, Pingping. 2019. Textbook interaction: A study of the language and cultural contextualisation of English learning textbooks. *Learning, Culture and Social Interaction* 21: 87–99.

doi Hughes, Rebecca. 2010. What a corpus tells us about grammar teaching materials. In *The Routledge Handbook of Corpus Linguistics*, Anne O'Keeffe & Michael McCarthy (eds), 401–412. New York, NY: Routledge.

Hundt, Marianne, Sand, Andrea & Siemund, Rainer. 1998. *Manual of information to accompany the Freiburg-LOB Corpus of British English ('FLOB')*. Albert-Ludwigs-Universität Freiburg. ⟨http://korpus.uib.no/icame/frown/⟩ (23 January 2022).

Hundt, Marianne, Sand, Andrea & Skandera, Paul. 1999. *Manual of information to accompany the Freiburg-Brown Corpus of American English*. Albert-Ludwigs-Universität Freiburg. ⟨http://korpus.uib.no/icame/flob/⟩ (23 January 2022).

doi Hunston, Susan. 2002. *Corpora in Applied Linguistics* [The Cambridge Applied Linguistics Series]. Cambridge: CUP.

doi Hunston, Susan & Francis, Gill. 2000. *Pattern Grammar: A Corpus-Driven Approach to the Lexical Grammar of English* [Studies in Corpus Linguistics 4]. Amsterdam: John Benjamins.

Husson, François, Cornillon, Pierre-André, Guyader, Arnaud, Jégou, Nicolas, Josse, Julie, Klutchnikoff, Nicolas, Le Pennec, Erwan, Matzner-Løber, Eric, Rouvière, Laurent & Thieurmel, Benoît. 2018. *R pour la statistique et la science des données*. Rennes: Presses universitaires de Rennes.

doi Husson, François, Lê, Sébastien & Pagès, Jérôme. 2017. *Exploratory Multivariate Analysis by Example Using R*, 2nd edn. Boca Raton, FL: Chapman and Hall/CRC Press.

doi Hyland, Ken. 1994. Hedging in academic writing and EAP textbooks. *English for Specific Purposes* 13(3): 239–256.

Hyland, Ken. 2013. Materials for developing writing skills. In *Developing Materials for Language Teaching*, Brian Tomlinson (ed.), 2nd edn, 391–406. London: Bloomsbury.

doi Hymes, Dell. 1984. Sociolinguistics: Stability and consolidation. *International Journal of the Sociology of Language* 45: 39–45.

Ide, Nancy. 1996. Corpus encoding standard. v. 1.5 (last updated March 2020). Expert Advisory Group on Language Engineering Standards (EAGLES). ⟨https://www.cs.vassar.edu/CES/⟩ (2 January 2022).

doi Jablonkai, Reka R. & Csomay, Eniko. 2022. *The Routledge Handbook of Corpora and English Language Teaching and Learning*. London: Routledge.

doi Jacobs, George M. & Ball, Jessica. 1996. An investigation of the structure of group activities in ELT coursebooks. *ELT Journal* 50(2): 99–107.

doi Jansen, Sandra, Mohr, Susanne & Forsberg, Julia. 2021. Standard language ideology in the English language classroom: Suggestions for EIL-informed teacher education. In *Glocalising Teaching English as an International Language*, Marcus Callies, Stefanie Hehner, Philipp Meer & Micahel Westphal (eds). London: Routledge.

doi Jenkins, Jennifer. 1998. Which pronunciation norms and models for English as an International Language? *ELT Journal* 52(2): 119–126.

Jenkins, Jennifer. 2000. *The Phonology of English as an International Language*. Oxford: OUP.

Jenkins, Jennifer. 2003. *World Englishes: A Resource Book for Students* [Routledge English Language Introductions]. New York, NY: Routledge.

doi Jiang, Xiangying. 2006. Suggestions: What should ESL students know? *System* 34(1): 36–54.

doi Johns, Tim. 1986. Micro-concord: A language learner's research tool. *System* 14(2): 151–162.

Johns, Tim. 1993. Data-driven learning: An update. *TELL & CALL* 3: 23–32.

doi Johns, Tim. 2002. Data-driven learning: The perpetual challenge. In *Teaching and Learning by Doing Corpus Analysis*, Bernhard Kettemann & Georg Marko (eds), 105–117. Amsterdam: Rodopi.

doi Johns, Tim. 2014. Contexts: The background, development and trialling of a concordance-based CALL program. In *Teaching and Language Corpora*, Anne Wichmann & Steven Fligelstone (eds), 100–115. New York, NY: Routledge.

Jolliffe, Ian T. 2002. *Principal Component Analysis* [Springer Series in Statistics], 2nd edn. New York, NY: Springer.

doi Kachru, Yamuna & Smith, Larry E. 2008. *Cultures, Contexts and World Englishes* [ESL & Applied Linguistics Professional Series]. New York, NY: Routledge.

doi Kaiser, Henry F. & Rice, John. 1974. Little Jiffy, Mark IV. *Educational and Psychological Measurement* 34(1): 111–117.

doi Karlsen, Petter Hagen & Monsen, Marte. 2020. Corpus literacy and applications in Norwegian upper secondary schools: Teacher and learner perspectives. *Nordic Journal of English Studies* 19(1): 118.

doi Kavanagh, Barry. 2021. Norwegian in-service teachers' perspectives on language corpora in teaching English. *Nordic Journal of Language Teaching and Learning* 9(2): 90–106.

doi Kerres, Michael. 2020. Against all odds: Education in Germany coping with Covid-19. *Postdigital Science and Education* 2(3): 690–694,

doi Kilgarriff, Adam, Baisa, Vít, Bušta, Jan, Jakubíček, Miloš, Kovář, Vojtěch, Michelfeit, Jan, Rychlý, Pavel & Suchomel, Vít. 2014. The Sketch Engine: Ten years on. *Lexicography* 1(1): 7–36.

doi Kim, Daejin & Hall, Joan Kelly. 2002. The role of an interactive book reading program in the development of second language pragmatic competence. *The Modern Language Journal* 86(3): 332–348.

Koch, Peter & Oesterreicher, Wulf. 1985. Language of immediacy – Language of distance: Orality and literacy from the perspective of language theory and linguistic history. In *Communicative Spaces. Variation, Contact, and Change: Papers in Honour of Ursula Schaefer*, Claudia Lange, Beatrix Weber & Göran Wolf (eds), 441–73. Frankfurt: Peter Lang.

doi Koch, Peter & Oesterreicher, Wulf. 2011. *Gesprochene Sprache in der Romania: Französisch, Italienisch, Spanisch* [Romanistische Arbeitshefte 31]. Berlin: De Gruyter.

doi Koprowski, Mark. 2005. Investigating the usefulness of lexical phrases in contemporary coursebooks. *ELT Journal* 59(4): 322–332,

doi Kosmas, Panagiotis, Parmaxi, Antigoni, Perifanou, Maria & Economides, Anastasios A. 2021. Open educational resources for language education: Towards the development of an e-toolkit. In *Learning and Collaboration Technologies: New Challenges and Learning Experiences. 8th International Conference, LCT 2021, Held as Part of the 23rd HCI International Conference, HCII 2021, Virtual Event, July 24–29, 2021, Proceedings, Part I* [Lecture Notes in Computer Science], Panayiotis Zaphiris & Andri Ioannou (eds), 65–79. Cham: Springer.

Krashen, Stephen. 1982. *Principles and Practice in Second Language Acquisition* [Language Teaching Methodology Series]. Oxford: Pergamon.

Krashen, Stephen. 1985. *Second Language Acquisition and Second Language Learning* [Language Teaching Methodology Series]. Reprinted. Oxford: Pergamon.

doi Kruger, Haidee & van Rooy, Bertus. 2018. Register variation in written contact varieties of English: A multidimensional analysis. *English World-Wide. A Journal of Varieties of English* 39(2): 214–242.

doi Kuhl, Patricia K. & Meltzoff, Andrew N. 1996. Infant vocalizations in response to speech: Vocal imitation and developmental change. *The Journal of the Acoustical Society of America* 100(401): 2425–2438.

Kultusministerkonferenz. 2003. Bildungsstandards für die erste Fremdsprache (Englisch/Französisch) für den Mittleren Schulabschluss. Sekretariat der Ständigen Konferenz der Kultusminister der Länder in der Bundesrepublik Deutschland. ⟨https://www.kmk.org/fileadmin/veroeffentlichungen_beschluesse/2003/2003_12_04-BS-erste-Fremdsprache.pdf⟩ (21 January 2017).

Kultusministerkonferenz. 2012. Bildungsstandards für die fortgeführte Fremdsprache (Englisch/Französisch) für die Allgemeine Hochschulreife. Beschluss der Kultusministerkonferenz vom 18.10.2012. Sekretariat der Ständigen Konferenz der Kultusminister der Länder in der Bundesrepublik Deutschland. ⟨http://www.kmk.org/bildung-schule/qualitaetssicherung-in-schulen/bildungsstandards/dokumente.html⟩ (26 November 2018).

Kurtz, Jürgen. 2019. Lehrwerkgestütztes Fremdsprachenlernen im digitalen Wandel. In *Das Lehren und Lernen von Fremd- und Zweitsprachen im digitalen Wandel: Arbeitspapiere der 39. Frühjahrskonferenz zur Erforschung des Fremdsprachenunterrichts* [Gießener Beiträge zur Fremdsprachendidaktik], Eva Burwitz-Melzer, Claudia Riemer & Lars Schmelter (eds), 114–25. Tübingen: Narr Francke Attempto.

doi Labov, William. 2004. Quantitative analysis of linguistic variation. In *Sociolinguistics / Soziolinguistik* [Handbücher Zur Sprach- Und Kommunikationswissenschaft / Handbooks of Linguistics and Communication Science [HSK]], Vol. 1, 6–21. Berlin: De Gruyter Mouton.

doi Lakoff, George & Johnson, Mark. 2003. *Metaphors We Live By*. Chicago, IL: The University of Chicago Press.

Landesregierung Nordrhein-Westfalen. 2016. Lernen im digitalen Wandel. Unser Leitbild 2020 für Bildung in Zeiten der Digitalisierung. ⟨https://www.land.nrw/sites/default/files/asset/document/leitbild_lernen_im_digitalen_wandel.pdf⟩ (22 January 2022).

Langacker, Ronald W. 1987. *Foundations of Cognitive Grammar: Theoretical Prerequisites.* Stanford, CA: Stanford University Press.

doi Langacker, Ronald W. 2001. Cognitive linguistics, language pedagogy, and the English present tense. In *Applied Cognitive Linguistics*, Vol. I: *Theory and Language Acquisition*, Martin Pütz, Susanne Niemeier & René Dirven (eds), 3–39. Berlin: De Gruyter.

doi Langacker, Ronald W. 2008. *Cognitive Grammar: A Basic Introduction*. Oxford: OUP.

doi Larsen-Freeman, Diane. 1997. Chaos/complexity science and second language acquisition. *Applied Linguistics* 18(2): 141–165.

Larsen-Freeman, Diane. 2006. The emergence of complexity, fluency, and accuracy in the oral and written production of five Chinese learners of English. *Applied Linguistics* 27(4): 590–619.

Larsen-Freeman, Diane. 2018. Looking ahead: Future directions in, and future research into, second language acquisition. *Foreign Language Annals* 51(1): 55–72.

Lavi-Rotbain, Ori & Arnon, Inbal. 2022. The learnability consequences of Zipfian distributions in language. *Cognition* 223: 105038.

Le Foll, Elen. 2017. Textbook English: A corpus-based analysis of language use in German and French EFL textbooks. Poster presented at the Corpus Linguistics 2017 Conference, University of Birmingham, July. ⟨https://www.birmingham.ac.uk/Documents/college-artslaw/corpus/conference-archives/2017/general/paper230.pdf⟩ (20 October 2017).

Le Foll, Elen. 2018a. "They were walking in a corridor when suddenly the mummy appeared." A corpus-based study of narrative texts in secondary school EFL textbooks. Presented at the 13th Teaching Language and Corpora (TaLC) Conference, Cambridge, UK.

Le Foll, Elen. 2018b. Raising, *discovering and *exploiting awareness: Using the Internet as a source of collocational knowledge. Presented at the OLLReN Annual Online Conference: Research into using Technology for Language Learning, October. ⟨https://www.researchgate.net/publication/328368290_Raising_discovering_and_exploiting_awareness_Using_the_Internet_as_a_source_of_collocational_knowledge⟩ (13 April 2024)

Le Foll, Elen. 2020a. Development and evaluation of a corpus linguistics seminar in pre-service teacher training. Presented at the Teaching and Language Corpora Conference (TaLC) 2020, Perpignan, July. ⟨https://youtu.be/PtgW5y-xFW8⟩ (13 April 2024).

Le Foll, Elen. 2020b. Issues in compiling and exploiting textbook corpora. Presented at the Japanese Association for English Corpus Studies 2020, Tokyo, October.

Le Foll, Elen. 2021a. A New Tagger for the Multi-Dimensional Analysis of Register Variation in English. M.Sc. thesis, Osnabrück University.

Le Foll, Elen. 2021b. About the project. In *Creating Corpus-Informed Materials for the English as a Foreign Language Classroom: A Step-by-Step Guide for (Trainee) Teachers Using Online Resources* [Open Educational Resource], 3rd edn. ⟨https://pressbooks.pub/elenlefoll⟩ (30 July 2021).

Le Foll, Elen. 2021c. Register variation in school EFL textbooks. *Register Studies* 3(2): 207–246.

Le Foll, Elen. 2021d. *Introducing the multi-feature tagger of English (MFTE). Perl.* Osnabrück University. ⟨https://github.com/elenlefoll/MultiFeatureTaggerEnglish⟩ (5 January 2022).

Le Foll, Elen. 2022a. "I'm putting some salt in my sandwich." The use of the progressive in EFL textbook conversation. In *Broadening the Spectrum of Corpus Linguistics: New Approaches to Variability and Change* [Studies in Corpus Linguistics 105], Susanne Flach & Martin Hilpert (eds), 93–132. Amsterdam: John Benjamins.

Le Foll, Elen. 2022b. *Making* tea and mistakes: The functions of *make* in spoken English and textbook dialogues. In *Multifunctionality in English: Corpora, Language and Academic Literacy Pedagogy* [Routledge Advances in Corpus Linguistics], Zihan Yin & Elaine Vine (eds), 157–78. New York, NY: Routledge.

Le Foll, Elen. 2022c. Textbook English: A Corpus-based Analysis of the Language of EFL Textbooks Used in Secondary Schools in France, Germany and Spain. PhD dissertation, Osnabrück University. https://osnadocs.ub.uni-osnabrueck.de/handle/ds-202303138538.

doi Le Foll, Elen. 2023a. "Opening up" corpus linguistics: An open education approach to developing corpus literacy among pre-service language teachers. *Journal of Second Language Teacher Education* 2(2): 161–86.

doi Le Foll, Elen. 2023b. The potential impact of EFL textbook language on learner English: A triangulated corpus study. In *Demystifying Corpus Linguistics for English Language Teaching*, Kieran Harrington & Patricia Ronan (eds), 259–287. Cham: Springer.

Le Foll, Elen. 2023c. A conceptual replication of the Multi-dimensional Model of General Spoken and Written English (Biber 1988): Challenges, limitations and potential solutions. Presented at the ICAME44, NWU Vanderbijlpark (South Africa), May. ⟨https://osf.io/f5496/⟩ (13 April 2024).

doi Le Foll, Elen. 2024a. *Schulenglisch*: A multi-dimensional model of the variety of English taught in German secondary schools. *AAA: Arbeiten aus Anglistik und Amerikanistik / Agenda: Advancing Anglophone Studies* 49(1): 15–50.

doi Le Foll, Elen. 2024b. Why we need Open Science and Open Education to bridge the corpus research–practice gap. In *Corpora for Language Learning: Bridging the Research-Practice Divide*, Peter Crosthwaite (ed.), 142–156. London: Routledge.

Le Foll, Elen. forthcoming. "To me, authenticity means credibility and correctness": A data-driven learning approach to encouraging pre-service teachers to re-evaluate their understanding of "authentic English". In *Multiliteracies-aligned Teaching and Learning in Digitally-mediated Second Language Teacher Education*, Carolyn Blume (ed.). London: Routledge. Preprint: https://hal.science/hal-04393791 (5 April 2024)

Le Foll, Elen & Brezina, Vaclav. 2023. Is multi-dimensional analysis replicable? Variables, parameters and transparency. Presented at CL2023, Lancaster University (UK), July.

doi Lê, Sébastien, Josse, Julie & Husson, François. 2008. FactoMineR: An R package for multivariate analysis. *Journal of Statistical Software* 25(1).

doi Leacock, Claudia, Chodorow, Martin, Gamon, Michael & Tetreault, Joel. 2010. *Automated Grammatical Error Detection for Language Learners* [Synthesis Lectures on Human Language Technologies 10]. San Rafael, CA: Morgan & Claypool.

Lee, David YW. 2001. Genres, registers, text types, domain, and styles: Clarifying the concepts and navigating a path through the BNC jungle. *Language Learning & Technology* 5(3): 37–72.

doi Lee, Hansol, Warschauer, Mark & Lee, Jang Ho. 2019. The effects of corpus use on second language vocabulary learning: A multilevel meta-analysis. *Applied Linguistics* 40(5): 721–753.

Lee, Yong Wey David. 2000. Modelling Variation in Spoken and Written Language: TheMmulti-dimensional Approach Revisited. PhD dissertation, Lancaster University.

Leńko-Szymańska, Agnieszka. 2017. Training teachers in data-driven learning: Tackling the challenge. *Language Learning & Technology* 21(3): 217–241.

doi Leńko-Szymańska, Agnieszka & Boulton, Alex. 2015. Introduction: Data-driven learning in language pedagogy. In *Multiple affordances of Language Corpora for Data-driven Learning* [Studies in Corpus Linguistics 69], Agnieszka Leńko-Szymańska & Alex Boulton (eds), 1–14. Amsterdam: John Benjamins.

Lenth, Russell. 2020. emmeans: Estimated marginal means, aka least-squares means. Manual. ⟨https://CRAN.R-project.org/package=emmeans⟩ (12 July 2020).

Leroy, Michel. 2012. Les manuels scolaires: Situation et perspectives. n° 2012-036. Inspection générale de l'éducation nationale. ⟨https://www.education.gouv.fr/les-manuels-scolaires-situation-et-perspectives-6017⟩ (1 August 2018).

Levshina, Natalia. 2015. *How to Do Linguistics with R: Data Exploration and Statistical Analysis*. Amsterdam: John Benjamins.

Lewis, Michael. 1993. *The Lexical Approach*. Hove: Language Teaching Publications.

Lewis, Michael. 1997. *Implementing the Lexical Approach: Putting Theory into Practice*. Hove: Language Teaching Publications.

Lewis, Michael. 2009. *The Lexical Approach: The State of ELT and a Way Forward*. London: Heinle.

Liedke, Martina. 2013. Mit Transkripten Deutsch lernen. In *Gesprochene Sprache im DaF-Unterricht: Grundlagen – Ansätze – Praxis*, Sandro M. Moraldo & Federica Missaglia (eds), 243–266. Heidelberg: Winter.

Limberg, Holger. 2016. "Always remember to say Please and Thank You": Teaching politeness with German EFL textbooks. In *Pragmatics & Language Learning*, Kathleen Bardovi-Harlig & César Félix-Brasdefer (eds), 265–292. Honolulu, HI: University of Hawai'i, National Foreign Language Resource Center.

Little, David, Devitt, Sean & Singleton, David. 1989. *Learning Foreign Languages from Authentic Texts: Theory and Practice*. Dublin: Authentik.

Little, David, Devitt, Seán & Singleton, David. 2002. The communicative approach and authentic texts. In *Teaching Modern Languages*, Ann Swarbrick (ed.), 51–55. London: Routledge.

Littlejohn, Andrew. 2011. The analysis of language teaching materials: Inside the Trojan horse. In *Materials Development in Language Teaching*, Brian Tomlinson (ed.), 179–211. Cambridge: CUP.

Liu, Dilin. 2011. The most frequently used English phrasal verbs in American and British English: A multicorpus examination. *Tesol Quarterly* 45(4): 661–688.

Liu, Eric T.K. & Shaw, Philip M. 2001. Investigating learner vocabulary: A possible approach to looking at EFL/ESL learners' qualitative knowledge of the word. *International Review of Applied Linguistics in Language Teaching* 39(3): 171–94.

Ljung, Magnus. 1990. *A Study of TEFL Vocabulary* [Stockholm Studies in English 78]. Stockholm: Almqvist & Wiksell International.

Ljung, Magnus. 1991. Swedish TEFL meets reality. In *English Computer Corpora: Selected Papers and Research Guide*, Stig Johansson & Anna-Brita Stenström (eds), 245–256. Berlin: De Gruyter.

Loewen, Shawn & Gonulal, Talip. 2015. Exploratory factor analysis and principal components analysis. In *Advancing Quantitative Methods in Second Language Research* [Second Language Acquisition Research Series], Luke Plonsky (ed.), 182–211. New York, NY: Routledge.

Love, Robbie, Dembry, Claire, Hardie, Andrew, Brezina, Vaclav & McEnery, Tony. 2017. The Spoken BNC2014. *International Journal of Corpus Linguistics* 22(3): 319–344.

Love, Robbie, Hawtin, Abi & Hardie, Andrew. 2018. The British National Corpus 2014: User manual and reference guide. ⟨http://corpora.lancs.ac.uk/bnc2014/doc/BNC2014manual.pdf⟩ (15 November 2018).

Lüdecke, Daniel. 2020. sjPlot: Data visualization for statistics in social science. Manual. ⟨https://CRAN.R-project.org/package=sjPlot⟩ (12 July 2020).

doi Luke, Steven G. 2017. Evaluating significance in linear mixed-effects models in R. *Behavior Research Methods* 49(4): 1494–1502.

doi MacWhinney, B. 2006. Emergentism--Use often and with care. *Applied Linguistics* 27(4): 729–40.

doi Madlener, Karin. 2018. Do findings from artificial language learning generalize to second language classrooms? In *Usage-inspired L2 Instruction: Researched Pedagogy* [Language Learning & Language Teaching 49], Andrea Tyler, Lourdes Ortega, Mariko Uno, & Hae In Park (eds), 211–234. Amsterdam: John Benjamins.

doi Manning, Christopher D. 2011. Part-of-speech tagging from 97% to 100%: Is it time for some linguistics? In *Computational Linguistics and Intelligent Text Processing* [Lecture Notes in Computer Science], Alexander F. Gelbukh (ed.), 171–89. Berlin: Springer.

Martin, James R. & Rose, David. 2008. *Genre Relations: Mapping Culture* [Equinox Textbooks and Surveys in Linguistics]. London: Equinox.

doi Martin, James R. 2009. Genre and language learning: A social semiotic perspective. *Linguistics and Education* 20(1): 10–21.

doi Martinez, Ron & Schmitt, Norbert. 2012. A phrasal expressions list. *Applied Linguistics* 33(3): 299–320.

doi Matthiessen, Christian M.I.M. 2019. Register in systemic functional linguistics. *Register Studies* 1(1): 10–41.

doi Mauranen, Anna. 2003. The corpus of English as lingua franca in academic settings. *TESOL Quarterly* 37(3): 513–527.

doi Mauranen, Anna. 2004a. Speech corpora in the classroom. In *Corpora and Language Learners* [Studies in Corpus Linguistics 17], Guy Aston, Silvia Bernardini & Dominic Stewart (eds), 195–211. Amsterdam: John Benjamins.

doi Mauranen, Anna. 2004b. Spoken – General. Spoken corpus for an ordinary learner. In *How to Use Corpora in Language Teaching* [Studies in Corpus Linguistics 12], John McH. Sinclair (ed.), 89–108. Amsterdam: John Benjamins.

doi Mauranen, Anna, Hynninen, Niina & Ranta, Elina. 2010. English as an academic lingua franca: The ELFA project. *English for Specific Purposes* 29(3): 183–90.

Mayring, Philipp. 2010. *Qualitative Inhaltsanalyse: Grundlagen und Techniken* [Beltz Pädagogik]. Weinheim: Beltz.

McCarthy, Michael. 1998. *Spoken Language and Applied Linguistics*. Cambridge: CUP.

doi McCarthy, Michael & Carter, Ronald. 1995. Spoken grammar: What is it and how can we teach it? *ELT journal* 49(3): 207–218.

doi McCarthy, Michael & Carter, Ronald. 2001. Size isn't everything: Spoken English, corpus, and the classroom. *Tesol Quarterly* 35(2): 337–340.

McCarthy, Michael, McCarten, Jeanne & Sandiford, Helen. 2005. *Touchstone*. First edition. Cambridge: CUP.

doi McEnery, Tony & Hardie, Andrew. 2011. *Corpus Linguistics: Method, Theory and Practice*. Cambridge: CUP.

McEnery, Tony & Xiao, Richard. 2011. What corpora can offer in language teaching and learning. In *Handbook of Research in Second Language Teaching and Learning* [ESL & Applied Linguistics Professional Series], Eli Hinkel (ed.), 364–380. New York, NY: Routledge.

doi McManus, Kevin. In press. Replication and open science in applied linguistics Research. In *Open Science in Applied Linguistics*, Luke Plonsky (ed.). ⟨Preprint: https://osf.io/bqr9w/⟩ (29 October 2021).

doi Meunier, Fanny & Gouverneur, Céline. 2007. The treatment of phraseology in ELT textbooks. In *Corpora in the Foreign Language Classroom*, Encarnación Hidalgo, Luis Quereda & Juan Santana (eds), 119–139. Amsterdam: Rodopi.

doi Meunier, Fanny & Gouverneur, Céline. 2009. New types of corpora for new educational challenges: Collecting, annotating and exploiting a corpus of textbook material. In *Corpora and Language Teaching* [Studies in Corpus Linguistics 33], Karin Aijmer (ed.), 179–201. Amsterdam: John Benjamins,

doi Meunier, Fanny & Reppen, Randi. 2015. Corpus versus non-corpus-informed pedagogical materials: Grammar as the focus. In *The Cambridge Handbook of English Corpus Linguistics* [Cambridge Handbooks in Language and Linguistics], Douglas Biber & Randi Reppen (eds), 498–514. Cambridge: CUP.

doi Meurers, Detmar. 2015. Learner corpora and natural language processing. In *The Cambridge Handbook of Learner Corpus Research*, Sylviane Granger, Gaetanelle Gilquin & Fanny Meunier (eds), 537–566. Cambridge: CUP.

doi Meurers, Detmar, De Kuthy, Kordula, Nuxoll, Florian, Rudzewitz, Björn & Ziai, Ramon. 2019. Scaling up intervention studies to investigate real-life foreign language learning in school. *Annual Review of Applied Linguistics* 39: 161–188.

Meurers, Detmar, Ziai, Ramon, Amaral, Luiz, Boyd, Adriane, Dimitrov, Aleksandar, Metcalf, Vanessa & Ott, Niels. 2010. Enhancing authentic web pages for language learners. In *Proceedings of the 5th Workshop on Innovative Use of NLP for Building Educational Applications*, 9. Los Angeles, CA. ⟨http://www.sfs.uni-tuebingen.de/~dm/papers/meurers-ziai-et-al-10.pdf⟩ (21 January 2022).

Miekley, Joshua. 2005. ESL textbook evaluation checklist. *The Reading Matrix* 5(2).

doi Miller, Don. 2011. ESL reading textbooks vs. university textbooks: Are we giving our students the input they may need? *Journal of English for Academic Purposes* 10(1): 32–46.

doi Milroy, James & Milroy, Lesley. 2012. *Authority in Language: Investigating Standard English* [Routledge Linguistics Classics]. New York, NY: Routledge.

Mindt, Dieter. 1987. *Sprache, Grammatik, Unterrichtsgrammatik: Futurischer Zeitbezug im Englischen* [Schule und Forschung]. Frankfurt: Diesterweg.

Mindt, Dieter. 1992. *Zeitbezug im Englischen: Eine didaktische Grammatik des Englischen Futurs* [Tübinger Beiträge Zur Linguistik]. Tübingen: Gunter Narr.

Mindt, Dieter. 1995a. *An Empirical Grammar of the English Verb: Modal Verbs*. Berlin: Cornelsen.

Mindt, Dieter. 1995b. Schulgrammatik vs. Grammatik der englischen Sprache. In *Perspektiven des Grammatikunterrichts*, Claus Gnutzmann & Frank G. Königs (eds), 47–68. Tübingen: Gunter Narr.

Mindt, Dieter. 1996. English corpus linguistics and the foreign language teaching syllabus. In *Using Corpora for Language Research*, Jenny Thomas & Mick Short (eds), 232–247. Harlow: Longman.

Mindt, Dieter. 1997. Corpora and the teaching of English in Germany. In *Teaching and Language Corpora* [Applied Linguistics and Language Study], Anne Wichmann (ed.), 40–50. London: Longman.

Mishan, F. 2005. *Designing Authenticity into Language Learning Materials* [Play Text Series]. Portland, OR: Intellect Books.

doi Mishra, Punya & Koehler, Matthew J. 2006. Technological pedagogical content knowledge: A framework for teacher knowledge. *Teachers College Record* 108(6): 1017–1054.

doi Mizumoto, Atsushi & Plonsky, Luke. 2016. R as a lingua franca: Advantages of using R for quantitative research in applied linguistics. *Applied Linguistics* 37(2): 284–291.

doi Mohr, Susanne, Jansen, Sandra & Forsberg, Julia. 2019. European English in the EFL classroom? Teacher attitudes towards target varieties of English in Sweden and Germany. *English Today*, 37(2): 85–91.

Möller, Stefan. 2016. Sourcebook rather than coursebook. Lernerorientiert mit dem Lehrwerk arbeiten. *Der fremdsprachliche Unterricht Englisch* 50(143): 12–18.

Möller, Verena. 2017. A statistical analysis of learner corpus data, experimental data and individual differences: Monofactorial vs. multifactorial approaches. In *Language, Learners and Levels: Progression and Variation*, Pieter de Haan, Rina de Vries & Sanne van Vuuren (eds), 409–439. Louvain-la-Neuve: Presses Universitaires de Louvain.

doi Möller, Verena. 2020. From pedagogical input to learner output: Conditionals in EFL and CLIL teaching materials and learner language. *Pedagogical Linguistics* 1(2): 95–124,

doi Moreno, Ana I. 2003. Matching theoretical descriptions of discourse and practical applications to teaching: The case of causal metatext. *English for Specific Purposes* 22(3): 265–295.

doi Moyer, Alene. 2008. Input as a critical means to an end: Quantity and quality of experience in L2 phonological attainment. In *Input Matters in SLA*, Thorsten Piske & Martha Young-Scholten (eds), 159–174. Multilingual Matters.

doi Moyer, Alene. 2013. *Foreign Accent: The Phenomenon of Non-Native Speech*. Cambridge: CUP.

doi Mukherjee, Joybrato. 2004. Bridging the gap between applied corpus linguistics and the reality of English language teaching in Germany. In *Applied Corpus Linguistics: A Multidimensional Perspective*, Ulla Connor & Thomas Upton (eds), 239–250. Amsterdam: Rodopi.

Mukundan, Jayakaran. 2010. Retrotext- E 1.0: The beginnings of computer-based ELT textbook evaluation. *Advances in Language and Literary Studies* 1(2): 270–280.

Mukundan, Jayakaran & Ahour, Touran. 2010. A review of textbook evaluation checklists across four decades (1970–2008). In *Research for Materials Development in Language Learning: Evidence for Best Practice*, Brian Tomlinson & Hitomi Masuhara (eds), 336–352. London: Bloomsbury.

doi Mukundan, Jayakaran, Leong Chiew Har, Amelia & Nimehchisalem, Vahid. 2012. Distribution of articles in Malaysian secondary school English language textbooks. *English Language and Literature Studies* 2(2): 62–70.

doi Mukundan, Jayakaran & Roslim, Norwati. 2009. Textbook representation of prepositions. *English Language Teaching* 2(4): 13–24.

Müller, Simone. 2005. *Discourse Markers in Native and Non-Native English Discourse* [Pragmatics & Beyond New Series 138]. Amsterdam: John Benjamins.

Mundry, Roger & Sommer, Christina. 2007. Discriminant function analysis with nonindependent data: Consequences and an alternative. *Animal Behaviour* 74(4): 965–976.

Munro, Murray J. & Derwing, Tracey M. 1998. The effects of speaking rate on listener evaluations of native and foreign-accented speech. *Language Learning* 48(2): 159–182.

Murphy, M. Lynne. 2003. *Semantic Relations and the Lexicon: Antonymy, Synonymy and Other Paradigms*. Cambridge: CUP.

Nakagawa, Shinichi, Johnson, Paul C. D. & Schielzeth, Holger. 2017. The coefficient of determination R^2 and intra-class correlation coefficient from generalized linear mixed-effects models revisited and expanded. *Journal of The Royal Society Interface* 14(134): 20170213.

Nelson, Mike. 2022. Corpora for English Language Learning Textbook Evaluation. In *The Routledge Handbook of Corpora and English Language Teaching and Learning* [Routledge Handbooks in Applied Linguistics], Reka R. Jablonkai & Eniko Csomay (eds). London: Routledge.

Nesselhauf, Nadja. 2005. *Collocations in a Learner Corpus* [Studies in Corpus Linguistics 14]. Amsterdam: John Benjamins.

Neumann, Stella & Evert, Stefan. 2021. A register variation perspective on varieties of English. In *Corpus-based Approaches to Register Variation* [Studies in Corpus Linguistics 103], Elena Seoane & Douglas Biber (eds), 144–78. Amsterdam: John Benjamins.

Nini, Andrea. 2014. Multidimensional Analysis Tagger (MAT), ⟨http://sites.google.com/site/multidimensionaltagger⟩ (18 September 2019).

Nini, Andrea. 2019. The multi-dimensional analysis tagger. In *Multi-Dimensional Analysis: Research Methods and Current Issues*, Tony Berber Sardinha & Marcia Veirano Pinto (eds), 67–96. London: Bloomsbury.

Ninio, Anat. 1999. Pathbreaking verbs in syntactic development and the question of prototypical transitivity. *Journal of Child Language* 26(3): 619–653.

Nold, Günter. 1998. Die Arbeit mit dem Lehrwerk. In *English lernen und lehren – Didaktik des Englischunterrichts*, Johannes P. Timm (ed.), 127–36. Berlin: Cornelsen.

Nordlund, Marie. 2016. EFL textbooks for young learners: A comparative analysis of vocabulary. *Education Inquiry* 7(1): 47–68.

Novakova, Iva & Siepmann, Dirk (eds). 2020. *Phraseology and Style in Subgenres of the Novel: A Synthesis of Corpus and Literary Perspectives*. Cham: Springer.

OECD, European Union, UNESCO Institute for Statistics. 2015. *ISCED 2011 Operational Manua: Guidelines for Classifying National Education Programmes and Related Qualifications*. Paris: OECD Publishing.

Oelkers, Jürgen. 2008. Lehrplanentwicklung, Lehrmittel und Bildungsstandards. presented at the Klausurtagung der Leitungskonferenz des Staatsinstituts für Schulentwicklung und Bildungsforschung, St. Quirin. ⟨https://www.ife.uzh.ch/research/emeriti/oelkersjuergen/vortraegeprofoelkers/vortraege2008/339_StQuirin.pdf⟩ (8 February 2022).

O'Keeffe, Anne, McCarthy, Michael & Carter, Ronald. 2007. *From Corpus to Classroom: Language Use and Language Teaching*. Cambridge: CUP.

Osborne, Jason W. & Fitzpatrick, David C. 2005. Replication analysis in exploratory factor analysis: What it is and why it makes your analysis better. *Practical Assessment, Research, and Evaluation* 17(7): 1–9.

Papert, Seymour A. 2020. *Mindstorms: Children, Computers, and Powerful Ideas.* New York, NY: Hachette.

Paquot, Magali & Plonsky, Luke. 2017. Quantitative research methods and study quality in learner corpus research. *International Journal of Learner Corpus Research* 3(1): 61–94.

Parsons, Sam, Azevedo, Flávio, Elsherif, Mahmoud M., Guay, Samuel, Shahim, Owen N., Govaart, Gisela H., Norris, Emma et al. 2022. A community-sourced glossary of open scholarship terms. *Nature Human Behaviour* 6(3): 312–318.

Peacock, Matthew. 1997. The effect of authentic materials on the motivation of EFL learners. *ELT Journal* 51(2): 144–156.

Pérez-Paredes, Pascual & Abad, Malena. Forthcoming. Integrating language teachers' voices in the design and exploitation of Spanish corpora in the UK. In *Applying Corpora in Teaching and Learning Romance Languages*, Henry Tyne & Stefania Spina (eds). Amsterdam: John Benjamins.

Pérez-Paredes, Pascual & Mark, Geraldine (eds). 2021. *Beyond Concordance Lines: Corpora in Language Education* [Studies in Corpus Linguistics 102]. Amsterdam: John Benjamins.

Pérez-Paredes, Pascual, Mark, Geraldine & O'Keeffe, Anne. 2020. The impact of usage-based approaches on second language learning and teaching [Cambridge Education Research Reports]. Cambridge: CUP. ⟨https://www.cambridge.org/partnership/research/impact-usage-based-approaches-second-language-learning-and-teaching⟩ (9 July 2021).

Phakiti, Aek & Plonsky, Luke. 2018. Reconciling beliefs about L2 learning with SLA theory and research. *RELC Journal* 49(2): 217–237.

Piaget, Jean. 2013. *The Construction of Reality in the Child.* Oxon: Taylor & Francis.

Picoral, Adriana, Staples, Shelley & Reppen, Randi. 2021. Automated annotation of learner English: An evaluation of software tools. *International Journal of Learner Corpus Research* 7(1): 17–52.

Pienemann, Manfred. 1984. Psychological constraints on the teachability of languages. *Studies in Second Language Acquisition* 6(2): 186–214.

Popescu, Marius. 2011. Studying translationese at the character level. In *Proceedings of Recent Advances in Natural Language Processing*, 634–639. Hissar, Bulgaria.

Porte, Graeme & McManus, Kevin. 2018. *Doing Replication Research in Applied Linguistics.* Routledge.

Posner, Michael I. & Keele, Steven W. 1968. On the genesis of abstract ideas. *Journal of Experimental Psychology* 77(3, Pt.1): 353–363.

Posner, Michael I. & Keele, Steven W. 1970. Retention of abstract ideas. *Journal of Experimental Psychology* 83(2, Pt. 1): 304–308.

Prabhu, Nagore Seshagiri. 1989. Materials as support; Materials as constraint. *Guidelines: A Periodical for Classroom Language Teachers* 11(1): 66–74.

Prodromou, Luke. 1992. What culture? Which culture? Cross-cultural factors in language learning. *ELT journal* 46(1): 39–50.

Prodromou, Luke. 1996. Correspondence. *ELT Journal* 50(1): 88–89.

Prodromou, Luke. 2003. In search of the successful user of English How a corpus of non-native speaker language could impact on EFL teaching. *Modern English Teacher* 12(2): 5–15.

Prowse, Philip. 1998. How writers write: Testimony from authors. In *Materials Development in Language Teaching*, Brian Tomlinson (ed.), 130–145. Cambridge: CUP.

Quaglio, Paulo. 2009. *Television Dialogue: The Sitcom* Friends *vs. Natural Conversation* [Studies in Corpus Linguistics 36]. Amsterdam: John Benjamins.

Quirk, Randolph. 1995. *Grammatical and Lexical Variance in English*. London: Routledge.

Quirk, Randolph, Greenbaum, Sidney, Leech, Geoffrey & Svartvik, Jan. 1985. *A Comprehensive Grammar of the English Language*. London: Longman.

R Core Team. 2022. R: A Language and Environment for Statistical Computing. *Manual.* Vienna, Austria: R Foundation for Statistical Computing. ⟨https://www.R-project.org/⟩ (29 January 2021).

Ramjattan, Vijay A. 2019. The white native speaker and inequality regimes in the private English language school. *Intercultural Education* 30(2): 126–140.

Ranalli, James M. 2003. The treatment of key vocabulary learning strategies in current ELT course books: Repetition, resource use, recording. MA thesis, University of Birmingham. ⟨http://www.birmingham.ac.uk/documents/college-artslaw/cels/essays/matefltesldissertations/ranallidiss.pdf⟩ (10 August 2017).

Rankin, Tom. 2010. Advanced learner corpus data and grammar teaching: Adverb placement. In *Corpus-Based Approaches to English Language Teaching*, Mari Carmen Campoy Cubillo, Begoña Bellés-Fortuño & Maria Lluïsa Gea-Valor (eds), 205–2015. London: Continuum.

Rasch, Björn, Friese, Malte, Hofmann, Wilhelm & Naumann, Ewald. 2014. Einfaktorielle Varianzanalyse. In *Quantitative Methoden, 2: Einführung in die Statistik für Psychologen und Sozialwissenschaftler* [Springer-Lehrbuch], Björn Rasch, Malte Friese, Wilhelm Hofmann & Ewald Naumann (eds), 1–34. Berlin: Springer.

Rautionaho, Paula & Deshors, Sandra C. 2018. Progressive or not progressive? Modeling the constructional choices of EFL and ESL writers. *International Journal of Learner Corpus Research* 4(2): 225–252.

Reda, Ghsoon. 2003. English coursebooks: Prototype texts and basic vocabulary norms. *ELT Journal* 57(3): 260–268.

Reder, Stephen, Harris, Kathryn & Setzler, Kristen. 2003. The multimedia adult ESL learner corpus. *TESOL Quarterly* 37(3): 546–557.

Reinders, Hayo & Ellis, Rod. 2009. The effects of two types of input on intake and the acquisition of implicit and explicit knowledge. In *Implicit and Explicit Knowledge in Second Language Learning, Testing and Teaching*, Rod Ellis, Shawn Loewen, Catherine Elder, Hayo Reinders, Rosemary Erlam & Jenefer Philp (eds), 281–302. Bristol: Multilingual Matters.

Reppen, Randi. 1994. Variation in Elementary Student Writing. PhD dissertation, Northern Arizona University.

Reppen, Randi. (2001) 2013. Register variation in student and adult speech and writing. In *Variation in English: Multi-dimensional Studies*, Susan Conrad & Douglas Biber (eds), 187–99. New York, NY: Routledge.

Revelle, William. 2020. *psych: Procedures for psychological, psychometric, and personality research*. Evanston, IL. ⟨https://CRAN.R-project.org/package=psych⟩ (20 April 2021).

doi Révész, Andrea & Brunfaut, Tineke. 2013. Text characteristics of task input and difficulty in second language listening comprehension. *Studies in Second Language Acquisition* 35(1): 31–65.

doi Richards, Jack C. 2001. *Curriculum Development in Language Teaching*. Cambridge: CUP.

doi Richards, Jack C. 2015. *Key Issues in Language Teaching*. Cambridge: CUP.

Richardson, Leonard. 2015. Beautiful Soup 4.4.0 documentation, 2015. ⟨https://beautiful-soup-4.readthedocs.io/en/latest/⟩ (7 January 2022).

doi Roberts, Celia & Cooke, Melanie. 2009. Authenticity in the adult ESOL classroom and beyond. *TESOL Quarterly* 43(4): 620–642.

doi Robinson, Peter J. & Ellis, Nick C. (eds). 2008. *Handbook of Cognitive Linguistics and Second Language Acquisition*. New York, NY: Routledge.

Rohleder, Bernhard. 2019. Smart school – Auf dem Weg zur digitalen Schule. presented at the Bitkom Research GmbH, Berlin, March 12. ⟨https://www.bitkom.org/sites/default/files/2019-03/Pr%C3%A4sentation%20Bitkom-PK%20Bildungskonferenz%2012.03.2019_final.pdf⟩ (29 September 2020).

doi Römer, Ute. 2004a. A corpus-driven approach to modal auxiliaries and their didactics. In *How to Use Corpora in Language Teaching* [Studies in Corpus Linguistics 12], John McH. Sinclair (ed.), 185–99. Amsterdam: John Benjamins.

doi Römer, Ute. 2004b. Comparing real and ideal language learner input: The use of an EFL textbook corpus in corpus linguistics and language teaching. In *Corpora and Language Learners* [Studies in Corpus Linguistics 17], Guy Aston, Silvia Bernardini & Dominic Stewart (eds), 151–168. Amsterdam: John Benjamins.

doi Römer, Ute. 2005. *Progressives, Patterns, Pedagogy: A Corpus-Driven Approach to English Progressive Forms, Functions, Contexts, and Didactics* [Studies in Corpus Linguistics 18]. Amsterdam: John Benjamins.

doi Römer, Ute. 2006. Pedagogical applications of corpora: Some reflections on the current scope and a wish list for future developments. *Zeitschrift für Anglistik und Amerikanistik* 54(2): 121–34.

Römer, Ute. 2007. Learner language and the norms in native corpora and EFL teaching materials: A case study of English conditionals. In *Proceedings of the Anglistentag 2006*, Sabine Volk-Birke & Julia Lippert (eds), 355–363. Trier: Wissenschaftlicher Verlag Trier.

Römer, Ute. 2010. Using general and specialized corpora in English language teaching: Past, present and future. In Mari Carmen Campoy Cubillo, Begoña Bellés Fortuño & Maria Lluïsa Gea-Valor (eds.), *Corpus-based approaches to English language teaching*, 18–38. London: Continuum.

doi Römer, Ute & Berger, Cynthia M. 2019. Observing the emergence of constructional knowledge: Verb patterns in German and Spanish learners of English at different proficiency levels. *Studies in Second Language Acquisition* 41(5): 1089–1111.

Rose, David & Martin, James R. 2012. *Learning to Write, Reading to Learn: Genre, Knowledge and Pedagogy in the Sydney School*. London: Equinox.

doi Rösler, Dietmar & Schart, Michael. 2016. Die Perspektivenvielfalt der Lehrwerkanalyse und ihr weißer Fleck: Einführung in zwei Themenhefte. *Info DaF* 5(43): 483–493.

Rühlemann, Christoph. 2008. A register approach to teaching conversation: Farewell to standard English? *Applied Linguistics* 29(4): 672–693.

Rundell, Michael. 2008. The corpus revolution revisited. *English Today* 24(1): 23–27.

Runte, Maren. 2015. *Lernerlexikographie und Wortschatzerwerb*. Berlin: Walter de Gruyter.

Rüschoff, Bernd & Wolff, Dieter. 1999. *Fremdsprachenlernen in der Wissensgesellschaft: zum Einsatz der neuen Technologien in Schule und Unterricht*. Munich: Hueber Verlag.

Scales, Julie, Wennerstrom, Ann, Richard, Dara & Wu, Su Hui. 2006. Language learners' perceptions of accent. *TESOL Quarterly* 40(4): 715.

Schaer, Ursula. 2007. Source books rather than course books – Die Bildungsreform im Fremdsprachenunterricht und die neue Rolle für die Lehr-mittel. *Beiträge zur Lehrerbildung* 25(2): 255–267.

Schäfer, Werner. 2003. Unterrichten ohne Lehrbuch? Einige unzeitgemäße Bemerkungen. *Praxis des neusprachlichen Unterrichts* 50(3): 305–311.

Schauer, Gila A. & Adolphs, Svenja. 2006. Expressions of gratitude in corpus and DCT data: Vocabulary, formulaic sequences, and pedagogy. *System* 34(1): 119–134.

Schegloff, Emanuel A. 1993. Reflections on quantification in the study of conversation. *Research on Language & Social Interaction* 26(1): 99–128.

Scheiwe, Lisa. 2022. Evaluating accents of English in ELT textbooks used at German secondary schools. *Anglistik* 33(2): 61–75.

Schildhauer, Peter, Schulte, Marion & Zehne, Carolin. 2020. Global Englishes in the classroom. *PFLB. Zeitschrift für Schul- und Professionsentwicklung* 2(4): 26–40.

Schlüter, Norbert. 2002. *Present Perfect: Eine Korpuslinguistische Analyse des Englischen Perfekts mit Vermittlungsvorschlägen für den Sprachunterricht* [Language in Performance 25]. Tübingen: Narr.

Schönbrodt, Felix D. 2016. *p*-hacker: Train your *p*-hacking skills! ⟨https://shinyapps.org/apps/p-hacker/⟩ (28 January 2022).

Schweinberger, Martin. 2020. Best practices in corpus linguistics. Presented at the ICAME41, Heidelberg University, May. ⟨http://martinschweinberger.de/docs/ppt/schweinberger-ppt-heidelberg-2020-05-21.pdf⟩ (26 July 2021).

Scott, Mike. 2011. *WordSmith Tools*. Stroud: Lexical Analysis Software.

Segermann, Krista. 2000. Eine neue Lehrwerk-Konzeption: Lehrbuch für Lehrer–Lernmaterialien für Schüler. *Praxis des neusprachlichen Unterrichts* 47(4): 339–348.

Seidlhofer, Barbara. 2001. Closing a conceptual gap: The case for a description of English as a lingua franca. *International Journal of Applied Linguistics* 11(2): 133–158.

Séré, Alain & Bassy, Alain-Marie. 2010. Le manuel scolaire à l'heure du numérique : Une 'nouvelle donne' de la politique de ressources pour l'enseignement. n° 2010-087. Inspection générale de l'éducation nationale. ⟨https://www.education.gouv.fr/le-manuel-scolaire-l-heure-du-numerique-1310⟩ (6 January 2022).

Siegel, A. 2014. What should we talk about? The authenticity of textbook topics. *ELT Journal* 68(4): 363–375.

Siepmann, Dirk. 2004. *Discourse Markers across Languages: A Contrastive Study of Second-Level Discourse Markers in Native and Non-Native Text with Implications for General and Pedagogic Lexicography*. London: Routledge.

Siepmann, Dirk. 2007. Wortschatz und Grammatik: Zusammenbringen, was zusammengehört. *Beiträge zur Fremdsprachenvermittlung* 46: 59–80.

Siepmann, Dirk. 2011. Any chance of a bloody drink sometime this century? Generische Strukturen einer Gesprächssituation analysieren. *Der fremdsprachliche Unterricht Englisch* 45(114): 22–26.

Siepmann, Dirk. 2014. Zur Repräsentation von Mehrwortausdrücken in deutschen Lehrwerken des Englischen. In *Sprachwissenschaft und Fremdsprachenunterricht: Spracherwerb und Sprachkompetenzen im Fokus*, Dirk Siepmann & Christoph Bürgel (eds). Baltmannsweiler: Schneider Verlag Hohengehren.

Siepmann, Dirk. 2018a. *A Grammar of Spoken and Written French*, Vol. 5: *Prepositions*. Leipzig: Independently published.

Siepmann, Dirk. 2018b. Zum Verhältnis von Fachwissenschaften, Fachdidaktik und Sprachpraxis in der universitären Lehrerausbildung: Theoretische Überlegungen und Anregungen für eine kohärentere Praxis. In *Universitäre Englischlehrerbildung: Wege zu mehr Kohärenz im Studium und Korrespondenz mit der Praxis*, Bärbel Diehr (ed.), 103–121. Berlin: Peter Lang.

Siepmann, Dirk. 2019. *Grammatik des gesprochenen und geschriebenen Französisch*, Bd. 3: *Das Adjektiv*. Leipzig: Amazon Distribution.

Siepmann, Dirk & Bürgel, Christoph. 2022. *Band 2: Das Nomen* [Grammatik des gesprochenen und geschriebenen Französisch]. Leipzig: Independently published.

doi Siepmann, Dirk, Gallagher, John D., Hannay, Mike & Mackenzie, J. Lachlan. 2011. *Writing in English: A Guide for Advanced Learners*, 2nd, rev. & ext. edn. Tübingen: Francke.

doi Sigley, Robert J. 1997. Text categories and where you can stick them: A crude formality index. *International Journal of Corpus Linguistics* 2(2): 199–237.

doi Simmons, Joseph P., Nelson, Leif D. & Simonsohn, Uri. 2011. False-positive psychology: Undisclosed flexibility in data collection and analysis allows presenting anything as significant. *Psychological Science* 22(11): 1359–1366.

Sinclair, John McH. 1983. Naturalness in language. In *Corpus Linguistics: Recent Developments in the Use of Computer Corpora in English Language Research* [Costerus 45], Jan Aarts & Willem Meijs (eds), 203–210. Amsterdam: Rodopi.

Sinclair, John McH. 1991. *Corpus, Concordance, Collocation*. Oxford: OUP.

doi Sinclair, John McH. 1992. The automatic analysis of corpora. In *Directions in Corpus Linguistics*, Jan Svartvik (ed.), 379–400. Berlin: De Gruyter Mouton.

doi Sinclair, John McH. (ed.). 2004. *How to Use Corpora in Language Teaching* [Studies in Corpus Linguistics 12]. Amsterdam: John Benjamins.

Sinclair, John McH., Fox, Gwyneth, Bullon, Stephen, Krishnamurthy, Ramesh, Manning, Elisabeth & Todd, John (eds). 1990. *Collins Cobuild English Grammar: Helping Learners with Real English*. Glasgow: Harper Collins.

Sinclair, John McH. & Renouf, Antoinette. 1988. A lexical syllabus for language learning. In *Vocabulary and Language Teaching*, Ronald Carter & Michael McCarthy (eds), 140–158. Harlow: Longman.

Singapore Wala, Duriya Aziz. 2013. The instructional design of a coursebook is as it is because of what it has to oo–An application of systemic functional theory. In *Developing Materials for Language Teaching*, Brian Tomlinson (ed), 2nd edn, 119–138. London: Bloomsbury.

Skehan, Peter. 2014. *Individual Differences in Second-Language Learning*. London: Routledge.

Smith, Christopher Arnold. 2020. A Triangulated Accounting of Top Notch 2: Negotiating Ideologies in the Multimodal Discourse of an EFL Textbook in Korean University Classrooms. PhD dissertation, Carleton University. ⟨https://curve.carleton.ca/00125d56-bc4c-4500-ab9a-d1fd4d8ccc02⟩ (13 February 2022).

Sommer, Roy. 2020. Lehrerbildung aus fachwissenschaftlicher Perspektive: Beispiel Anglistik. In *Die Stimmen der Fächer hören: Fachprofil und Bildungsanspruch in der Lehrerbildung*, Michaela Heer & Ulrich Heinen (eds), 307–324. Paderborn: Ferdinand Schöningh.

Spada, Nina & Lightbown, Patsy M. 1999. Instruction, first language influence, and developmental readiness in second language acquisition. *The Modern Language Journal* 83(1): 1–22.

Spoustová, Drahomíra, Hajič, Jan, Raab, Jan & Spousta, Miroslav. 2009. Semi-supervised training for the averaged perceptron POS tagger. In *Proceedings of the 12th Conference of the European Chapter of the Association for Computational Linguistics on – EACL '09*, 763–771. Athens, Greece: Association for Computational Linguistics.

Spring, Ryan. 2018. Teaching phrasal verbs more efficiently: Using corpus studies and cognitive linguistics to create a particle list. *Advances in Language and Literary Studies* 9(5): 121–135.

Starkey, Louise, Shonfeld, Miri, Prestridge, Sarah & Cervera, Mercè Gisbert. 2021. Special issue: *Covid-19 and the Role of Technology and Pedagogy on School Education during a Pandemic. Technology, Pedagogy and Education* 30(1): 1–5.

Stefanowitsch, Anatol. 2020. *Corpus Linguistics: A Guide to the Methodology* [Textbooks in Language Science 7]. Berlin: Language Science Press.

Stein, Marcy, Stuen, Carol, Carnine, Douglas & Long, Roger M. 2001. Textbook evaluation and adoption. *Reading & Writing Quarterly* 17(1): 5–23.

Stranks, Jeff. 2013. Materials for the teaching of grammar. In *Developing Materials for Language Teaching*, 2nd edn, 337–350. London: Bloomsbury.

Sun, Zhuomin. 2010. Language teaching materials and learner motivation. *Journal of Language Teaching and Research* 1(6): 889–892.

Swaffar, Janet K. 1985. Reading authentic texts in a foreign language: A cognitive model. *The Modern Language Journal* 69(1): 15–34.

Syndicat national de l'édition. 2021. Chiffres clés de l'édition. *Syndicat national de l'édition*, 21 July 2021. ⟨https://www.sne.fr/economie/chiffres-cles/⟩ (2 January 2022).

Tabachnick, Barbara G. & Fidell, Linda S. 2014. *Using Multivariate Statistics* [Always Learning]. 6th edn. Harlow: Pearson.

Tan, Melinda. 2003. Language corpora for language teachers. *Journal of Language and Learning* 1(2): 98–105.

Tateyama, Yumiko. 2019. Pragmatics in a language classroom. In *The Routledge Handbook of Second Language Acquisition and Pragmatics*, Naoko Taguchi (ed.), 400–413. London: Routledge.

Taylor, Charlotte. 2008. What is corpus linguistics? What the data says. *ICAME Journal* 32: 179–200.

Tesch, Felicitas. 1990. *Die Indefinitpronomina Some und Any im Authentischen Englischen Sprachgebrauch und in Lehrwerken: Eine Empirische Untersuchung* [Tübinger Beiträge zur Linguistik 345]. Tübingen: Gunter Narr.

Thompson, Paul, Hunston, Susan, Murakami, Akira & Vajn, Dominik. 2017. Multi-dimensional analysis, text constellations, and interdisciplinary discourse. *International Journal of Corpus Linguistics* 22(2): 153–186.

Thompson, Paul & Sealey, Alison. 2007. Through children's eyes? Corpus evidence of the features of children's literature. *International Journal of Corpus Linguistics* 12(1): 1–23.

Thornbury, Scott. 2000. Plenary: Deconstructing grammar. In *IATEFL 2000: Dublin Conference Selections*, Alan Pulverness (ed.), 59–67. Faversham: IATEFL.

Thornbury, Scott. 2002. Training in instructional conversation. In *Language in Language Teacher Education* [Language Learning & Language Teaching 4], Hugh Trappes-Lomax & Gibson Ferguson (eds), 95–106. Amsterdam: John Benjamins.

Timmis, Ivor. 2003. Corpora, Classroom and Context: The Place of Spoken Grammar in English Language Teaching. PhD dissertation, University of Nottingham.

Timmis, Ivor. 2013. Corpora and materials: Towards a working relationship. In *Developing Materials for Language Teaching*, Brian Tomlinson (ed.), 2nd edn, 461–474. London: Bloomsbury.

Timmis, Ivor. 2015. *Corpus Linguistics for ELT: Research and Practice* [Routledge Corpus Linguistics Guides]. London: Routledge.

Timmis, Ivor. 2016. Humanising coursebook dialogues. *Innovation in Language Learning and Teaching* 10(2): 144–153.

Tognini-Bonelli, Elena. 2001. *Corpus Linguistics at Work* [Studies in Corpus Linguistics 6]. Amsterdam: John Benjamins.

Tomasello, Michael. 2005. *Constructing a Language: A Usage-Based Theory of Language Acquisition*. Cambridge, MA: Harvard University Press.

Tomlinson, Brian. 2001. Materials development. In *The Cambridge Guide to Teaching English to Speakers of Other Languages*, David Nunan & Ronald Carter (eds), 66–71. Cambridge: CUP.

Tomlinson, Brian (ed.). 2008. *English Language Learning Materials: A Critical Review*. London: Continuum.

Tomlinson, Brian. 2012. Materials development for language learning and teaching. *Language Teaching* 45(2): 143–179.

Tomlinson, Brian (ed.). 2013a. *Applied Linguistics and Materials Development*. London: Bloomsbury.

Tomlinson, Brian (ed.). 2013b. *Developing Materials for Language Teaching*. 2nd edn. London: Bloomsbury.

Tomlinson, Brian, Dat, Bao, Masuhara, Hitomi & Rugdy, Rani. 2001. Survey review. EFL courses for adults. *ELT Journal* 55(1): 80–101.

Tono, Yukio. 2004. Multiple comparisons of IL, L1 and TL corpora: The case of L2 acquisition of verb subcategorization patterns by Japanese learners of English. In *Corpora and Language Learners* [Studies in Corpus Linguistics 17], Guy Aston, Silvia Bernardini & Dominic Stewart (eds), 45–66. Amsterdam: John Benjamins,

Tony, Bex. 1999. *Standard English: The Widening Debate*. Hove: Psychology Press.

Torres-Martínez, Sergio. 2019. *Applied Cognitive Construction Grammar: A Cognitive Guide to the Teaching of Phrasal Verbs*. Medellín: Lulu.com.

Toutanova, Kristina, Klein, Dan, Manning, Christopher D. & Singer, Yoram. 2003. Feature-rich part-of-speech tagging with a cyclic dependency network. In *Proceedings of the 2003 Conference of the North American Chapter of the Association for Computational Linguistics on Human Language Technology*, Vol. 1, 173–80. Stroudsburg, PA: Association for Computational Linguistics.

Toutanova, Kristina & Manning, Christopher D. 2000. Enriching the knowledge sources used in a maximum entropy part-of-speech tagger. In *Proceedings of the 2000 Joint SIGDAT Conference on Empirical Methods in Natural Language Processing and Very Large Corpora Held in Conjunction with the 38th Annual Meeting of the Association for Computational Linguistics*, Vol. 13, 63–70. Hong Kong: Association for Computational Linguistics,

Trabelsi, Soufiane, Tomlinson, Brian & Masuhara, Hitomi. 2010. Developing and trialling authentic materials for business English students at a Tunisian university. In *Research for Materials Development in Language Learning: Evidence for Best Practice*, Brian Tomlinson & Hitomi Masuhara (eds), 103–120. London: Bloomsbury.

Tracy-Ventura, Nicole & Paquot, Magali. 2020. *The Routledge Handbook of Second Language Acquisition and Corpora*. London: Routledge.

Tsaroucha, Efthymia. 2018. A Cognitive Linguistics Approach to English Phrasal Verbs. PhD dissertation, Aristotle University of Thessaloniki. ⟨http://ikee.lib.auth.gr/record/299055⟩ (14 April 2024).

Tyler, Andrea. 2012. *Cognitive Linguistics and Second Language Learning: Theoretical Basics and Experimental Evidence*. London: Routledge.

Tyler, Andrea E. & Ortega, Lourdes. 2018. Usage-inspired L2 instruction: An emergent, researched pedagogy. In *Usage-Inspired L2 Instruction: Researched Pedagogy* [Language Learning & Language Teaching 49], Andrea E. Tyler, Lourdes Ortega, Mariko Uno & Hae In Park (eds), 3–26. Amsterdam: John Benjamins,

Tyler, Andrea, Ortega, Lourdes, Uno, Mariko & Park, Hae In (eds). 2018. *Usage-Inspired L2 Instruction: Researched Pedagogy* [Language Learning & Language Teaching 49]. Amsterdam: John Benjamins.

Ur, Penny. 2011. Research, theory, and practice. In *Handbook of Research in Second Language Teaching and Learning* [ESL & Applied Linguistics Professional Series], Eli Hinkel (ed.), Vol. 2, 507–22. New York, NY: Routledge.

Usó-Juan, Esther. 2008. A pragmatic-focused evaluation of requests and their modification devices in textbook conversations. In *Learning How to Request in an Instructed Language Learning Context*, Eva Alcón Soler (ed.), 65–90. Bern: Peter Lang.

Usó-Juan, Esther & Martínez-Flor, Alicia. 2010. The teaching of speech acts in second and foreign language instructional contexts. In *Pragmatics across Languages and Cultures*, 423–442. Berlin: Walter de Gruyter.

Valero Garcés, Carmen. 1998. Some pedagogical and practical implications of contrastive studies in ELT. *Revista Española de Lingüística Aplicada* 13: 27–36.

van de Werfhorst, Herman, Kessenich, Emma & Geven, Sara. 2020. The digital divide in online education. Inequality in digital preparedness of students and schools before the start of the COVID-19 pandemic. Pre-print published on OSF. ⟨https://osf.io/preprints/socarxiv/58d6p/⟩ (1 February 2022).

van Lier, Leo. 2013. *Interaction in the Language Curriculum: Awareness, Autonomy and Authenticity*. Hoboken, NJ: Taylor and Francis.

Van Rossum, Guido & Drake, Fred L. 2009. Python 3 Reference Manual. *Python Software Foundation*, ⟨https://docs.python.org/3/reference/⟩ (4 January 2019).

Varmış Kiliç, Zerhan & Genç İlter, Binnur. 2015. The effect of authentic materials on 12th grade students' attitudes in EFL Classes. *ELT Research Journal* 4(1): 2–15.

doi Veirano Pinto, Marcia. 2019. Using discriminate function analysis in multi-dimensional analysis. In *Multi-Dimensional Analysis: Research Methods and Current Issues*, Tony Berber Sardinha & Marcia Veirano Pinto (eds), 217–230. London: Bloomsbury Academic.

doi Velicer, Wayne F. & Jackson, Douglas N. 1990. Component analysis versus common factor analysis: Some issues in selecting an appropriate procedure. *Multivariate Behavioral Research* 25(1): 1–28.

Vellenga, Heidi. 2004. Learning pragmatics from ESL & EFL textbooks: How likely? *TESL-EJ Teaching English as a Second or Foreign Language* 8(2).

doi Verspoor, Marjolijn. 2017. Complex dynamic systems theory and L2 pedagogy. In *Complexity Theory and Language Development: In Celebration of Diane Larsen-Freeman* [Language Learnung & Language Teaching 48], Lourdes Ortega & Han ZhaoHong (eds), 143–162. Amsterdam: John Benjamins.

doi Verspoor, Marjolijn, Lowie, Wander & van Dijk, Marijn. 2008. Variability in second language development from a dynamic systems perspective. *The Modern Language Journal* 92(2): 214–231.

Viana, Vander (ed.). 2023. *Teaching English with Corpora: A Resource Book*. New York, NY: Routledge.

Vielau, Axel. 2005. Lehrwerk, quo vadis? Einflüsse auf die Lehrwerkentwicklung. In *Niemals Zu Früh und Selten Zu Spät: Fremdsprachenunterricht in Schule und Erwachsenenbildung. Festschrift für Jürgen Quetz*, Eva Burwitz-Melzer & Gert Solmecke (eds), 137–147. Berlin: Cornelsen.

Vine, Elaine W. 2013. Corpora and coursebooks compared: Category ambiguous words. In *Twenty Years of Learner Corpus Research. Looking Back, Moving Ahead: Proceedings of the First Learner Corpus Research Conference (LCR 2011)*, Vol. 1, 463–78. Louvain-la-Neuve: Presses Universitaires de Louvain.

Vogt, Karin. 2011. *Fremdsprachliche Kompetenzprofile: Entwicklung und Abgleichung von GeR-Deskriptoren für Fremdsprachenlernen mit einer beruflichen Anwendungsorientierung*. Tübingen: Gunter Narr.

doi Volansky, Vered, Ordan, Noam & Wintner, Shuly. 2015. On the features of translationese. *Digital Scholarship in the Humanities* 30(1): 98–118.

Volkmann, Laurenz. 2010. *Fachdidaktik Englisch: Kultur und Sprache*. Tübingen: Narr.

doi Vyatkina, Nina. 2020. Corpora as open educational resources for language teaching. *Foreign Language Annals* 53(2): 359–370,

Waibel, Birgit. 2005. Corpus-based approaches to learner interlanguage: Case studies based on the "International Corpus of Learner English". *AAA: Arbeiten aus Anglistik und Amerikanistik* 30(1–2): 143–176.

doi Wallis, Sean. 2020. *Statistics in Corpus Linguistics Research: A New Approach*. London: Routledge.

Weninger, Csilla & Kiss, Tamas. 2013. Culture in English as a foreign language (EFL) textbooks: A semiotic approach. *TESOL Quarterly* 47(4): 694–716.

Werner, Valentin. 2021. Text-linguistic analysis of performed language: Revisiting and re-modeling Koch and Oesterreicher. *Linguistics* 59(3): 541–575.

Whitelaw, Casey & Argamon, Shlomo. 2004. Systemic functional features in stylistic text classification. *AAAI Technical Report* (7).

Widdowson, Henry G. 1978. *Teaching Language as Communication*. Oxford: OUP.

Widdowson, Henry G. 1984. *Explorations in Applied Linguistics*, 2nd edn. Oxford: OUP.

Widdowson, Henry G. 1989. Knowledge of language and ability for use. *Applied Linguistics* 10(2): 128–137.

Widdowson, Henry G. 2003. *Defining Issues in English Language Teaching* [Oxford Applied Linguistics]. Oxford: OUP.

Wieling, Martijn, Rawee, Josine & van Noord, Gertjan. 2018. Reproducibility in computational linguistics: Are we willing to share? *Computational Linguistics* 44(4): 641–649.

Wiese, Heike, Mayr, Katharina, Krämer, Philipp, Seeger, Patrick, Müller, Hans-Georg & Mezger, Verena. 2017. Changing teachers' attitudes towards linguistic diversity: Effects of an anti-bias programme. *International Journal of Applied Linguistics* 27(1): 198–220.

Wilkinson, Mark D., Dumontier, Michel, Aalbersberg, IJsbrand Jan, Appleton, Gabrielle, Axton, Myles, Baak, Arie, Blomberg, Niklas et al. 2016. The FAIR Guiding Principles for scientific data management and stewardship. *Scientific Data* 3(1): 160018.

Willis, Dave. 2009. *Rules, Patterns and Words: Grammar and Lexis in English Language Teaching* [Cambridge Language Teaching Library]. Cambridge: CUP.

Winter, Bodo. 2019. *Statistics for Linguists: An Introduction Using R*. New York, NY: Routledge.

Winter, Tatjana & Le Foll, Elen. 2022. Testing the pedagogical norm: Comparing *if*-conditionals in EFL textbooks, learner writing and English outside the classroom. *International Journal of Learner Corpus Research* 8(1): 31–66.

Wolff, Dieter. 1984. Lehrbuchtexte und Verstehensprozesse in einer zweiten Sprache. *Neusprachliche Mitteilungen aus Wissenschaft und Praxis* 37(1): 4–11.

Wolk, Christoph, Götz, Sandra & Jäschke, Katja. 2021. Possibilities and drawbacks of using an online application for semi-automatic corpus analysis to investigate discourse markers and alternative fluency variables. *Corpus Pragmatics* 5: 7–36.

Wood, David. 2010. Lexical clusters in an EAP textbook corpus. In *Perspectives on Formulaic Language: Acquisition and Communication*, David Wood (ed.), 88–106. London: Continuum.

Wood, David & Appel, Randy. 2014. Multiword constructions in first year business and engineering university textbooks and EAP textbooks. *Journal of English for Academic Purposes* 15: 1–13.

Wulff, Stefanie, Ellis, Nick C., Römer, Ute, Bardovi-Harlig, Kathleen & Leblanc, Chelsea J. 2009. The acquisition of tense-aspect: Converging evidence from corpora and telicity ratings. *The Modern Language Journal* 93(3): 354–369.

Wulff, Stefanie & Gries, Stefan Th. 2021. Exploring individual variation in learner corpus research: Methodological suggestions. In *Learner Corpus Research Meets Second Language Acquisition* [Cambridge Applied Linguistics], Bert Le Bruyn & Magali Paquot (eds), 191–213. Cambridge: CUP.

doi Xiao, Richard. 2009. Theory-driven corpus research: Using corpora to inform aspect theory. In *Corpus Linguistics: An International Handbook* [Handbücher Zur Sprach- Und Kommunikationswissenschaft = Handbooks of Linguistics and Communication Science], Anke Lüdeling & Merja Kytö (eds), Vol. 2, 987–1007. Berlin: Walter de Gruyter.

doi Yoo, Isaiah WonHo. 2009. The English definite article: What ESL/EFL grammars say and what corpus findings show. *Journal of English for Academic Purposes* 8(4): 267–278.

doi Yoo, Soyung. 2013. *Hypothetical Would-Clauses in Korean EFL Textbooks: An Analysis Based on a Corpus Study and Focus on Form Approach.* Portland State University M.A. .

doi Zarifi, Abdolvahed & Mukundan, Jayakaran. 2012. Phrasal verbs in Malaysian ESL textbooks. *English Language Teaching* 5(5): 9–18.

Zipf, George Kingsley. 1935. *The Psycho-Biology of Language: An Introduction to Dynamic Philology*. Cambridge, MA: The MIT Press.

Zipf, George Kingsley. 1949. *Human Behavior and the Principle of Least Effort: An Introduction to Human Ecology*. Cambridge, MA: The MIT Press.

Appendices

All appendices can be found in the Online Supplements on the project's webpage: ⟨https://elenlefoll.github.io/TextbookMDA/⟩. This page is linked to the project's GitHub repository, where the data and source code can be found: ⟨https://github.com/elenlefoll/TextbookMDA/⟩. The repository is also archived at https://doi.org/10.17605/OSF.IO/JPXAE.

Appendix A. Literature Review Data
Appendix B. Corpus Data
Appendix C. Linguistic Features
Appendix D. Evaluation of the Multi-Feature Tagger of English (MFTE)
Appendix E. Data Preparation for the Model of Intra-Textbook Variation
Appendix F. Data Analysis for the Model of Intra-Textbook Variation
Appendix G. Data Preparation for the Model of Textbook English vs. 'real-world' English
Appendix H. Data Analysis for the Model of Textbook English vs. 'real-world' English

Index